THE LAW OF ATHENS

VOLUME II

Procedure

A.R.W. Harrison

New Edition
Foreword and Bibliography by
D.M. MacDowell

Published in the U.K. by
Gerald Duckworth & Co. Ltd
London

Published in North America by
Hackett Publishing Company, Inc.
Indianapolis/Cambridge

Cover illustration: from busts of Aischines and Demosthenes

First published in 1971 by Oxford University Press
This edition published, with permission, in 1998 by
Bristol Classical Press
an imprint of
Gerald Duckworth & Co. Ltd
The Old Piano Factory
48 Hoxton Square, London N1 6PB
and by
Hackett Publishing Company, Inc.
P.O. Box 44937
Indianapolis, Indiana 46244-0937

U.K. edition:
ISBN 1-85399-571-1

A CIP Catalogue record for this book is available from the British Library

U.S. edition:
ISBN 0-87220-412-X paperback
ISBN 0-87220-413-8 cloth
ISBN 0-87220-414-6 paperback set (Vols. I and II)
ISBN 0-87220-415-4 cloth set (Vols. I and II)
LC number 98-13464

The paper used in this publication meets the minimum requirements of American National Standard for Information Sciences - Permanence of Paper for Printed Library Materials, ANSI Z39.48-1984

∞

Printed in the United States of America

THE LAW OF ATHENS

Vol. II

FOREWORD

THE law of classical Athens is a subject which straddles two academic professions, law and classics. For historians of law its special interest is that it is almost the only developed but pre-Roman system of which a fairly full reconstruction is possible, thanks to the survival of about a hundred forensic speeches of the Attic orators and a substantial quantity of Athenian inscriptions on stone. For classical scholars Athenian law is an essential part of Athenian life, revealing much of politics, religion, and moral beliefs. These two approaches have often been divided by geography. In continental Europe, especially Germany, Athenian law has been studied mainly by academic lawyers, who see it as a remote ancestor of their own civil law systems. In anglophone countries, on the other hand, it has received little attention from lawyers, but more from classicists having a historical and literary background.

A.R.W. Harrison struck a happy medium. He was an ancient historian by profession, but he had a sound knowledge of Roman law, and, as the preface to his first volume shows, he saw himself as a successor to the great European writers on Athenian law, especially Beauchet and Lipsius. His first volume does in fact largely supersede their works as far as the family and property are concerned. His second volume remained incomplete (as explained in its preface), so that for the topics omitted from it Lipsius remains indispensable.

In the years since Harrison's death no one else has attempted to produce a detailed study of the entire field. I have myself offered a shorter account of the whole subject in *The Law in Classical Athens*, and more recently Todd has produced another, *The Shape of Athenian Law*, concentrating more on the law's social implications. At a more specialized level European legal historians have continued to produce good studies of particular problems: Thür's *Beweisführung vor den Schwurgerichtshöfen Athens* is an outstanding example. On procedural and constitutional topics there are several important books by Hansen. Britain has been the principal location for editions of the relevant Greek texts, including a new edition of *Inscriptiones Graecae*, vol. i, by the late David Lewis, a commentary by Rhodes on the Aristotelian *Athenaion Politeia,* and commentaries by myself and others on several of the forensic speeches. In America the early history of Athenian law (mainly before Harrison's period) has been elucidated in Gagarin's *Drakon and Early Athenian Homicide Law* and *Early Greek Law.* Court procedures and buildings are discussed in Edward E. Cohen's *Ancient Athenian Maritime Courts* and in Boegehold's *The Lawcourts at Athens.* At the sociological end of the subject there are two important books by David Cohen: *Law, Sexuality, and Society*; and *Law, Violence, and Community in Classical Athens.*

These books and others of the last three decades are listed in the selective bibliography which I have compiled for this reissue of Harrison's work (pp xxi-xxiii in vol I; pp xvi-xviii in vol II). They exemplify a wide diversity of approaches to Athenian law—still, it seems, with a geographical basis: head west if you want sociology, east if you want jurisprudence. But it would not be right to imply that there is a schism among the scholars in this field. The contrary is the case; and this is due in large part to an initiative taken by the late H.J. Wolff. A German scholar who had spent the period of the Second World War in America, he inaugurated in 1971 a series of colloquia on ancient Greek law which has continued at intervals of two or three years until the present time. These meetings bring together scholars from many different countries, and their papers are published together in the volumes entitled *Symposion,* which give a good impression of the range of work in progress. Harrison died too soon to participate in these colloquia. He worked largely alone, and thus it is the more remarkable that he produced the best work of the last half-century on Athenian law.

June 1997 D.M. MacDowell

PREFACE

THE first volume of *The Law of Athens*, on the law of the family and of property, was published in February 1968. By the time it appeared the author had already done much work towards the second volume, which was to be on the law of obligations and of procedure. He continued work on it throughout 1968, but early in 1969 he was taken ill, and he died in May.

When his papers were examined, they were found to include drafts of chapters amounting to nearly the whole of the account of procedure; that is, to about half of the intended second volume. It is sometimes not easy to know what action to take when a scholar dies leaving a book unfinished; but in this case there can be little doubt that students of ancient law will be glad of the chance to read these chapters even in their unrevised state, and will be grateful to Mrs. Harrison and to the Delegates of the Oxford University Press for agreeing to their publication.

Readers will find that most aspects of procedure in Athenian courts are covered. The principal omissions, which were to have been discussed in further chapters or sections, are the procedure in homicide courts, the procedure before arbitrators, and cases involving foreigners, especially *δίκαι ἀπὸ συμβόλων* and *δίκαι ἐμπορικαί*. The sections on penalties and on procedures connected with liturgies are clearly unfinished.

In preparing the typescript for the printer, I have inserted the majority of the quotations from Greek texts and a smaller number of other references, which were omitted or incomplete in the draft. I have clarified the wording in some places, and here and there I have deleted one or two sentences which I was sure would not have survived the author's own revision. But I have not added or changed any statements of fact or opinion—not even in those places (which are anyway not very numerous) in which I happen to take a different view from his. If he had lived, he would certainly have revised these chapters, and might have made considerable modifications in them; but I felt it was not my business to put into his mouth modifications which he might not have cared to make. For the same reason I have not attempted to add references to relevant books (most notably R. S. Stroud's *Drakon's Law on Homicide*, published at the end of 1968) which appeared too late for him to take account of them.

A. R. W. Harrison spent nearly the whole of his academic life in Merton College, of which he was successively Postmaster, Fellow, and (from 1963) Warden. A few months before his death the College, on his proposal, did me the honour of electing me to a Visiting Research Fellowship for the Michaelmas term of 1969. I should like to record here my gratitude to the College for electing me, to the University of Manchester for granting me leave of absence, and to those of my colleagues in Manchester who undertook extra teaching and other duties to make my absence possible. It was a great sorrow to me that the hopes which the Warden and I both had of working on Athenian law in consultation with each other during that term came to nothing. But it was some slight consolation that I was able in his memory to devote part of the term to working on his manuscript in the beautiful and peaceful College which he served so long.

D. M. MacDOWELL

December 1969

CONTENTS

LIST OF ABBREVIATIONS

AAW	*Anzeiger der Akademie der Wissenschaften.* Philosophisch-historische Klasse (Vienna).
AJA	*American Journal of Archaeology.*
AJP	*American Journal of Philology.*
An. Bekk.	I. Bekker, *Anecdota Graeca* (Berlin, 1814–21).
AP	*Archiv für Papyrusforschung.*
Ath. Mitt.	*Mitteilungen des Deutschen Archäologischen Instituts: Athenische Abteilung.*
ATL	B. D. Meritt, H. T. Wade-Gery, M. F. McGregor, *The Athenian Tribute Lists* (Princeton, 1939–53).
BCH	*Bulletin de correspondance hellénique.*
Beauchet	L. Beauchet, *L'Histoire du droit privé de la république athénienne* (Paris, 1897).
Berneker, *ZGR*	E. Berneker (ed.), *Zur griechischen Rechtsgeschichte* (Darmstadt, 1968).
Böckh, *Staatsh.*	A. Böckh, *Die Staatshaushaltung der Athener* (3. Auflage, Berlin, 1886).
Bonner, *Evidence*	R. J. Bonner, *Evidence in Athenian Courts* (Chicago, 1905).
Bo. Sm.	R. J. Bonner and G. Smith, *The Administration of Justice from Homer to Aristotle* (Chicago, 1930–8).
BPW	*Berliner Philologische Wochenschrift.*
Bu. Sw.	G. Busolt and H. Swoboda, *Griechische Staatskunde* (Munich, 1920–6).
Calhoun, *Clubs*	G. M. Calhoun, *Athenian Clubs in Politics and Litigation* (Austin, 1913).
Calhoun, *Criminal Law*	G. M. Calhoun, *The Growth of Criminal Law in Ancient Greece* (Berkeley, 1927).
Colin, *Hyper.*	G. Colin, *Hypéride: Discours* (Paris, 1946).
CP	*Classical Philology.*
CQ	*Classical Quarterly.*
CR	*Classical Review.*
Dareste, *Dem.*	R. Dareste, *Plaidoyers civils de Démosthène* (Paris, 1875).
Demisch, *Schuldenerb.*	E. Demisch, *Die Schuldenerbfolge im attischen Recht* (Borna–Leipzig, 1910).

F.Gr.H.	F. Jacoby, *Die Fragmente der griechischen Historiker* (Berlin, Leiden, 1923 onwards).
Fine, *Horoi*	J. V. A. Fine, 'Horoi: studies in mortgage, real security, and land tenure in ancient Athens' (*Hesperia*, Suppl. 9, Baltimore, 1951).
Finley, *Land*	M. I. Finley, *Studies in Land and Credit in Ancient Athens, 500–200 B.C.* (New Brunswick, 1951).
Fränkel, *Att. Geschw.*	M. Fränkel, *Die attischen Geschworenengerichte* (Berlin, 1877).
Gernet, *Ant.*	L. Gernet, *Antiphon: Discours* (Paris, 1923).
Gernet, *Dem.*	L. Gernet, *Démosthène: Plaidoyers civils* (Paris, 1954–60).
Gernet, *DSGA*	L. Gernet, *Droit et société dans la Grèce ancienne* (Paris, 1955).
Gernet, *Plat.*	L. Gernet, 'Introduction, deuxième partie: *Les Lois* et le droit positif', in É. des Places, *Platon: Œuvres complètes, tome xi: Les Lois* (Paris, 1951).
Gernet, *Recherches*	L. Gernet, *Recherches sur le développement de la pensée juridique et morale en Grèce* (Paris, 1917).
Gernet and Bizos, *Lys.*	L. Gernet and M. Bizos, *Lysias: Discours* (Paris, 1924–6).
Glotz, *Solidarité*	G. Glotz, *La Solidarité de la famille dans le droit criminel en Grèce* (Paris, 1904).
Hignett, *HAC*	C. Hignett, *A History of the Athenian Constitution* (Oxford, 1952).
Hommel, *Heliaia*	H. Hommel, *Heliaia* (*Philologus*, Suppl. 19, Heft 2, Leipzig, 1927).
HSCP	*Harvard Studies in Classical Philology.*
IG	*Inscriptiones Graecae.*
IJ	R. Dareste, B. Haussoulier, T. Reinach, *Recueil des inscriptions juridiques grecques* (Paris, 1891–1904).
Jones, *LLTG*	J. W. Jones, *The Law and Legal Theory of the Greeks* (Oxford, 1956).
JP	*Journal of Philology.*
Kahrstedt, *Mag.*	U. Kahrstedt, *Untersuchungen zur Magistratur in Athen* (Stuttgart, 1936).
Kahrstedt, *Staatsg.*	U. Kahrstedt, *Staatsgebiet und Staatsangehörige in Athen* (Stuttgart, 1934).
Kränzlein, *Eig. und Bes.*	A. Kränzlein, *Eigentum und Besitz im griechischen Recht* (Berlin, 1963).
Lacey, *Family*	W. K. Lacey, *The Family in Classical Greece* (London, 1968).
Lämmli, *Prozeß.*	F. Lämmli, *Das attische Prozeßverfahren in seiner Wirkung auf die Gerichtsrede* (Paderborn, 1938).

Latte, *HR*	K. Latte, *Heiliges Recht* (Tübingen, 1920).
Lavency, *Logographie*	M. Lavency, *Aspects de la logographie judiciaire attique* (Louvain, 1964).
Leisi, *Zeuge*	E. Leisi, *Der Zeuge im attischen Recht* (Frauenfeld, 1907).
Lipsius, *AR*	J. H. Lipsius, *Das attische Recht und Rechtsverfahren* (Leipzig, 1905–15).
Lofberg, *Sycophancy*	J. O. Lofberg, *Sycophancy in Athens* (Chicago, 1917).
MacDowell, *Homicide*	D. M. MacDowell, *Athenian Homicide Law* (Manchester, 1963).
MacDowell, *Mysteries*	D. M. MacDowell, *Andokides: On the Mysteries* (Oxford, 1962).
Meyer-Laurin, *Ges. Bill.*	H. Meyer-Laurin, *Gesetz und Billigkeit im attischen Prozeß* (Weimar, 1965).
Mitteis, *RV*	L. Mitteis, *Reichsrecht und Volksrecht in den östlichen Provinzen des römischen Kaiserreichs* (Leipzig, 1891).
MSL	M. H. E. Meier, G. F. Schömann, J. H. Lipsius, *Der attische Proceß* (Berlin, 1883–7).
NJ	*Neue Jahrbücher für klassische Philologie.*
Paoli, *St. Dir.*	U. E. Paoli, *Studi di diritto attico* (Florence, 1930).
Paoli, *St. Proc.*	U. E. Paoli, *Studi sul processo attico* (Padua, 1933).
Partsch, *GB*	J. Partsch, *Griechisches Bürgschaftsrecht* (Leipzig, 1909).
Pringsheim, *GLS*	F. Pringsheim, *The Greek Law of Sale* (Weimar, 1950).
RE	*Paulys Real-Encyclopädie der classischen Altertumswissenschaft.*
RÉG	*Revue des études grecques.*
Rentzsch, ψευδομ.	J. Rentzsch, *De* δίκῃ ψευδομαρτυρίων *in iure Attico* (Leipzig, 1901).
RHD	*Revue historique de droit français et étranger.*
RIDA	*Revue internationale des droits de l'antiquité.*
Schodorf, *Beiträge*	K. Schodorf, *Beiträge zur genaueren Kenntnis der attischen Gerichtssprache* (Würzburg, 1904).
Schömann, *Isai.*	G. F. Schömann, *Isaei orationes xi* (Greifswald, 1831).
SEG	*Supplementum Epigraphicum Graecum.*
SIFC	*Studi italiani di filologia classica.*
SIG	W. Dittenberger, *Sylloge Inscriptionum Graecarum* (editio tertia, Leipzig, 1915–24).
Steinwenter, *Streit.*	A. Steinwenter, *Die Streitbeendigung durch Urteil, Schiedsspruch und Vergleich nach griechischem Rechte* (Munich, 1925).
TAPA	*Transactions of the American Philological Association.*

Tod, *GHI*	M. N. Tod, *Greek Historical Inscriptions* (Oxford, 1946–8).
Wade-Gery, *EGH*	H. T. Wade-Gery, *Essays in Greek History* (Oxford, 1958).
Wayte, *Dem.*	W. Wayte, *Demosthenes: Against Androtion and Against Timocrates* (second edition, Cambridge, 1893).
Weiss, *GP*	E. Weiss, *Griechisches Privatrecht auf rechtsvergleichender Grundlage* (Leipzig, 1923).
Wilamowitz, *A. und A.*	U. von Wilamowitz-Moellendorff, *Aristoteles und Athen* (Berlin, 1893).
Wolff, *Beitr.*	H. J. Wolff, *Beiträge zur Rechtsgeschichte Altgriechenlands und des hellenistisch-römischen Ägypten* (Weimar, 1961).
Wolff, *Paragraphe*	H. J. Wolff, *Die attische Paragraphe* (Weimar, 1966).
WS	*Wiener Studien.*
Wyse, *Isai.*	W. Wyse, *The Speeches of Isaeus* (Cambridge, 1904).
Z	*Zeitschrift der Savigny-Stiftung für Rechtsgeschichte* (Romanistische Abteilung).

SELECT BIBLIOGRAPHY, 1967-97

Bauman, R.A., *Political Trials in Ancient Greece* (London, 1990).

Behrend, D., *Attische Pachturkunden* (Munich, 1970).

Biscardi, A. *Diritto greco antico* (Milan, 1982).

Boegehold, A.L., *The Lawcourts at Athens* (The Athenian Agora, vol. xxviii; Princeton, 1995).

Cantarella, E., *Studi sull'omicidio in diritto greco e romano* (Milan, 1976).

Carey, C., *Lysias: Selected Speeches* (Cambridge, 1989).

——, *Trials from Classical Athens* (London, 1997).

Carey, C. and Reid, R.A., *Demosthenes: Selected Private Speeches* (Cambridge, 1985).

Cartledge, P., Millett, P. and Todd, S. (editors), *Nomos: Essays in Athenian Law, Politics, and Society* (Cambridge, 1990).

Cohen, D., *Law, Sexuality, and Society* (Cambridge, 1991).

——, *Law, Violence, and Community in Classical Athens* (Cambridge, 1995).

——, *Theft in Athenian Law* (Munich, 1983).

Cohen, E.E., *Ancient Athenian Maritime Courts* (Princeton, 1973).

——, *Athenian Economy and Society* (Princeton, 1992).

Dimakis, P.D., Αττικό δίκαιο (Athens, 1986).

Fisher, N.R.E., *Hybris* (Warminster, 1992).

Foxhall, L. and Lewis, A.D.E. (editors), *Greek Law in its Political Setting* (Oxford, 1996).

Gagarin, M., *Antiphon: The Speeches* (Cambridge, 1997).

——, *Drakon and Early Athenian Homicide Law* (New Haven, 1981).

——, *Early Greek Law* (Berkeley, 1986).

Garner, R., *Law and Society in Classical Athens* (London, 1987).

Gauthier, P., *Symbola: les étrangers et la justice dans les cités grecques* (Nancy, 1972).

Hansen, M.H., *Apagoge, Endeixis and Ephegesis against Kakourgoi, Atimoi and Pheugontes* (Odense, 1976).

——, *The Athenian Democracy in the Age of Demosthenes* (Oxford, 1991).

——, *Eisangelia: the Sovereignty of the People's Court in Athens in the Fourth Century* BC *and the Impeachment of Generals and Politicians* (Odense, 1975).

——, *The Sovereignty of the People's Court in Athens in the Fourth Century* BC *and the Public Action against Unconstitutional Proposals* (Odense, 1974).

Hillgruber, M., *Die zehnte Rede des Lysias* (Berlin, 1988).

Hunter, V. J., *Policing Athens: Social Control in the Attic Lawsuits, 420-320* BC (Princeton, 1994).

Isager, S. and Hansen, M.H., *Aspects of Athenian Society in the Fourth Century* BC (Odense, 1975).

Just, R., *Women in Athenian Law and Life* (London, 1989).

Koch, C., *Volksbeschlüsse in Seebundangelegenheiten: das Verfahrensrecht Athens im Ersten attischen Seebund* (Frankfurt, 1991).

Lambert, S.D., *The Phratries of Attica* (Ann Arbor, 1993).

Lewis, D.M., *Inscriptiones Graecae,* vol. i, editio tertia, fasc. 1 et 2 (Berlin, 1981, 1994).

MacDowell, D.M., *Demosthenes: Against Meidias* (Oxford, 1990).

——, *The Law in Classical Athens* (London, 1978).

Manville, P.B., *The Origins of Citizenship in Ancient Athens* (Princeton, 1990).

Millett, P., *Lending and Borrowing in Ancient Athens* (Cambridge, 1991).

Ogden, D., *Greek Bastardy* (Oxford, 1996).

Osborne, M.J., *Naturalization in Athens,* vols. i, ii, iii-iv (Brussels, 1981, 1982, 1983).

Osborne, R. and Hornblower, S., *Ritual, Finance, Politics: Athenian Democratic Accounts presented to David Lewis* (Oxford, 1994).

Ostwald, M., *From Popular Sovereignty to the Sovereignty of Law* (Berkeley, 1986).

——, *Nomos and the Beginnings of Athenian Democracy* (Oxford, 1969).

Patterson, C., *Pericles' Citizenship Law of 451-50* BC (New York, 1981).

Pomeroy, S.B., *Families in Classical and Hellenistic Greece* (Oxford, 1997).

Quass, F., *Nomos und Psephisma* (Munich, 1971).

Rhodes, P.J., *The Athenian Boule* (Oxford, 1972).

——, *A Commentary on the Aristotelian* Athenaion Politeia (Oxford, 1981).

Rhodes, P.J. and Lewis, D.M., *The Decrees of the Greek States* (Oxford, 1997).

Roberts, J.T., *Accountability in Athenian Government* (Madison, 1982).

Rubinstein, L., *Adoption in IV. Century Athens* (Copenhagen, 1993).

Ruschenbusch, E., *Untersuchungen zur Geschichte des athenischen Strafrechts* (Cologne, 1968).

Schaps, D.M., *Economic Rights of Women in Ancient Greece* (Edinburgh, 1979).

Sealey, R., *The Justice of the Greeks* (Ann Arbor, 1994).

——, *Women and Law in Classical Greece* (Chapel Hill, 1990).

Spina, L., *Il cittadino alla tribuna: diritto e libertà di parola nell' Atene democratica* (Naples, 1986).

Stroud, R.S., *Drakon's Law on Homicide* (Berkeley, 1968).

Thompson, W.E., *De Hagniae hereditate* (Leiden, 1976).

Thür, G., *Beweisführung vor den Schwurgerichtshöfen Athens* (Vienna, 1977).

Todd, S.C., *The Shape of Athenian Law* (Oxford, 1993).

Tulin, A., *Dike phonou: the Right of Prosecution and Attic Homicide Procedure* (Stuttgart, 1996).

Wallace, R.W., *The Areopagos Council* (Baltimore, 1989).

Wankel, H., *Demosthenes: Rede für Ktesiphon über den Kranz* (Heidelberg, 1976).

Whitehead, D., *The Demes of Attica* (Princeton, 1986).

——, *The Ideology of the Athenian Metic* (Cambridge, 1977).

Wolff, H.J., *'Normenkontrolle' und Gesetzesbegriff in der attischen Demokratie* (Heidelberg, 1970).

Worthington, I., *A Historical Commentary on Dinarchus* (Ann Arbor, 1992).

The *Akten der Gesellschaft für griechische und hellenistische Rechtsgeschichte* are published by Böhlau at Cologne as follows:

Symposion 1971, edited by H.J. Wolff (1975).
Symposion 1974, edited by A. Biscardi (1979).
Symposion 1977, edited by J. Modrzejewski and D. Liebs (1982).
Symposion 1979, edited by P.D. Dimakis (1983).
Symposion 1982, edited by F.J. Fernandez Nieto (1989).
Symposion 1985, edited by G. Thür (1989).
Symposion 1988, edited by G. Nenci and G. Thür (1990).
Symposion 1990, edited by M. Gagarin (1991).
Symposion 1993, edited by G. Thür (1994).
Symposion 1995, edited by G. Thür and J. Velissaropoulos-Karakostas (1997).

PART III

PROCEDURE

I · THE JUDICIAL MACHINE

§ 1. *Introduction*

THE aim of this Part is to examine the judicial procedure available for remedying wrongs, whether against the state or the individual. Questions of historical development are sometimes more insistent here than elsewhere in the book, but discussion of them has been kept to a minimum, since we are concerned with the law as it was in the fourth century.

§ 2. *Organs of jurisdiction: historical development*

We have first to examine the organs provided by the state for making and enforcing judicial decisions. When the city state was being formed and the judicial system was but an embryo, the king was that organ. In Attica the king's functions, military, religious, and civil, gradually devolved on a number of magistrates, who were at first aristocratic in character. By the time of Solon, the earliest date from which anything approaching detailed knowledge of the system survives, the king had been replaced by nine archons, six of whom (the thesmothetai) were concerned almost wholly with judicial business. From that time down to the fourth century two parallel developments were transforming the system. On the one hand the archons were becoming progressively less and less aristocratic in character. These offices were annual, and iteration was forbidden (though strangely we do not know whether this meant that a man could not hold one particular kind of archonship, the office of polemarch for example, twice, or that having been an archon of any kind he could never be archon again). Eligibility was at first restricted to the highest of Solon's census classes, but by the fourth century any male citizen was eligible, though by the strict letter of the law even then members of the lowest class, the thetes, were excluded.[1] In the year 487/6 straight election had been replaced by mixed sortition (*κλήρωσις ἐκ προκρίτων*): the people elected five hundred persons out of whom nine were selected as archons by lot.[2]

Parallel with this moderate democratization of the board of archons itself there was during the same period the creation or evolution of other organs which derogated from the powers, both judicial and other, exercised by the archons. In military and administrative matters the most important development was the supplanting of the archons by the board of ten strategoi: they were re-eligible year after year, and this fact of itself gave the office an authority which threw the office of archon into the shade. In the judicial sphere however the change was of minor importance, since the strategoi only took over judicial powers related to their other functions, as we shall see later, and in this respect they shared with the archons a loss of direct power to the popular organs of government.

This last was a much more important change than the proliferation of other offices. The seed had been sown by Solon, so at least the historians of the fourth century believed, when he introduced appeal from the magistrates' judicial decisions to the people.[3] We do not know either what cases could be so appealed or the procedure followed when appeals occurred; what is clear is that by the mid fifth century this right of the people to hear cases on appeal had developed into the right—or duty—to hear many cases in the first instance, that to perform this duty 'the

[1] Ar. *Ath. Pol.* 7. 4.

[2] Ar. *Ath. Pol.* 22. 5. Not a marked democratic advance, as is sometimes assumed. The electors, instead of being able to elect directly to the office, had to choose this large number of candidates (and at that date it was from the top two census classes only; the office of archon was not opened to the third class, the zeugitai, until 457/6, Ar. *Ath. Pol.* 26. 2), and the lot did the rest. Thus used the lot was anything but democratic. What it, combined with the rule against iteration, did secure, was that no tinge of expertise could develop in the holders of these offices.

[3] Ar. *Ath. Pol.* 7. 3 *τοῖς δὲ τὸ θητικὸν τελοῦσιν ἐκκλησίας καὶ δικαστηρίων μετέδωκε μόνον*, 9. 1 *τρίτον δέ* (the third most democratic feature of Solon's constitution), ⟨*ᾧ*⟩ *μάλιστά φασιν ἰσχυκέναι τὸ πλῆθος, ἡ εἰς τὸ δικαστήριον ἔφεσις· κύριος γὰρ ὢν ὁ δῆμος τῆς ψήφου κύριος γίγνεται τῆς πολιτείας.*

people' (known in its judicial capacity as the heliaia) had been organized into a number of dikasteries varying between 200 and 1,500 in size, and that the function of the magistrates, whether archons or others, had been reduced to preparing the case for adjudication (*ἀνακρίνειν*) and presiding over the court which tried it (*ἡγεμονία*: the verb is *εἰσάγειν*).[1] It was this development which led Aristotle to the surprising but perceptive judgement that it was appeal to the dikastery which, of all the reforms of Solon, contributed most to putting power in the hands of the people; 'for', he says, 'when the people is master of the vote' (and this means the vote in the dikasteries) 'it becomes master of the constitution'.[2]

The boule too, as newly constituted by Kleisthenes, probably gained some judicial power at the expense of the magistrates on the one hand and of the Areopagos on the other. These gains however seem to have been temporary, and by the fourth century its judicial powers were strictly limited.[3]

The Areopagos, which at one time had enjoyed very wide and vaguely defined powers, had been virtually restricted by the fourth century to certain cases of homicide and of impiety.[4]

We shall have to consider later (Chapter II) precisely what a magistrate had to do both when he was conducting the preliminaries in a case and when he was presiding, and we shall find that the former function was rather more and the latter rather less important than we might at first glance suppose. What we

[1] Ar. *Ath. Pol.* 3. 5 speaking of the archons before Solon says *κύριοι δ' ἦσαν καὶ τὰς δίκας αὐτοτελεῖς [κρίν]ειν καὶ οὐχ ὥσπερ νῦν προανακρίνειν.* For *εἰσάγειν δίκην* see p. 21 and especially n. 2.

[2] Ar. *Ath. Pol.* 9. 1 (p. 2, n. 3 above). This historical development is the subject of the first volume of *The Administration of Justice from Homer to Aristotle* by R. J. Bonner and G. Smith (Chicago, 1930); see also Hignett, *HAC* index s.v. 'Dikasteria', especially 216 ff., Kahrstedt, *Mag.* 201 ff.

[3] Ar. *Ath. Pol.* 45. 1 *ἡ δὲ βουλὴ πρότερον μὲν ἦν κυρία καὶ χρήμασιν ζημιῶσαι καὶ δῆσαι καὶ ἀποκτεῖναι. . . . ὁ δὲ δῆμος ἀφείλετο τῆς βουλῆς τὸ θανατοῦν καὶ δεῖν καὶ χρήμασιν ζημιοῦν, καὶ νόμον ἔθετο, ἄν τινος ἀδικεῖν ἡ βουλὴ καταγνῷ ἢ ζημιώσῃ, τὰς καταγνώσεις καὶ τὰς ἐπιζημιώσεις εἰσάγειν τοὺς θεσμοθέτας εἰς τὸ δικαστήριον, καὶ ὅ τι ἂν οἱ δικασταὶ ψηφίσωνται, τοῦτο κύριον εἶναι.* The date of the restriction referred to in the second sentence quoted is not known, but it may have been when the bouleutic oath was instituted in the archonship of Hermokreon (501/0 B.C.), Ar. *Ath. Pol.* 22. 2.

[4] Ar. *Ath. Pol.* 25. 2, Philochoros, *F.Gr.H.* 328 F 64b: the reform of Ephialtes of 462/1 left the Areopagos with little judicial power beyond homicide cases. U. Kahrstedt, *Klio* 30 (1937) 10 ff., stakes out rather more for the fourth-century Areopagos than is usually allowed.

have now to do is to outline in brief all the judicial organs of the state and their functions.

§ 3. *Magistrates*

(i) *All magistrates*

It is clear that high among the powers of the magistrates which were gradually curtailed by the development of the powers of other organs of state ranked the right to pronounce judgements on their own initiative (αὐτοτελεῖς). These judgements might be employed either against those who interfered with them in the discharge of their official duties or more generally for the settlement of disputes brought before them by litigants. Vestiges of this power survived right into the classical period. There was a specific term, ἐπιβολαί, for fines imposed by magistrates, and we have at least one statement from the fourth century which implies that a distinguishing mark of a magistrate was this power to impose fines (ἐπιβολὰς ἐπιβάλλειν).[1]

By classical times the rights of magistrates in this respect were limited in two ways. First there was an upper limit in value to the fines they could impose: this is expressed in general terms in a law quoted in a Demosthenic speech which lays down that the magistrate (in that case the archon) is empowered to impose a fine within the limits allowed to him (κατὰ τὸ τέλος) for offences against widows or orphans. If he deems the wrongdoer should pay a greater penalty, he is to cite him to appear before a heliastic court, stating on the citation what penalty he proposes: the court first decides whether the man is guilty, and then fixes the penalty by the process of τίμησις; presumably this means that the

[1] On ἐπιβολαί see Lipsius, *AR* 53 f., 954, Thalheim, *RE* s.v. ἐπιβολή, Bu. Sw. 1054, Bo. Sm. i. 279 ff., ii. 138 f., 245 f., Kahrstedt, *Mag.* 212 ff. According to Aischin. 3 *Ktes.* 27 Demosthenes, when a teichopoios, ἐπιβολὰς ἐπέβαλλε, καθάπερ οἱ ἄλλοι ἄρχοντες, where ἄρχοντες clearly means 'magistrates' in general, not 'archons'. Evidence for the following specific organs of government: the Areopagos, Aischin. 2 *Embassy* 93; the archons, Lys. 30 *Nikom.* 3; the eponymous archon, Dem. 21 *Meid.* 179, 43 *Makart.* 75, Ar. *Ath. Pol.* 56. 7; the basileus, Lys. 6 *Andok.* 21 (assuming that Taylor's emendation of ἐπιβουλῆς to ἐπιβολῆς is correct and that the magistrate referred to is the basileus); the generals, Lys. 9 *Soldier* 6, 15 *Alk.* ii. 5, Ar. *Ath. Pol.* 61. 2; the overseer of the διωβελία, Xen. *Hell.* 1. 7. 2; the teichopoioi, Aischin. 3 *Ktes.* 27; the hieropoioi, *IG* i². 84. 26 ff. (see p. 6, n. 2); the demarch of the deme Peiraeus, *IG* ii². 1177; and possibly the proedroi, Aischin. 1 *Timarch.* 35 (the law quoted is not genuine, but the reconstruction may be based on a genuine law).

defendant puts in his estimate of the appropriate penalty and the court decides between it and that proposed by the archon.[1] This upper limit to the value of the fine which a magistrate could inflict without reference to a court differed for the various magistrates. The only figure for which we have definite evidence is 50 drachmai for the hieropoioi and the proedroi; but we can conjecture that it was at least as high for other more important magistrates.[2]

The existence of the other limitation is more speculative; but it is possible that there could be appeal to a court even from those penalties which a magistrate was allowed to impose on his own initiative (αὐτοτελής). The evidence for this is in Lys. 9 *Soldier*, a speech written in defence of Polyainos. According to the speaker the strategoi had imposed a fine on him for abusing them; the law, so he alleges, forbade abuse of magistrates in a public office (συνέδριον), whereas his had been spoken in a bank; it was this which made the fine illegal (there is no hint that the strategoi had exceeded the limit of value allowed them). But though they had imposed the fine the strategoi did not attempt to exact it (6

[1] Dem. 43 *Makart.* 75 ὁ ἄρχων . . . κύριος ἔστω ἐπιβάλλειν κατὰ τὸ τέλος. ἐὰν δὲ μείζονος ζημίας δοκῇ ἄξιος εἶναι, προσκαλεσάμενος πρόπεμπτα καὶ τίμημα ἐπιγραψάμενος, ὅ τι ἂν δοκῇ αὐτῷ, εἰσαγέτω εἰς τὴν ἡλιαίαν. ἐὰν δ' ἁλῷ, τιμάτω ἡ ἡλιαία περὶ τοῦ ἁλόντος, ὅ τι χρὴ αὐτὸν παθεῖν ἢ ἀποτεῖσαι. There is some doubt as to the meaning of the words κατὰ τὸ τέλος. For example MSL 49, n. 22, Lipsius, *AR* 53, n. 2, Thalheim, *RE* s.v. ἐπιβολή, Bo. Sm. i. 279, ii. 245 interpret them as in the text above. Dareste, *Dem.* ii. 49, on the other hand, translates 'le frapper d'une amende proportionnée à sa fortune', the penalty was to be proportional to the census class of the wrongdoer. This rendering is accepted by Kahrstedt, *Mag.* 216, in the course of an argument to establish that in the fourth century ἐπιβολή as a term of art was restricted to penalties imposed by a court (or by the boule or ekklesia) on the motion of a magistrate because they exceeded the limit allowed to him, as opposed to penalties imposed by him within that limit. In the interests of the same argument he would like to substitute καί for ἤ in the following sentence from Ar. *Ath. Pol.* 56. 7: κύριός ἐστι (ὁ ἄρχων) τοῖς ἀδικοῦσιν ἐπιβάλ[λειν ἢ εἰσάγειν εἰς] τὸ δικαστήριον. These arguments are perhaps rather fine drawn; but Kahrstedt is right to draw a distinction between the fines which a magistrate could impose merely to keep order (at festivals, for example, or dramatic performances for which he might be responsible) and those which served a much wider purpose as sanctions for the whole body of laws in his domain (the protection, for example, if he was archon, of widows and orphans).

[2] *IG* i². 84. 26 ff. (quoted on p. 6, n. 2), Aischin. 1 *Timarch.* 35 (but on this see p. 4, n. 1). We must distinguish from this right to impose a fine up to a certain value the right enjoyed by certain magistrates to adjudicate without reference to a dikastery cases involving claims of less than a certain value. Thus the apodektai and the Forty were allowed to adjudicate on cases involving ten drachmai or less (Ar. *Ath. Pol.* 52. 3, 53. 2).

ἐπιβαλόντες δὲ τὸ ἀργύριον πράξασθαι μὲν οὐκ ἐπεχείρησαν, ἐξιούσης δὲ τῆς ἀρχῆς γράψαντες εἰς λεύκωμα τοῖς ταμίαις παρέδοσαν). On laying down office they recorded it on a tablet which was handed to the treasurers of Athena, and made no reference to it in their own official accounts at their εὔθυνα. The treasurers took it upon themselves to remit the fine, but none the less Polyainos was prosecuted by the procedure known as ἀπογραφή. We look elsewhere at this procedure (pp. 211 ff.) and also at the procedure at a magistrate's εὔθυνα (pp. 208 ff.). For our present purpose the story seems to establish three points: first that there was no direct right of appeal in such a case, for if there had been Polyainos would surely have availed himself of it: second that indirectly the victim of a fine could get his case before a court simply by not paying the fine; it then lay with the magistrate to get the fine confirmed by a court (11 οὔτε γὰρ εὐθύνας ὑπέσχον, οὔτε εἰς δικαστήριον εἰσελθόντες τὰ πραχθέντα ψήφῳ κύρια κατέστησαν): third that the legitimacy of the fine could be challenged at the magistrate's εὔθυνα; this might lead to his being penalized and, one would suppose, though there is no evidence for this, to restitution for the victim.

One of the peculiarities of this vestigial power of the magistrates was that in certain circumstances it was a magistrate and not a private citizen who had to take the initiative in bringing a matter before a court. The circumstances had to be special, for at one point Lykourgos correctly implies that at Athens without a prosecutor there is no judge, and there was no public prosecutor at Athens.[1] In these exceptional cases the magistrate might either be the equivalent of a private citizen and bring the suit in the court of another magistrate, or he might initiate proceedings in a court presided over by himself. An example of the former class would be the hieropoioi who had resort to the court of the archon,[2] and perhaps the basileus who, on one view of a passage in Andokides, proceeds against a man alleged in an

[1] Lykourg. *Leokr.* 4 οὔθ' ὁ νόμος οὔθ' ἡ τῶν δικαστῶν ψῆφος ἄνευ τοῦ παραδώσοντος αὐτοῖς τοὺς ἀδικοῦντας ἰσχύει. Kahrstedt, *Mag.* 222. On the role of ὁ βουλόμενος in certain suits see pp. 76 f.

[2] *IG* i². 84. 26 ff. (a decree of 421/0 B.C.) τε̃ς δὲ πονπε̃ς hόπος [ἂν hος κάλλιστα] πενφθε̃ι, hο[ι hι]εροπ[οι]οὶ ἐπιμελόσθον, καὶ ἄν τίς τι ἀκοσμε̃[ι, κύριοι ἔστον αὐ]τοὶ μὲν ζεμ[ιο̃ν μέχρι πε]ντέκοντα δραχμο̃ν καὶ ἐκγράφεν ἐκ [το̃ν πενπόντον. ἐὰν] δέ τις ἄχσ[ιος ε̃ι μέζον]ος ζε[μ]ίας, τὰς ἐπιβολὰς ποιό[ντ]ον [hοπόσας ἂν δοκε̃ι κα]ὶ ἐσαγ[όντον ἐς τὸ δικαστ]έρ[ιο]ν τὸ το̃ ἄρχοντος.

ἔνδειξις to be guilty of impiety by bringing him first before the boule; the boule passes the case on to a dikastery presided over, on this view, by some magistrate other than the basileus.[1] We must assume that in such cases the prosecuting magistrate was in all material respects on all fours with an ordinary prosecutor (ὁ βουλόμενος).

Better attested and juristically more interesting are the cases where the magistrate had to refer a penalty imposed—perhaps one had better say proposed—by him for decision of a court sitting under his own presidency. We have seen above (p. 4) that the archon had to bring before a court fines for the maltreatment of widows and orphans, and the court for the trial of such cases was the archon's. Similarly when in *IG* i². 55. 5 ff. the polemarch is given the duty of bringing before a court cases infringing the rights of a certain Thessalian, we may assume that the court trying any such case would be the polemarch's. In this same class would have fallen the agoranomoi,[2] the strategoi,[3] and possibly the overseers of the docks.[4] Unfortunately we are unable to say with certainty how the magistrate discharged this double role; but we may accept as likely the surmise that where he was a member of a board, a strategos for example, he preferred the charge and his colleagues presided, whilst where he was a single magistrate such as archon or polemarch he was represented in one capacity or the other by one of his paredroi (on whom see pp. 11 f.).[5]

(ii) *The nine archons*

The most important single group of magistrates judicially was the nine archons. They did not however function in this capacity as a board, at least in the classical period.

Taking them separately, there was first the archon, called for convenience the eponymous archon because he gave his name to

[1] So Kahrstedt, *Mag.* 232; the evidence is in Andok. 1 *Myst.* 111. Lipsius, *AR* 62, n. 34, deduces from this passage that the basileus presided at the trial. MacDowell, *Mysteries* 142, is right in saying that we cannot gather from the speech what the exact procedure was. We cannot assume, as Kahrstedt does, that the basileus did *not* preside, and the other cases alleged by him to fall into this category are equally doubtful.

[2] Aristoph. *Ach.* 824, 968, *Wasps* 1406 ff.

[3] Lys. 15 *Alk.* ii. 1.

[4] Dem. 47 *Euerg.* 24; but it is by no means self-evident that this court was presided over by the overseers of the docks.

[5] Kahrstedt, *Mag.* 233 f.

the official year (though the epithet does not occur in fact until Roman imperial times). On assuming office his first act was a solemn promise that everyone would enjoy occupation of his property undisturbed during the archon's year of office.[1] This suggests that at one stage the archon was responsible for all cases dealing with property, but by the fourth century this sphere had been narrowed to cases concerning the family, whether property cases or other. The following list of archon's cases is drawn from Ar. *Ath. Pol.* 56. 6: cases concerning the maltreatment of parents, of orphans or of heiresses, mismanagement of orphans' estates, suits against guardians, against parents alleged to be dissipating the family property through insanity or idleness, for the division of property held in common, for instituting a guardianship or deciding between rival claims to be a guardian, for the discovery of property or documents, for claims to be a guardian, for an inheritance or the hand of an heiress. The archon also had executive functions out of which jurisdiction might arise: he had general oversight over orphans, over heiresses, and over widows who claimed to be pregnant by their dead husbands; he was responsible for letting out the estates of orphans and of heiresses till they reached the age of fourteen, and for receiving the official valuations of the properties offered as security by lessees of such estates;[2] he had to manage dramatic and other contests and the allotment of liturgies connected therewith, which involved jurisdiction both when a man raised an objection (*σκῆψις*) to being drafted and when he challenged some other citizen to take on the liturgy or exchange estates with him (*ἀντίδοσις*); finally, he was responsible for certain processions and festivals.[3]

The basileus took over most of the religious functions of the old kings. In the executive field this involved the management of the Mysteries, the Lenaian Dionysia, torch races, and in general 'all the ancestral festivals', to use the words of Aristotle.[4] In this capacity he had jurisdiction where two litigants were claiming a priesthood, or where families or priests were at odds about cult

[1] Ar. *Ath. Pol.* 56. 2.

[2] Ar. *Ath. Pol.* 56. 7, *An. Bekk.* (*Λέξ. Ῥητ.*) 310. 1 ff., Dem. 35 *Lakrit.* 48, 43 *Makart.* 75, Hyper. 3 *Euxen.* 6.

[3] Ar. *Ath. Pol.* 56. 3–5. Dem. 21 *Meid.* 60 mentions the possibility of a choregos' being sued in the archon's court for including a foreigner in his chorus.

[4] Ar. *Ath. Pol.* 57. 1, Plato, *Pol.* 290 e, Lys. 6 *Andok.* 4, Dem. 35 *Lakrit.* 48, 39 *Boiot.* i. 9.

matters.[1] He had oversight over land belonging to the gods, and he reported to the boule leases of sacred precincts.[2] The basileus was responsible for two branches of jurisdiction, both in primitive times religious in tendency, suits concerning impiety and homicide; these latter embraced wounding with intent to kill, arson, and poisoning.[3] Homicide cases had many peculiarities in regard to procedure which were due to the religious implications of the act: it had polluted the community and an essential element in the procedure was the elimination of this taint. These peculiarities affected both the venue and the part played by the *ἡγεμών* of the court; see the discussion of the homicide courts below (pp. 36 ff.). Here it will suffice to stress three points. First, for religious reasons homicide suits always remained in form private suits (*δίκαι*) and there was never a *γραφὴ φόνου*.[4] Second, and in a sense inconsistently with this first fact, the basileus took an important executive step early in the proceedings, when he made a proclamation telling the accused to keep away from 'the Mysteries and other places laid down by custom' or some such formula.[5] Third, the function of the basileus in these trials is sometimes described by the word *δικάζειν*, while the function of the jury is called *διαγνῶναι*.[6]

The polemarch ceased to be a military official early in the fifth century, but the powers, executive and judicial, which remained to him were recognizable survivals of a military function. The sacrifices and contests which fell to his care were connected with war.[7] He was charged with the care of the

[1] Ar. *Ath. Pol.* 27. 2. The reading *ἱερῶν* is to be preferred to the conjectured *γερῶν*: the latter is taken from *An. Bekk.* (*Λέξ. Ῥητ.*) 219. 20, but id. 310. 9 has *ἱερῶν*. Lipsius, *AR* 61, n. 33.

[2] Ar. *Ath. Pol.* 47. 4, 57. 2, *SIG* 83. 54, 204. 25.

[3] Ar. *Ath. Pol.* 57. 2–3; MacDowell, *Homicide* 33 ff.

[4] See p. 77, n. 2.

[5] Ar. *Ath. Pol.* 57. 2 *λαγχάνονται δὲ καὶ αἱ τοῦ φόνου δίκαι πᾶσαι πρὸς τοῦτον, καὶ ὁ προαγορεύων εἴργεσθαι τῶν νομίμων οὗτός ἐστιν*, *An. Bekk.* (*Λέξ. Ῥητ.*) 310. 6–9 *ὁ βασιλεὺς εἰσάγει τὰς φονικὰς ἁπάσας, ἐπεὶ καὶ προαγορεύει τὸν ἀνδροφόνον εἴργεσθαι τῶν νόμων* (read *νομίμων*), *καὶ περὶ τῶν ἱερῶν καὶ τοῖς γένεσι δικάζει*, Poll. 8. 90 *προαγορεύει δὲ τοῖς ἐν αἰτίᾳ ἀπέχεσθαι μυστηρίων καὶ τῶν ἄλλων νομίμων*. MacDowell, *Homicide* 25, is right to point out that this proclamation of the basileus followed the denunciation to him of the accused by the victim's relatives and was neither prior to nor contemporaneous with it.

[6] *IG* i^2. 115. 11 ff. There is some doubt here whether *βασιλέας* in the plural means the successive holders of the office of basileus or the basileus sitting with the phylobasileis; on this see p. 43. On the significance of *δικάζειν* see p. 38, n. 1.

[7] Ar. *Ath. Pol.* 58. 1.

children of those who had been killed in war; these children were brought up at the public expense.[1]

In jurisdiction he was mainly concerned with cases in which metics were involved, particularly their family cases; Aristotle closes his account of the polemarch's duties by saying that he stood to metics in the same relation as the archon to citizens.[2] The precise role of the polemarch and its bearing on the duties and privileges of metics have been discussed in detail in vol. i, pp. 193 ff. It was argued there that resort to the polemarch's court was a privilege reserved for metics, ἰσοτελεῖς, and πρόξενοι among non-citizens, though we cannot be certain exactly how this worked as a privilege, nor whether the rule was simply that metic defendants had to be sued in that court or whether metic plaintiffs could also sue there irrespective of the status of the defendant.[3] Probability seemed to lie with the view that a metic plaintiff had the right to sue before the polemarch, and that this was a privilege because the right to sue at all in a city's courts was likely *a priori* to belong to citizens only and the polemarch was the official who vouched for the plaintiff's being in the class of non-citizens privileged to sue. Foreigners who were not metics might of course have this right, but it would not be automatic, and the method of its application would have depended on the existence and terms of a treaty (σύμβολα) between the foreigner's home city and Athens. Thus in the preliminaries to a trial in which one of the litigants was a metic the polemarch played a role quite distinct from that of any other magistrate with judicial competence.[4]

In one other matter at the preliminary stage the polemarch's role was unique. In certain cases where a metic was defendant the plaintiff could demand sureties for his appearance in court up to

[1] Plato, *Menex.* 248 e, schol. Dem. 24 *Timokr.* 20.

[2] Ar. *Ath. Pol.* 58. 3.

[3] Vol. i, p. 194, n. 2.

[4] For the details of the procedure see vol. i, pp. 193 ff. For the polemarch's role in the mid fifth century see *IG* i². 16. Wade-Gery, *EGH* 182 ff., deduces from the wording of that inscription (especially 9 f. παρὰ τῷ πολεμάρχῳ and 18 f. καταδικάσῃ) that when it was inscribed, perhaps between 469 and 462, the polemarch and other magistrates actually gave the decisions still; but on this see p. 38, n. 1. The provisions of *IG* i². 55 (a decree of *c.* 431) support the view that the polemarch had to protect the interests of the metic plaintiff: there the polemarch is instructed, under pain of a fine of 1,000 drachmai in case of disobedience, to introduce a case against anyone who wrongs Aristonous or his children. G. E. M. de Ste Croix, *CQ* 11 (1961) 273 f., rightly regards the prospective prosecutor in such a case as the wronged metic.

a sum related to the matter in dispute. This he did before the polemarch.[1]

Once the preliminary stage was passed cases fell into two broad categories. There were those which were remitted to the Forty. These cases the polemarch did not see again. But there were others in which he acted as *ἡγεμών* throughout. These were, first, suits dealing with family matters, mostly between metic and metic, such as guardianship, inheritance, heiresses; probably private suits only, since it is unlikely that there were *γραφαί* protecting metic orphans, heiresses, and parents parallel to the *εἰσαγγελίαι κακώσεως* for citizens of these classes. Another private suit falling to the polemarch was for the protection of a master who had manumitted a slave under conditions which the freedman was not observing (*δίκη ἀποστασίου*). The defendant in such a suit was most likely to be a metic, and the plaintiff might also be. The only *γραφή* which came before the polemarch was the *γραφὴ ἀπροστασίου*, a suit against a metic for 'not having a patron', which may mean either not having a patron at the moment of his enrolment or, more probably, not being able to produce a patron at the moment of the charge (vol. i, pp. 189 ff.).

The eponymous archon, the basileus, and the polemarch (but not the thesmothetai) had each two assistants (*πάρεδροι*), whose position was slightly anomalous, in that they were selected by the archon whom they served, but were yet public officials who could act for him and who had therefore to pass both the test of eligibility before taking up office, the *δοκιμασία*, and the examination of accounts on laying it down, the *εὔθυνα*.[2] We have instances of the eponymous archon's nominating his father as paredros and of a man's buying the post from an impoverished basileus; in one passage we are told that Aristophon of Azenia was the archon's paredros, and in another that a certain Mnesarchides, the archon's paredros, received a deposition as his deputy.[3] Not only was the selection of paredroi free from the chances of the lot, but so far as we know there was no rule against iteration. These officials may therefore in fact have contributed some small degree of professionalism to the administration of the law. There is some

[1] See below, p. 87, and vol. i, p. 273, n. 1. It is not certain whether the surety was for appearance in court or for carrying out the court's award.

[2] Ar. *Ath. Pol.* 56. 1; Lipsius, *AR* 66 f., Bu. Sw. 1059 f., Kahrstedt, *Mag.* 124 ff.

[3] Dem. 21 *Meid.* 178, 59 *Neair.* 72, Aischin. 1 *Timarch.* 158, Dem. 58 *Theokr.* 32.

direct evidence that they did: we are told that the basileus who was alleged to have sold the office of paredros had done so to remedy his own lack of skill in affairs;[1] and Aristophon must certainly have been deeply versed in at least one type of case, for he boasted that he had been acquitted seventy-five times in *γραφαὶ παρανόμων*.[2]

The remaining six archons, the thesmothetai, were in some respects the most important in the judicial sphere. Unlike the others, it seems that they never had any strictly executive functions save those that were concerned with the administration of justice.

The origins of the office are obscure, but in practice it seems to have worked out that they took over jurisdiction in all fields which did not naturally come within the purview of the other archons. Thus they would have been the first magistrates whose duties were solely judicial, while, looked at in sum, the cases they took were rather miscellaneous. According to Ar. *Ath. Pol.* 3. 4 they were instituted for the purpose of recording ordinances and preserving them for the judging of disputes between litigants: *θεσμοθέται δὲ πολλοῖς ὕστερον ἔτεσιν* (sc. than the other archons) *ᾑρέθησαν . . . ὅπως ἀναγράψαντες τὰ θέσμια φυλάττωσι πρὸς τὴν τῶν ἀμφισβητούντων κρίσιν*. There is some dispute as to the meaning of this sentence and as to its value historically. It may be no more than a guess on Aristotle's part; not a very good guess, since occasionally the word is applied to all nine archons and this account does not explain how the thesmothetai acquired independent jurisdiction.[3] Nevertheless the sentence may have value as indicating what Aristotle reckoned from survivals the thesmothetai originally did. There are two views as to what this was. On one view the thesmothetai originally acted as assessors to the other archons when these latter were sitting in judgement, and recorded their decisions, making as it were a book of precedents. But it seems unlikely that if this had been the case they would have subsequently acquired jurisdiction in quite other spheres, or that the paredroi of the other archons would have been needed. Moreover it would be strange that the use of precedent in this

[1] Dem. 59 *Neair.* 81 *διὰ τὴν ἀπειρίαν τῶν πραγμάτων καὶ τὴν ἀκακίαν τὴν ἑαυτοῦ τοῦτον πάρεδρον ποιήσαιτο, ἵνα διοικήσῃ τὴν ἀρχήν.*

[2] Aischin. 3 *Ktes.* 194.

[3] Dem. 57 *Euboul.* 66 and 70, Plut. *Solon* 25. 3 (taken with Plato, *Phaidr.* 235 d), *An. Bekk.* (*Λέξ. Ῥητ.*) 311. 11. Cf. Hignett, *HAC* 77.

way should have entirely disappeared. It seems more likely that they recorded rules which they intended to follow in giving judgement on matters falling outside the competence of other magistrates; these *θέσμια* would have been something like the praetor's edict at Rome, and at some stage or stages (the codifications, for example, of Drakon, Solon, and Kleisthenes) would have crystallized into written and published *νόμοι*.[1] So much for *ἀναγράψαντες*. As to guardianship (*φυλάττωσι*), it is possible that the thesmothetai from the first played a leading part in conjunction with the Areopagos in applying sanctions for unconstitutional behaviour, a function described by the rather vague term *νομοφυλακία*.

This sketchy outline of the historical development of the office goes some way to account for some of its main functions in the classical period. First there was an executive task, but one directly concerned with the administration of justice: the thesmothetai fixed the dates of trials and assigned the courts to the several other magistrates.[2] This was more than a mere piece of business organization; on its efficient discharge depended the avoidance both of unnecessary delays and of possible corruption.

Of judicial functions proper the most important category of case falling to the thesmothetai was that concerned with offences against the state. According to the *Ath. Pol.* they played a leading part in three special procedures which were all of the nature of impeachments: *εἰσαγγελία*, *καταχειροτονία*, and *προβολή*. The common factor in these procedures was that the boule, the ekklesia, or both took cognizance of an alleged wrong against the state, and if the vote went against him the wrongdoer was as a rule (not always in the case of *προβολαί*) then arraigned before

[1] Hignett, *HAC* 77, quotes with approval Thirlwall, *History of Greece* ii. 17: probably the thesmothetai were so called 'because, in the absence of a written code, those who declare and interpret the laws may properly be said to make them'. See also Wilamowitz, *A. und A.* i. 244, Lipsius, *AR* 68 ff., Bu. Sw. 1096 ff., Bo. Sm. i. 87 f., Latte, *RE* s.v. 'Thesmotheten', Lacey, *Family* 55 (their duty was 'to assemble the case-law of the community by recording (though not publishing) judgements').

[2] Ar. *Ath. Pol.* 59. 1 *οἱ δὲ θεσμοθέται πρῶτον μὲν τοῦ προγράψαι τὰ δικαστήριά εἰσι κύριοι τίσιν ἡμέραις δεῖ δικάζειν, ἔπειτα τοῦ δοῦναι ταῖς ἀρχαῖς*. In Dem. 21 *Meid.* 47 the *νόμος τῆς ὕβρεως* lays down: *οἱ δὲ θεσμοθέται εἰσαγόντων εἰς τὴν ἡλιαίαν τριάκοντα ἡμερῶν ἀφ' ἧς ἂν ⟨ῇ⟩ ἡ γραφή, ἐὰν μή τι δημόσιον κωλύῃ, εἰ δὲ μή, ὅταν ᾖ πρῶτον οἷόν τε*. But here of course the thesmothetai are acting in a dual capacity, as presidents of the relevant court and as responsible for arranging the calendar of trials; had this been, say, an archon's case, we do not know how a similar provision would have run. Cf. *IG* ii². 1629. 204 ff. (quoted on p. 32, n. 7).

a dikastery. The *Ath. Pol.* leaves us in doubt as to the exact role of the thesmothetai in these cases; the most probable view is that they presided at the dikastery hearing whenever this occurred (though, *pace* the *Ath. Pol.*, cases of impiety arising out of *προβολαί* most likely fell to the basileus), but not at the hearings before the boule or the ekklesia.[1] The function described as 'introducing' (*εἰσάγειν*) was exactly parallel to that of any other *ἡγεμών*. Closely related to this type of case, where the offence was some act or neglect directly threatening the constitution or safety of the state, were those public suits, *γραφαί*, directed against unconstitutional acts in the course of legislation. The principal of these were the *γραφαὶ παρανόμων* and *νόμον μὴ ἐπιτήδειον θεῖναι*, together with three closely related suits known to us by name only, the *γραφαὶ πρυτανική, προεδρική, ἐπιστατική*.[2]

There is another class of case which it is difficult to specify precisely, but which perhaps belongs here. It is a class which may have disappeared with the first Athenian empire. These were cases involving the penalty of death, exile, or *ἀτιμία*, where the defendant was the citizen of an allied city. According to the terms imposed on Chalkis in 446/5 there was in such cases *ἔφεσις* to 'the heliaia of the thesmothetai'.[3]

The thesmothetai presided over two kinds of case arising out of a magistrate's accountability, his *εὔθυνα*. For a period—its length is not known—after a magistrate had laid down office he was liable to be accused on some specific charge of malpractice during his year of office. Such charges were made to a *εὔθυνος* (probably of the magistrate's tribe). That official could reject the

[1] Ar. *Ath. Pol.* 59. 2 *ἔτι δὲ τὰς εἰσαγγελίας εἰσαγγέλλουσιν εἰς τὸν δῆμον καὶ τὰς καταχειροτονίας καὶ τὰς προβολὰς ἁπάσας εἰσάγουσιν οὗτοι*. We have to distinguish three things, which this text does not: (1) initiating an impeachment (for which one would expect the verb *εἰσαγγέλλειν*); (2) presiding at meetings of the boule or ekklesia at which the impeachment was presented (for which there is no term of art); (3) presiding over the court to which the boule or ekklesia might have remitted the case (for which the verb would be *εἰσάγειν*). Lipsius, *AR* 207, n. 99, followed by Blass, would insert *ἃς* before *εἰσαγγέλλουσιν*. Wilamowitz, *A. und A.* i. 244, n. 117, suggests omitting *εἰσαγγέλλουσιν εἰς τὸν δῆμον*, but as Lipsius points out these words must have stood in the text read by Pollux (8. 87) and Photios (s.v. *θεσμοθέται*). D. M. Lewis suggests *τοῖς* before *εἰσαγγέλλουσιν*.

[2] Ar. *Ath. Pol.* 59. 2, and for the *γραφὴ πρυτανική* Harpokr. s.v. *ῥητορικὴ γραφή*, *An. Bekk.* (*Λέξ. 'Ρητ.*) 299. 24 f.; this suit no doubt gave place to the *γραφὴ προεδρική*.

[3] *IG* i². 39. 75 f.; de Ste Croix, *CQ* 11 (1961) 271.

charge, but if he accepted it he referred it, if the act charged was a wrong against an individual, to the Forty, or, if it was a wrong against the state, to the thesmothetai; these officials then had to direct the further proceedings in the case. Exceptionally the strategoi were liable to this process of *εὔθυνα* at any time during their tenure of office (as well of course as being liable to the ordinary *εὔθυνα*); the thesmothetai presided in cases brought against the strategoi in this way.[1]

Next comes a group of cases described, rather misleadingly, by Ar. *Ath. Pol.* 59. 3 as suits in which the *παράστασις* (a small fee payable to the state by the prosecutor) was due.[2] Aristotle's list of these *γραφαί* is as follows: *ξενίας, δωροξενίας* (*ἄν τις δῶρα δοὺς ἀποφύγῃ τὴν ξενίαν*), *συκοφαντίας, δώρων, ψευδεγγραφῆς, ψευδοκλητείας, βουλεύσεως, ἀγραφίου, μοιχείας*. It does not help to describe this group of suits as directed against delicts which militated primarily against a private, and only mediately against a public, interest.[3] This description fits some of the suits in the group, but not all; and the same is true of the next group, for which, though they are omitted by Aristotle, we have evidence in the orators and Aristophanes. These were *δεκασμοῦ*,[4] *ὕβρεως*,[5] *ἑταιρήσεως*,[6] *ἀδίκως εἱρχθῆναι ὡς μοιχόν*,[7] *κλοπῆς*,[8] *ἀναπογράφου μετάλλου*,[9] *διαφθείρειν τὸ*

[1] Ar. *Ath. Pol.* 59. 2 (the strategoi), 48. 5 (other magistrates).

[2] On the *παράστασις* see p. 94. Aristotle's wording is misleading, both because his list is incomplete, and because there were *γραφαί* which came before the thesmothetai which did not incur the *παράστασις*, the *γραφὴ ὕβρεως* for example (Isok. 20 *Loch.* 2).

[3] As does Lipsius, *AR* 72, followed by Bu. Sw. 1097. Lipsius withdraws the suggestion on p. 410, n. 134, but returns to it on p. 828.

[4] Law in Dem. 46 *Steph.* ii. 26.

[5] Law in Dem. 21 *Meid.* 47. Cf. Aischin. 1 *Timarch.* 16, Dem. 37 *Pant.* 33, Isok. 20 *Loch.* 2 (on which see n. 2 above).

[6] Dem. 22 *Androt.* 21.

[7] Dem. 59 *Neair.* 66.

[8] We have evidence for the presidency of the thesmothetai only for suits *κλοπῆς δημοσίων χρημάτων* (Aristoph. *Wasps* 935), but it is a fair assumption that they presided in other suits for theft. These might be either *γραφαί* or *δίκαι*. Cf. Bo. Sm. ii. 109 f. Although MSL give *δίκαι κλοπῆς* to the thesmothetai, Lipsius, *AR* 627 ff., does not list them in his chapter on their private suits. For the *γραφή* see vol. i, p. 235, n. 2.

[9] Suda s.v. *ἀγράφου μετάλλου δίκη· οἱ τὰ ἀργύρεια μέταλλα ἐργαζόμενοι ὅπου βούλοιντο καινοῦ ἔργου ἄρξασθαι, φανερὸν ἐποιοῦντο τοῖς ἐπ' ἐκείνοις τεταγμένοις ὑπὸ τοῦ δήμου καὶ ἀπεγράφοντο τοῦ τελεῖν ἕνεκα τῷ δήμῳ εἰκοστὴν τετάρτην τοῦ καινοῦ μετάλλου. εἴ τις οὖν ἐδόκει λάθρα ἐργάζεσθαι μέταλλον, τὸν μὴ ἀπογραψάμενον ἐξῆν τῷ βουλομένῳ γράφεσθαι καὶ ἐλέγχειν.* There is no evidence as to the presidency, but the fact that *δίκαι μεταλλικαί* fell to the thesmothetai (Ar. *Ath. Pol.* 59. 5) may confirm the view that *γραφαὶ ἀναπογράφου μετάλλου* also fell to them.

νόμισμα.[1] A *γραφὴ ὑποβολῆς* available against one who had been smuggled into the citizen body is vouched for only by a grammarian.[2]

Certain private suits came to the thesmothetai in addition to the *δίκη κλοπῆς* (on which see p. 15, n. 8). First there were the *δίκαι ἀπὸ συμβόλων*, suits brought under treaties (*σύμβολα*) existing between Athens and other cities. Such treaties had to be ratified by a court sitting under the thesmothetai, and it was natural that suits arising out of them should have the same venue.[3] Allied to them were the *δίκαι ἐμπορικαί*; these belonged to the category of monthly suits (*δίκαι ἔμμηνοι*), so called because they had to be decided within thirty days of being initiated. They were probably created as a special class of case around 355 B.C. and entrusted to the thesmothetai at the same time; before that date suits of a similar kind, though probably not defined in exactly the same terms, had come before the nautodikai (on whom see pp. 23 f.). The *δίκαι μεταλλικαί* (private suits arising out of the working of mines) were also monthly suits and under the competence of the thesmothetai.[4]

It is not easy to give a reason why the thesmothetai should have been responsible, as they were, for *δίκαι* against slaves for the slandering of free men and against perjurers in a trial before the Areopagos.[5] But the *ad hoc* assignment to them of *διαδικασίαι* on claims for rewards by informers about the mutilation of the Hermai seems natural.[6]

The thesmothetai presided in certain judicial proceedings which were neither *δίκαι* nor *γραφαί*. One such proceeding was any *δοκιμασία* of a magistrate which came before a court; it is a matter of dispute whether every *δοκιμασία* after being voted on by the boule was submitted thereafter to a dikastery, or only cases of appeal against an adverse judgement by the boule. They also presided over cases where the boule either wished to impose a penalty beyond the limit allowed or had imposed a penalty which the defendant desired to resist by way of *ἔφεσις*

[1] Dem. 24 *Timokr.* 212 ff., 20 *Lept.* 167; assigned to the thesmothetai on *a priori* grounds.

[2] *An. Bekk.* (*Λέξ. Ῥητ.*) 311. 33 ff.

[3] Ar. *Ath. Pol.* 59. 6.

[4] Ar. *Ath. Pol.* 59. 5. On the dating see Gernet, *DSGA* 173 ff.

[5] Ar. *Ath. Pol.* 59. 5–6. We should have expected the latter suit to be under the basileus, since normally trials for false witness came before the same magistrate as had presided in the original suit.

[6] Andok. 1 *Myst.* 28.

(τὰς καταγνώσεις τὰς ἐκ τῆς βουλῆς). Where a man had been excluded from a deme, he could bring suit against the demesmen to have his name accepted; the thesmothetai presided over the court which heard the case.[1]

Two passages in orators state that the thesmothetai had the duty of putting to death any man who illegally returned after having been banished for murder or treason. Though they may at one time have had this executive power, what is probably meant in the classical period is that the thesmothetai brought such a man before a court by ἀπαγωγή and then presided at his trial; a man at that period would surely have had the opportunity to plead before a court, maintaining for example that it was a case of mistaken identity.[2]

Allied to this was their responsibility for certain kinds of ἔνδειξις, including ἔνδειξις against a man who was occupying a magistracy in spite of being in debt to the state.[3]

(iii) *The Eleven*

The Eleven (there is no satisfactory explanation of their number) were primarily executive officers, elected by lot. They were charged with the conviction and punishment of common criminals, technically classified as κακοῦργοι, and with the care of the city prison. Hence they were sometimes called ἐπιμεληταὶ τῶν κακούργων or δεσμοφύλακες. They also supervised the infliction of the death penalty and execution upon property forfeit to the state.[4]

In the classical period they had certain judicial functions arising out of this police activity, and they afford a striking instance of the failure of the Athenians to distinguish sharply between executive and judicial powers. Originally (and as an office they went back at least as far as Solon)[5] they had probably

[1] Ar. *Ath. Pol.* 55. 2–5, 59. 4.

[2] Dem. 23 *Aristokr.* 31, Lykourg. *Leokr.* 121; MacDowell, *Homicide* 121 f., 140.

[3] Ar. *Ath. Pol.* 52. 1, Dem. 24 *Timokr.* 22 (both quoted on p. 229, n. 6).

[4] Ar. *Ath. Pol.* 52. 1, Ant. 5 *Her.* 17, Dem. 24 *Timokr.* 105, schol. Dem. 22 *Androt.* 26, 24 *Timokr.* 80, Poll. 8. 102. If we may believe Isai. 4 *Nikostr.* 28, one board of Eleven were all condemned to death for letting prisoners go. Cf. Kahrstedt *Mag.* 204.

[5] If we can trust Ar. *Ath. Pol.* 7. 3 on this point; Wilamowitz, *A. und A.* i. 222.

been empowered to put to death common criminals who were caught red-handed in certain crimes. By the fourth century this power was restricted to cases where the criminal admitted the charge. In these cases the Eleven acted in a kind of judicial capacity in accepting his confession and convicting him. We do not know what safeguards other than the εὔθυνα there were against the abuse of this power.[1] If the man protested his innocence, he was entitled to trial by a jury, and in that case the Eleven presided.[2] The procedures under which this might occur were those known as ἀπαγωγή, ἔνδειξις, and ἐφήγησις, which are fully discussed elsewhere (pp. 221 ff.). We discuss there too the definition of the technical term κακοῦργοι, against whom alone, in theory at least, these procedures were available.

When, exceptionally, ἀπαγωγή was made by decree of the people to extend beyond the sphere of κακοῦργοι (for example, to metics who had left Attica in a period of war) we may presume that the Eleven presided.[3] Out of their executive power to deal with property forfeit to the state developed their responsibility for cases falling under the special procedure known as ἀπογραφή (on which see pp. 211 ff.).[4]

(iv) *The Forty*

The Forty as officials were the lineal descendants of the deme judges (δικασταὶ κατὰ δήμους) instituted by Peisistratos as circuit judges to discourage country people from coming into the city for the settlement of their legal differences.[5] At some date between Peisistratos and 453/2 B.C. the office must have been abolished, for we are told that in that year they were restored, being then thirty in number. After the rule of the Thirty their number was increased to forty. They were chosen by lot, four from each tribe. They were sometimes still called δικασταὶ κατὰ δήμους, though they now operated in the city.[6] They acted not as a single board,

[1] Paoli, *Z* 76 (1959) 100, rather strains language when he equates 'confessed wrongdoing' with 'being caught ἐπ' αὐτοφώρῳ'. In Aischin. 1 *Timarch.* 91 the two things are distinguished.

[2] Ar. *Ath. Pol.* 52. 1, Aristoph. *Wasps* 1108, Aischin. 1 *Timarch.* 91, Dem. 24 *Timokr.* 63, 105, 113, 35 *Lakrit.* 47, Poll. 8. 102.

[3] Hyper. 5 *Athenog.* 29.

[4] Ar. *Ath. Pol.* 52. 1.

[5] Ar. *Ath. Pol.* 16. 5.

[6] Ar. *Ath. Pol.* 26. 3, 48. 5, 53. 1, Dem. 24 *Timokr.* 112. On the historical development of the office see Gernet, *DSGA* 105 f.

but in their tribal groups of four. Each tribal group was responsible for those cases in which the defendant was of their tribe.[1] When a case came before them, if the matter at issue was worth less than ten drachmai they could pronounce judgement forthwith. We may conjecture that each case was assigned to one of the four appropriate members of the Forty, since if all four sat on each case it would have been hard to deal with an equally divided vote on any issue.

If the matter at issue was greater than ten drachmai (we must suppose that for this purpose the value was that stated in his claim by the plaintiff), the case was handed over to one of the public arbitrators (see pp. 66 ff.). If he could not reconcile the litigants, he gave a decision which, if accepted, counted as a judgement and brought proceedings to an end. If either party declined to accept the award, the evidence, the challenges, and the laws cited by each party during the hearing were sealed up in separate caskets, the written decision of the arbitrator was attached, and all these documents were handed over by the arbitrator to the four members of the Forty. They had to bring all such cases to trial before a dikastery under their presidency; at the trial no material not used before the arbitrator could be used by either litigant (see pp. 101 f.).

There has been considerable controversy on the exact definition of cases which were remitted to the Forty. Aristotle describes them loosely in *Ath. Pol.* 53. 1 as 'the other δίκαι', having just been dealing with suits which came before the Eleven, the eisagogeis, and the apodektai, but before he has come to the functions of the archons. The right view probably is that the Forty were responsible for all suits that would in the normal course (if relating to matters worth more than ten drachmai) come before arbitrators; that is to say, all private suits except monthly suits (which fell either to the eisagogeis or to the thesmothetai), homicide suits (which were technically private and fell to the basileus), and suits dealing with the family and family property (which fell to the archon or, for metic families, to the polemarch). Where the defendant in these cases was a metic, ἰσοτελής, or πρόξενος, he had to be cited in the first instance before the polemarch.

[1] Ar. *Ath. Pol.* 53. 2; but Paoli, *Studi Betti* (Milan, 1962) iii. 7, believes that in this context ὁ φεύγων is he who refused to accept the arbitrator's award and used ἔφεσις.

The latter, if he was satisfied of the status of the defendants, distributed these cases into ten groups and assigned each group by lot to one of the ten tribes. The cases were then dealt with by the Forty in their appropriate tribes on exactly the same footing as cases where the defendant was a citizen. These were cases other than family cases, which on this view did not go to an arbitrator but were referred direct to a dikastery by the polemarch.[1]

According to the rival view even cases of family property, which came in the first instance to the archon (or for metics to the polemarch), had then to be remitted through the Forty for arbitration. The main support for this view is the fact that certain cases dealing with guardianship are known from the orators to have involved arbitration. In none of these cases, however, is there evidence that the archon was involved; and it has been plausibly suggested that guardianship cases came before the archon only so long as the ward was a minor, and that where a δίκη ἐπιτροπῆς involved arbitration we should assume that it was being brought by a ward after he had come of age. One might in fact argue *a priori* that arbitrational procedure was not appropriate until the ward was in a position to agree to an arbitrator's award.[2]

There was a reason why the metic cases had to have the preliminary procedure before the polemarch. The metic status of the defendant was relevant to the issue; and, since metics had no deme (and therefore no tribe), there had to be special machinery

[1] Ar. *Ath. Pol.* 53. 2, 58. 2. For a list of cases from the orators which certainly or probably went before arbitrators see Bo. Sm. ii. 115 f., drawing on H. C. Harrell, *Public Arbitration in Athenian Law* (University of Missouri Studies xi, no. 1). Doubtful items are the δίκη ἐπιτροπῆς (on which see the text above) and the δίκη προικός. The δίκη προικός (on which see vol. i, pp. 50 ff.) is called a monthly suit in Ar. *Ath. Pol.* 52. 2, and falls there as such to the eisagogeis. A suit between Boiotos and Mantitheos mentioned in Dem. 40 *Boiot.* ii. 16 f. went before an arbitrator; it was classified by Lipsius, *AR* 497, as a δίκη προικός, probably wrongly; it was rather a δίκη βλάβης. Another doubtful item is Isai. 12 *Euphil.*: according to that speech Euphiletos' deme had removed him from its register and this decision had become the subject of an arbitration. Gernet, *Mélanges offerts à A.-M. Desrousseaux* (1937) 171 ff., regards such a rule as so improbable that on this and other grounds he rejects the speech as a forgery. Dem. 59 *Neair.* 60 is, he claims, no parallel, since the excluding body there is a genos, a private organization. This distinction between the status of the deme and the genos hardly bears this weight.

[2] Lipsius, *AR* 532 ff., refuted by Bo. Sm. ii. 102 ff. The cases are referred to in Lys. 32 *Diogeit.*, Dem. 27 *Aphob.* i, 29 *Aphob.* iii (to be used with caution: Lipsius is inconsistent; cf. *AR* 533 with 346, n. 25, and 822, n. 68), 38 *Nausim.* 15.

not needed in citizen cases to distribute their cases among the tribes.[1]

The δίκη αἰκείας, the suit for assault, is rather anomalous. We are told in Dem. 37 *Pant.* 33 that it came before the Forty; this speech was delivered about 346 B.C. But it had become a monthly suit under the eisagogeis by the time of the *Ath. Pol.* (52. 2), that is by about 323 B.C.

(v) *The eisagogeis*

The word εἰσαγωγεύς, introducer, is derived from εἰσάγειν, which describes the function of any magistrate who brings a case as president before a court, and the noun is used occasionally in this very general sense.[2] There was however a moment when special officers with this title were instituted to deal with a group of cases whose common factor, in Aristotle's time at least, was that they had to be decided within one month. At that time the eisagogeis were five in number, each dealing with the business of two tribes, and they were elected by lot. There has been much discussion on the date and circumstances of their institution. Here it must suffice to say that on the most probable view they were instituted between 346 and 322 B.C. to relieve other magistrates of a number of suits in what was then a fairly new, but growing, class of cases in which litigants were guaranteed as a privilege a decision within thirty days.[3]

The eisagogeis mentioned in an inscription of 425 B.C., who have a function in connection with the collection of tribute, have probably no relation with the officials we are here discussing. Certainly the duties of the two bodies bear no close resemblance to each other.[4]

[1] We are ill informed on the procedure which had to be followed when either litigant was a foreigner who was not a metic.

[2] For example Dem. 37 *Pant.* 34 οὐκ ὄντων εἰσαγωγέων τῶν θεσμοθετῶν, *An. Bekk.* (Λέξ. Ῥητ.) 246. 14. For a discussion of εἰσάγειν δίκην see Wade-Gery, *EGH* 178 f.

[3] Convincingly argued by Gernet, *DSGA* 173 ff. His most telling point is that Dem. 37 *Pant.* 33 f. twice, in speaking of various magistrates competent to do this or that, uses εἰσαγωγεῖς in the general sense, which would have been impossible if there had been at the time a special group of magistrates with that name.

[4] *IG* i². 63 (*ATL* A 9). See Gernet, *DSGA* 174. Wilamowitz, *A. und A.* i. 223, had already suggested that these eisagogeis had to do with contentious matters concerning the allies, not with cases which were as such given the speedy thirty-day treatment. See also *ATL* iii. 71, 77, 79.

Aristotle's list of suits dealt with by the eisagogeis is as follows:[1] for a dowry, if a man who owes it does not return it;[2] for money lent at 12 per cent interest (we may assume that this means not more than 12 per cent);[3] for capital lent for the setting up of a business in the market place (presumably irrespective of the rate of interest);[4] for assault (*αἴκεια*);[5] for the return of friendly loans (*ἐρανικαί*);[6] suits arising out of banking transactions (*τραπεζιτικαί*);[7] out of associations (probably not, as they are usually taken, suits against or by corporations);[8] out of holding a trierarchy (*τριηραρχικαί*);[9] finally, suits called *ἀνδραπόδων* and *ὑποζυγίων*, which are either concerning property in slaves and beasts or, more probably, concerning damage done by slaves or beasts.[10]

[1] Ar. *Ath. Pol.* 52. 2 *εἰσὶ δ' ἔμμηνοι προικός, ἐάν τις ὀφείλων μὴ ἀποδῷ, κἄν τις ἐπὶ δραχμῇ δανεισάμενος ἀποστερῇ, κἄν τις ἐν ἀγορᾷ βουλόμενος ἐργάζεσθαι δανείσηται παρά τινος ἀφορμήν· ἔτι δ' αἰκείας καὶ ἐρανικαὶ καὶ κοινωνικαὶ καὶ ἀνδραπόδων καὶ ὑποζυγίων καὶ τριηραρχικαὶ καὶ τραπεζιτικαί.*

[2] Vol. i, pp. 50 ff. and literature there cited.

[3] The privilege of speedy redress was restricted to those who charged what was then considered a reasonable rate of interest; cf. Dem. 27 *Aphob.* i. 23, 35, Aischin. 3 *Ktes.* 104.

[4] Dem. 36 *For Phorm.* was spoken in a *παραγραφή* in such a suit (hyp. 2).

[5] Dem. 37 *Pant.* 33 (delivered about 346/5 B.C.) refers to this suit as coming before the Forty. It was probably transferred to the eisagogeis when the latter were instituted.

[6] On *ἔρανοι* see Finley, *Land* 100 ff. (especially 103). He holds that the normal *ἔρανος* loan was interest free. We cannot tell what particular aspects of *ἔρανοι* needed the remedy of a special suit.

[7] Designedly thus loosely translated. Lipsius, *AR* 85, calls them 'Klagen gegen Wechsler'. But Gernet, *DSGA* 176, n. 2, rightly makes the point that bankers' books enjoyed particular credit in judicial affairs and that it was likely that this suit, when invented, would have been equally for plaintiff bankers as for plaintiffs against them. He also argues plausibly that the actions concerning the bank of Pasion in the decade 370–360 B.C., for which we have considerable evidence, were not monthly suits.

[8] Lipsius, *AR* 771, describes them as suits in which one party was an association ('ein Verein'), but there is some doubt whether the Athenians achieved the juristic idea of a corporation as a legal person (see vol. i, p. 242).

[9] As Gernet, *DSGA* 177, points out, these were concerned neither with claims of the state against trierarchs (these were *γραφαί* or *ἀπογραφαί* and came under the overseers of the docks; see pp. 34, 211 ff.) nor with the attribution of a trierarchy between two contestants (these were *διαδικασίαι* under the direction of the strategoi; see p. 32). They were rather what he describes as quasi-contractual cases, where a retiring trierarch wishes to recover from his successor expenses incurred on his behalf. There is a typical case in Dem. 50 *Polykl.*, dated probably to 358 B.C., but the suit was not at that time monthly; it may have become so because witnesses would be hard to come at after an interval.

[10] Lipsius, *AR* 640, 682, 745, followed by Bu. Sw. 1114, holds that they were the former. But why should property in slaves or beasts have needed the protection of speedy suits more than any other property? On the other hand special suits

None of the suits mentioned went before an arbitrator. We must suppose that the eisagogeis, like any other magistrate, had to decide whether the suit lay, and that if either litigant challenged their decision the matter would have been the subject of a παραγραφή (pp. 106 ff.).

(vi) *The nautodikai and the xenodikai*

We are less well informed about these magistrates, since they had been superseded by Aristotle's time and therefore get no mention in the *Ath. Pol.* We first hear of nautodikai in a decree dated about 444 B.C.; all we can say about this piece of evidence is that it shows them presiding over a court that has nothing to do with merchants.[1] We find them in a speech of Lysias presiding over a case where the defendants, the possessors of some land, challenged the competence of an ordinary magistrate to deal with the case on the ground that they, the defendants, were merchants: πέρυσι μὲν οὖν διεγράψαντό μου τὰς δίκας, ἔμποροι φάσκοντες εἶναι· νυνὶ δὲ λαχόντος ἐν τῷ Γαμηλιῶνι μηνὶ οἱ ναυτοδίκαι οὐκ ἐξεδίκασαν. This indicates that it was the calling of the litigant rather than the matter being litigated which in this case determined the court.[2] We must assume that, as a privilege, merchants (in this case note that these merchants were citizens, for if they had been foreigners or metics they could not have been in possession of land) could have a case tried by special procedure, involving perhaps peculiarities of time and place. Finally, Krateros preserved a decree to the effect that a γραφή in the court of the nautodikai lay against anyone who, though both his parents were foreigners, posed as a member of a phratry. This may justify the hypothesis built on it that, when Perikles in 451/0 made it a condition of citizenship that both parents should be citizens, the resulting γραφὴ ξενίας to give sanction to the rule was entrusted to the nautodikai. But note that the rule envisaged in the Krateros

dealing with damage done by slaves or beasts are easily understandable, and difficulties of proof might well have suggested their inclusion in this class.

[1] *IG* i². 41. On the nautodikai see Paoli, *St. Dir.* 111 ff., A. Körte, *Hermes* 68 (1933) 238 ff., U. Kahrstedt, *Klio* 32 (1939) 148 ff., Gernet, *DSGA* 180, Wolff, *Paragraphe* 28, n. 24.

[2] Lys. 17 δημ. ἀδ. 5; Perrot, *Essai sur le droit public d'Athènes* 311, n. 1, Gernet, *DSGA* 180. Cf. *An. Bekk.* (Λέξ. Ῥητ.) 283. 3–4.

decree is the less strict rule that prevailed before 451/0 (and probably for a period again just before the end of the century), namely that at least one parent had to be a citizen. The decree of Krateros therefore cannot be identical with the law of Perikles.[1] However that may be, the nautodikai were certainly at one stage charged with γραφαὶ ξενίας.[2] By the time of Aristotle these suits came before the thesmothetai.[3]

We seem then to have evidence for cases where the merchant calling of the litigant (certainly when he was defendant; only conjecturally when he was plaintiff) brought the issue before the nautodikai, and similarly with cases where the citizen status of the defendant was at stake. There is not so much in common between these two types of case as is sometimes supposed. In both the status of the parties has some relevance, and it is perhaps legitimate to assume that in a good many alien cases the defendant would have been of foreign merchant extraction; but that is about all.

It seems likely that the nautodikai were still deciding merchants' cases as late as the date of Xenophon's *Revenues* (probably 355 B.C.), since in 3. 3 of that work he describes the magistracy responsible for merchants' cases as ἡ τοῦ ἐμπορίου ἀρχή, which he would hardly have done had it been the thesmothetai.[4]

For a time officials named xenodikai exercised jurisdiction in matters in which foreigners were involved. But unfortunately we cannot say for certain either what that period was or what precisely were the matters referred to them.[5]

The magistrates dealt with so far, except for the archon and the basileus, were primarily judicial officers. The rest are magis-

[1] Krateros, *F.Gr.H.* 342 F 4 and Jacoby ad loc., Kratinos fr. 233, Wilamowitz, *A. und A.* i. 223, n. 75.

[2] And surely at that stage all γραφαὶ ξενίας. It is hard to believe with Bu. Sw. 1095, n. 1 that in the second half of the fifth century the polemarch took γραφαὶ ξενίας except where the defendant was accused of having both parents non-citizens, when they went to the nautodikai.

[3] Ar. *Ath. Pol.* 59. 3.

[4] Gernet, *DSGA* 180.

[5] They occur in *IG* i². 342. 38, 343. 89, ii². 46, 144 (cf. A. G. Woodhead, *Hesperia* 26 (1957) 221 ff., and D. M. Lewis, *Hesperia* 28 (1959) 248 ff.). *IG* ii². 46 is a treaty with Troizen from the early fourth century; the fragments seem to refer largely to torts and crimes and not to contracts; see de Ste Croix, *CQ* 11 (1961) 109. Cf. also A. W. Gomme, *Essays in Greek History and Literature* 80, n. 2, 83 f., U. Kahrstedt, *Klio* 32 (1939) 152 ff., Jacoby, commentary to Philochoros, *F.Gr.H.* 328 F 119, n. 29, *ATL* iii. 10.

trates whose judicial functions were strictly subordinate to their executive functions.

(vii) *Street and market officials*

The more important of these were the astynomoi, the agoranomoi, the metronomoi, the sitophylakes, and the overseers of the market. Each of these boards consisted of ten members elected by lot; in each of the first four boards five members functioned in Athens and five in Peiraeus.[1]

The astynomoi were responsible for cleanliness and order in the streets. They could punish both slaves and free men for resistance to their orders, but would have to take a free man to court, presided over probably by them, if they wished to secure a penalty higher than that allowed to them. They probably also presided over *διαδικασίαι* to settle disputes arising out of the encroachment of private buildings on the highway, particularly projecting first-floor buildings.[2]

The agoranomoi had similar duties in the market places of Athens and Peiraeus. There was a *νόμος ἀγορανομικός*, which, among other things, laid down certain prices, and by virtue of which the agoranomoi were charged with seeing that order was kept, that the wares offered were pure and genuine and that neither buyers nor sellers were cheated.[3] They too could impose penalties up to a limit, and for more serious breaches of order bring the offenders before a court under their presidency. Parties

[1] Ar. *Ath. Pol.* 50 f.

[2] Ps.-Xen. *Ath. Pol.* 3. 4 *δεῖ δὲ καὶ τάδε διαδικάζειν, εἴ τις . . . κατοικοδομεῖ τι δημόσιον*, Ar. *Ath. Pol.* 50. 2 *καὶ τὰς ὁδοὺς κωλύουσι κατοικοδομεῖν καὶ δρυφάκτους ὑπὲρ τῶν ὁδῶν ὑπερτείνειν καὶ ὀχετοὺς μετεώρους εἰς τὴν ὁδὸν ἔκρουν ἔχοντας ποιεῖν καὶ τὰς θυρίδας εἰς τὴν ὁδὸν ἀνοίγειν*. In Isai. 1 *Kleonym.* 14 f. a testator has deposited his will with the astynomoi, but Lipsius, *AR* 91 f., is right in saying that this implies no connection between these officers and the administration of the law of testament, though Kahrstedt, *Mag.* 159, uses of the action of the astynomoi in this case the puzzling phrase 'Akte freiwilliger Gerichtsbarkeit'.

[3] Ar. *Ath. Pol.* 51. 1 *τούτοις δὲ ὑπὸ τῶν νόμων προστέτακται τῶν ὠνίων ἐπιμελεῖσθαι πάντων, ὅπως καθαρὰ καὶ ἀκίβδηλα πωλήσεται*, schol. *Iliad* 21. 203 *ἐν τῷ ἀγορανομικῷ νόμῳ Ἀθηναίων διέσταλται ἰχθύων καὶ ἐγχελύων τέλη*, Hyper. 5 *Athenog.* 14 *ὁ μὲν τοίνυν εἷς νόμος κελεύει ἀψευδεῖν ἐν τῇ ἀγορᾷ*, Harpokr. s.v. *κατὰ τὴν ἀγορὰν ἀψευδεῖν* (after quoting Hypereides)· *ἔοικεν ὁ νόμος περὶ τῶν ὠνίων κεῖσθαι· Θεόφραστος γοῦν ἐν τοῖς περὶ νόμων φησὶ δυοῖν τούτων ἐπιμελεῖσθαι δεῖν τοὺς ἀγορανόμους, τῆς τε ἐν τῇ ἀγορᾷ εὐκοσμίας καὶ τοῦ ἀψευδεῖν μὴ μόνον τοὺς πιπράσκοντας ἀλλὰ καὶ τοὺς ὠνουμένους*, Lys. 22 *Corn-dealers* 16, Dem. 20 *Lept.* 9; H. J. Wolff, *Freiburger Rechts- und Staatswissenschaftliche Abhandlungen* 27 (1967) 173.

wronged in transactions in the market could bring a *δίκη βλάβης* before a court sitting under the agoranomoi.[1]

The metronomoi had to see that sellers used correct weights and measures. They probably had judicial competence similar to that of the other officers here under discussion, but we have no direct evidence of it.[2]

The sitophylakes had important duties connected with the supply and marketing of corn. According to a speech of Lysias they had oversight of all those measures which had been taken to prevent an artificial raising of the price of corn, in particular a law which imposed the death penalty for selling more than fifty phormoi; presumably this meant a limit on sales in any one day.[3] At the time of Demosthenes' speech against Leptines they had to keep records of imports of corn.[4]

In Aristotle's account the sphere of the sitophylakes' activity has shrunk to the control of retail trade in corn. They had to see that unmilled corn (*σῖτος ἀργός*) was on sale in accordance with the law, that millers sold meal in accordance with the price of barley and bakers bread in accordance with the price of wheat and at proper weights. In spite of this apparent decrease in the transactions which they had to supervise, their number had increased from ten to thirty-five, twenty for Athens and fifteen for Peiraeus.[5]

Again we must assume, though Aristotle does not say so, that their punitive and judicial powers followed the same pattern as those of other market officials. In Lysias' time certainly we are explicitly told that they played in relation to dealings in corn exactly the same part as the agoranomoi in relation to dealings in other wares.[6] Whether the case against the corn-dealers dealt with in the relevant speech of Lysias came before the thesmothetai, because it had its origin in an *εἰσαγγελία*,[7] or before the sitophylakes cannot be determined from the speech itself.

[1] Aristoph. *Wasps* 1406 ff. *προσκαλοῦμαί σ' ὅστις εἶ πρὸς τοὺς ἀγορανόμους βλάβης τῶν φορτίων, κλητῆρ' ἔχουσα Χαιρεφῶντα τουτονί*, *Ach.* 723, 968.

[2] Ar. *Ath. Pol.* 51. 2 *οὗτοι τῶν μέτρων καὶ τῶν σταθμῶν ἐπιμελοῦνται πάντων, ὅπως οἱ πωλοῦντες χρήσονται δικαίοις*, Harpokr. s.v. *μετρονόμοι*, Poll. 4. 167.

[3] Lys. 22 *Corn-dealers* 5, 16; Wilamowitz, *A. und A.* i. 220, ii. 374 ff.

[4] Dem. 20 *Lept.* 32.

[5] Ar. *Ath. Pol.* 51. 3.

[6] Lys. 22 *Corn-dealers* 16.

[7] Lipsius, *AR* 97, says categorically that it did, but apparently only on *a priori* grounds; this may be a circular argument.

The overseers of the market (ἐπιμεληταὶ τοῦ ἐμπορίου) administered the law controlling shipments of corn.[1] Aristotle only mentions the provision that two-thirds of any cargo had to be brought to Athens; that is, must not be re-exported.[2] A law quoted in a Demosthenic speech goes much further: by it any citizen or metic who lent money on a ship which was not going to bring corn back to Athens was liable to φάσις before these officials, and another law (or another provision of the same law) forbade the transport of corn by a metic or citizen to any other destination than Peiraeus.[3]

(viii) *The apodektai*

The receivers (ἀποδέκται) were first instituted by Kleisthenes. It was their function to receive public revenues from various sources and pay them over to the appropriate chests. The main sources of revenue which came to them in the fourth century were proceeds of sales of public property and rents of public property leased out. Under this last head were included rents from the leasing of the right to collect certain taxes (τέλη). Suits arising out of the collection of these taxes, whether brought by or against the collectors (τελῶναι), were decided by the apodektai if the matter at issue was worth less than ten drachmai; if more, the cases were brought by them as monthly cases before a dikastery. They could probably impose fines up to ten drachmai on their own motion, while referring more serious tax offences to a dikastery.[4]

[1] Xen. *Poroi* 3. 3 has been quoted to prove that when that work was published, about 355 B.C., this office did not yet exist (Lipsius, *AR* 98, n. 177, Gernet, *DSGA* 182, n. 7), but the argument is hardly conclusive.

[2] Ar. *Ath. Pol.* 51. 4 *τούτοις δὲ προστέτακται τῶν τ' ἐμπορίων ἐπιμελεῖσθαι, καὶ τοῦ σίτου τοῦ καταπλέοντος εἰς τὸ σιτικὸν ἐμπόριον τὰ δύο μέρη τοὺς ἐμπόρους ἀναγκάζειν εἰς τὸ ἄστυ κομίζειν.* (There is no need to read with some editors Ἀττικὸν for σιτικόν.)

[3] Dem. 35 *Lakrit.* 51 *ἀργύριον δὲ μὴ ἐξεῖναι ἐκδοῦναι Ἀθηναίων καὶ τῶν μετοίκων τῶν Ἀθήνησι μετοικούντων μηδενί, μηδὲ ὧν οὗτοι κύριοί εἰσιν, εἰς ναῦν ἥτις ἂν μὴ μέλλῃ ἄξειν σῖτον Ἀθήναζε. . . . ἐὰν δέ τις ἐκδῷ παρὰ ταῦτα, εἶναι τὴν φάσιν καὶ τὴν ἀπογραφὴν τοῦ ἀργυρίου πρὸς τοὺς ἐπιμελητάς, καθάπερ τῆς νεὼς καὶ τοῦ σίτου εἴρηται, κατὰ ταὐτά,* 35 *Lakrit.* 50, 34 *Ag. Phorm.* 37, Lykourg. *Leokr.* 27 (all quoted on p. 221, n. 3).

[4] Ar. *Ath. Pol.* 52. 3 *οἱ δ' ἀποδέκται τοῖς τελώναις καὶ κατὰ τῶν τελωνῶν, τὰ μὲν μέχρι δέκα δραχμῶν ὄντες κύριοι, τὰ δ' ἄλλ' εἰς τὸ δικαστήριον εἰσάγοντες ἔμμηνα.* Lipsius, *AR* 100, takes the limit as applying merely to the amount at issue; Kahrstedt, *Mag.* 213, is right to take the phrase as including the right to fine up to ten drachmai.

Although the poletai had much business which would have given rise to litigation, for example the selling into slavery of metics who failed to pay the metic tax (vol. i, p. 184), there is no evidence that they had any jurisdiction in these matters.[1]

(ix) *Accounting officers*

These form a special category owing to the very elaborate machinery worked out in the fifth century at Athens to ensure the accountability of all magistrates.[2] They fall into two groups, one concerned with accountability in the strict financial sense, the other with accountability in a much more general sense.

The first body of officials in the former category were the logistai. We find in Ar. *Ath. Pol.* two bodies with this title. In 48. 3 he tells us that the bouleutai choose by lot ten logistai from their own number, who have to check the accounts of magistrates every prytany. We may assume that irregularities which emerged during these examinations could be brought to trial on the initiative of the boule, but there is nothing to suggest that this committee of the boule had any hand in the judicial process, and they therefore do not concern us further.[3]

In 54. 2 Aristotle describes the functions of what must be a quite distinct body of ten logistai. They also were chosen by lot, but from the whole people, we may assume, rather than from the boule. To assist them they had ten synegoroi, also chosen by lot. All magistrates, together with members of the boule, ambassadors, and priests, if they had had any dealings in public funds or property, were required on laying down office to present their accounts to the logistai and the synegoroi (λόγον ἐγγράφειν or ἀποφέρειν). If, exceptionally, they had had no such dealings, they

[1] So Lipsius, *AR* 100 f., quoting Dem. 25 *Aristogeit.* i. 57. He is hardly right to follow H. Schenkl, *WS* 2 (1880) 185, in the view that the question whether the μετοίκιον had been paid could not be a matter for decision by a court, but rightly decides that the question whether the accused was *liable* or not was one for the polemarch's court. That would also be the tribunal where a matter of disputed payment would be resolved.

[2] On the constitutional significance of this see Kahrstedt, *Mag.* 170 ff., Hignett, *HAC* 203 ff.

[3] Ar. *Ath. Pol.* 48. 3 κληροῦσι δὲ καὶ λογιστὰς ἐξ αὑτῶν οἱ βουλευταὶ δέκα τοὺς λογιουμένους ταῖς ἀρχαῖς κατὰ τὴν πρυτανείαν ἑκάστην. It is to this body that Lys. 30 *Nikom.* 5 refers. Lipsius, *AR* 102, n. 195, Bu. Sw. 1032 f., Schulthess, *RE* s.v. λογισταί 1012, Kahrstedt, *Mag.* 180.

had to make a formal statement to that effect.[1] The logistai had then within thirty days to bring the accounts before a dikastery sitting under their presidency. They might propose that the accounts should be passed; if no private citizen came forward with a counter-proposal, and if the court so voted, the magistrate was discharged from this stage of accountability. Alternatively the logistai might oppose the passing of the accounts and wish to propose some penalty on the magistrate. In this case one of the synegoroi would conduct the case for the prosecution. Besides mere failure to square the accounts, which could well be due to simple incompetence, the magistrate could be charged under this procedure with the specific offences of embezzlement (*κλοπῆς*) or receiving bribes (*δῶρα λαβόντα*) or perhaps more generally with an improper use of public funds or property (this may have been the import of the *γραφὴ ἀδικίου*).[2] We may conjecture that each of the ten logistai and the ten synegoroi dealt with the accounts of the magistrates belonging to their respective tribes.[3]

[1] Aischin. 3 *Ktes.* 15 *λόγον καὶ εὐθύνας ἐγγράφειν πρὸς τὸν γραμματέα καὶ τοὺς λογιστάς*, 22 *καὶ τοῦτον ἀποφέρειν κελεύει λόγον πρὸς τοὺς λογιστάς. καὶ πῶς ὅ γε μηδὲν λαβὼν μηδ' ἀναλώσας ἀποίσει λόγον τῇ πόλει; αὐτὸς ὑποβάλλει καὶ διδάσκει ὁ νόμος ἃ χρὴ γράφειν· κελεύει γὰρ αὐτὸ τοῦτο ἐγγράφειν, ὅτι "οὔτ' ἔλαβον οὐδὲν τῶν τῆς πόλεως οὔτ' ἀνήλωσα"*. A copy of the account had to be lodged in the Metroon, if we may argue back from evidence of a later date, viz. *IG* ii^2. 847 (*c.* 215 B.C.), 956 (*c.* 161 B.C.), 958 (*c.* 155 B.C.); hence the reference to the *γραμματεύς*.

[2] Ar. *Ath. Pol.* 54. 2, Harpokr. s.v. *λογισταί* for the thirty days, *Lex. Cant.* s.v. *λογισταὶ καὶ συνήγοροι· Ἀριστοτέλης ἐν τῇ Ἀθηναίων πολιτείᾳ οὕτω· λογισταὶ δὲ κληροῦνται δέκα παρ' οἷς διαλογίζονται πᾶσαι αἱ ἀρχαὶ τά τε λήμματα καὶ τὰς γεγενημένας δαπάνας καὶ ἄλλοις δέκα συνηγόροις, οἵτινες συνανακρίνουσι τούτοις· καὶ οἱ τὰς εὐθύνας διδόντες παρὰ τούτοις ἀνακρίνονται πρῶτον, εἶτα ἐφίενται εἰς τὸ δικαστήριον εἰς ἕνα καὶ πεντακοσίους.* Wade-Gery, *EGH* 193, n. 4, would read *ἀφίενται* for *ἐφίενται*, comparing Dem. 34 *Ag. Phorm.* 21 (with the reading *ἀφῆκεν*, not *ἐφῆκεν*). Although the grammarian professes to be quoting from Aristotle, he expands what appears in the *Ath. Pol.* Note the use of the technical *ἀνακρίνειν* for the function of the *λογισταί* and *συνήγοροι*: Bo. Sm. ii. 35. Kahrstedt, *Mag.* 234, stresses the important role of the synegoroi as prosecutors where the logistai as *εἰσάγουσα ἀρχή* may wish to prefer a charge (cf. Dem. 18 *Crown* 117). Aischin. 3 *Ktes.* 23 for the herald of the logistai asking 'Who wishes to accuse?' On *ἀδικίου* see Lipsius, *AR* 380 f., Bu. Sw. 1077, Bo. Sm. ii. 257.

[3] No evidence survives on this point. The procedure set out in the text obtained in Aristotle's day. In the fifth century there are some references to a body of thirty logistai in inscriptions concerned with the tribute, for example in the decree of Kallias (*ATL* D1. 7 ff.). These references are not to an annual clearance of magistrates' accounts; the only fifth-century reference to this is Eupolis fr. 223 *ἄνδρες λογισταὶ τῶν ὑπευθύνων χορῶν*. It is a fair assumption, however, that these thirty logistai were the forerunners of the ten logistai and ten synegoroi of the fourth century.

Failure by an outgoing magistrate to comply with this procedure might lead to a *γραφὴ ἀλογίου*. We do not know who would preside at such a trial. Analogy would suggest that it was again the logistai themselves. However, in the absence of direct evidence, there is some *a priori* support for the view that the thesmothetai presided: it would be more than usually harsh to expect a defendant who had in fact presented his accounts to prove this in the teeth of a denial by the board which furnished the presiding magistrate of the court; at least one of that board would be a material witness.[1]

So much for strictly financial accounting. There was however a more general accountability for which magistrates known as euthynoi were responsible. These were ten in number, selected by lot, one from each tribe, and assisted each by two paredroi. Their function was to sit by the statue of the eponymous hero of each tribe for three (possibly thirty) days after the magistrate's accounts had passed the first procedure, and receive from complainants written charges against any retiring magistrate. The charges might refer either to private or to public wrongs. The euthynos examined these charges (the technical word *ἀνακρίνειν* is possibly used) and, if he thought fit, rejected them; but if he thought the charge made out he remitted it, if it was a private wrong, to the deme judges, if a public wrong, to the thesmothetai. In neither case did he play any further part in the proceedings; he was not, as was the logistes, competent *εἰσάγειν εἰς τὸ δικαστήριον*.[2]

There has been some discussion as to whether this second stage of the examination of magistrates' conduct during office did not violate the principle *ne bis in idem*. This principle was certainly recognized in Athenian law, and some scholars have thought that here was a derogation from it.[3] The better view is that the

[1] *Lex. Cant.* and Suda s.v. *ἀλογίου δίκη*, *An. Bekk.* (*Συν. Λέξ. Χρησ.*) 436. 5, Eupolis fr. 349, Poll. 8. 54 refer to this suit without indicating what magistrate presided. Though *Lex. Cant.* and Suda use the word *δίκη*, the suit must have been a *γραφή*: *ἀλογίου* cannot have been a private wrong. Lipsius, *AR* 399, surmises that the thesmothetai presided, though in n. 92 alleging that the suit is attributed to the logistai in the *Ath. Pol.*; but the *Ath. Pol.* does not name this suit.

[2] Ar. *Ath. Pol.* 48. 4–5.

[3] Dem. 20 *Lept.* 147 *οἱ νόμοι δ' οὐκ ἐῶσι δὶς πρὸς τὸν αὐτὸν περὶ τῶν αὐτῶν οὔτε δίκας οὔτ' εὐθύνας οὔτε διαδικασίαν οὔτ' ἄλλο τοιοῦτ' οὐδὲν εἶναι*, and other passages cited on p. 119, n. 3. If, as Lipsius and others have thought, the passing of a magistrate's accounts by the logistai did not free him from further examination so far as those accounts went, this would have been more than 'ein gewisser Abfall von dem Rechtsgrundsatze', as Lipsius, *AR* 293, describes it.

second examination, the εὔθυνα properly so-called as opposed to the λόγος (though this terminology is not always strictly adhered to), was confined to matters which lay outside the purview of the logistai, and that the power of the euthynoi to reject a complaint was intended to cover particularly a case where the accused magistrate had already been cleared by the logistai.[1]

(x) *Military officers*

Far the most important of these were the ten strategoi. They had during the first quarter of the fifth century replaced the nine archons as the most powerful executive organ in the state. The office had two attributes which were part cause, part effect, of its encroachment on the power of the archonship: firstly the lot played no part in the election of the strategoi, and secondly there was no rule against holding the office in succeeding years; Perikles for example held it for fifteen years in unbroken succession from the year 443/2 B.C.

Originally each strategos had been commander of his tribal contingent, but in the fifth century this duty was taken over by the taxiarchs and the strategoi became commanders-in-chief in commission. Nevertheless the strategoi continued to be elected one from each tribe till about the middle of the fourth century. In Aristotle's time he expressly tells us that they were elected from all (ἐξ ἁπάντων). By his time too various members of the board were assigned specific areas of military authority, whether geographic or administrative.[2]

The jurisdiction of the strategoi, as of other executive officers of state, arose out of their executive functions. These fell into two broad categories, command in the field and matters of defence in peacetime. Under the first head their summary jurisdiction had at one time embraced the right to put to death,[3] but by

[1] So Kahrstedt, *Mag.* 172 ff., Bo. Sm. ii. 257 ff. See also Bu. Sw. 1080, n. 2. Wilamowitz, *A. und A.* ii. 231 ff., is still basic, in spite of criticism by Lipsius, *AR* 101 ff.; cf. also E. Koch, *De Atheniensium logistis euthynis synegoris* (Zittau, 1894), Boerner, *RE* s.v. εὔθυνα 1515.

[2] Ar. *Ath. Pol.* 61. 1. The exceptional cases where in a given year one tribe appears to have double representation do not concern us; neither does the vexed question whether in these or other years there was any provision for a president of the board or commander-in-chief.

[3] For the death penalty in the fifth and early fourth century see Xen. *Hell.* 1. 1. 15, Lys. 13 *Agorat.* 67.

Aristotle's day this summary jurisdiction had been reduced to the right to remand in custody, to cashier (⟨ἐκ⟩κηρῦξαι: we do not know what precisely this entailed), and to impose a fine (ἐπιβολὴν ἐπιβάλλειν). Aristotle adds that the imposition of fines by them had fallen into disuse (by which he surely means the imposition of fines without right of appeal to a court).[1] Serious offences against military discipline were dealt with by the following *γραφαί*: *ἀστρατείας, λιποταξίου, ἀποβεβληκέναι τὴν ἀσπίδα, ἀποναυτίου, ἀναυμαχίου*. These cases were tried by juries composed of the defendant's fellow soldiers[2] under the presidency of the strategos.[3] The strategos might take the initiative in having the case brought into court, but any of these suits could be initiated by ὁ βουλόμενος.[4]

The home duties of the strategoi included the enrolment of soldiers,[5] the designation of trierarchs, and the control of schedules of those liable to the extraordinary tax known as εἰσφορά and of the trierarchic symmory lists.[6] Suits arising out of these duties of the strategoi were mainly private, in the shape of διαδικασίαι concerned with rival claims to evade payment of the εἰσφορά or serving as trierarch;[7] but there must also have been some public suit as sanction against evasion of enrolment.

The strategoi had certain subordinate officers to assist them in their command. At some date in the first half of the fifth century the command of the tribal regiments of hoplites was entrusted to ten taxiarchs; these were elected.[8] A speech of Demosthenes indicates the possibility that a taxiarch might have to receive a charge of λιποτάξιον and bring the case into court, acting either as prosecutor or as president of the court; the

[1] Ar. *Ath. Pol.* 61. 2 κύριοι δέ εἰσιν ὅταν ἡγῶνται καὶ δῆσαι τὸν ἀτακτοῦντα καὶ ⟨ἐκ⟩κηρῦξαι καὶ ἐπιβολὴν ἐπιβάλλειν· οὐκ εἰώθασι δὲ ἐπιβάλλειν. An instance of ἐκκήρυξις in Lys. 3 *Sim.* 45; of threatened remand in custody in Lys. 9 *Soldier* 5, Dem. 50 *Polykl.* 51. Kahrstedt, *Mag.* 245 ff.

[2] Lys. 14 *Alk.* i. 5.

[3] Lys. 15 *Alk.* ii. 1.

[4] Lys. 15 *Alk.* ii. 1, Dem. 21 *Meid.* 103, 110, Aischin. 2 *Embassy* 148.

[5] Lys. 9 *Soldier* 4, 14 *Alk.* i. 6.

[6] Dem. 39 *Boiot.* i. 8, 42 *Phain.* 5.

[7] Ar. *Ath. Pol.* 61. 1 ἕνα δ' (sc. στρατηγὸν διατάττουσιν) ἐπὶ τὰς συμμορίας, ὃς τούς τε τριηράρχους καταλέγει καὶ τὰς ἀντιδόσεις αὐτοῖς ποιεῖ καὶ τὰς διαδικασίας αὐτοῖς εἰσάγει, Dem. 42 *Phain.* 5, 14, *IG* ii². 1629. 204 ff. ὅπω[ς] δ' ἂν [καὶ] αἱ σκήψεις εἰσαχθῶσι, [τοὺ]ς θεσμοθέτας παρα[πλ]ηρῶσαι δικαστήρια εἰς [ἕν]α καὶ διακοσίους τῶι [στ]ρατηγῶι τῶι ἐπὶ τὰς συμ[μ]ορίας ἡιρημένωι.

[8] Ar. *Ath. Pol.* 61. 3.

wording of the passage does not allow us to say which, though it slightly favours the latter.[1]

For cavalrymen the hipparchs and phylarchs had much the same functions as the strategoi and taxiarchs had for hoplites. These officers too were elected, the two hipparchs ἐξ ἁπάντων, the ten phylarchs one from each tribe.[2] A passage of Xenophon indicates that when it was written a hipparch had the duty of seeing that those liable to service in the cavalry actually served, and that if persuasion failed him he could have recourse to compulsion through a court; but here again we cannot be sure whether the court was presided over by a hipparch or by some other magistrate.[3] Cavalry cases are further complicated by the possibility that ἱπποτροφία was a liturgy and, if the trierarchy may be used as an analogy, failure to serve might lead to a διαδικασία; though one would suppose that the question at issue in such a case would be primarily whether the defendant's financial situation excused him from this service.[4] By the time of Aristotle there was a special procedure, supervised by the boule, for

[1] Dem. 39 *Boiot.* i. 17 λιποταξίου προσεκλήθη, κἀγὼ ταξιαρχῶν τῆς φυλῆς ἠναγκαζόμην κατὰ τοὐνόματος τοῦ ἐμαυτοῦ πατρόθεν δέχεσθαι τὴν λῆξιν· καὶ εἰ μισθὸς ἐπορίσθη τοῖς δικαστηρίοις, εἰσῆγον ἂν δῆλον ὅτι. A. T. Murray in the Loeb edition mistranslates '. . . was compelled to receive the summons, since it was against my name'; this suggests that 'receive the summons' is here being used of the defendant, not of the magistrate. But the point is that the speaker had, as taxiarch, to receive a plea in which the name given to the defendant was his (the speaker's) own. Kahrstedt, *Mag.* 232 f., does not allude to this case when discussing the distinction between cases brought by magistrates as prosecutors in the courts of other magistrates and those where the presiding magistrate was himself the initiator of the prosecution. Use of the word εἰσάγειν is not conclusive to prove that here the taxiarch would have presided, since that word can be used of a prosecutor (as in Dem. 18 *Crown* 121, 21 *Meid.* 39, 25 *Aristogeit.* i. 36, 59 *Neair.* 12). On the other hand, the phrase δέχεσθαι τὴν λῆξιν is appropriate to the magistrate who was to preside (in Dem. 58 *Theokr.* 32 a plaintiff gives the λῆξις to the archon's paredros).

[2] Ar. *Ath. Pol.* 61. 4–5.

[3] Xen. *Hipparch.* 1. 9 τοὺς μὲν τοίνυν ἱππέας δῆλον ὅτι καθιστάναι δεῖ κατὰ τὸν νόμον τοὺς δυνατωτάτους καὶ χρήμασι καὶ σώμασιν ἢ εἰσάγοντα εἰς δικαστήριον ἢ πείθοντα. Kahrstedt, *Mag.* 231, n. 4, points out that the question before the court would not be a penalty, but whether the defendant was or was not liable for service; and on p. 233 he specifically removes the hipparchs from the category of εἰσάγουσαι ἀρχαί (and therefore presumably by analogy the taxiarchs; cf. n. 1 above).

[4] Lipsius, *AR* 114, assumes that ἱπποτροφία was a liturgy; cf. Lykourg. *Leokr.* 139, Hyper. 2 *Lyk.* 16. But there is reason in M. Fränkel's objection in Böckh, *Staatsh.* ii. 110*, n. 755, that everyone of the relevant age in the class of hippeis would have been liable for cavalry service, whereas a liturgy implied a list within that body.

enrolling cavalry. We are not told what sanctions existed for the evasion of this procedure, nor whether the enrolled men had any appeal from the boule's decision; but it is an oversimplification to say that this procedure of itself eliminated the need for a court.[1]

This picture suggests that there might have been considerable overlapping of judicial competence between the various military officers so far discussed. While the general looseness of Athenian juridical concepts would make this overlapping not wholly unacceptable as an hypothesis, the picture would certainly be simplified if we adopted the conjecture, which nothing absolutely contradicts, that in this sphere the strategoi were the only *εἰσάγουσα ἀρχή*.

Finally there were the overseers of the docks (*ἐπιμεληταὶ τῶν νεωρίων*) chosen, probably by lot, one from each tribe. Their function was to see that the ships of the fleet were properly equipped and ready for service. They would be especially active at the crucial time of the year when one set of trierarchs handed over to their successors. Hence they presided in *διαδικασίαι* where there were disputes between incoming and outgoing trierarchs as to the equipment handed or due to be handed over, or lost equipment liable to be replaced.[2]

(xi) *Extraordinary officers*

For a short time after the restoration of the full democracy at Athens at the end of the fifth century there is evidence for the existence of a board of commissioners (*σύνδικοι*) concerned with the many property cases arising out of confiscations, exiles, and so forth during the recent political upheavals. As with so many other officers whom we have considered, their primary function was probably administrative, to look after the interests of the state treasury; but this did not prevent their presiding over cases not

[1] Ar. *Ath. Pol.* 49. 2; Wilamowitz, *A. und A.* i. 212, Bu. Sw. 1050, n. 4.

[2] Dem. 47 *Euerg.* 26 *πρῶτον μὲν ἀπῄτουν τὰ σκεύη· ὡς δὲ τοῦτό μου εἰπόντος οὐκ ἀπεδίδου, ὕστερον αὐτῷ περιτυχὼν περὶ τὸν Ἑρμῆν τὸν πρὸς τῇ πυλίδι προσεκαλεσάμην πρός τε τοὺς ἀποστολέας καὶ πρὸς τοὺς τῶν νεωρίων ἐπιμελητάς· οὗτοι γὰρ εἰσῆγον τότε τὰς διαδικασίας εἰς τὸ δικαστήριον περὶ τῶν σκευῶν.* Lipsius, *AR* 114, n. 242, suggests that *τότε* indicates a temporary association of the apostoleis (see p. 35) with the overseers of the docks in this matter. For other instances of the overseers of the docks as presiding officers see *IG* ii². 1631. 351 ff., *SEG* x. 142. 3 ff.; for their tribal connection, *IG* ii². 1622. 478 ff., 1631. 369. Dem. 47 *Euerg.* 28 shows the working of the procedure.

only between private citizens, but also where the state was in effect a party.[1] The syndikoi who were members of this short-lived board are to be distinguished from syndikoi who are occasionally mentioned as pleaders appointed by the state, by corporations, or on behalf of individuals.[2] Only those appointed by the state are here relevant, and of these we need only say that syndikoi of this type were never presidents of a court.

An elected board of syllogeis was probably contemporaneous with the former type of syndikoi mentioned in the preceding paragraph. They were apparently charged with identifying property of oligarchs due to be confiscated and conducting cases in court against the holders of the property, but it seems likely that they did not themselves preside at the hearing of the cases.[3] A somewhat similar, though more generalized, task seems to have been allotted to officials known as *ζητηταί*. The grammarians regard these as an *ἀρχή* and assume that they presided over cases arising out of their activities, but there is no satisfactory contemporary evidence of this.[4]

In the latter half of the fourth century there is frequent mention of an extraordinary board of ten, elected from the whole people and called *ἀποστολεῖς*. They had to ensure the speedy and efficient embarkation of the fleet, and to this end could either imprison defaulting trierarchs or, in concert with the overseers of the docks, bring before a court, over which they presided, cases regarding the equipment for which an outgoing trierarch was responsible.[5]

[1] Lys. 19 *Prop. Arist.* 32 *καὶ πρότερον πρὸς τοὺς συνδίκους καὶ νῦν ἐθέλομεν πίστιν δοῦναι* (this shows the syndikoi presiding), 16 *Mantith.* 7, 17 *δημ. ἀδ.* 10, 18 *Prop. Nik. brother* 26. These speeches fall roughly in the decade 397–387 B.C.

[2] For syndikoi for the defence of a law which it was proposed to abrogate see Dem. 20 *Lept.* 146, cf. 24 *Timokr.* 23; for a syndikos with a more general remit, Dem. 18 *Crown* 134. No man could be a syndikos of this kind more than once (Dem. 20 *Lept.* 152), and convictions for certain moral offences disqualified from holding such a post (Aischin. 1 *Timarch.* 19). For a deme's syndikoi see *IG* ii². 1196. 17. For syndikoi appointed by a man's fellow tribesmen to assist him in his defence, Andok. 1 *Myst.* 150, Dem. 23 *Aristokr.* 206.

[3] *An. Bekk.* (*Λέξ. Ῥητ.*) 304. 4 f. *συλλογεῖς· ἄρχοντες ὑπὸ τοῦ δήμου χειροτονητοί, οἵτινες ἀπεγράφοντο τὰς οὐσίας τῶν ὀλιγαρχικῶν.*

[4] Lys. 21 *ἀπολ. δωρ.* 16, Dem. 24 *Timokr.* 11, Phot. and Suda s.v. *ζητηταί*, *An. Bekk.* (*Λέξ. Ῥητ.*) 261. 4 ff. Different are the zetetai appointed to inquire into the mutilation of the Hermai, Andok. 1 *Myst.* 14, 36, 40. Kahrstedt, *Mag.* 223, scouts the idea that zetetai of either kind were an *ἀρχή*.

[5] *IG* ii². 1629 (Tod, *GHI* no. 200) 251 ff. *ἑλέσθαι δὲ καὶ ἀποστολέας τὸν δῆμον δέκα ἄνδρας ἐξ Ἀθηναίων ἁπάντων, τοὺς δὲ αἱρεθέντας ἐπιμελεῖσθαι τοῦ ἀποστόλου,*

Officials known down to 378 B.C. (when the symmories were instituted) as ἐπιγραφεῖς and thereafter as διαγραφεῖς, whose function it was to determine the amount of individuals' liability to εἰσφορά, did not, as is sometimes supposed, preside over a court when disputes as to these amounts arose; this was the duty of the strategoi (see p. 32). They rather had to present the state's case to the court.[1]

Finally, *ad hoc* boards set up either by the people or by tribes on the instruction of a decree of the people had jurisdiction over matters coming under their purview, provided they were in charge of any public funds for more than thirty days. This applies for example to the overseers of public works (ἐπιστάται τῶν δημοσίων ἔργων).[2]

(xii) *Demarchs*

Demarchs had no jurisdiction, and the phrase εἰσάγειν εἰς τὸ δικαστήριον is used of one only in a loose sense.[3] They had some importance however in connection with the execution of judgements (see pp. 186, 189, 212).

§ 4. *Courts*

(i) *The homicide courts*

The Athenians of the classical period rightly believed that for religious reasons their forebears had been extremely conservative with regard to the law of homicide, and that the substance of it went back to the codification of Drakon, so that a full description of the code as it stood in that period was 'the laws of Drakon and Solon'.[4] Although we are not concerned with the

καθάπερ τῆι βουλῆι προστέτακται, Dem. 47 *Euerg.* 26 (quoted on p. 34, n. 2), 18 *Crown* 107.

[1] Harpokr. s.v. ἐπιγραφέας· τοὺς καθεστηκότας ἐπὶ τῷ γράφειν ὁπόσον ὀφείλουσιν εἰσφέρειν εἰς τὸ δημόσιον· Λυσίας ἐν τῷ περὶ τῆς εἰσφορᾶς, s.v. διάγραμμα· . . . διαγραφεὺς μέντοι ἐστὶν ὁ καθιστάμενος ἐν ταῖς συμμορίαις ἐπὶ τῷ διακρῖναι πόσον ἕκαστος ἀνὴρ εἰσενεγκεῖν ὀφείλει, ὡς ὁ αὐτός (Hypereides) πάλιν φανερὸν ποιεῖ ἐν τῷ κατὰ Πολυεύκτου, Isok. 17 *Trapez.* 41.

[2] Aischin. 3 *Ktes.* 14, 27, 29 f., Ἐφ. Ἀρχ. (1900) 93, line 32.

[3] *IG* ii^2. 1177. 15. Equally untechnical is the use of δικάζειν of the deme itself in *IG* ii^2. 1196A. 11, and of διαδικασία of the phratry of the Demotionids in *IG* ii^2. 1237.

[4] Ant. 5 *Her.* 14 (repeated in 6 *Chor.* 2), And. 1 *Myst.* 81 ff., Dem. 20 *Lept.* 158, 23 *Aristokr.* 51, 47 *Euerg.* 71; Harrison, *CQ* 11 (1961) 3 ff., MacDowell, *Homicide* 5 ff.

historical development, this fact about their origin does explain certain peculiar features of the homicide courts.

At the earliest period known to us, before Solon had sown the seed of the popular courts, jurisdiction in homicide cases, and possibly in those cases alone, was not left to the magistrate's unfettered decision, but the magistrate concerned, the basileus, had to bring each case, after it had been initiated by the relatives of the dead man, before a court. Where the death was attributed to an identified man, the court was composed either of the whole council of the Areopagos or of a body of fifty-one ephetai, who on the most likely hypothesis were originally drawn from the members of the Areopagos; that body itself was manned by ex-archons who remained members of it for life. In order to avoid pollution from the killer, all such cases were tried in the open air, and at a different venue according to the type of homicide: on the Areopagos premeditated, at the Palladion unpremeditated, at the Delphinion justifiable, at Phreatto on the coast cases against a man already in exile for homicide who was accused of another homicide (the accused remained on a boat to avoid the pollution which his return to Attica before due time would have involved). Where the death was attributed to an unknown person, an animal, or an inanimate object, the court was composed of the basileus and the phylobasileis and sat at the Prytaneion.[1]

Here we are concerned with the composition of the various courts in the fourth century.[2] The Areopagos remained what it had always been, a council made up of ex-archons who became life-members of it as soon as they had passed their εὔθυνα: they were probably not even temporary members during their year of office as archons.[3] It has been suggested that the basileus, besides introducing the case as ἡγεμών of the court, also voted

[1] MacDowell, *Homicide* 58 ff.

[2] Kahrstedt, *Klio* 30 (1937) 10 ff. (Berneker, *ZGR* 196 ff.), MacDowell, *Homicide* 39 ff.

[3] Ar. *Ath. Pol.* 3. 6, 60. 3, Poll. 8. 118. Lipsius, *AR* 122, holds that archons were members of the Areopagos while in office; but the only passage of the three cited by him which gives some colour to his view, Lys. 7 *Sacr. Ol.* 22 τοὺς ἐννέα ἄρχοντας . . . ἢ ἄλλους τινὰς τῶν ἐξ Ἀρείου πάγου, should be translated 'the nine archons or some members of the Areopagos', and not 'the nine archons or some other members of the Areopagos' (Gernet and Bizos, *Lys.* ad loc., MacDowell, *Homicide* 40). The other passages cited by Lipsius are Dem. 54 *Kon.* 28, Lys. 26 *Euandr.* 12.

upon it as a member of the Areopagos. This view is based on the use of δικάζειν in several passages to denote the function of the basileus in homicide cases; normally this word is used of the dikasts. In one important context however, the law relating to unpremeditated homicide partially preserved in a late-fifth-century inscription, there is a verbal distinction between the function of the presiding basileis (the meaning of the plural here is discussed on p. 43), δικάζειν, and that of the jury or ephetai, διαγνῶναι. It is probably better therefore to suppose that the word δικάζειν as applied in this context to the basileus is an anachronistic survival due to conservatism in matters affecting homicide, and that in effect he stood in the same relation to the homicide courts as did other magistrates to the courts over which they presided.[1] A further anachronism was the trial of cases concerning the sacred olives by the Areopagos, whereas other kinds of impiety were tried by the ordinary courts.[2]

We know almost nothing directly about the functioning of the Areopagos as a jury, but *a priori* we can infer certain differences between it and other Athenian juries. The ex-archons who made it up had all had some quite intensive experience of judicial administration as presidents of courts, and in this respect they were superior to the average member of a dikastery. Since they remained members of the Areopagos for life, the body as a whole acquired a collective experience unlike any other jury. Their life

[1] *IG* i². 115. 11 ff., Ar. *Ath. Pol.* 57. 4 δικάζουσι δ' οἱ λαχόντες ταῦτα ⟨να'⟩ ἄνδρες (for this reading see R. S. Stroud, *CP* 63 (1968) 212) πλὴν τῶν ἐν Ἀρείῳ πάγῳ γιγνομένων, εἰσάγει δ' ὁ βασιλεύς, καὶ δικάζουσιν ἐν ἱερῷ καὶ ὑπαίθριοι, καὶ ὁ βασιλεὺς ὅταν δικάζῃ περιαιρεῖται τὸν στέφανον. Those who believe that this last phrase implies that the basileus voted have not noted that in *Ath. Pol.* 52. 3 it is said of the eisagogeis ταύτας δικάζουσιν ἐμμήνους εἰσάγοντες, but no one believes that they voted with the jury. In Lys. 26 *Euandr.* 12 (*pace* MacDowell, *Homicide* 37) φόνου δίκας δικάζοντα is used not of a basileus but of an archon who would eventually become an Areopagite. H. J. Wolff, *Traditio* 4 (1946) 76, says 'δικάζειν denotes the issuing of a definite and authoritative statement that an execution may or may not take place, διαγιγνώσκειν is the term for a verdict stating the legal situation from the viewpoint of substantive law'; cf. MacDowell, *Homicide* 38. In the Phaselis inscription, *IG* i². 16, probably of the mid fifth century, καταδικάζειν is used of the act of any ἀρχή controlling a court which has condemned a man. Wade-Gery, *EGH* 183, deduces from the use of this word for the magistrate's function that at the time of the inscription magistrates were still deciding cases without reference to dikasteries; he does not discuss the possibly anachronistic use of δικάζειν in the passages quoted above.

[2] Ar. *Ath. Pol.* 60. 2. Dem. 59 *Neair.* 80 refers to some other limited powers of punishment vested in the Areopagos in religious matters.

membership also meant that they were comparatively free from ephemeral popular pressures. The fact that, unlike other juries, they must have been known by name to litigants might have meant that they were more open than they to bribery. But we hear no hint of this happening or even being a danger; on the contrary the Areopagos remained a highly respected tribunal which in times of stress was entrusted with special powers of judicial examination.[1] There is one point on which we are not informed. It seems just possible that the Areopagos was permitted, as no other jury was, to discuss its verdict before giving it. If this was so, it would have constituted a major difference between the Areopagos and other tribunals.[2]

The early history of the ephetai has been the subject of endless and still unsettled controversy. It seems fairly certain that they go back at least as far as Drakon, and that they were at that time fifty-one in number and were chosen on an aristocratic basis. Some scholars have thought that they were a commission of the Areopagos, selected out of that body to act as jury for cases of qualified homicide; the evidence on this is inconclusive.[3] It is more important for our purpose to determine how they were appointed in the fourth century.

[1] For extraordinary powers entrusted to the Areopagos see for example Lykourg. *Leokr.* 52, Dein. 1 *Dem.* 62; cf. Bo. Sm. i. 365.

[2] According to a probable emendation Athena is made to describe the court of the Areopagos as δικαστῶν βουλευτήριον in Aisch. *Eum.* 684: an ordinary dikastery could hardly be described as a βουλευτήριον; see Jacoby on Androtion, *F.Gr.H.* 324 F 3–4, n. 46 (on p. 111 of notes to commentary). But Dem. 47 *Euerg.* 44, 50 *Polykl.* 3 show that even in ordinary dikasteries some discussion between dikasts was possible.

[3] An inscription of 409/8 B.C., *IG* i². 115, shows that what was then described as 'the law of Drakon about homicide' prescribed a jury of fifty-one ephetai for cases of unpremeditated (μὴ ἐκ προνοίας) homicide. Dem. 43 *Makart.* 57 proves that the terms of the law were the same in the fourth century. The following evidence from grammarians is likely to have been drawn largely from the orators: Harpokr. s.v. ἐφέται· οἱ δικάζοντες τὰς ἐφ' αἵματι κρίσεις ἐπὶ Παλλαδίῳ καὶ ἐπὶ Πρυτανείῳ καὶ ἐπὶ Δελφινίῳ καὶ ἐν Φρεαττοῖ ἐφέται ἐκαλοῦντο, Poll. 8. 125 ἐφέται τὸν μὲν ἀριθμὸν εἷς καὶ πεντήκοντα, Δράκων δ' αὐτοὺς κατέστησεν ἀριστίνδην αἱρεθέντας· ἐδίκαζον δὲ τοῖς ἐφ' αἵματι διωκομένοις ἐν τοῖς πέντε δικαστηρίοις. Σόλων δ' αὐτοῖς προσκατέστησε τὴν ἐξ Ἀρείου πάγου βουλήν. We are not concerned with the historical development; but these passages suggest that the ephetai were still sitting at the Palladion, the Delphinion, and Phreatto. We shall see later (p. 42) that it is improbable that they were also sitting at the Prytaneion. Andok. 1 *Myst.* 78 and Dem. 23 *Aristokr.* 37 f. also refer to ephetai as jurors. The derivation of the word is too uncertain to shed any light on the origins or functions of the body. See MacDowell, *Homicide* 48 ff.

The commonly accepted view until recently has been that, either at the time of Perikles or during the revision of the laws which took place towards the end of the fifth century, in 409/8 or 403/2 B.C., trials of cases of qualified homicide were transferred from the ephetai to ordinary heliastic courts, but owing to religious conservatism the jurors when sitting in these courts were still called ephetai. This thesis rests upon two pieces of evidence. In Isok. 18 *Kallim.* 51 ff. we have the strange story of a slave woman who was alleged to have died of wounds inflicted on her in an affray by Kratinos. Kallimachos' brother-in-law prosecuted Kratinos for homicide at the Palladion, and Kallimachos was a witness for the prosecution. But the woman had in fact been abducted by Kallimachos and his brother-in-law; Kratinos was able to get hold of her and produce her in the court. The speaker (54) describes the result: *ἑπτακοσίων μὲν δικαζόντων, τεττάρων δὲ καὶ δέκα μαρτυρησάντων ἅπερ οὗτος* (Kallimachos), *οὐδεμίαν ψῆφον μετέλαβε*. At first sight this story implies a jury of seven hundred at the Palladion, but there is a difficulty: grammatically the man who did not get one vote must be Kallimachos, but in the trial at the Palladion it was Kallimachos' brother-in-law who was prosecuting. This leads MacDowell to suggest that what really happened was that Kratinos was acquitted at the Palladion and then Kallimachos was prosecuted for false witness, and it was at this trial that he did not secure a single vote; Isokrates has telescoped the story, and it therefore does not prove a jury of seven hundred at the Palladion. This is a rather desperate remedy, and it seems at least possible that Isokrates' inexactitude consisted in speaking of Kallimachos rather than his brother-in-law as the loser of the suit; if we ask why Kallimachos was not prosecuted by a *δίκη ψευδομαρτυρίων* (and if he had been Isokrates would surely have brought it into the speech), we can only surmise that Kratinos was content with his own resounding acquittal (and after all there were fourteen other witnesses involved).

The second piece of direct evidence which has been adduced for a large court at the Palladion is in Dem. 59 *Neair.* 10. From that passage we learn that Stephanos prosecuted Apollodoros at the Palladion for killing a slave woman. The speaker alleges that Stephanos perjured himself and left the court discredited, *ὀλίγας ψήφους μεταλαβὼν ἐκ πεντακοσίων δραχμῶν* (vulg.: *δικαστῶν* Q *γρ.*

D). Reiske, followed by most modern editors, bracketed δραχμῶν, and this would make this passage evidence for five hundred jurors at the Palladion. But MacDowell is right to protest that δραχμῶν gives an acceptable sense ('he got few votes from his expenditure of five hundred drachmai'; the previous words refer to a bribe); this passage therefore falls out as evidence for a large jury at the Palladion.

Nor should any weight be attached to the fact that a defendant at the Palladion addresses the jury as ἄνδρες δικασταί (Ant. 6 *Chor.* 1), or that a defendant at the Delphinion addresses them as ὦ Ἀθηναῖοι (Lys. 1 *Killing of Erat.* 6 f.). These forms of address would have been perfectly appropriate to a jury of fifty-one ephetai of the old style.

We are therefore reduced to the one passage in Isokrates for the view that the jurors in cases of qualified homicide, though still called ephetai, were ordinary dikasts, and that these juries were no longer fifty-one in number. Difficult though MacDowell's reading of the passage is, we should probably accept it, since *a priori* considerations are rather in favour of the continuance of the old ephetic courts. It would have been strange to retain the aristocratic court of the Areopagos (aristocratic in origin, and still so in the sense of being a body of life-membership) for cases of unqualified homicide, and hand over to fully popular courts the more difficult cases of qualified homicide.[1] For it is a misconception that the Areopagos' cases were, as it is often put, more important. Both from the state's point of view and from the defendant's it was just as important to decide whether a particular killing had been unpremeditated or justified as to decide whether the defendant had or had not actually been the killer, and the difficulty of arriving at the right decision would probably on balance have been greater in the former than in the latter type of case.

If we do accept, albeit cautiously, the view that jurors at the Palladion, Delphinion, and Phreatto were fifty-one ephetai, we still do not know how they were chosen; but, again arguing *a priori*, there is much to be said for thinking that they were Areopagites selected by lot; otherwise we should have expected

[1] Dem. 23 *Aristokr.* 66 says that no tyrant, oligarchy, or democracy had dared to remove from the Areopagos τὰς φονικὰς δίκας. This language strongly suggests that no change had taken place in procedure relating to homicide cases as a whole.

some definite information as to how they were selected.[1] It seems quite likely that they had to be at least fifty years of age.[2]

The court at the Prytaneion was manned by the basileus and the phylobasileis. These latter were archaic survivals from very early days, when they had been tribal kings of the four Ionic tribes. This tribal system had been largely superseded constitutionally by Kleisthenes, but had survived in certain religious contexts, this among them. We have no evidence how they were selected in the fourth century; but we can be fairly certain that they, with the basileus, formed the court at the Prytaneion without any ephetai.[3] But it is not right to speak of their function, as

[1] The view in the text follows MacDowell, *Homicide* 52 ff. For the other view see G. Smith, *CP* 19 (1924) 353 ff., followed by Bo. Sm. i. 270 ff. They hold that the only plausible explanation of Perikles' having 'taken some things from the Areopagites' (Ar. *Ath. Pol.* 27. 1 *τῶν Ἀρεοπαγιτῶν ἔνια παρείλετο*) is that he removed from the ephetai (whom Bonner and Smith take to have been commissions of Areopagites) trials of qualified homicide and entrusted them to heliastic jurors, who were still called ephetai. Lipsius, *AR* 41, assumes a similar change, but puts it shortly after 403/2 B.C. Ar. *Ath. Pol.* 57. 4 (quoted on p. 38, n. 1) describes those who manned these courts; in this passage *λαχόντες* is usually translated 'appointed by lot'. But T. J. Saunders, *JHS* 85 (1965) 225, rightly prefers 'take these cases for hearing in an order they determine by lot'. Even so it is improbable that they were appointed by merit, as some grammarians state (see n. 2 below), though if they were Areopagites a fourth-century Athenian might have regarded them as reverend seniors. The meaning of Androtion, *F.Gr.H.* 324 F 4a (Philochoros, *F.Gr.H.* 328 F 20b) *ἐκ γὰρ τῶν ἐννέα καθισταμένων ἀρχόντων Ἀθήνησι τοὺς Ἀρεοπαγίτας ἔδει συνεστάναι δικαστάς* is uncertain: either 'at Athens the Areopagite judges had to be drawn from the nine men who were appointed archons', the Areopagite *judges* being the ephetai (so Bo. Sm. i. 99 f.); or 'the Areopagites appointed the judges out of the nine archons' (so Jacoby on Androtion, *F.Gr.H.* 324 F 3–4, n. 32, on p. 108 of notes to commentary). The former translation implies, the latter does not, that in the writer's view the ephetai were also Areopagites. Cf. MacDowell, *Homicide* 51 f.

[2] Suda (= Photios) s.v. *ἐφέται· ἄνδρες ὑπὲρ πεντήκοντα ἔτη γεγονότες καὶ ἄριστα βεβιωκέναι ὑπόληψιν ἔχοντες· οἳ καὶ τὰς φονικὰς δίκας ἔκρινον.* Cf. *An. Bekk.* (*Δικ. 'Ον.*) 188. 30 ff.

[3] Dem. 23 *Aristokr.* 76 *ἐὰν λίθος ἢ ξύλον ἢ σίδηρος ἤ τι τοιοῦτον ἐμπεσὸν πατάξῃ, καὶ τὸν μὲν βαλόντ' ἀγνοῇ τις, αὐτὸ δ' εἰδῇ καὶ ἔχῃ τὸ τὸν φόνον εἰργασμένον, τούτοις ἐνταῦθα λαγχάνεται*, Patmos schol. ad loc. (*BCH* 1 (1877) 139) *ἐπὶ πρυτανείῳ· ἐν τούτῳ τῷ δικαστηρίῳ δικάζονται φόνου, ὅταν ὁ μὲν ἀνῃρημένος δῆλος ᾖ, ζητεῖται δὲ ὁ τὸν φόνον δράσας. καὶ ἀποφέρει τὴν γραφὴν πρὸς τὸν βασιλέα, καὶ ὁ βασιλεὺς διὰ τοῦ κήρυκος κηρύττει καὶ ἀπαγορεύει τόνδε τὸν ἀνελόντα τὸν δεῖνα μὴ ἐπιβαίνειν ἱερῶν καὶ χώρας Ἀττικῆς. ἐν τῷ αὐτῷ δὲ τούτῳ δικαστηρίῳ κἄν τι ἐμπεσὸν πατάξῃ τινὰ καὶ ἀνέλῃ τῶν ἀψύχων, δικάζεται τούτῳ καὶ ὑπερορίζεται*, Poll. 8. 120 *τὸ ἐπὶ πρυτανείῳ δικάζει περὶ τῶν ἀποκτεινάντων, κἂν ὦσιν ἀφανεῖς, δικάζει δὲ καὶ περὶ τῶν ἀψύχων τῶν ἐμπεσόντων καὶ ἀποκτεινάντων. προειστήκεσαν δὲ τούτου τοῦ δικαστηρίου οἱ φυλοβασιλεῖς, οὓς ἔδει τὸ ἐμπεσὸν ἄψυχον ὑπερορίσαι*, Ar. *Ath. Pol.* 57. 4 *ὅταν δὲ μὴ εἰδῇ τὸν ποιήσαντα, τῷ δράσαντι λαγχάνει. δικάζει δ' ὁ βασιλεὺς καὶ οἱ φυλοβασιλεῖς καὶ τὰς τῶν ἀψύχων καὶ τῶν ἄλλων ζῴων.* Harpokr. s.v. *ἐφέται* and Poll. 8. 125 (both

some do, as purely formal. In determining whether a death was due to an unknown killer, an animal, or an inanimate object, this court was performing something of the function of an English coroner's court, besides the ritual act of ridding the community of pollution. It is significant that, in a well-known amnesty law attributed to Solon, among those excluded from the amnesty are those 'condemned from the Prytaneion'; these would seem most likely to be unknown murderers whom it was obviously necessary to include in the exceptions to the amnesty. As the terms of this law were almost exactly repeated in the decree of Patrokleides of 405 B.C., the Prytaneion must at that date have been pronouncing sentence of exile against 'persons unknown'.[1] The use of the plural (βασιλεῖς) in the law of Drakon recorded in 409/8 has been taken by some to mean that in all homicide cases the phylobasileis assisted the basileus in presiding or in the preliminary procedures. On the whole, however, it seems more likely that the plural here is a way of saying 'the basileus for the time being'.[2]

(ii) *The dikasteries*

Aristotle (*Ath. Pol.* 7. 3) asserts that the only share in the constitution granted by Solon to the lowest class, the thetes, was membership of the ekklesia and of the dikasteries, and later (9. 1) he says that appeal to the dikasteries was what contributed most

quoted on p. 39, n. 3) give ephetai as jurors at the Prytaneion. Cf. MacDowell, *Homicide* 85 ff.

[1] Solon's amnesty law (Plut. *Solon* 19. 4): *ὅσοι ἐξ Ἀρείου πάγου ἢ ὅσοι ἐκ τῶν ἐφετῶν ἢ ἐκ πρυτανείου καταδικασθέντες . . . ἔφευγον.* Decree of Patrokleides (Andok. 1 *Myst.* 78): *πλὴν ὅποσα* (sc. *ὀνόματα*) *ἐν στήλαις γέγραπται τῶν μὴ ἐνθάδε μεινάντων ἢ ⟨οἷς, ἢ⟩ ἐξ Ἀρείου πάγου ἢ τῶν ἐφετῶν ἢ ἐκ πρυτανείου ἢ Δελφινίου δικασθεῖσιν* (Lipsius: *ἐδικάσθη ἢ* codd.) *ὑπὸ τῶν βασιλέων, ἢ ἐπὶ φόνῳ τίς ἐστι φυγὴ ἢ θάνατος κατεγνώσθη ἢ σφαγεῦσιν ἢ τυράννοις.* G. Smith, *CP* 16 (1921) 345 ff., disposes of the view that there is a reference here to a treason court at the Prytaneion. Cf. A. Ledl, *Studien zur älteren athenischen Verfassungsgeschichte* (Heidelberg, 1914) 312, Hignett, *HAC* 312.

[2] *IG* i². 115. 12. MacDowell, *Homicide* 87, leaves this question open. Bo. Sm. i. 116 ff. reject the view that the phrase could mean 'the king-archons in succession'. They sum up: 'the phylobasileis continued to act as an advisory committee in the preliminary investigation' of any homicide; 'that is, they helped to determine the nature of the homicide and consequently the proper jurisdiction for the case'. But it is quite unrealistic to suppose that a magistrate or committee could determine thus in advance 'the nature of the homicide' in abstraction from the question whether the defendant had committed it.

to the people's power (τρίτον δέ, ⟨ᾧ⟩ μάλιστά φασιν ἰσχυκέναι τὸ πλῆθος, ἡ εἰς τὸ δικαστήριον ἔφεσις). Although there is much that is anachronistic in this report, in particular the attribution to Solon of popular courts in the plural, the appraisal of the importance of the dikasteries is likely to be accurate for the fourth century.[1]

We have not here to trace the steps by which what started probably as appeal from the decision of a magistrate in more serious cases to the whole people sitting as a court (the heliaia) turned into hearings in the first instance of almost all cases by dikasteries of varying size, selected from among those citizens qualified to serve.[2] Our present business is to determine how these popular courts were organized at the time of Aristotle.

The method of manning the courts earlier in the fourth and at the end of the fifth centuries is briefly considered in Appendix F (pp. 239 ff.).[3] Any citizen over the age of thirty was eligible to be a heliast, provided that he was not in any sense ἄτιμος and in particular that he was not in debt to the state; sitting in defiance of this last disqualification might be punished with death.[4] By the time of Aristotle it is probable that the roll of heliasts consisted of all those qualified by age and status who presented themselves and took the heliastic oath (on which see p. 48) at the beginning of the official year. The number of six thousand, which perhaps started as a quorum needed when the assembly was sitting as a court in certain particularly important cases or was performing the semi-judicial act of ostracism, had by Aristotle's time ceased to have any significance which it may have had earlier. Every man on first presenting himself and being accepted as a heliast was given a ticket (πινάκιον) which he retained through life as documentary evidence of his right to sit as a dikast.[5]

[1] For an assessment of the juristic consequences of the popular control of the courts in the fourth century see E. Ruschenbusch, *Historia* 6 (1957) 257 ff., especially 265: 'Die Rechtsprechung lief damit auf reine Willkür hinaus, die dann infolge des primitiven Prozeßverfahrens und der Rabulistik der Advokaten nicht mehr zu überbieten war.' This emphasis on the orators' 'Rabulistik' is perhaps overdone; cf. vol. i, p. 122, n. 1 and p. 309 on Isaios, and H. J. Wolff, *Demosthenes als Advokat* (Berlin, 1968) 6 ff.

[2] On ἔφεσις see pp. 72 ff.

[3] Hommel, *Heliaia*, though out of date on some points, is still useful. See also Bo. Sm. i. 365 ff.

[4] Ar. *Ath. Pol.* 63. 3, Dem. 21 *Meid.* 182 (both quoted on p. 231, n. 6).

[5] For πινάκια see S. Dow, *BCH* 87 (1963) 653 ff. A number of them have been

No attempt is made here to examine in detail the evidence for the manner in which, in the first place, jurymen were selected each day for service in the courts and, in the second place, how these selected men were distributed among the separate courts. The principal evidence on this is contained in Ar. *Ath. Pol.* 63–9, amended and interpreted in the light of recently discovered archaeological material, principally from the Agora at Athens. In using the very detailed, though not always satisfactory, account of the *Ath. Pol.* as evidence we must never lose sight of the fact that it is evidence only for the time at which it was written.[1]

On any day on which the courts were due to sit all dikasts who wished to sit assembled by tribes outside the courts. Each had his ticket as evidence of his right to sit. It is worth noting that the tribe was a unit containing approximately one tenth of the total male citizen body, and that it was used for other administrative and military purposes, so that members were likely to be known to one another and the chances of impersonation or fraudulent entry, for which as we have seen there were severe penalties, were therefore small. The selection of the jurors who were to sit for that day was now made by the use of the allotment machines under the supervision of officials for each tribe. The very elaborate procedure followed was designed to secure two aims: first that on the body of jurors as a whole on any given day each of the ten tribes was fairly represented; and second that every juror who presented himself on that day had an equal chance of being chosen. These were not wholly compatible aims. The latter could only have been secured by a wholly random selection each day from among the total number presenting themselves. This would

found. They were often buried with their owners. Some have had more than one owner, presumably having been sold by the heirs of the first owner. This would perhaps indicate that the original holders were men of small means. Those found are of bronze, but in Aristotle's time they were of boxwood (*Ath. Pol.* 63. 4).

[1] In this particular problem Hommel, *Heliaia* has been largely superseded as a result of the discovery in the Agora of objects which have been identified as machines for the allotment of jurors on a given day and as being Hellenistic counterparts of those *κληρωτήρια* which figure in Ar. *Ath. Pol.* 63 ff. It is now clear that in these chapters this word always means 'a machine for allotting' and not sometimes, as Hommel and others have thought, 'an allotment chamber'. For these machines and their supposed method of operation see S. Dow, *Hesperia* Supp. 1 (1937) 198 ff., *HSCP* 50 (1939) 1 ff.; for a useful summary of the procedure as worked out by Dow see K. von Fritz and E. Kapp, *Aristotle: Constitution of Athens* (New York, 1950) 197 ff.

have taken far too long and would not have secured equal representation of the tribes. The method adopted was a reasonable compromise.[1]

There must have been some procedure, the details of which we cannot recover, for making a special selection of jurors in two types of case. In those which involved matters connected with the Mysteries only those initiated into the Mysteries could sit as jurors,[2] and in cases of military indiscipline in the field juries were composed of men who had been serving on the campaign in question.[3]

It has been contended that a *δίκη ψευδομαρτυρίων* was tried before the same dikasts as had been sitting over the case in which the allegedly false evidence had been given.[4] If this was so, it is difficult to imagine how in fact anything approaching an identical jury could have been reassembled if the cases were not held on the same day.

When all the jurors needed to fill the courts for the day had been selected, there followed another elaborate procedure for allotting to each court the complement of jurors needed. A tentative deduction from Aristotle is that after being allotted to a court each juror received a token which determined in what part of the court he was to take his seat; this will have been to discourage the formation of claques to intimidate or encourage the litigants by shouting.[5]

Not much is known for certain of the physical structure and location of the courts either in Aristotle's day or earlier. The procedure outlined by Aristotle does entail, however, that in his day there was an entrance for each tribe through which the designated jurors for each day's sitting were admitted, that once they had passed through these entrances they were in a forecourt inaccessible to other members of the public, and that they then passed from this forecourt into the respective courts for which they had been designated. The general public had access to the

[1] For the statistical effects of the procedure, S. Dow, *HSCP* 50 (1939) 31 ff. For numbers in the tribes, C. W. J. Eliot, *Phoenix* 22 (1968) 3 ff.

[2] Andok. 1 *Myst.* 28, 31.

[3] Lys. 14 *Alk.* i. 5.

[4] Leisi, *Zeuge* 124, Berneker, *RE* s.v. *ψευδομαρτυρίων δίκη* 1367.

[5] A. L. Boegehold, *Hesperia* 29 (1960) 393 ff., suggests this as the explanation of the *σύμβολον δημοσίᾳ* of Ar. *Ath. Pol.* 65. 2, for which no other plausible explanation has been advanced.

courts from the side opposite to this forecourt in some manner not clear to us.[1]

The size of any particular dikastery varied in accordance with the seriousness of the matter in issue. We have evidence for juries of 200 members and various multiples of 100 up to 2,500, and one jury in an important political trial in 415 B.C. numbered 6,000. These are round numbers, since it was usual to have juries of odd numbers (201, etc.).[2] The theoretical reason for the odd number may have been to avoid a tie, and at least one ancient authority states that it was so. But in practice this can hardly have been the result; for on the one hand we are told that when the votes were equal the case went to the defendant, and on the other there is at least one recorded case where the votes cast added up to 499; this confirms the suspicion that it must have been difficult with such large juries to ensure that every juror cast his vote, and unless this was done the odd vote had no point.[3]

As we shall see later (pp. 161 f.), for the purpose of allocating time to hearings cases were divided into public and private, and it was the normal practice to allow a whole day for the hearing of public cases, while probably four private cases were fitted into one day.[4] On a day devoted to hearing private suits, when juries would normally number 200, the statistical chances of being selected

[1] S. Dow, *HSCP* 50 (1939) 15 f. for correction of the layout of the courts suggested in Hommel, *Heliaia* 140 f. For the latest views on the early seat of the heliaia see H. Thompson, *AJA* 69 (1965) 177. In Aischin. 3 *Ktes.* 207 supporters of the two sides congregate near their respective platforms.

[2] Plut. *Per.* 32: 1,500 jurors for the trial of Perikles. Andok. 1 *Myst.* 17: 6,000 jurors tried a *γραφὴ παρανόμων* against Speusippos in 415 B.C. Ar. *Ath. Pol.* 53. 3: 201 jurors for private suits involving sums of less than a thousand drachmai, 401 jurors where the value was over that sum. *IG* ii². 1629 (Tod, *GHI* no. 200). 208: 201 jurors in the general's court dealing with appeals against having to perform a trierarchy. Isai. 5 *Dikaiog.* 20: 500 jurors for a *δίκη ψευδομαρτυρίων*. Dem. 24 *Timokr.* 9: 1,001 jurors for a *γραφὴ παρανόμων*; perhaps for this case two juries were joined together to form a single jury (see Wayte ad loc.). Dein. 1 *Dem.* 107: 1,500 jurors. Lys. 13 *Agorat.* 35: 2,000 jurors, just before the revolution of the Thirty in 404 B.C. Dein. 1 *Dem.* 52: 2,500 jurors.

[3] Schol. Dem. 24 *Timokr.* 9 states that the odd member was added to avoid a tie. For a tie as equal to a verdict for the defendant, see Ant. 5 *Her.* 51, Aischin. 3 *Ktes.* 252, Ar. *Prob.* 29. 13 and 15 (with a discussion of the rationale of the rule), *Ath. Pol.* 69. 1. For the 499 votes, *IG* ii². 1641. 30 ff. Cf. Bo. Sm. i. 239 ff.

[4] Ar. *Ath. Pol.* 67. 1 *ταῦτα δὲ ποιήσαντες εἰσκαλοῦσι τοὺς ἀγῶνας, ὅταν μὲν τὰ ἴδια δικάζωσι, τοὺς ἰδίους, τῷ ἀριθμῷ [ὃς ἂ]ν ῇ* (δ′ [ἐ]ξ Kenyon) *ἑκάστων τῶν δικῶν τῶν ἐκ τοῦ νόμου, καὶ δ[ιο]μνύ[ουσι]ν οἱ ἀντίδικοι εἰς αὐτὸ τὸ πρᾶγμα ἐρεῖν· [ὅταν] δὲ τὰ δημόσια, τοὺς δημοσίους, καὶ ἕν[α μόνον ἐ]κδικάζουσι.* The hearing of four private suits in a day depends on Kenyon's reading of the papyrus.

were very much lower than on those days when public suits, which needed juries of 500 or more, were to be tried. It is a reasonable conjecture that for this reason the dikast who dwelt in the country would have tended to favour public as against private days.[1]

At the beginning of each year all the heliasts had to take an oath known as the heliastic oath. What purports to be a text of the oath is given in Dem. 24 *Timokr.* 149–51. It is doubtful whether this is an authentic text; it certainly omits some clauses which we know from other sources formed part of the oath. We can however piece together a probable version of the oath. The jurors swore that they would vote according to the laws and decrees of the Athenian people and of the council of five hundred or, in a case not covered by a law, in accordance with what was most just and without fear or favour, that they would vote on the matter in issue after listening to both sides, and that they would take no bribe either direct or indirect.[2] The general tenor of the oath suggests that the juror is to vote according to his conscience; there would certainly have been many cases not completely or not at all covered by law or decree.[3] It has been wrongly supposed that besides this annual oath heliasts took another oath before each case.[4]

Pay for jurors was instituted by Perikles, probably early in the decade 460–450 B.C. His motive, according to the partisan account in Ar. *Ath. Pol.* 27. 4, was to overtrump the largesse of

[1] Hommel, *Heliaia* 119, Bo. Sm. i. 371, n. 3.

[2] Isok. 15 *Antid.* 21 *ὀμνύναι μὲν καθ' ἕκαστον τὸν ἐνιαυτὸν ἦ μὴν ὁμοίως ἀκροάσεσθαι τῶν κατηγορούντων καὶ τῶν ἀπολογουμένων*, Dem. 39 *Boiot.* i. 40 *γνώμῃ τῇ δικαιοτάτῃ δικάσειν ὀμωμόκατε*, 57 *Euboul.* 63 *γνώμῃ τῇ δικαιοτάτῃ καὶ οὔτε χάριτος ἕνεκ' οὔτ' ἔχθρας*, 24 *Timokr.* 150 f. *οὐδὲ δῶρα δέξομαι τῆς ἡλιάσεως ἕνεκα οὔτ' αὐτὸς ἐγὼ οὔτ' ἄλλος ἐμοὶ οὔτ' ἄλλη εἰδότος ἐμοῦ, οὔτε τέχνῃ οὔτε μηχανῇ οὐδεμιᾷ. . . . καὶ ἀκροάσομαι τοῦ τε κατηγόρου καὶ τοῦ ἀπολογουμένου ὁμοίως ἀμφοῖν, καὶ διαψηφιοῦμαι περὶ αὐτοῦ οὗ ἂν ἡ δίωξις ᾖ*, Harpokr. s.v. *Ἀρδηττός· . . . ἐν τούτῳ φασὶ δημοσίᾳ πάντες ὤμνυον Ἀθηναῖοι τὸν ὅρκον τὸν ἠλιαστικόν. . . . Θεόφραστος δ' ἐν τοῖς περὶ νόμων δηλοῖ ὡς κατελέλυτο τὸ ἔθος τοῦτο*, Dem. 19 *Embassy* 179, Hyper. 3 *Euxen.* 40. Possibly when the number of 6,000 heliasts fell into abeyance, if it had ever operated, all citizens over the age of thirty were required to take the oath. See Bo. Sm. ii. 152 ff.

[3] J. F. Cronin, *The Athenian Juror and his Oath* (Chicago, 1936) 18 ff. For cases not covered by laws see E. Ruschenbusch, *Historia* 6 (1957) 257 ff.

[4] Poll. 8. 122, *An. Bekk.* (*Δικ. 'Ον.*) 184. 9 f. posit oaths before each case. But Isok. 18 *Kallim.* 34 *δύ' ὅρκους ὀμόσαντες δικάζετε, τὸν μὲν ὅνπερ ἐπὶ ταῖς ἄλλαις εἴθισθε, τὸν δ' ὃν ἐπὶ ταῖς συνθήκαις ἐποιήσασθε* refers to the heliastic oath and the oath taken at the amnesty; if there had been another oath, the speaker here could hardly have failed to mention it.

Kimon by bribing the people with their own money. In point of fact some pay for jurors was essential if the poorer section of the community was to play its part in the rapidly increasing litigation of the period. The pay was at first two obols a day. It was soon increased to three obols, and remained at that figure in Aristotle's day.[1] Although Plato *Gorg.* 515 e makes Sokrates say ἀκούω Περικλέα πεποιηκέναι Ἀθηναίους ἀργοὺς καὶ δειλοὺς καὶ λάλους καὶ φιλαργύρους, εἰς μισθοφορίαν πρῶτον καταστήσαντα, and although this probably refers in the main to dikastic pay, it is unlikely that pay at this rate was, for those in the prime of life, ever more than a rather inadequate compensation for the loss of a day's work, and with the fall in the value of money during the fourth century it became more rather than less inadequate. In fact there is much to be said for the view that in the time of Demosthenes juries tended to be manned not by the poor, but by those of middling circumstances.[2] On the other hand, even if a dikast's pay did not bulk so large in his budget as critics of the extreme democracy were apt to assume, their total pay must have bulked large in the state budget. Certainly there were times of stringency when court sittings had to be curtailed owing to lack of funds to pay the jurors.[3]

The payment on each day was restricted by elaborate rules to those who had actually voted on the prescribed occasions.[4]

(iii) *The ekklesia and the boule*

As we have seen (p. 44), the dikasteries had their origin in a much simpler system, under which the whole body of the

[1] Schol. Aristoph. *Wasps* 88 ἐδίδοτο δὲ αὐτοῖς χρόνον μέν τινα δύο ὀβολοί, ὕστερον δὲ Κλέων στρατηγήσας τριώβολον ἐποίησε ἀκμάζοντος τοῦ πολέμου τοῦ πρὸς Λακεδαιμονίους, ibid. 300, Ar. *Ath. Pol.* 62. 2; Lipsius, *AR* 163, Hignett, *HAC* 342 f.

[2] According to Aristoph. *Wasps* 661 ff., 6,000 dikasts cost the state 150 talents a year. This may be an exaggeration, but it implies an average earning of 150 drachmai a year for each juryman, earned (if the rate was then 3 obols) by sitting on 300 days. Böckh, *Staatsh.* i. 141 f., reckoned that a working-class family of four grown people at the end of the fifth century needed in the region of 400 drachmai to live on. In 329 B.C. casual free labour earned 1½ drachmai a day and skilled labour 2 to 2½ drachmai (*IG* ii². 1672). For the composition of juries in Demosthenes' time cf. A. H. M. Jones, *Athenian Democracy* (Oxford, 1957) 36 f.

[3] Making full allowance for the exaggeration of Aristophanes (see previous note) the annual cost of jury pay must have been in the region of 100 talents. Curtailment of sittings owing to lack of funds is mentioned in Dem. 39 *Boiot.* i. 17.

[4] Ar. *Ath. Pol.* 65. We can see that the procedure was elaborate, although we cannot describe it precisely owing to the defective text.

people sat as a court of appeal, and perhaps on occasion as a court of first instance. It was a survival of this system when in the fourth century the ekklesia and its steering committee, the boule, either tried cases throughout or remitted them, with or without a prejudicial resolution as to guilt and recommended penalty, to a dikastery.[1]

The procedures under which the boule and ekklesia might act in a judicial capacity were three: *εἰσαγγελία, ἀποχειροτονία, προβολή.*

(a) *εἰσαγγελία*

Surviving first-hand evidence about this procedure is not plentiful. We have only one speech delivered before the ekklesia in such a case, Lys. 28 *Ergokl.* of 388 B.C. Speeches delivered before dikasteries in *εἰσαγγελίαι* are Lys. 30 *Nikom.*, Lykourg. *Leokr.*, Hyper. 2 *Lyk.* and 3 *Euxen.* The last named is particularly important as providing citations from the so-called *νόμος εἰσαγγελτικός* (on which see pp. 52 ff.).[2] In view of the paucity of direct

[1] There had been a period when the boule had been competent to fine, imprison, and put to death: Ar. *Ath. Pol.* 45. 1 *ἡ δὲ βουλὴ πρότερον μὲν ἦν κυρία καὶ χρήμασιν ζημιῶσαι καὶ δῆσαι καὶ ἀποκτεῖναι.* Cf. Bo. Sm. i. 335 ff. There is much controversy as to the exact date at which the boule lost these powers; Aristotle gives no clue, but it was certainly before the time which concerns us. The oath taken by each councillor is known to have contained, among other promises of a general kind such as to discharge his duties in the best interests of the state (Lys. 31 *Phil.* 1), at least one specific undertaking, not to detain a man who produced bail save in cases allied to treason or cases of fiscal default: Dem. 24 *Timokr.* 144 *οὐδὲ δήσω Ἀθηναίων οὐδένα, ὃς ἂν ἐγγυητὰς τρεῖς καθιστῇ τὸ αὐτὸ τέλος τελοῦντας, πλὴν ἐάν τις ἐπὶ προδοσίᾳ τῆς πόλεως ἢ ἐπὶ καταλύσει τοῦ δήμου συνιὼν ἁλῷ, ἢ τέλος πριάμενος ἢ ἐγγυησάμενος ἢ ἐκλέγων μὴ καταβάλῃ.* It possibly also included a clause against enforcing exile or the death penalty without due trial: Andok. 4 *Alk.* 3 (but the evidential value of this speech is dubious). On the oath see Bo. Sm. ii. 151 f.

[2] Lys. 22 *Corn-dealers* is sometimes cited as having been delivered in an *εἰσαγγελία*, but it was more probably an *ἀπαγωγή*; cf. Gernet and Bizos, *Lys.* ii. 82 f. Similarly Lys. 24 *Invalid* is not, in spite of its title in the manuscripts *πρὸς τὴν εἰσαγγελίαν*, an *εἰσαγγελτικὸς λόγος*; cf. Gernet and Bizos, *Lys.* ii. 101. Of the lost speeches the most important must have been that of Antiphon *περὶ τῆς μεταστάσεως* in his own defence (frr. 1–6 Thalheim). There were also speeches of Lykourgos *Against Menesaichmos* (with possibly one in his defence by Deinarchos) and two *Against Lykophron* (answered by one, possibly two, speeches by Hypereides), and speeches of Deinarchos *Against Himeraios, Against Pistias* (said in Harpokr. s.v. *βουλεύσεως* to have been delivered before the Areopagos), *Against Agasikles* (who was accused of having been corruptly enrolled in the deme Halimous; cf. Hyper. 3 *Euxen.* 3, Harpokr. s.v. *Ἀγασικλῆς*), *Against Kallisthenes, Against Pheidiades,* and (wrongly attributed to Deinarchos) *Against Timokrates.* Cf. Philochoros, *F.Gr.H.* 328 F 199, with Jacoby's commentary.

evidence from the orators the evidence of the grammarians is important.[1]

The verb *εἰσαγγέλλειν* (with its cognate *εἰσαγγελία*) has both a general sense 'report', 'give information about', and a technical sense of initiating the legal procedure of that name, for which the best translation is 'impeach'.[2] The distinguishing marks of this procedure were that the act charged was deemed a particularly serious threat to public order, even though in some cases it had only affected a private individual, that it called for speedy redress, and that the initiator or prosecutor was not subject to a fine of a thousand drachmai if he failed to secure one-fifth of the votes or did not persist in the prosecution, as were prosecutors in *γραφαί*. In the latter half of the fourth century this last privilege had been so much abused, however, that prosecutors in *εἰσαγγελίαι* were made liable to the fine in the circumstances stated, though still not to *ἀτιμία*.[3]

[1] Harpokr. s.v. *εἰσαγγελία* describes three types, of which only the first concerns us here: *ἡ μὲν γὰρ ἐπὶ δημοσίοις ἀδικήμασι μεγίστοις καὶ ἀναβολὴν μὴ ἐπιδεχομένοις, καὶ ἐφ' οἷς μήτε ἀρχὴ καθέστηκε μήτε νόμοι κεῖνται τοῖς ἄρχουσι καθ' οὓς εἰσάξουσιν, ἀλλὰ πρὸς τὴν βουλὴν ἢ τὸν δῆμον ἡ πρώτη κατάστασις γίνεται, καὶ ἐφ' οἷς τῷ μὲν φεύγοντι, ἐὰν ἁλῷ, μέγισται ζημίαι ἐπίκεινται, ὁ δὲ διώκων, ἐὰν μὴ ἕλῃ, οὐδὲν ζημιοῦται, πλὴν ἐὰν τὸ ε′ μέρος τῶν ψήφων μὴ μεταλάβῃ· τότε γὰρ χιλίας ἐκτίνει.* Poll. 8. 51 f. *ἡ δ' εἰσαγγελία τέτακται ἐπὶ τῶν ἀγράφων δημοσίων ἀδικημάτων. κατὰ τὸν νόμον τὸν εἰσαγγελτικόν . . . (ἀμφοτέρως γὰρ λέγουσιν), ὃς κεῖται . . . περὶ ὧν οὐκ εἰσὶ νόμοι, ἀδικῶν δέ τις ἁλίσκεται ἢ ἄρχων ἢ ῥήτωρ, εἰς τὴν βουλὴν εἰσαγγελία δίδοται κατ' αὐτοῦ, κἂν μὲν μέτρια ἀδικεῖν δοκῇ, ἡ βουλὴ ποιεῖται ζημίας ἐπιβολήν, ἂν δὲ μείζω, παραδίδωσι δικαστηρίῳ· τὸ δὲ τίμημα, ὅ τι χρὴ παθεῖν ἢ ἀποτῖσαι. ἐγίνοντο δὲ εἰσαγγελίαι καὶ κατὰ τῶν καταλυόντων τὸν δῆμον ῥητόρων, ἢ μὴ τὰ ἄριστα τῷ δήμῳ λεγόντων, ἢ πρὸς τοὺς πολεμίους ἄνευ τοῦ πεμφθῆναι ἀπελθόντων, ἢ προδόντων φρούριον ἢ στρατιὰν ἢ ναῦς, ὡς Θεόφραστος ἐν τῷ πρώτῳ περὶ νόμων.* *Lex. Cant.* s.v. *εἰσαγγελία· κατὰ καινῶν καὶ ἀγράφων ἀδικημάτων. αὕτη μὲν οὖν ἡ Καικιλίου δόξα. Θεόφραστος δὲ ἐν τῷ τετάρτῳ περὶ νόμων φησὶ γενέσθαι, ἐάν τις καταλύῃ τὸν δῆμον ῥήτωρ ἢ μὴ τὰ ἄριστα συμβουλεύῃ χρήματα λαμβάνων, ἢ ἐάν τις προδιδῷ χωρίον ἢ ναῦς ἢ πεζὴν στρατιάν, ἢ ἐάν τις εἰς τοὺς πολεμίους ἀφικνῆται ἢ μετοικῇ παρ' αὐτοῖς ἢ στρατεύηται μετ' αὐτῶν ἢ δῶρα λαμβάνῃ. συνομολογεῖ δὲ τοῖς ὑπὸ Θεοφράστου ἡ κατὰ Θεμιστοκλέους εἰσαγγελία, ἣν εἰσήγγειλε κατὰ Κράτερον Λεωβώτης Ἀλκμαίωνος Ἀγρυλῆθεν. ἔνιοι δὲ τῶν ῥητόρων εἰώθεσαν καλεῖν καὶ τὰ μὴ μεγάλα ἀδικήματα εἰσαγγελίαν. ἔστι δ' ὅτε ἐμβάλλοντες τοὺς συκοφαντουμένους εἰσήγγελλον, ὡς μὲν Φιλόχορος, χιλίων καθεζομένων, ὡς δὲ Δημήτριος ὁ Φαληρεύς, χιλίων πεντακοσίων. Καικίλιος δὲ οὕτως ὡρίσατο· εἰσαγγελία ἐστὶν ὃ περὶ καινῶν ἀδικημάτων δεδώκασιν ἀπενεγκεῖν οἱ νόμοι. ἔστι δὲ τὸ μελετώμενον ἐν ταῖς τῶν σοφιστῶν διατριβαῖς.*

[2] For the former usage Lys. 12 *Ag. Erat.* 48, 13 *Agorat.* 50, 56; instances of the latter in the following paragraphs. On the procedure in general see H. Hager, *JP* 4 (1872) 74 ff., Thalheim, *RE* s.v. *εἰσαγγελία*, Lipsius, *AR* 176 ff., Bo. Sm. i. 294 ff., Colin, *Hyper.* 146 ff.

[3] Poll. 8. 52 f. *ὅτι δὲ ὁ εἰσαγγείλας καὶ οὐχ ἑλὼν ἀζήμιος ἦν, Ὑπερείδης ἐν τῷ ὑπὲρ Λυκόφρονός φησιν. καίτοι γε ὁ Θεόφραστος τοὺς μὲν ἄλλας γραφὰς γραψαμένους χιλίας*

There were three distinct categories of *εἰσαγγελία*. First, it was available against those who wronged orphans or heiresses (see vol. i, pp. 117 ff.); second, against official misconduct of arbitrators (see p. 68); finally, against those guilty of acts threatening the stability of the state, the state sometimes being equated with the democracy. We are here concerned with cases of the third category, since only in these did either the boule or the ekklesia or both play a role.[1]

At some stage in the development the wrongful acts chargeable under this third procedure, and presumably the steps in the procedure itself, were laid down in a separate law, the *νόμος εἰσαγγελτικός*, and we may perhaps conjecture that this was among the laws of the thesmothetai. Aristotle attributes the original law to Solon. Speaking in *Ath. Pol.* 8. 4 of the Areopagos he says *καὶ τοὺς ἐπὶ καταλύσει τοῦ δήμου συνισταμένους ἔκρινεν, Σόλωνος θέντος νόμον εἰσαγγελίας περὶ αὐτῶν*. Though it may be doubted whether there was a specific law as early as this, there existed early in the fifth century a special procedure for dealing with serious political misdeeds, conducted at first throughout before the Areopagos, later initiated before the boule and carried through either before it or before the ekklesia or remitted by one or other of these bodies to a dikastery.[2] The date at which the

τ' ὀφλισκάνειν, εἰ τὸ πέμπτον τῶν ψήφων μὴ καταλάβοιεν, καὶ προσατιμοῦσθαι, τοὺς δὲ εἰσαγγέλλοντας μὴ ἀτιμοῦσθαι μέν, ὀφλεῖν δὲ τὰς χιλίας· ἔοικε δὲ τοῦτο διὰ τοὺς ῥᾳδίως εἰσαγγέλλοντας ὕστερον προσγεγράφθαι. Hyper. 2 *Lyk.* 8 and 12 imply that the prosecutor in an *εἰσαγγελία* ran no risk; the most probable date of that speech is 333 B.C. Dem. 18 *Crown* 250, on the other hand, implies that immediately after the battle of Chaironeia in 338 this privilege did not exist; however, Demosthenes is actually speaking in 330, and it may well be that he is projecting back the rule as it then stood. There is no mention of the privilege in Hyper. 3 *Euxen.*, and we may therefore conclude that it was curtailed between 333 and 330 B.C.; cf. Colin, *Hyper.* 149.

[1] Kahrstedt, *Mag.* 206 ff., argues a case for regarding the boule in respect to litigation as an *εἰσάγουσα ἀρχή*. It may be that there was an analogy between the boule's power to fine, imprison, and put to death and similar powers originally enjoyed by magistrates. But it is difficult to see how in practice it could ever have exercised the sort of powers which developed into the hegemony of a court. These are almost by definition such as could only be exercised by an individual, or at most by a very small committee.

[2] The fifth-century cases are conveniently collected in Bo. Sm. i. 299 ff. Note especially Plut. *Alk.* 22, which gives what purports to be the actual text of the indictment by *εἰσαγγελία* against Alkibiades for profanation of the Mysteries in 415 B.C., and *IG* i². 76. 58 f., an early use of the word in its technical sense in a contemporary document (the date is uncertain, but not later than 416 and possibly as early as 446; the offence here too is against religion).

law in its latest form, the form which obtained in the last half of the fourth century, was passed has been variously placed either immediately after the fall of the Four Hundred in 411 B.C. or at the general revision of the laws in 403/2 B.C. or about the middle of the fourth century. On the whole the first of these three dates is to be preferred. The succeeding discussion aims at depicting the rules as they stood at this final stage, whenever that was.[1]

For the content of the law of impeachment in its final form we are largely indebted to the third speech of Hypereides, *For Euxenippos*. This speech was delivered soon after 330 B.C. and certainly before 324 B.C. It was a defence of Euxenippos, a wealthy but non-political Athenian, who had been impeached by Polyeuktos. One of the main lines of defence was that *εἰσαγγελία* was a totally inappropriate procedure for the act alleged against the defendant. In developing this defence Hypereides gives what we may assume to be a fairly complete, though not necessarily exhaustive, account of the wrongful acts mentioned in the law as rendering the actor liable to impeachment. In an attempt then to reconstruct the law we may start with this speech, making such additions as are deducible from other sources. We should all the time bear in mind that the Athenians were much looser than we should be in defining acts rendering a man liable to various types of process. (We can see a striking parallel to their looseness here in their failure to define what was meant by *ὕβρις* in the action named after it.) Acts specified tended to be regarded rather as *exempli gratia* than as excluding other vaguely similar acts. It is true that Hyper. 3 *Euxen.* 4 argues that in public trials (*δημόσιοι ἀγῶνες*) defendants should be able to insist on a strict interpretation of the relevant law, and he even goes so far as to suggest that, because the law of impeachment has a clause directed against orators, it is not available against all Athenians indiscriminately. But this is special pleading, and elsewhere (5 *Athenog.* 13 ff.) Hypereides uses the exactly opposite thesis, that the spirit rather than the letter of the law is what should count.

With this *caveat* in mind we can say that the law named the following grounds for impeachment:

1. Attempt to overthrow the constitution.[2]

[1] For the dating of the law Bo. Sm. i. 302 ff.

[2] Hyper. 3 *Euxen.* 7 f. *ἐάν τις . . . τὸν δῆμον τὸν Ἀθηναίων καταλύῃ . . . ἢ συνίῃ ποι ἐπὶ καταλύσει τοῦ δήμου ἢ ἑταιρικὸν συναγάγῃ.*

2. Treason.[1]

3. Taking of bribes by an orator.[2]

4. Allied to this last was the charge of making deceptive promises to the people (ἀπάτη τοῦ δήμου). It would perhaps not have been necessary either to prove bribery or to show that the man charged was in any technical sense an orator. It may have been under some such clause in a law that the great Miltiades was arraigned; it certainly remained a possible charge in the middle of the fourth century.[3]

5. A number of miscellaneous charges allied to treason, such as damage to naval establishments or to commerce, the burning of public buildings or records, and acts of sacrilege, are mentioned in various contexts as fit occasions for εἰσαγγελία. We cannot be sure whether these were specified in the law or were by the practice of the courts subsumed under treason.[4]

It has sometimes been held that one function of εἰσαγγελία was to deal with extraordinary crimes against the state which had not been foreseen by the legislators. This view was taken by Caecilius as against Theophrastos, who believed that the process was restricted to the first three charges mentioned above.[5] The probability is that technically a prosecutor was required to bring a charge under one of the heads named in the law, but that there was wide latitude as to the acts which could be thus subsumed. Leokrates for example was probably prosecuted by Lykourgos not for an ἄγραφον ἀδίκημα but for treason (the word προδοσία is used in Lykourg. *Leokr.* 59), though it was obviously stretching the meaning of the word to extend it to leaving the city at a time of stress.[6] It is this stretching of the law to cover acts which it was

[1] Hyper. 3 *Euxen.* 8 ἢ ἐάν τις πόλιν τινὰ προδῷ ἢ ναῦς ἢ πεζὴν ἢ ναυτικὴν στρατιάν, *Lex. Cant.* s.v. εἰσαγγελία (quoted on p. 51, n. 1).

[2] Hyper. 3 *Euxen.* 8 ἢ ῥήτωρ ὢν μὴ λέγῃ τὰ ἄριστα τῷ δήμῳ τῷ Ἀθηναίων χρήματα λαμβάνων, 29 ῥήτορα ὄντα λέγειν μὴ τὰ ἄριστα τῷ δήμῳ τῷ Ἀθηναίων χρήματα λαμβάνοντα καὶ δωρεὰς παρὰ τῶν τἀναντία πραττόντων τῷ δήμῳ, 39.

[3] Dem. 49 *Timoth.* 67 νόμων ὄντων, ἐάν τις τὸν δῆμον ὑποσχόμενος ἐξαπατήσῃ, εἰσαγγελίαν εἶναι περὶ αὐτοῦ. For Miltiades see Hdt. 6. 136; Partsch, *GB* 388, n. 2.

[4] Hyper. 2 *Lyk.* fr. III Jensen ἢ νεωρίων προδοσίαν ἢ ἀρχείων ἐμπυρισμὸν ἢ κατάληψιν ἄκρας (cf. Poll. 9. 156), *IG* ii². 1631. 398 ff. εἶναι δὲ καὶ εἰσαγγελίαν αὐτῶν εἰς τὴμ βουλὴν καθάπερ ἐάν τις ἀδικεῖ περὶ τὰ ἐν τοῖς νεωρίοις, D.H. *Dein.* 10 κατὰ Πυθέου περὶ τῶν κατὰ τὸ ἐμπόριον εἰσαγγελία. H. Hager, *JP* 4 (1872) 93 f.

[5] Poll. 8. 51 f., *Lex. Cant.* s.v. εἰσαγγελία (both quoted on p. 51, n. 1).

[6] A stretching intelligible, however, to those who have become accustomed to the mentality which dictated the Berlin Wall.

not intended to cover to which Hypereides takes exception in the opening of his speech *For Euxenippos*.[1] There is a modern parallel in England in recent attempts to exploit the concept of Parliamentary privilege.

We turn now to the procedure followed in εἰσαγγελία.[2] This requires special treatment here, as it was in important respects different from the procedure followed in other suits, whether public or private, which forms the subject of Chapter II.

Two pre-eminent aims seem to have dictated the extraordinary procedures available for impeachment. The first, emphasized by Harpokration, was to bring the wrongdoer to book with the minimum of delay.[3] The second was to give the widest latitude to informers to initiate proceedings without fear of reprisals from men of wealth or power, the sort of aim which in a modern society a free press is supposed to attain.

An information could be laid (it probably had to be in writing) before the boule at any moment and, so far as we know, by any person, slave or free, foreigner or citizen.[4] This information could be against anyone, whether officer of the state or private person. Several courses were then open to the boule.[5] It could reject the information out of hand; there would be considerable risk in so doing if the charge was of a serious nature and seemed

[1] Hager, *JP* 4 (1872) 78, thinks that under the law the prosecutor had to bring his charge under one of the statutory headings. We cannot deduce with certainty from Hypereides whether under the regime which he is criticizing impeachments had or had not been brought under one of these. For instance, he says that two men had been impeached for hiring out flute-girls at above the permitted price. This may well have been brought technically under the clause dealing with commerce (cf. p. 54, n. 4). Again, he says that Agasikles was impeached because he registered with the deme Halimous. We learn only from Harpokr. s.v. Ἀγασικλῆς that Agasikles was an alien who had bribed the demesmen to enrol him; he may well therefore have been arraigned under a natural extension of the third head above.

[2] For the Greek technical terminology see Hager, *JP* 4 (1872) 98, n. 1.

[3] Harpokr. s.v. εἰσαγγελία (quoted on p. 51, n. 1).

[4] Aristoph. *Knights* 475 ff., Isok. 15 *Antid.* 314, 16 *Chariot* 6, Dem. 21 *Meid.* 116. For written informations (also named εἰσαγγελίαι) Plut. *Alk.* 22, Hyper. 2 *Lyk.* 3, 4, 12, 3 *Euxen.* 29, 30, 40, Lykourg. *Leokr.* 34, 137.

[5] We ignore here the wider powers once enjoyed by the boule (see p. 50, n. 1). The curtailment of these powers is an early recognition of the desirability of separating judicial from executive power. The boule of five hundred was in some respects no different from a court of five hundred; each was a body of fully qualified citizens chosen at random; but the boule had considerable executive power and, after experience for an unknown length of time, it was realized that there would be danger in leaving it with large judicial powers also.

plausible.[1] If the boule decided that there was a *prima facie* case, the prytaneis fixed a day in the near future for a hearing before the boule; sureties were taken for the appearance of the accused, save that if the charge was one of treason or conspiracy to overthrow the democracy no sureties were allowed, but the accused had to be held in custody.[2] On the day fixed for the second hearing the boule might itself impose a penalty of up to five hundred drachmai; but even so, in the fourth century at least, there could be an appeal against this fine to a dikastery.[3] We do not know whether the prosecutor could appeal if the defendant was acquitted.

If the boule deemed the offence too serious to be dealt with by a fine of five hundred drachmai, it again had two courses open to it. The more normal course was for a decree to be passed referring the matter to a dikastery. This decree, known technically as *κατάγνωσις*, might, though it need not, contain a recommendation as to the fitting penalty. The secretary to the prytany communicated the terms of the decree to the thesmothetai, who then had to bring the case before a court. This court finally decided the issue and, if they condemned, determined the penalty, choosing, we must presume, between that proposed by the boule and that put forward by the defendant.[4] As a rule the original informer would be the prosecutor in the court, though his place could be taken by a substitute.[5] Where a defendant was being

[1] For possible rejection of a case by the boule see Lys. 30 *Nikom.* 22. In Dem. 47 *Euerg.* 42 f. what seemed quite a serious case was compromised for the trifling fine of twenty-five drachmai; in this case the boule had invited the informer to bring an *εἰσαγγελία*.

[2] Dem. 24 *Timokr.* 144 (quoted on p. 50, n. 1). The word *ἁλῷ* there means not 'convicted' (Demosthenes says in the next sentence but one that such men are still *ἄκριτοι*) but 'against whom a *prima facie* case has been made out'.

[3] Dem. 47 *Euerg.* 43 *ἐν τῷ διαχειροτονεῖν ἣν ἡ βουλὴ πότερα δικαστηρίῳ παραδοίη ἢ ζημιώσειε ταῖς πεντακοσίαις, ὅσου ἦν κυρία κατὰ τὸν νόμον*, Ar. *Ath. Pol.* 45. 2 *ἔξεστι δὲ καὶ τοῖς ἰδιώταις εἰσαγγέλλειν ἣν ἂν βούλωνται τῶν ἀρχῶν μὴ χρῆσθαι τοῖς νόμοις· ἔφεσις δὲ καὶ τούτοις ἐστὶν εἰς τὸ δικαστήριον ἐὰν αὐτῶν ἡ βουλὴ καταγνῷ*, 41. 2 *καὶ γὰρ αἱ τῆς βουλῆς κρίσεις εἰς τὸν δῆμον ἐληλύθασιν*. Lipsius, *AR* 198, n. 67, holds that there was appeal, Bo. Sm. ii. 240 ff. that there was not.

[4] Dem. 24 *Timokr.* 63 *Τιμοκράτης εἶπεν· ὁπόσοι Ἀθηναίων κατ' εἰσαγγελίαν ἐκ τῆς βουλῆς ἢ νῦν εἰσιν ἐν τῷ δεσμωτηρίῳ ἢ τὸ λοιπὸν κατατεθῶσι, καὶ μὴ παραδοθῇ ἡ κατάγνωσις αὐτῶν τοῖς θεσμοθέταις ὑπὸ τοῦ γραμματέως τοῦ κατὰ πρυτανείαν κατὰ τὸν εἰσαγγελτικὸν νόμον, δεδόχθαι τοῖς νομοθέταις εἰσάγειν τοὺς ἕνδεκα εἰς τὸ δικαστήριον τριάκονθ' ἡμερῶν ἀφ' ἧς ἂν παραλάβωσιν, ἐὰν μή τι δημοσίᾳ κωλύῃ, ἐὰν δὲ μή, ὅταν πρῶτον οἷόν τ' ᾖ. κατηγορεῖν δ' Ἀθηναίων τὸν βουλόμενον οἷς ἔξεστιν. ἐὰν δ' ἁλῷ, τιμάτω ἡ ἡλιαία περὶ αὐτοῦ ὅ τι ἂν δοκῇ ἄξιος εἶναι παθεῖν ἢ ἀποτεῖσαι. ἐὰν δ' ἀργυρίου τιμηθῇ, δεδέσθω τέως ἂν ἐκτείσῃ ὅ τι ἂν αὐτοῦ καταγνωσθῇ.*

[5] Ant. 6 *Chor.* 36.

held in custody, the Eleven had to secure that his case was brought before a court within thirty days of his arrest.[1] The second and rarer course was for the boule to pass a decree referring the matter for trial by the ekklesia.[2] There is yet a third theoretical possibility (whether it was actual or not we do not know): the boule on this second hearing might reverse its previous decision and dismiss the case. In the procedure hitherto sketched the boule acted as the chief executive organ of the state, and it could itself initiate action by getting one of its own members or some other person to bring an *εἰσαγγελία*.[3]

An information might be laid direct to the ekklesia. In such a case it was the immediate duty of the boule to formulate a *προβούλευμα* on the matter; this might contain proposals that the case should be tried by the ekklesia itself or that it be remitted to a dikastery, and in the latter case that the jury should number such-and-such and the penalty be such-and-such. This *προβούλευμα* was subject to amendment and was passed upon by the ekklesia.[4] In this type of case the proposal for a penalty, if

[1] Dem. 24 *Timokr.* 63 (quoted on p. 56, n. 4).

[2] Lipsius, *AR* 201, draws a distinction between the boule's acting as the chief executive power in the state and its acting as the ekklesia's steering (probouleutic) committee. This is important, and it is probable that when acting in the latter capacity all that it could do was to put forward a decree for decision by the ekklesia, though that decree might propose either that the issue should be tried by a dikastery or that it should be tried in full assembly.

[3] Ar. *Ath. Pol.* 46. 2 *ἐξετάζει δὲ καὶ τὰ οἰκοδομήματα τὰ δημόσια πάντα, κἄν τις ἀδικεῖν αὐτῇ δόξῃ, τῷ τε δήμῳ τοῦτον ἀποφαίνει καὶ καταγνοῦσα παραδίδωσι δικαστηρίῳ.* Kahrstedt, *Mag.* 206 f.

[4] Plut. *Per.* 32 quotes a motion of Drakontides, as amended by a motion of Hagnon, for the trial of Perikles, probably an *εἰσαγγελία*. Xen. *Hell.* 1. 7. 1 ff. gives the procedure in the trial of the generals after the battle of Arginousai in 406 B.C.; although the circumstances were exceptional and there were acknowledged irregularities, the pattern of procedure is probably typical. Plut. *Mor.* 833 e–f gives the decree for the prosecution of Antiphon, Archeptolemos, and Onomakles after the fall of the Four Hundred in 411 B.C. (text as in Gernet, *Ant.* 29): *ἔδοξεν τῇ βουλῇ, μιᾷ καὶ εἰκοστῇ τῆς πρυτανείας, Δημόνικος Ἀλωπεκῆθεν ἐγραμμάτευε, Φιλόστρατος Παλληνεὺς ἐπεστάτει, Ἄνδρων εἶπε· περὶ τῶν ἀνδρῶν οὓς ἀποφαίνουσιν οἱ στρατηγοὶ πρεσβευσαμένους εἰς Λακεδαίμονα ἐπὶ κακῷ τῆς πόλεως τῆς Ἀθηναίων καὶ [ἐκ] τοῦ στρατοπέδου πλεῖν ἐπὶ πολεμίας νεὼς καὶ πεζεῦσαι διὰ Δεκελείας, Ἀρχεπτόλεμον καὶ Ὀνομακλέα καὶ Ἀντιφῶντα συλλαβεῖν καὶ ἀποδοῦναι εἰς τὸ δικαστήριον, ὅπως δῶσι δίκην· παρασχόντων δ' αὐτοὺς οἱ στρατηγοὶ καὶ ἐκ τῆς βουλῆς οὕστινας ἂν δοκῇ τοῖς στρατηγοῖς προσελομένοις μέχρι δέκα, ὅπως ἂν περὶ παρόντων γένηται ἡ κρίσις· προσκαλεσάσθων δ' αὐτοὺς οἱ θεσμοθέται ἐν τῇ αὔριον ἡμέρᾳ, καὶ εἰσαγόντων, ἐπειδὰν αἱ κλήσεις ἐξήκωσιν, εἰς τὸ δικαστήριον περὶ προδοσίας. κατηγορεῖν ⟨δὲ⟩ τοὺς ᾑρημένους συνηγόρους καὶ τοὺς στρατηγοὺς καὶ ἄλλος ἄν τις βούληται· ὅτου δ' ἂν καταψηφίσηται τὸ δικαστήριον, περὶ αὐτοῦ ποιεῖν κατὰ τὸν νόμον ὃς κεῖται περὶ τῶν προδοτῶν.* This decree, whether by a usurpation or by mandate from the ekklesia,

accepted by the ekklesia, was mandatory on the dikastery if it found the defendant guilty.[1]

We have not much fourth-century evidence for the procedure followed when a case was heard right through in the ekklesia. If we may judge from Xenophon's account of the trial of the generals after the battle of Arginousai, the law prescribed that a certain time should be allowed to defendants to put their case (this provision was flouted on that occasion); each tribe had two urns, one for condemnation and the other for acquittal, though it was the majority of all votes cast that carried the motion; the motion included the penalty (death, to be supervised by the Eleven, and confiscation of property, of which one-tenth was dedicated to Athena).[2] In other cases the verdict seems to have been given by show of hands, like other decisions in the ekklesia; at least there is in the brief statements about them nothing to indicate a special voting procedure such as that set out in Xenophon.[3] Whether decrees of this kind were subject to the rule that any νόμος ἐπ' ἀνδρί needed a quorum of six thousand, we cannot be sure. If it did, it would seem that voting by pebbles in urns would have been necessary in order to ensure that this provision was met. On the whole, the fact that this quorum is never mentioned in connection with procedure by εἰσαγγελία leads us to suppose that it did not apply here.[4]

seems to have been passed by the boule without reference back to the ekklesia, but it probably followed the pattern of προβουλεύματα. In *IG* ii². 125 (Tod, *GHI* no. 154), a decree of 357/6 B.C., the ekklesia instructs the boule to bring forward a προβούλευμα to deal with the trial of invaders of Eretria.

1 Xen. *Hell.* I. 7. 22, Lykourg. *Leokr.* 113. The assumption here is that the law did not itself prescribe penalties. This assumption may seem to be refuted by the last clause of the decree on Antiphon and his fellows (quoted on p. 57, n. 4), but at that date the νόμος ἐπὶ προδοσίᾳ and the νόμος εἰσαγγελτικός were distinct; they were later, it would seem, run together (see p. 59).

2 Xen. *Hell.* I. 7. 9 f.

3 Lys. 29 *Philokr.* 2 Ἐργοκλέους . . . ὑμεῖς θάνατον κατεχειροτονήσατε, Dem. 19 *Embassy* 277, 49 *Timoth.* 10. See Dem. 23 *Aristokr.* 167 for a money fine rather than the death penalty (by three votes).

4 For the law prohibiting laws against individuals see Andok. 1 *Myst.* 87, Dem. 23 *Aristokr.* 86, 24 *Timokr.* 59, 46 *Steph.* ii. 12. We should not argue that the law prohibits only *laws* against individuals unless there is a quorum of six thousand and does not mention *decrees*; the distinction between νόμος and ψήφισμα was always liable to be blurred, and it would have been absurd to ban a νόμος of this kind, when νόμοι were in any case much harder to get through than ψηφίσματα, while leaving it open to pass ψηφίσματα which would have had just the same effect. Nevertheless it is quite possible that a ψήφισμα condemning a man which had been reached through the regular procedure of εἰσαγγελία was either by express

Treason (*προδοσία*), together with temple-robbing, was, at least as late as 406 B.C., the subject of a special law, with the stated penalty of death, no burial in Attica, and confiscation of property. We must assume that at some stage between then and the date of the final *νόμος εἰσαγγελτικός* the former had been assimilated into the latter law.[1] Treason might be the subject of an ordinary *γραφή*, but in view of the privileges which were enjoyed by the prosecutor in an *εἰσαγγελία* over those of the prosecutor in a *γραφή* the latter procedure would have been rarely used when the former was available.

(*b*) *ἀποχειροτονία*

At the *κυρία ἐκκλησία* in each prytany anyone, according to Ar. *Ath. Pol.* 43. 4, could prefer an *εἰσαγγελία*; such a case would follow the course outlined in the preceding paragraphs. But there was also a vote taken on all magistrates to determine whether they were governing rightly;[2] we learn later (61. 2) that if the vote was adverse the magistrate concerned had to appear before a dikastery, which could either condemn him and fix the penalty, or acquit him, in which case he took up his office again. This procedure was in effect an *εἰσαγγελία*. It was of major importance politically; a notorious instance was its use against Perikles in 430 B.C.[3]

(*c*) *προβολή*

προβολή was a peculiar form of procedure, which was rather the preliminary stage (whether mandatory or not remains to be seen) to certain actions than an integral part of an action. Under it the perpetrator of certain public wrongs could be reported to the ekklesia by means of a written complaint addressed to the prytaneis. The proedroi had then to bring up the matter at a meeting of the ekklesia, at which both sides were heard and the

exception or by custom not regarded as a *νόμος ἐπ' ἀνδρί*. Bu. Sw. 1009 assume that the quorum applied and that the voting was by pebble.

[1] Xen. *Hell.* 1. 7. 22 *κατὰ τόνδε τὸν νόμον κρίνατε, ὅς ἐστιν ἐπὶ τοῖς ἱεροσύλοις καὶ προδόταις, ἐάν τις ἢ τὴν πόλιν προδιδῷ ἢ τὰ ἱερὰ κλέπτῃ, κριθέντα ἐν δικαστηρίῳ, ἂν καταγνωσθῇ, μὴ ταφῆναι ἐν τῇ Ἀττικῇ, τὰ δὲ χρήματα αὐτοῦ δημόσια εἶναι*, Plut. *Mor.* 833 f (quoted on p. 57, n. 4); E. Berneker, *RE* s.v. *προδοσία* 94.

[2] Ar. *Ath. Pol.* 43. 4 *κυρίαν, ἐν ᾗ δεῖ τὰς ἀρχὰς ἐπιχειροτονεῖν εἰ δοκοῦσι καλῶς ἄρχειν.*

[3] Thuc. 2. 65.

people then voted by show of hands.[1] A *προβολή* could be put forward even by a foreigner, but the accused had to be either a citizen or a metic.[2]

The vote in the ekklesia, though it is sometimes described as *καταχειροτονία* or *ἀποχειροτονία*, had in itself no effect. If it was in favour of the accused there is no evidence that he was thereby immune from prosecution, though no prosecutor would have been likely to be forthcoming in that event.[3] Contrariwise, if the vote was adverse to the accused, the initiator of it did not have to proceed.[4]

The acts which qualified for this procedure were quite specific. They fell into two categories. First there were sycophancy and deceiving the people by making unfulfilled promises.[5] There is the usual difficulty in defining precisely what these general terms covered, and consequently in understanding why they are thus conjoined. Deceiving the people (which included deceiving the boule or a dikastery) was, according to Demosthenes, an offence made punishable by death in an ancient law.[6] A famous early instance of a prosecution for this offence was that of the great Miltiades, who failed in his promise to take Paros and, according

[1] Dem. 21 *Meid.* 9 *ὁ μὲν νόμος οὗτός ἐστιν . . . καθ' ὃν αἱ προβολαὶ γίγνονται, λέγων . . . ποιεῖν τὴν ἐκκλησίαν ἐν Διονύσου μετὰ τὰ Πάνδια, ἐν δὲ ταύτῃ ἐπειδὰν χρηματίσωσιν οἱ πρόεδροι περὶ ὧν διῴκηκεν ὁ ἄρχων, χρηματίζειν καὶ περὶ ὧν ἄν τις ἠδικηκὼς ᾖ περὶ τὴν ἑορτὴν ἢ παρανενομηκώς*, 206 *καθῆτ' Εὔβουλος ἐν τῷ θεάτρῳ, ὅθ' ὁ δῆμος κατεχειροτόνησε Μειδίου, καὶ καλούμενος ὀνομαστὶ καὶ ἀντιβολοῦντος τούτου καὶ λιπαροῦντος, ὡς ὑμεῖς ἴστε, οὐκ ἀνέστη. καὶ μὴν εἰ μὲν μηδὲν ἠδικηκότος ἡγεῖτο τὴν προβολὴν γεγενῆσθαι, τότ' ἔδει τόν γε φίλον δήπου συνειπεῖν καὶ βοηθῆσαι*, 214, *An. Bekk.* (*Λέξ. Ῥητ.*) 288. 18 ff., Poll. 8. 46. Poll. 8. 87 says *οἱ μὲν θεσμοθέται . . . τὰς προβολὰς εἰσάγουσι.* Lipsius, *AR* 215, and Bu. Sw. 1010 are wrong in saying that the *προβολή* only came before the people if the boule decided that the wrong was greater than could be dealt with under its power to impose a fine of five hundred drachmai; as Berneker, *RE* s.v. *προβολή* 44, points out, the *προβολή* is simply confined to pronouncing whether the accused had done the wrong act alleged. In Dem. 21 *Meid.* 8 the phrase *ὅσαι ἂν μὴ ἐκτετισμέναι ὦσιν* is not genuine.

[2] Ar. *Ath. Pol.* 43. 5 *ἐπὶ δὲ τῆς ἕκτης πρυτανείας . . . συκοφαντῶν προβολὰς τῶν Ἀθηναίων καὶ τῶν μετοίκων μέχρι τριῶν ἑκατέρων, κἄν τις ὑποσχόμενός τι μὴ ποιήσῃ τῷ δήμῳ.* In Dem. 21 *Meid.* 175 a Karian moves.

[3] Dem. 21 *Meid.* 214 *καὶ γὰρ εἰ μέν, ὦ ἄνδρες Ἀθηναῖοι, τόθ' ὅτ' ἦν ἡ προβολή, τὰ πεπραγμέν' ὁ δῆμος ἀκούσας ἀπεχειροτόνησε Μειδίου, οὐκ ἂν ὁμοίως ἦν δεινόν· καὶ γὰρ μὴ γεγενῆσθαι, καὶ μὴ περὶ τὴν ἑορτὴν ἀδικήματα ταῦτ' εἶναι, καὶ πόλλ' ἂν εἶχέ τις αὐτὸν παραμυθήσασθαι.*

[4] Aischin. 3 *Ktes.* 52 shows that Demosthenes dropped the case against Meidias though he had secured a favourable vote at the *προβολή*. Dem. 21 *Meid.* 216 implies that it was open to him to do so.

[5] Ar. *Ath. Pol.* 43. 5 (quoted in n. 2 above).

[6] Dem. 20 *Lept.* 100, 135.

to the story, was punished not with death but with a fine of fifty talents.[1] A paradigm case of such deceptive promises in the fourth century would be the expectations roused by informers against very rich men of punitive fines which would accrue to the treasury if they were convicted.[2] It may have been this aspect of the offence which caused it to be linked with sycophancy; though here we must beware of arguing in a circle, since we cannot be sure what sycophancy meant in this context. At first glance one would take it to mean irresponsible or malicious prosecution, a meaning which it certainly could bear and which would consort with the foregoing explanation of its association with deception of the people by false promises. Some scholars however have found it difficult to believe that there was a specific offence of malicious prosecution, in view of the severe penalties which attached to prosecutors who failed to secure one-fifth of the votes of the jury or who abandoned a public prosecution once it had been launched. These scholars therefore take sycophancy in this context to be something more akin to criminal libel or to blackmail, with the proviso that the wrongful act had to be shown as harming the interests of the state as well as those of the individual libelled or blackmailed.[3] We do not get much help from the ancient texts here. Aischines in one passage purports to give a definition of sycophancy which will distinguish it from common rumour; it is sycophancy, he says, when a man fixes a charge upon another and slanders him in every meeting of the people and before the boule.[4] Nor do the few known cases help much. Kallixenos and others who had led the attack on the generals after Arginousai were subsequently arraigned by the procedure of *προβολή* for having deceived the people and, perhaps exceptionally, had to furnish sureties until the time of trial.[5] Agoratos,

[1] Hdt. 6. 136.

[2] Striking instances are cited in Hyper. 3 *Euxen.* 33 ff., on which see Bo. Sm. ii. 49 f.

[3] Latte, *RE* s.v. *συκοφαντίας γραφή* 1031, says 'es den Verbreiter übler Nachrede bedeutet, nicht den verleumderischen Ankläger'. He thinks it possible that a *προβολή* was a necessary step before the bringing of a *γραφὴ συκοφαντίας*, and that this was a slight safeguard against the uncertainty due to the vagueness of the term. He is followed by Berneker, *RE* s.v. *προβολή* 45.

[4] Aischin. 2 *Embassy* 145.

[5] Xen. *Hell.* 1. 7. 35 *ἐψηφίσαντο, οἵτινες τὸν δῆμον ἐξηπάτησαν, προβολὰς αὐτῶν εἶναι, καὶ ἐγγυητὰς καταστῆσαι, ἕως ἂν κριθῶσιν, εἶναι δὲ καὶ Καλλίξενον τούτων. προυβλήθησαν δὲ καὶ ἄλλοι τέτταρες, καὶ ἐδέθησαν ὑπὸ τῶν ἐγγυησαμένων, ὕστερον δὲ . . . ἀπέδρασαν οὗτοι πρὶν κριθῆναι.* This does not seem quite to fit 'deceiving the people by false promises', but is closer to Aischines' definition of sycophancy.

the accused in Lys. 13 *Agorat.*, had practised sycophancy through δίκαι, γραφαί, and ἀπογραφαί; he was condemned before the people and before a dikastery, and fined ten thousand drachmai.[1] It is highly probable that the condemnation before the people was a προβολή.[2] Isokrates has a rhetorical passage deploring the plague of sycophancy against which, he says, Solon had provided γραφαί to the thesmothetai, εἰσαγγελίαι to the boule, and προβολαί to the people; but although he enumerates the savagery, the inhumanity, and the maliciousness of the sycophant, he does not give any precise definition of his activity.[3]

One peculiarity of the procedure relating to this type of offence was that it could only be attacked by προβολή in the κυρία ἐκκλησία of the sixth prytany and that the number of προβολαί on each occasion was limited to six, three against citizens and three against metics.[4] It looks as if the Athenians were a little nervous lest this brake upon the activities of the informer should be too efficient. The informer was, in fact, a necessary evil in the administration of Athenian justice.

The second category of act which qualified for treatment by προβολή was behaviour prejudicial to the sanctity of certain festivals. At first it was the Greater Dionysia only, but to this were added by subsequent laws the Dionysia at Peiraeus, the Lenaia, and the Thargelia. The qualifying act was described in general terms as ἀδικεῖν περὶ τὴν ἑορτήν; more specifically this included assault on the persons of festival officials or those attending the festival, corrupting or threatening of festival officials, damaging or appropriating sacred objects, and even what would in other circumstances have been lawful arrest of persons for debt, including judgement debtors.[5]

It has been argued that for a γραφὴ συκοφαντίας and a γραφὴ ἀσεβείας relating to the specified festivals a necessary precondition was a προβολή.[6] If this was so, it would have been the duty of the appropriate ἡγεμών (the thesmothetai and the basileus respectively) to determine at the ἀνάκρισις whether there had

[1] Lys. 13 *Agorat.* 65.

[2] So Lofberg, *Sycophancy* 92, followed by Latte, *RE* s.v. συκοφαντίας γραφή 1032, Bo. Sm. ii. 66; Lipsius, *AR* 449, n. 109, is doubtful. If Lofberg is right, this case seems to tell against Latte's formulation (p. 61, n. 3 above).

[3] Isok. 15 *Antid.* 314.

[4] Ar. *Ath. Pol.* 43. 5 (quoted on p. 60, n. 2).

[5] Dem. 21 *Meid.* 1, 11, 16 ff., 176 ff., 218.

[6] See p. 61, n. 3.

been an adverse vote in a *προβολή*, and if not to throw out the case as *οὐκ εἰσαγώγιμος*. But it is probably better to hold that in principle either of these *γραφαί* could be brought without a previous *προβολή*. The rule that a vote against an accused in a *προβολή* did not necessarily entail his prosecution would have been logically balanced by a rule that he could be prosecuted even in the absence of an adverse vote.

Kallixenos and his coadjutors in 406 B.C. were required to furnish sureties after an adverse vote in a *προβολή*. This might seem inconsistent with the view that such a vote did not necessarily entail prosecution, but it may be that in that case the vote was followed immediately by a summons and that the demand for sureties was connected with that summons.[1] We are told that on one occasion Aristophon by returning some crowns annulled the *προβολή*.[2] We should assume not that the *προβολή* had been passed and was hanging over him, but that he averted any vote on the *προβολή* by returning the crowns.[3]

An action based on a *προβολή* followed a normal course before the dikastery. It is certainly not the case, as has sometimes been maintained, that the court could not acquit an accused who had been voted down in the ekklesia, and had merely to determine the penalty. In several passages in 21 *Meid.* Demosthenes assumes that Meidias might be acquitted, and he contemplates two votes, one convicting and the other sentencing Meidias.[4] There is however some dispute as to whether in case of conviction the procedure for fixing the penalty differed from that followed in other *ἀγῶνες τιμητοί*. In these latter, as we shall see later (pp. 80 ff., 166 f.), the jury, if it convicted, had to choose between the penalty proposed by the prosecutor and the counter-proposition of the defendant; but in certain passages in 21 *Meid.* Demosthenes suggests the possibility of more than two alternatives. We need not

[1] Xen. *Hell.* 1. 7. 35 (quoted on p. 61, n. 5). But here the demand for sureties is part of the decree. W. W. Goodwin, *Demosthenes: Against Midias* (Cambridge, 1906) 159, n. 2, holds that this *προβολή* had nothing in common with the procedure of the fourth century.

[2] Dem. 21 *Meid.* 218 Ἀριστοφῶν ἀποδοὺς τοὺς στεφάνους ἔλυσε τὴν προβολήν.

[3] Schol. Dem. 21 *Meid.* 218.

[4] Dem. 21 *Meid.* 151 ἐπὶ ταῦτα δ' ἀπήντων ὡς "ἑάλωκεν ἤδη καὶ κατεψήφισται· τίνος τιμήσειν αὐτῷ προσδοκᾷς τὸ δικαστήριον;" Lipsius, *AR* 217, n. 135, rightly follows Weil in taking the perfects as presupposed results of the trial in court; the vote in the ekklesia would have been *κατακεχειροτόνηται* rather than *κατεψήφισται*.

make too much of the phrase 'whatever penalty you think just';[1] but later he speaks of death *or* confiscation of property, which implies at least three possible penalties, since Meidias' proposal must have been less than either of these.[2] He also records a case where a Karian, Menippos, had been arrested by Euandros during the Mysteries for a judgement debt for two talents in a *δίκη ἐμπορική*; Menippos prosecuted him after a *προβολή*, and the court, according to Demosthenes, convicted Euandros and was ready to punish him with death; but the prosecutor was prepared to come to terms, which involved Euandros' resigning his claim to the two talents and paying Menippos damages for time lost in prosecuting the case.[3] These phrases can be adequately explained by supposing that in cases arising out of *προβολαί* the *τίμημα* of the prosecutor was not put forward with his indictment but only after the accused had been declared guilty.[4]

We are probably justified in assuming, in the absence of direct evidence, that the people's vote against the accused in a *προβολή* freed any future prosecutor from the penalties for securing less than one-fifth of the votes.

§ 5. *Arbitrators*

(i) *Private arbitrators*

Although private arbitrators (*διαιτηταὶ αἱρετοί*) were by definition not officers of the state, they were in a sense converted into a kind of officer by the fact that the state laid down certain rules governing the decisions they arrived at. It may therefore be convenient to treat of their functions here.[5] It is probable that

[1] Dem. 21 *Meid.* 21 ἐν τίμημα ποιήσασθε, ὅ τι ἂν δίκαιον ἡγῆσθε.

[2] Dem. 21 *Meid.* 152 οὐδ' ὑπολαμβάνω τιμήσειν οὐδὲν ἐλάττονος τούτῳ ἢ ὅσον καταθεὶς οὗτος παύσεται τῆς ὕβρεως· τοῦτο δ' ἐστὶ μάλιστα μὲν θάνατος, εἰ δὲ μή, πάντα τὰ ὄντ' ἀφελέσθαι.

[3] Dem. 21 *Meid.* 176 εἰσελθόντα δ' εἰς τὸ δικαστήριον ἐβούλεσθε μὲν θανάτῳ κολάσαι, τοῦ δὲ προβαλλομένου πεισθέντος τὴν δίκην τε πᾶσαν ἀφεῖναι ἠναγκάσατ' αὐτόν, ἣν ᾑρήκει πρότερον (ἦν δὲ δυοῖν αὕτη ταλάντοιν), καὶ προσετιμήσατε τὰς βλάβας, ἃς ἐπὶ τῇ χειροτονίᾳ μένων ἐλογίζεθ' αὐτῷ γεγενῆσθαι πρὸς ὑμᾶς ἄνθρωπος.

[4] So Lipsius, *AR* 218, n. 137. Goodwin, *Demosthenes: Against Midias* 162, suggests that the court could ignore both *τιμήματα* and fix its own penalty; but it is difficult to imagine how this could have been done.

[5] On *διαιτηταί* see Thalheim, *RE* s.v., Lipsius, *AR* 220 ff., Bu. Sw. 1111 ff. (with literature cited in 1111, n. 4), Steinwenter, *Streit.* 63 ff., Bo. Sm. i. 346 ff., ii. 97 ff.,

these rules were laid down in their final form in a law concerned with arbitration (known as 'the law about the arbitrators'), perhaps one of the Forty's laws, carried in the archonship of Eukleides (403/2 B.C.).[1]

Under certain conditions the decision of an arbitrator or joint arbitrators agreed upon by two possible litigants was equally binding with the decision of a court, in the sense that the losing party was liable, if he did not conform to the decision, to a *δίκη ἐξούλης*,[2] and that both parties were barred from raising the same issue before a court.[3] The primary condition for a legally binding private arbitration was agreement on the person or persons who were to arbitrate. This is laid down in the law incorporated in Dem. 21 *Meid.*,[4] and we have an example of disputants trying abortively to agree on arbitrators in Dem. 33 *Apatour.* 14 ff. This agreement could be incorporated in a document (*συνθῆκαι*). Thus in the Apatourios case there was, so the speaker alleges, a document appointing three arbitrators, and he implies that a majority decision by them would have been binding. As against him Apatourios maintained that two of the three men named were empowered merely to act as reconcilers, and only the third was arbitrator in the strict sense of one who could give a binding decision.[5] The case was bedevilled by the fact that

Gernet, *DSGA* 103 ff., N. J. Pantazopoulos, *Festschrift Koschaker* (Weimar, 1939) iii. 199 ff., Meyer-Laurin, *Ges. Bill.* 41 ff.

[1] Lys. fr. 16 Th. *οὐδεπώποτε ἠθέλησε συνελθεῖν οὐδὲ λόγον περὶ ὧν ἐνεκάλει ποιήσασθαι, οὐδὲ δίαιταν ἐπιτρέψαι, ἕως ὑμεῖς τὸν νόμον τὸν περὶ τῶν διαιτητῶν ἔθεσθε.* *IG* ii². 179. 8 mentions *[τὸ]ν διαιτητικὸν νόμον*. For the inclusion of *διαιτηταὶ αἱρετοί* in the law, Dem. 21 *Meid.* 94 *ΝΟΜΟΣ. ἐὰν δέ τινες περὶ συμβολαίων ἰδίων πρὸς ἀλλήλους ἀμφισβητῶσι καὶ βούλωνται διαιτητὴν ἑλέσθαι ὁντινοῦν, ἐξέστω αὐτοῖς αἱρεῖσθαι ὃν ἂν βούλωνται. ἐπειδὰν δ' ἕλωνται κατὰ κοινόν, μενέτωσαν ἐν τοῖς ὑπὸ τούτου διαγνωσθεῖσι, καὶ μηκέτι μεταφερέτωσαν ἀπὸ τούτου ἐφ' ἕτερον δικαστήριον ταὐτὰ ἐγκλήματα, ἀλλ' ἔστω τὰ κριθέντα ὑπὸ τοῦ διαιτητοῦ κύρια*: this document is probably a grammarian's interpolation, but none the less contains the gist of a genuine clause in the law; so Lipsius, *AR* 222, n. 6, Steinwenter, *Streit.* 61, n. 1 (but see Latte, *Gnomon* 2 (1926) 211, Gernet, *DSGA* 104, n. 7). Andok. 1 *Myst.* 87 f. shows that even before the law of 403/2 a *δίαιτα* might be equally binding with a court decision: *τὰς δὲ δίκας καὶ τὰς διαίτας κυρίας εἶναι, ὁπόσαι ἐν δημοκρατουμένῃ τῇ πόλει ἐγένοντο· τοῖς δὲ νόμοις χρῆσθαι ἀπ' Εὐκλείδου ἄρχοντος.*

[2] Dem. 52 *Kallip.* 16 *ὡς δὲ ἐγὼ μὲν ἀληθῆ λέγω, οὗτοι δὲ ψεύδονται, πρῶτον μὲν αὐτὸ ὑμῖν τοῦτο γενέσθω τεκμήριον, ὅτι κατεγνώκει ἂν αὐτοῦ ὁ Λυσιθείδης, καὶ ὅτι ἐγὼ ἐξούλης ἂν ἔφευγον νῦν, ἀλλ' οὐκ ἀργυρίου δίκην.*

[3] Isok. 18 *Kallim.* 11 *οὐκ εἰσαγώγιμος ἦν ἡ δίκη διαίτης γεγενημένης*, Poll. 8. 57.

[4] Dem. 21 *Meid.* 94; see n. 1 above.

[5] Dem. 33 *Apatour.* 17 *καὶ ἦλθεν ἐπὶ τὸ ἀμφισβητεῖν ὡς αὐτῷ διαιτητὴς εἴη ὁ Ἀριστοκλῆς, τὸν δὲ Φώκριτον καὶ ἐμὲ οὐδενὸς κυρίους ἔφησεν εἶναι ἀλλ' ἢ τοῦ διαλῦσαι.*

Apatourios had succeeded in suppressing the document. The general tenor of what is said in the case suggests that a written agreement was normally to be expected, though we cannot say that it was mandatory.[1] There would have been considerable variety in the degree to which the matter to be arbitrated was defined and the methods of execution of a judgement were spelt out in the document.

A second condition for a legally binding private arbitration was that the arbitrator should give his decision under oath. This has been denied, mainly on the ground of a passage in Dem. 52 *Kallip.*; but the better interpretation of this speech confirms the rule.[2]

(ii) *Public arbitrators*

All male citizens had to serve as public arbitrators during the official year following that in which they reached the age of

[1] Dem. 33 *Apatour.* 30 *καίτοι ὁπότε περὶ τῆς μελλούσης γνώσεως γενήσεσθαι ἑτέρας ἐνεχείρουν συνθήκας γράφεσθαι, ἐπειδὴ αἱ ὑπάρχουσαι ἀπώλοντο, πῶς ἐνῆν μὴ γραφεισῶν συνθηκῶν ἑτέρων ἢ δίαιταν γενέσθαι ἢ ἐγγύην;*

[2] Lysitheides, a private arbitrator, gave a decision against Apollodoros and in favour of Kallippos without taking an oath. Kallippos, for some reason not stated by Apollodoros (the speaker of Dem. 52), did not proceed to execution. It is simplest to suppose, with Lipsius, *AR* 223, followed by S. Huwardas, *Zeitschr. vergl. Rechtswiss.* 49 (1934) 303 ff., Gernet, *DSGA* 109, that he did not do so because a private arbitrator's decision, when not given under oath, did not empower him to. Unfortunately the language of Apollodoros, a notoriously slovenly speaker, does not support this view unambiguously. In 30 f. he says *οὗτος δὲ τὸν κατὰ τοὺς νόμους ἀπενηνεγμένον διαιτητὴν ἔπεισεν ἀνώμοτον διαιτῆσαι, ἐμοῦ διαμαρτυρομένου κατὰ τοὺς νόμους ὀμόσαντα διαιτᾶν, ἵνα αὐτῷ ᾖ πρὸς ὑμᾶς λέγειν ὅτι καὶ Λυσιθείδης, ἀνὴρ καλὸς κἀγαθός, ἔγνω περὶ αὐτῶν. Λυσιθείδης γάρ, ὦ ἄνδρες δικασταί, ἕως μὲν ὁ πατὴρ ἔζη, καὶ ἄνευ ὅρκου καὶ μεθ' ὅρκου ἴσως ἂν οὐκ ἠδίκησεν ἐκεῖνον· ἔμελε γὰρ αὐτῷ ἐκείνου. ἐμοῦ δὲ ἄνευ μὲν ὅρκου οὐδὲν αὐτῷ ἔμελεν, μεθ' ὅρκου δὲ ἴσως ἂν οὐκ ἠδίκησεν διὰ τὸ αὑτοῦ ἴδιον· διόπερ ἀνώμοτος ἀπεφήνατο.* The clear implication of the phrase *ἐμοῦ διαμαρτυρομένου κατὰ τοὺς νόμους ὀμόσαντα διαιτᾶν* is that Apollodoros had the right to insist on the arbitrator's taking an oath. But the words *καὶ ἄνευ ὅρκου καὶ μεθ' ὅρκου* seem to indicate the contrary, and these, together with the fact that the law in Dem. 21 *Meid.* 94 (see p. 65, n. 1) does not mention an oath as a necessary condition of a private arbitration, lead Thalheim, *Hermes* 41 (1906) 152, followed by Steinwenter, *Streit.* 93 ff., to deny the necessity for an oath. This might justify the phrase *καὶ ἄνευ ὅρκου καὶ μεθ' ὅρκου*, but it is arbitrary to regard, as Thalheim does, the words *κατὰ τοὺς νόμους* as due simply to a rhetorical flourish by Apollodoros. As Gernet, *DSGA* 110, explains, in the hypothetical case envisaged (and rejected as absurd) by Apollodoros (15 f.) his father, Pasion, refused to take an oath asserting the justice of his defence; in such a case judgement would have automatically gone against him, and it would have been a matter of indifference whether the arbitrator took an oath or not. Cf. J. Caimo, *SIFC* 5 (1927) 15 ff.

fifty-nine.[1] Their names stood on the register of their demes (*ληξιαρχικὸν γραμματεῖον*); service was compulsory, and only holding of office or absence from the country could excuse; failure to serve was punishable with *ἀτιμία*.[2] Probably at the beginning of the year the arbitrators were divided into ten sections, irrespective of their own tribal origin, and one section was allotted to each tribe; each tribe had for the year its own arbitrators.[3] As each case arose, it was the function of the four members of the Forty (or one of them) who belonged to the tribe of the defendant to assign the case by lot to one of the arbitrators serving for that tribe.[4] The tribe to which the arbitrator himself belonged was immaterial; thus we find that in Demosthenes' *δίκη κακηγορίας* against Meidias the arbitrator, Straton, belonged neither to Demosthenes' nor to Meidias' tribe.[5] An arbitrator's term of duty ended exactly with the end of the official year. His pay consisted of one drachma from each of the two litigants, and a further drachma from each for every day the hearing was prolonged by adjournments known as *ὑπωμοσίαι* (on which see p. 155).[6] If these postponements lasted beyond the official year, the arbitrator had to complete the case though his year of service was strictly over.[7] A successful plea by a litigant that he had been

[1] Ar. *Ath. Pol.* 53. 4, *An. Bekk.* (*Λέξ. 'Ρητ.*) 235. 20 ff., Hesych. s.v. *διαιτηταί*. This was the last of the forty-two years during which an Athenian was liable for service. It is not certain whether the first of these years was that in which the man became seventeen or eighteen, but for our purposes this is immaterial (see vol. i, p. 74, n. 3). *An. Bekk.* (*Δικ. 'Ον.*) 186. 1, Suda s.v. *διαιτηταί* wrongly give the age as 'over fifty'; perhaps a change was introduced by Demetrios of Phaleron, who refers to the *διαιτηταί* in a corrupt passage, *F.Gr.H.* 228 F 13. Cf. Lipsius, *AR* 226, Bu. Sw. 1112, n. 1, Kahrstedt, *Mag.* 19.

[2] Ar. *Ath. Pol.* 53. 5 *ὁ γὰρ νόμος, ἄν τις μὴ γένηται διαιτητὴς τῆς ἡλικίας αὐτῷ καθηκούσης, ἄτιμον εἶναι κελεύει, πλὴν ἐὰν τύχῃ ἀρχὴν ἄρχων τινὰ ἐν ἐκείνῳ τῷ ἐνιαυτῷ ἢ ἀποδημῶν· οὗτοι δ' ἀτελεῖς εἰσι μόνοι*, Poll. 8. 126. (Poll. 8. 89, cited by Kahrstedt, *Mag.* 227, probably does not belong here, since the reading should be *εἰς δατητῶν αἵρεσιν*.)

[3] Dem. 47 *Euerg.* 12 *ἡ μὲν γὰρ δίαιτα ἐν τῇ ἡλιαίᾳ ἦν· οἱ γὰρ τὴν Οἰνῇδα καὶ τὴν Ἐρεχθῇδα διαιτῶντες ἐνταῦθα κάθηνται.*

[4] Ar. *Ath. Pol.* 53. 5 *οἱ τετταράκοντα διανέμουσιν αὐτοῖς τὰς διαίτας καὶ ἐπικληροῦσιν ἃς ἕκαστος διαιτήσει.* Gernet, *DSGA* 115, n. 6, is right, as against Bo. Sm. i. 347, to see concealed in Aristotle's words the two distinct operations described in the text above.

[5] Dem. 21 *Meid.* 83.

[6] Harpokr. s.v. *παράστασις*, Poll. 8. 39, 127, *An. Bekk.* (*Λέξ. 'Ρητ.*) 290. 19 ff. It is not entirely clear from these passages whether the fee was paid by the plaintiff only (so Bu. Sw. 1112) or by both parties (so G. Gilbert, *Greek Constitutional Antiquities* (London, 1895) 389); Lipsius takes opposite views at *AR* 231 and 824.

[7] Ar. *Ath. Pol.* 53. 5 *ἀναγκαῖον ἃς ἂν ἕκαστος λάχῃ διαίτας ἐκδιαιτᾶν.*

wronged by a particular arbitrator meant ἀτιμία for that arbitrator. The plea was made by εἰσαγγελία, and, if we take the text of Ar. *Ath. Pol.* 53. 6 as it stands, the case was decided by the body of arbitrators as a whole: ἔστιν δὲ καὶ εἰσαγγέλλειν εἰς τοὺς διαιτητάς, ἐάν τις ἀδικηθῇ ὑπὸ τοῦ διαιτητοῦ, κἄν τινος καταγνῶσιν, ἀτιμοῦσθαι κελεύουσιν οἱ νόμοι· ἔφεσις δ' ἔστι καὶ τούτοις. This is such a strange provision that it is tempting to accept the conjecture of δικαστάς for διαιτητάς and suppose that such an εἰσαγγελία was heard before an ordinary court.[1] The only objection to this is that it leaves obscure who is supposed to have made the decision from which there might be ἔφεσις.

We learn from Ar. *Ath. Pol.* 55. 5 that there was a stone at which arbitrators took an oath before giving their decision: τὸν λίθον ἐφ' οὗ τὰ τόμι' ἐστίν, ἐφ' οὗ καὶ οἱ διαιτηταὶ ὀμόσαντες ἀποφαίνονται τὰς διαίτας. The wording of this statement precludes the view that this oath was taken by arbitrators at the beginning of their year of service. It can mean either that on each occasion they swore that they would give a fair decision, or that the decision which they had reached and were about to announce was just. There is no suggestion anywhere that the parties had to go with the arbitrator at the end of proceedings to the stone, and the former view is slightly preferable.[2]

Public arbitrators were not technically ἀρχαί, and therefore were not liable to εὔθυνα.[3] Nevertheless their conduct as arbitrators was subject to control by the courts, in that any one of them could be arraigned by way of εἰσαγγελία, as explained above.

[1] So Kahrstedt, *Mag.* 110, n. 4, 148, n. 2, citing Harpokr. s.v. εἰσαγγελία, which says εἰ γάρ τις ὑπὸ διαιτητοῦ ἀδικηθείη, ἐξῆν τοῦτον εἰσαγγέλλειν πρὸς τοὺς δικαστάς, καὶ ἁλοὺς ἠτιμοῦτο. In Dem. 21 *Meid.* 87 the πρυτανεύων who puts to the vote the charge against Straton for absenting himself from duty is probably the member of the Forty before whom the case had been initiated, not the leader of all the arbitrators (Kahrstedt, *Mag.* 164, n. 2).

[2] For this view Lipsius, *AR* 228, Bo. Sm. ii. 156 f.; for the other Latte, *HR* 42, Gernet, *DSGA* 107 f.

[3] Bu. Sw. 1112, n. 1, Kahrstedt, *Mag.* 39.

II · PROCESS AT LAW

§ 1. *Historical development*

ALTHOUGH it is our aim to depict procedure as it was in the classical period, this cannot be understood without a brief glance at the development of process at law at Athens. Something was said of this in describing the evolution of judicial organs of the state (pp. 1 ff.). Here we have to consider the more difficult, because less tangible, development of the concept of process at law.

There has been a good deal of discussion recently of the origins of the judicial process in Greece and specifically in Athens. As a result largely of a closely reasoned and documented study published in 1925 by Steinwenter, it became the widely accepted view that jurisdiction by an organ or organs of the state had its sole origin in voluntarily accepted arbitration.[1] Contestants began by submitting disputes voluntarily to arbitration and thus *pro hac vice* forgoing self-help in asserting their claims. Though they tended to choose as arbitrators men who had a special gift or skill in drawing decisions from divine inspiration, the fact that these men were also kings or princes was almost accidental.[2] This system, if such it can be called, is the only system for settlement of disputes between members of the community which can be detected in Homeric society. In the society depicted in Hesiod's *Works and Days* its gift-devouring kings are evidence that the process of submitting disputes to arbitration has ceased to be voluntary. Oppression of the poor by the rich was being facilitated by crooked decisions of these kings; but this would only have been

[1] Steinwenter, *Streit.* 29 ff. This view is in the main accepted by Bo. Sm. i. 42 ff., G. M. Calhoun, *Introduction to Greek Legal Science* (Oxford, 1944), 7 ff. See also E. Gerner, *Z* 67 (1950) 1 ff.

[2] *Iliad* 1. 238 f. *δικασπόλοι, οἵ τε θέμιστας πρὸς Διὸς εἰρύαται.* To be able to draw upon these *θέμιστες* and secure their observance is the mark of a civilized community in the Homeric poems. Thus the Cyclopes are distinguished as *ἀθέμιστοι* or not knowing *θέμιστες* (*Odyssey* 9. 106, 112, 215). *Odyssey* 12. 439 f. shows that the decision of such cases was a normal feature of public life.

possible if arbitration had become obligatory 'in case either party to a dispute desired it'.[1]

Well-founded objections to this view have been voiced by H. J. Wolff and L. Gernet.[2] Its fundamental defect is that it glosses over the vital step in the development, the step which associated the making of a decision to end a dispute (a judgement) with the sovereign power in the state, whether that power was a king, a body of nobles, or the popular assembly. It is not plausible to suggest that voluntary submission of disputes to arbitration became compulsory simply by the efflux of time and the force of custom. On the contrary, an essential element in the situation must from the very beginning have been the power of the community acting through its organs (king, nobles, assembly) to limit the bounds of self-help or to bring to an end disputes which were always a potential threat to public order. Thus settlement of disputes by arbitration and the intervention of an organ of state to bring to an end a kind of minor civil war were rather two parallel processes than two stages of a single process.[3]

In primitive, pre-Solonian, Athens we may suppose that procedures were highly formalized. Each party would have sworn an oath, each would have had the support of oath-helpers, the contest was of the nature of a ritual or joust, and the function of the judge was to declare the victor in accordance with the rules of the joust; this was δικάζειν.[4] In a system with such origins the

[1] Hes. *Works and Days* 38 f., 220 f. for the gift-devouring kings with their crooked judgements; 27 ff. implies that litigiousness might be a profitable business. The words in the text are quoted from Bonner, *CP* 7 (1912) 17.

[2] H. J. Wolff, 'The origin of judicial litigation among the Greeks', *Traditio* 4 (1946) 31 ff.; L. Gernet, 'Sur le notion du jugement en droit grec', *DSGA* 61 ff.; Gernet, 'Droit et prédroit en Grèce ancienne', *L'Année sociologique* 3 (1948–9) 21 ff. See also N. J. Pantazopoulos, *Festschrift Koschaker* (Weimar, 1939) iii. 204.

[3] H. J. Wolff, *Traditio* 4 (1946) 49. In a new interpretation of the Shield Scene (*Iliad* 18. 497–508) he argues that we have here not, as is usually supposed, a dispute voluntarily submitted by the two parties for settlement by a public procedure, but one in which the 'defendant' has taken the initiative (it is significant, Wolff argues, that he speaks first) to prevent the 'plaintiff' proceeding by self-help, his ground being that he has offered a sufficient ποινή which the 'plaintiff' is rejecting as inadequate. What is in question is whether the offered composition should or should not put an end to the blood feud.

[4] Latte, *HR* 40, Gernet, *DSGA* 63 and *Plat.* p. cxl, Lavency, *Logographie* 75 f. For the original meaning of the word δίκη, on which Gernet, *DSGA* 68, is cautious, see L. R. Palmer, *Trans. Phil. Soc.* (1950) 149 ff.; he shows that its basic meaning is not 'path' or 'pronouncement', but 'boundary mark', and that it was part of a group of ideas which saw the world as an ordered universe, where gods, men,

essential function of a judgement is not, to quote Gernet, 'the recognition and consecration of subjective rights. From this point of view it remains subordinate to the primitive conception of the sentence which terminates a "quarrel". Every δίκη merely, and by definition, grants a preference. The preference does not imply that the right of the winning party antedates, in a world of ideas, the declaration of the judge.'[1] Or, as H. J. Wolff puts it, 'the public authority acted on behalf of internal peace—not so much by placing itself at the disposal of those who sought peaceful adjudication of their claims as by lending its protection to an attacked member of the community as long as the aggressor's right to the attack was not established'; and later, dealing with the important issue of the litigants' resistance to or acquiescence in the judicial process, Wolff writes, 'the public authority simply would have extended its protection over the debtor indefinitely if the creditor had refused to plead, or would have withdrawn its protection if the debtor had failed to accept the trial in a form which was deemed appropriate'.[2]

It is important to note that on this theory the judgement of the authority is determining whether the plaintiff is or is not to be allowed to proceed against the defendant by self-help, and, if it goes against the defendant, it has achieved not so much peace as a further licensed outbreak of war. We shall have to deal with this aspect of the matter in considerably more detail when we come to the question of the execution of judgements in the classical law (pp. 187 ff.). What must be noted here is that judgement is by its nature delictual. Acquittal of the defendant means of course that *pro hac vice* the issue is closed, and any unilateral action by the plaintiff will render him liable to punishment; but conviction means that the plaintiff can proceed with force against the defendant as against a disturber of the settled order, and any resistance can be countered with a further process, the δίκη ἐξούλης, which will render the defendant liable not only for the original restitution to the plaintiff, but to a penalty exacted by the community.[3] This is a situation fundamentally different

and natural objects had each their allotted portion whose bounds it was dangerous to overstep.

[1] Gernet, *DSGA* 81.

[2] H. J. Wolff, *Traditio* 4 (1946) 47, 49.

[3] For the application of this suit to cases of property see vol. i, pp. 217 ff., 311 f. There was probably reference to it on the fifth ἄξων of Solon (Ox. Pap. 221 col. 14 = Solon F 36b Ruschenbusch).

from, though obviously able to exist beside and to react upon, the settlement of a dispute by an agreed arbitrator.

A further point to bear in mind is that at this primitive stage anything recognizable as judicial process is confined to disputes between individuals (though at this stage the individual would normally have at his back his whole family). Any threat to public order which did not take the form of a threat to some individual or individuals (mutiny, for example, or sedition) must have been checked in some way; but we must suppose that the organs of the community secured public order by exercising powers of coercion without restraint of anything resembling legal process.

In the late seventh and early sixth century B.C. a major advance is traceable owing to the legislation of Drakon and of Solon. We know little in detail of the former save for the law of homicide. Much more is known of the work of Solon, some of it from the unimpeachable evidence of his own poems. We learn from them that one major preoccupation of Solon was to reform the system of giving judgement, since it had become one of the main instruments in the hands of the rich in oppressing the poor.[1] As to detail, we are told that it was Solon who introduced ἔφεσις from a magistrate's decision to the people, called in this capacity the heliaia.

There has been much discussion as to the exact meaning of the word ἔφεσις. The simplest and most natural sense might be thought to be 'appeal', and it has been so taken by many scholars.[2] Objections have been raised to this straightforward view. There are certainly cases where the word seems to be used of a reference required by law, and therefore not appeal, since appeal only arises if one or other party moves. On this second view ἔφεσις is to be interpreted not as a recourse to justice at second instance, but as the removal of the issue from one plane to

[1] Solon 3. 32 ff. Diehl εὐνομίη . . . εὐθύνει δὲ δίκας σκολιὰς ὑπερήφανά τ' ἔργα πραΰνει.

[2] Lipsius, *AR* 28, 954, n. 2, Bu. Sw. 851. Wade-Gery, *EGH* 192 says ἔφεσις 'is always, I believe, the act of a "litigating party" who, being dissatisfied with an authoritative pronouncement made about his case, *appeals against it* to some other authority'. He cites Ar. *Ath. Pol.* 42. 1, Dem. 57 *Euboul.* 6, Isai. fr. VI Thalheim, to which should be added Isai. 12 *Euphil.* hyp. (appeals from demesmen); Ar. *Ath. Pol.* 45. 3, 55. 2 (from δοκιμασία by the boule); 53. 2 (from arbitrators). No reliance should be placed on the list of decisions open to ἔφεσις in Poll. 8. 62. Cf. M. Just, *Die Ephesis in der Geschichte des attischen Prozeßes* (Würzburg, 1965), reviewed by H. J. Wolff, *Z* 84 (1967) 404 ff.

another. In other words, the act of the litigant in ἔφεσις (and note Wade-Gery's view that by derivation ἔφεσις is the act of the litigant) in itself, irrespective of any subsequent judgement passed, annuls the previous decision.[1] It may seem that the difference between the two views is insignificant, but this is not so. It is true that in the classical period we are only marginally concerned with the relation of ἔφεσις to the function of the magistrates, since, as we have seen (pp. 4 ff.), the right of a magistrate to take any action to which ἔφεσις might apply was vestigial. But ἔφεσις was a matter of common occurrence when an arbitrator had given a decision. The question then is whether the hearing or hearings, for they might be many, before the arbitrator were hearings in the first instance and the single hearing before the dikastery, when there was ἔφεσις, was exactly like an appeal in a modern system. The holders of the second view maintain that the two hearings were fundamentally different in kind, governed in two important respects by different principles of decision. First, an arbitrator could give a compromise decision, neither wholly for nor wholly against the plaintiff; a dikastery could not do this. Second, arbitrators were given more latitude in equity than dikasteries, whose oath bound them strictly to the laws, at least in matters which were specifically covered by laws.[2]

On the whole the second view seems preferable, though its supporters have not perhaps given sufficient attention to the fact that where there was ἔφεσις from an arbitrator there were

[1] Steinwenter, *Streit.* 68 ff., Bo. Sm. ii. 232 ff., Gomme, *Commentary on Thucydides* i. 342, n. 2, Gernet, *DSGA* 114, n. 2, Wolff, *Traditio* 4 (1946) 78 ff., Gernet, *Plat.* p. cxxxiv. Paoli, *RIDA* 5 (1950) 325 ff., holds that in ἔφεσις εἰς τὸ δικαστήριον the defendant, by declining to accept (ἐμμένειν) the decision of a magistrate as arbitrator, removes the case from the level where a decision has an arbitrational element (is agreed to by both parties) to one where the sovereignty of the state rules; cf. *Studi Betti* (Milan, 1962) iii. 3 ff. In *Z* 76 (1959) 104 f. he maintains that after ἔφεσις the initiative for continuing the case rested with the plaintiff or prosecutor. Ruschenbusch, *Z* 78 (1961) 386 ff., holds that ἔφεσις must always have meant 'reference', and that it was impossible to determine its exact sense without knowing by whom the reference was to be made: it could, for example, be made by an arbitrator who did not pronounce judgement but referred the matter to a court (Dem. 34 *Ag. Phorm.* 21; but Wade-Gery, *EGH* 193, n. 4, is probably right to reject the reading ἐφῆκεν in favour of ἀφῆκεν). Ruschenbusch gives a useful (but not exhaustive) list of the uses of ἔφεσις and its cognates.

[2] Ar. *Rhet.* 1374^b20 ff. ὁ γὰρ διαιτητὴς τὸ ἐπιεικὲς ὁρᾷ, ὁ δὲ δικαστὴς τὸν νόμον· καὶ τούτου ἕνεκα διαιτητὴς εὑρέθη, ὅπως τὸ ἐπιεικὲς ἰσχύῃ, *Pol.* 1268^b4 ff. But it must be noted that Steinwenter, *Streit.* 106, followed by Meyer-Laurin, *Ges. Bill.* 41 f., argues that Aristotle in these passages is referring exclusively to private arbitrators.

elaborate procedural rules to ensure that the dikastery had before it all the evidence (and probably only the evidence) which had been before the arbitrator, together with the arbitrator's decision. This needs explaining if we are asked to regard the hearing before the dikastery as a hearing completely *de novo* and not an appeal.[1] The explanation may be that without these rules there would have been a serious tendency for the litigant against whom the arbitrator ruled to reject his ruling, and thus the aim of the institution of public arbitration, to relieve the courts, would have been frustrated.

§ 2. *Classification of actions*

We have now to determine the main categories of process which were available at Athens in the classical period. As usual the Greek terminology is anything but clear-cut. The word δίκη, besides meaning what a court awards, as in the phrases δίκην διδόναι and δίκην λαβεῖν, was a general and inclusive term for any action at law, though it was also, as we shall see, the name of a particular category of actions.[2] Another general term for an

[1] On this see Steinwenter, *Streit.* 72; the rule against the admission of new evidence is simply due to economy of procedure, and this only gives the outward appearance of appeal. He rightly emphasizes the need to spell out what is meant in the use of modern legal terms such as 'appeal'. He raises (p. 73, n. 1) the question, which will concern us later, whether evidence given before an arbitrator could be challenged by a δίκη ψευδομαρτυρίων in a case where the arbitrator's decision had not been subjected to ἔφεσις. His argument that the judgement of the heliaia or dikastery cannot be regarded as a quashing or amending judgement, owing to the fact that it is the entering of the ἔφεσις rather than that judgement which made the decision of the magistrate or arbitrator of no effect, is rejected by J. D. Ralph, *Ephesis in Athenian Litigation* (Chicago, 1936) 7, followed by Bo. Sm. ii. 234, n. 3; but see Wolff, *Traditio* 4 (1946) 79. See also E. Gerner, *Z* 67 (1950) 22 ff.

[2] For the root meaning of δίκη see p. 70, n. 4. Gernet, *Recherches* 459, discusses the phrase δίκην διδόναι in an appendix. He makes the point on p. 167 that in this phrase the subject is always one of the parties, not the judge who pronounces judgement. See Dem. 23 *Aristokr.* 66, Isai. 7 *Apollod.* 3 (with Wyse ad loc.), Ps.-Xen. *Ath. Pol.* 1. 18; R. Hirzel, *Themis, Dike und Verwandtes* (Leipzig, 1907) 127, n. 1. Gernet, *Recherches* 35 ff., throws much light on the word by studying its privative form ἀδικεῖν. Actively 'injustice' has in origin religious overtones; it is offence against the gods, sacrilege, involving not only the doer but the community in pollution. Hence the concept of the ἄγος, still strong enough to be used, in propaganda at least, against Perikles in the second half of the fifth century, and of the scapegoat or φαρμακός (Lys. 6 *Andok.* 53). Passively there may be ἀδίκημα πρὸς ἕνα (cf. Ar. *Rhet.* 1373^{b}19 ff.); this produced the category of private delicts, of which the two distinguishing characteristics were (1) a sanction secured by process of law, (2) recognition that the wronged individual took precedence over the community

action was ἀγών or 'match', a word which also reveals something of the nature of the original suit at law.[1]

The most important subdivision of suits, one recognized by the Athenians themselves, though not always in the same terms, was into public and private, δίκαι (ἀγῶνες) δημόσιαι and ἴδιαι.[2] We have to tread carefully here. This is not the same division as that between γραφαί and δίκαι, to which we shall return immediately. There is a very significant passage in Dem. 21 *Meid.* 42 ff. Demosthenes there makes a distinction between wrongs which are simply wrongs to individuals and wrongs to individuals which are also common wrongs (κοίν' ἀδικήματα). His language suggests that the latter are very often acts of violence, but we need not press it to imply that they are exclusively so. For wrongs of this latter kind the difference in procedural remedies is simply one of penalty; besides restitution to the wronged plaintiff a convicted defendant has to pay an additional penalty, whether it be to the state or to the prosecutor. Demosthenes produces four instances: first, wilful damage (ἂν μὲν ἑκὼν βλάψῃ), where the defendant in a δίκη βλάβης if convicted had to pay double (note that there is no suggestion that the damage had to be by way of violence); second, wilful murder, where the convicted defendant was liable to death (or, if he went into voluntary exile, exile for life) with the confiscation of his property; third, resistance to execution of a court's judgement, where Demosthenes uses the revealing words ἄν τις ὀφλὼν δίκην μὴ ἐκτίνῃ, οὐκέτ' ἐποίησ' ὁ νόμος τὴν ἐξούλην ἰδίαν, ἀλλὰ προστιμᾶν ἐπέταξε τῷ δημοσίῳ; fourth, ὕβρις, about which he says καὶ τῆς ὕβρεως αὐτῆς τὰς μὲν γραφὰς ἔδωκεν ἅπαντι τῷ βουλομένῳ, τὸ δὲ τίμημ' ἐποίησεν ὅλον δημόσιον· τὴν γὰρ πόλιν ἡγεῖτ' ἀδικεῖν, οὐ τὸν παθόντα μόνον, τὸν ὑβρίζειν ἐπιχειροῦντα, καὶ δίκην ἱκανὴν τὴν τιμωρίαν εἶναι τῷ παθόντι, χρήματα δ' οὐ

in seeking redress, though the community was by definition indirectly wronged as well as the individual.

[1] Ar. *Ath. Pol.* 67. 1 εἰσκαλοῦσι τοὺς ἀγῶνας, ὅταν μὲν τὰ ἴδια δικάζωσι, τοὺς ἰδίους . . .· [ὅταν] δὲ τὰ δημόσια, τοὺς δημοσίους. The verb ἀγωνίζεσθαι is used of both parties, though more usually of the defendant. Cf. Schodorf, *Beiträge* 18 ff.

[2] Dem. 46 *Steph.* ii. 26 ἐπὶ ταῖς δίκαις ταῖς ἰδίαις ἢ δημοσίαις (a phrase meant to cover all actions at law), 24 *Timokr.* 99, Ar. *Ath. Pol.* 59. 5, 67. 1 (quoted in preceding note). On the other hand, in Dem. 18 *Crown* 210 τάς τ' ἰδίας δίκας καὶ τὰς δημοσίας κρίνειν the public suits are limited in the context to those which are specifically political in character, and the phrase as a whole therefore leaves out of account suits where the public element is recognized but not predominant; cf. Lipsius, *AR* 240, n. 7.

προσήκειν τῶν τοιούτων ἐφ' ἑαυτῷ λαμβάνειν. Thus the instances Demosthenes gives of suits dealing with public wrongs are three kinds of δίκη and a γραφή. In this context he is concerned only with cases where an individual has been wronged. There were however all those cases of κοινὰ ἀδικήματα which involved no injury to a specific individual; doubtless these would have been included by him among δίκαι δημόσιαι had he been writing a jurisprudential treatise. They embraced all the γραφαί dealing with specifically public wrongs, such as the γραφαὶ παρανόμων, λιποταξίου, and so forth, and such special procedures as ἀπαγωγή, ἔνδειξις, and ἐφήγησις (on which see pp. 221 ff.).

A different, and overlapping, distinction is that between δίκαι in a narrower, technical sense of the word, and γραφαί.[1] Procedurally the main *differentia* of the γραφή was that it could be initiated by any person qualified to plead (ὁ βουλόμενος), whereas a δίκη in the narrower sense could only be initiated by the wronged person, or his or her κύριος, or in homicide cases by the dead person's relatives in an elaborately prescribed order. The γραφή was a type of remedy invented by Solon,[2] and it is important, though not easy, to determine what motive lay behind the innovation, since the origin of an institution is some guide to the true nature of that institution in its fully developed form. There is some danger of our equating procedure by γραφή with criminal procedure.[3] This would be a serious misconception. The concept of crime is not very clear, even as applied to modern systems; it

[1] In Isai. 11 *Hagn.* 28, 32, 35 the distinction is between γραφαί, here including εἰσαγγελίαι, and δίκαι ἴδιαι; Theopompos is making a sophistic point in arguing that he should not have been sued by way of a public suit; if his opponents had a ground of action at all, it was enforceable by way of εἰσαγγελία as well as by δίκη; the suggestion in 32 that where a δίκη lay a γραφή (which here equals εἰσαγγελία) was barred is certainly false. Dem. 21 *Meid.* 28: the law allows both δίκαι ἴδιαι and γραφὴ ὕβρεως in the circumstances alleged against Meidias. Ibid. 32: insulting behaviour towards a private citizen renders the doer liable to a γραφὴ ὕβρεως or a δίκη κακηγορίας. Dem. 45 *Steph.* i. 4: Apollodoros, being unable to bring a δίκη ἰδία because there was a temporary ban on all δίκαι, brought a γραφὴ ὕβρεως on the same facts. Dem. 54 *Kon.* 1: a plaintiff, having been assaulted, brings a δίκη ἰδία αἰκείας though he could have brought a γραφὴ ὕβρεως. See also Isok. 18 *Kallim.* 51, Lys. 1 *Killing of Erat.* 44, Poll. 8. 41 ἐκαλοῦντο γὰρ αἱ γραφαὶ καὶ δίκαι, οὐ μέντοι καὶ αἱ δίκαι γραφαί.

[2] According to Ar. *Ath. Pol.* 9. 1, τὸ ἐξεῖναι τῷ βουλομένῳ τιμωρεῖν ὑπὲρ τῶν ἀδικουμένων was one of the three most democratic innovations of Solon.

[3] The account of Solon's initiation of the γραφή in Calhoun, *Criminal Law* 72 ff., is marred by the author's assumption that the concept of crime is an easily identifiable and useful one.

has in fact been said that the only satisfactory definition of a crime is an act so classified in a criminal justice act. We might tentatively accept the definition of crime as wrongdoing which directly and in a serious degree threatens the security and well-being of society and which for that reason demands a penalty beyond the compensation of the party injured. There is however nothing in the tradition to suggest that it was the recognition of this element in a class of wrong acts which led Solon to single them out for prosecution by ὁ βουλόμενος. It is much more plausible to suppose that one most important plank in his platform was in danger of collapse so long as process at law was restricted to suits brought by the injured party. This plank was his prohibition of enslavement for debt and his release of slave debtors. Under the old system victims of such enslavement, being *de facto* slaves, might have found it extremely hard to procure a hearing, and children delivered into slavery by their parents would have been automatically barred by the fact that their fathers would have been the sole persons entitled to sue for them. But if in origin ὁ βουλόμενος was the champion of wronged citizens who but for him might have remained without effective remedy before the courts,[1] he stood ready as a convenient instrument for championing the state in those cases where no individual had been wronged, but only the community as such. Originally such wrongs had presumably been dealt with by the magistrates' coercive power; it was now possible to bring them into the stream of judicial decision by the device of ὁ βουλόμενος.

How misleading it is to equate γραφαί with criminal proceedings can be seen from two facts. Homicide, the crime *par excellence* in modern thought, was never the subject of a γραφή at Athens.[2] It was thought of as solely a matter between the victim (and his family) and the killer; and there was a rule, which would be quite repugnant to modern criminal law, that the victim, if he survived long enough to do so, could release the killer from all liability at law for the act.[3] And there were circumstances in

[1] See vol. i, pp. 72 f., 80, 115 f., for instances of actions in which ὁ βουλόμενος was an essential instrument for securing a remedy for the wronged party.

[2] MacDowell, *Homicide* 133 ff., believes in a γραφὴ φόνου and quotes in its support Dem. 23 *Aristokr.* 80. But that passage refers to the procedure of ἀπαγωγή of a slayer caught ἐπ' αὐτοφώρῳ, and hardly justifies the assertion of Poll. 8. 40 that there was a γραφὴ φόνου.

[3] The rule is stated in Dem. 37 *Pant.* 59, though there is no known instance of its operation.

which the defendant in a γραφή, if convicted, was yet not punished.[1]

Another way of distinguishing public from private suits might be by looking at the destination of the damages or penalty and cataloguing as public those suits where the penalty was a fine paid to the state or loss of liberty, status, or life inflicted on the defendant, and as private those where the penalty, whether simple restitution or restitution with an added punitive element, went to the wronged plaintiff.[2] But this approach again does not give a neat and tidy classification. We must again, as always, leave out of account homicide cases subject to the δίκη φόνου. Here there was some element of private restitution in so far as, in cases of unpremeditated homicide, the relatives of the dead man could accept a composition payment (αἴδεσις) which would release the defendant from further penalty. But it is not very enlightening to describe as only apparent exceptions to this classification such suits as the δίκαι ἐξούλης, βιαίων, and ἐξαιρέσεως, where a convicted defendant paid to the state a penalty equal to the value of the successful plaintiff's claim, or the δίκη κλοπῆς, where the court could impose imprisonment for five days and nights over and above restitution, or the δίκη ψευδομαρτυρίων, where a defendant, if convicted on three separate occasions, was automatically punished with ἀτιμία. Again it is not a merely apparent exception when in many clearly public suits (for example certain ἀπογραφαί and φάσεις) the prosecutor received a part of the penalty as remuneration.[3] Then there were γραφαί, such as those ἀδίκως εἰρχθῆναι ὡς μοιχόν, βουλεύσεως, and ψευδεγγραφῆς, the main effect of which, if the defendant was convicted, was to release the plaintiff from bondage or from a payment (though there may of course have been a penalty attached as well), and, as we saw above (n. 1), at least one γραφή which did not involve a penalty at all.

[1] In a γραφὴ παρανόμων, a suit which lay against the mover of a decree or law passed unconstitutionally, if the decree or law in issue had been passed more than a year before the bringing of the suit and the defendant was convicted, that decree or law was annulled but the defendant suffered no penalty.

[2] It is significant that for Demosthenes the 'public' element in the γραφὴ ὕβρεως is marked by the fact that the penalty goes wholly to the state; see 21 *Meid.* 45 (quoted on p. 75).

[3] Lipsius, *AR* 245, describes these as apparent exceptions only. For details of the suits see pp. 211 ff.

Yet another elusive distinction is that between δίκαι πρός τινα and δίκαι κατά τινος. The most obvious and the generally accepted view is that the latter were penal suits whereas in the former there was, to use Lipsius' terminology, either no personal delict or not one which was still liable to punishment.[1] But Gernet has thrown doubt on this classification. The only passage directly quoted for it, from Isai. 11 *Hagn.*,[2] does not fit it, since Theopompos is there distinguishing between a διαδικασία for the property in question (πρός) and an action for failure to execute a contract (κατά), while on the other hand there are two cases dealing with contracts for which the term κατά is well authenticated, namely Dem. 48 *Olymp.* and 56 *Dionysod.* For Gernet all δίκαι are of the delictual type; the normal action for breach of contract is the δίκη βλάβης, certainly a δίκη κατά τινος. There is no satisfactory evidence for a suit to protect contract as such, nor are there as a rule suits denominated by the particular type of contract which they were designed to sanction. All actions alike follow the same procedural pattern. They open with an ἔγκλημα or plaint, which ends with an assessment of the damage suffered (τίμημα). Gernet believes—though he admits it is a debated point and we shall have to return to it—that a condemnation was always pecuniary and never *ad ipsam rem.*[3] On this view, which has much to commend it, we have on the one side διαδικασίαι, where there is no defendant or plaintiff and the function of the court is simply to decide which of the parties before it has the better right to a thing

[1] Lipsius, *AR* 246. For him the description of the suit against Leptines, Dem. 20 *Lept.*, as πρὸς Λεπτίνην is significant, since, though a γραφή, it carried no penalty (see p. 78, n. 1). Cf. Böckh, *Staatsh.* i. 440. The view commonly accepted until Gernet's article referred to in n. 3 below was that the distinction corresponded to that between redress for breaches of ἑκούσια συναλλάγματα and wrongs suffered by ἀκούσια συναλλάγματα, as set out in Ar. *Nik. Eth.* 1130ᵇ ff.

[2] Isai. 11 *Hagn.* 34 εἰ δὲ μήτε πρὸς ἐμὲ μήτε κατ' ἐμοῦ δίκην εἶναί φησι τῷ παιδί, τὸν κωλύοντα νόμον εἰπάτω. . . . εἰ δ' αὖ μήτ' ἐπιδικάσασθαί φησι δεῖν τοῦ ἡμικληρίου μήτ' ἐμοὶ δικάσασθαι, . . .

[3] Gernet, *DSGA* 72 ff.; cf. Harrison, *JHS* 77 (1957) 46. There was no δίκη συνθηκῶν παραβάσεως, *pace* Beauchet iv. 415 (who relies on Poll. 8. 31). The δίκη χρέως is feebly attested, as is the δίκη ἀφορμῆς. The δίκη ἀργυρίου is very rare, though it should be common if it were simply for money due. There is no firm evidence for a δίκη παρακαταθήκης for restitution of a thing deposited, or a δίκη μισθώσεως for enforcement of *locatio operis faciendi* or *locatio operarum*, or an *actio empti venditi*. The exact nature of the δίκαι ἐνοικίου and καρποῦ is obscure. The only exception is the δίκη ἐγγύης, which provided the sanction for the obligation of a guarantor; this is the exception which proves the rule, for this suit had a delictual character and was instituted to replace an extra-judicial execution.

or to escape from a duty, and on the other all those processes, whether *δίκαι*, *γραφαί*, or other public processes, in which the defendant is regarded as guilty of a delict and the court inflicts on the defendant, if convicted, a penalty which is in the form either of damages to the plaintiff, or of a fine paid to the state (or partly to the state, partly to the plaintiff), or of loss of liberty or status or life.

Then there is the classification into *ἀγῶνες τιμητοί* and *ἀτίμητοι*. The function of the 'estimation' or *τίμημα* was to fix the damages or penalty, the *poena*. *τιμᾶσθαι* was used of the plaintiff, *ἀντιτιμᾶσθαι* of the defendant, their activity was *τίμησις*, the figure each fixed on was his *τίμημα*, the act of the judge (or jury) was *τιμᾶν*, and his determination of the figure was also the *τίμημα*. *ἀγῶνες τιμητοί* were those suits in which the law had not fixed in advance the amount or nature of the penalty or damages; *ἀγῶνες ἀτίμητοι* were suits where the law had so fixed.[1]

We have to decide which suits would in practice have fallen into either category. Here we should surely follow the opinion of Gernet, as against Lipsius, that any suit concerning a contractual obligation must have been *τιμητός*.[2] The plaintiff in such a suit had to state in his claim what the amount of that claim was, just as did the plaintiff in a *δίκη ἐπιτροπῆς* for example;[3] we must suppose that the defendant was formally permitted, in case of conviction, to submit a counter-estimate, and that the court could then choose between the two.[4] It was only an apparent exception to this rule if, as is clearly shown to be possible by Dem. 37 *Pant.* 40, litigants in what would normally have been an *ἀγὼν*

[1] Lipsius, *AR* 248 ff., Gernet, *DSGA* 78 f., O. Schulthess, *RE* s.v. *τιμηταὶ δίκαι*. Harpokr. s.v. *ἀτίμητος ἀγὼν καὶ τιμητός· ὁ μὲν τιμητὸς ἐφ' ᾧ τίμημα ὡρισμένον ἐκ τῶν νόμων οὐ κεῖται, ἀλλὰ τοὺς δικαστὰς ἔδει τιμᾶσθαι ὅ τι χρὴ παθεῖν ἢ ἀποτῖσαι· ὁ δὲ ἀτίμητος τοὐναντίον ᾧ πρόσεστιν ἐκ τῶν νόμων ὡρισμένον τίμημα, ὡς μηδὲν δεῖν τοὺς δικαστὰς διατιμῆσαι*: this definition is right, as against *An. Bekk.* (*Λέξ. Ῥητ.*) 202. 7 ff., (*Συν. Λέξ. Χρησ.*) 459. 26 ff., Suda s.v. *ἀτίμητος ἀγών*. In the orators *τιμητός* occurs only once, where Demosthenes describes his suit against Aphobos, a *δίκη ἐπιτροπῆς*, as *τιμητός* (27 *Aphob.* i. 67); Aischin. 3 *Ktes.* 210 calls his suit *οὐκ ἀτίμητος*. For *δίκη ἀτίμητος* see Dem. 21 *Meid.* 90, 37 *Pant.* 40, 55 *Kallikl.* 18, 25, 28. For the procedure followed in the *τίμησις* see p. 166.

[2] Gernet, *DSGA* 79. Lipsius, *AR* 258, includes among *ἀγῶνες ἀτίμητοι* those 'über die Berechtigung einer Schuldforderung'.

[3] Dem. 27 *Aphob.* i. 67.

[4] Dem. 56 *Dionysod.* 43 proves that a convicted defendant could put in an estimate of the sum to be adjudged lower than the estimate of the plaintiff; Gernet, *Dem.* iii. 148, n. 2.

τιμητός agreed before the case came into court upon the amount at issue, thus making the suit in effect ἀτίμητος. It is also conceivable that, where in cases of this type a defendant appealed from the award of an arbitrator, the plaintiff could, if he wished, elect to make the case ἀτίμητος, in which event the award of the arbitrator would have been the obligatory τίμημα. This is one way of explaining the otherwise puzzling fact that Dem. 55 *Kallikl.* is an ἀγὼν ἀτίμητος for 1,000 drachmai, though the defendant, the son of Teisias, maintains that the actual damage suffered by Kallikles was nothing like that sum.[1] Other suits certainly or probably in this category were the δίκαι ἐπιτροπῆς,[2] κλοπῆς,[3] αἰκείας,[4] ἐξαιρέσεως,[5] ψευδομαρτυρίων,[6] λιπομαρτυρίου,[7] κακοτεχνιῶν,[8] βιαίων.[9] The δίκαι ἐξούλης[10] and βλάβης were as a rule τιμητοί. The δίκαι ἀποστασίου and κακηγορίας were both ἀτίμητοι; in the former a convicted defendant was punished by relapse into slavery,[11] in the latter by penalties differing at different periods and according to the circumstances.

Suits other than δίκαι might be either τιμητοί or ἀτίμητοι. Of the three kinds of εἰσαγγελία (enumerated on p. 52) that dealing with wrongs against orphans and heiresses must clearly have been

[1] See vol. i, pp. 250 f. The plaintiff by this choice would be gambling on all or nothing. The language used by the defendant would fit this supposition, but less well the supposition that 1,000 drachmai was either a fixed penalty for the particular wrong with which the defendant was charged (building a wall which caused the flooding of Kallikles' land), irrespective of the damage caused, or a fixed charge by which the defendant could avoid the forfeiture of the land on which the offending wall stood; so H. J. Wolff, *AJP* 64 (1943) 316 ff. (*Beitr.* 91 ff.), *Traditio* 4 (1946) 51 ff. (*Beitr.* 36 ff.).

[2] See p. 80, n. 1.

[3] Dem. 24 *Timokr.* 114: the convicted thief pays double the amount stolen; this amount must have been the subject of τίμησις.

[4] Isok. 20 *Loch.* 19.

[5] Dem. 58 *Theokr.* 19: in addition to restitution a convicted defendant in a suit for the return to his master of a slave had to pay a penalty equal to the value of the slave, as in the δίκη κλοπῆς; the slave therefore had to be valued.

[6] Dem. 45 *Steph.* i. 46: Apollodoros' statement of claim in a δίκη ψευδομαρτυρίων includes an estimate of the loss suffered. Three convictions in δίκαι ψευδομαρτυρίων made a man automatically ἄτιμος; see p. 172.

[7] Phot. and Suda s.v. λειπομαρτυρίου δίκη.

[8] Assumed to be τιμητός by analogy with λιπομαρτυρίου.

[9] Plut. *Solon* 23 attributes to Solon a law by which there was a statutory penalty of 100 drachmai for the violation of a free woman, but by Lysias' time the damage had to be estimated (1 *Killing of Erat.* 32).

[10] Always, if we take the view of that suit worked out by Rabel and commended by Gernet; see vol. i, pp. 217 ff., 311 f.

[11] See vol. i, p. 185.

τιμητός.[1] εἰσαγγελία of an arbitrator was ἀτίμητος: conviction of an arbitrator for misconduct in an arbitration was punished with ἀτιμία (see p. 68). The third type of εἰσαγγελία was in this respect hybrid: as shown on pp. 55 ff., the penalty might be prescribed by the ekklesia in remitting a case to a dikastery, it might be left to the process of estimation, or, as in cases of προδοσία for example, it might be prescribed by statute.

The προβολή was technically an ἀγὼν τιμητός, but with the peculiarity that the accuser proposed the penalty not at the time when he made his charge, but only if and when the defendant was convicted (see pp. 63 f.).

Procedures under φάσις were τιμητοί; those under δοκιμασία ἀτίμητοι; those under εὔθυνα as a rule τιμητοί; those under ἀπαγωγή, ἔνδειξις, and ἐφήγησις as a rule ἀτίμητοι.

Whether a γραφή was τιμητός or ἀτίμητος depended on its content. The following were ἀτίμητοι: ἱεροσυλίας, ψευδεγγραφῆς, βουλεύσεως, ἀδίκως εἰρχθῆναι ὡς μοιχόν, ξενίας, ἀστρατείας, δειλίας, λιποταξίου, ἀναυμαχίου, μοιχείας, ἑταιρήσεως, προαγωγείας, ἀργίας, and probably δωροξενίας and ὑποβολῆς. The following were τιμητοί: ἀσεβείας (with certain exceptions), δώρων, δεκασμοῦ, παρανόμων, παραπρεσβείας, ψευδοκλητείας, ὕβρεως, κλοπῆς, συκοφαντίας. The following are doubtful: προδοσίας, ἀπροστασίου, ἀγραφίου, ἀγράφου μετάλλου, ἀλογίου.

§ 3. *Capacity*

In the sphere of law a person's status may affect his or her right to appear in court as plaintiff, defendant, or witness, or to perform certain acts with legal consequences, such as contracting, marrying, or making a will. Here we are concerned only with capacity in legal proceedings.

Unrestricted capacity over the whole field belonged in Athens only to male citizens of age who had not been deprived by partial or total ἀτιμία of some or all of these rights.[2] Total ἀτιμία em-

[1] Theopompos, a defendant in such a suit, indicates that, if convicted, he will be liable to heavy penalties, but his failure to specify them exactly suggests that they would have depended on the decision of the court, choosing, we must suppose, between his opponent's and his own τίμημα (Isai. 11 *Hagn.* 13, 35).

[2] Lipsius, *AR* 789 ff., Weiss, *GP* 164 ff., Paoli, *St. Dir.* 294 ff. For ἀτιμία as a punishment see pp. 169 ff.

braced within it the loss of all procedural rights, so that the man on whom it had been imposed was in the same position as a *ξένος* from a city with which Athens had no treaty. State debtors were subject to total *ἀτιμία* until their debt was paid off, and this *ἀτιμία* passed to their heirs with the same condition. This meant that they were barred not merely from bringing *γραφαί*, but also from bringing *δίκαι* and even from giving evidence in court. It is going too far to say that they lost the capacity to own property, but the ban on their suing by way of *δίκαι* must have rendered them very vulnerable to attack not only on their property but on their persons.[1] It is commonly held that a prosecutor in a public suit who either dropped the prosecution or failed to secure one-fifth of the votes was barred from ever bringing a *γραφή* in the future. It is more likely that he was fined 1,000 drachmai and was *ἄτιμος* (and therefore unable to bring suit at all, either public or private) until he had paid.[2] The phrase commonly found in laws dealing with *γραφαί*, "*γραφέσθω ὁ βουλόμενος Ἀθηναίων οἷς ἔξεστιν*", is obviously inserted with these prohibitions in view.[3]

As we saw in the section on wills (vol. i, pp. 151 ff.), neither

[1] Lys. 6 *Andok.* 24, Isai. 10 *Aristarch.* 20, Dem. 21 *Meid.* 87. On the capacity to own see vol. i, p. 236.

[2] Andok. 1 *Myst.* 33 *ἐὰν γὰρ μὴ μεταλάβῃ τὸ πέμπτον μέρος τῶν ψήφων καὶ ἀτιμωθῇ ὁ ἐνδείξας ἐμὲ Κηφίσιος οὑτοσί*, 76 *ἑτέροις οὐκ ἦν γράψασθαι, τοῖς δὲ ἐνδεῖξαι*, Dem. 21 *Meid.* 47 *ὅσοι δ' ἂν γράφωνται γραφὰς ἰδίας κατὰ τὸν νόμον, ἐάν τις μὴ ἐπεξέλθῃ ἢ ἐπεξιὼν μὴ μεταλάβῃ τὸ πέμπτον μέρος τῶν ψήφων, ἀποτεισάτω χιλίας δραχμὰς τῷ δημοσίῳ*, 103 *ἐκεῖνος ἠτίμωκεν αὑτὸν οὐκ ἐπεξελθών*, 24 *Timokr.* 7 *τὸ πέμπτον μέρος τῶν ψήφων οὐ μεταλαβὼν ὦφλε χιλίας*, 26 *Aristogeit.* ii. 9 *ὅταν τις ἐπεξιὼν μὴ μεταλάβῃ τὸ πέμπτον μέρος τῶν ψήφων, ἐφ' οἷς οἱ νόμοι κελεύουσι τὸ λοιπὸν μὴ γράφεσθαι μηδ' ἀπάγειν μηδ' ἐφηγεῖσθαι*, 58 *Theokr.* 6 *ὁ νόμος οὑτοσί, ὦ ἄνδρες δικασταί, τοῖς προαιρουμένοις ἢ γράφεσθαι γραφὰς ἢ φαίνειν ἢ ἄλλο τι ποιεῖν τῶν ἐν τῷ νόμῳ τούτῳ γεγραμμένων προλέγει διαρρήδην, ἐφ' οἷς ἕκαστόν ἐστιν τούτων ποιητέον. ἔστι δὲ ταῦτα, ὥσπερ ἠκούσατε ἐξ αὐτοῦ τοῦ νόμου, ἐὰν ἐπεξιών τις μὴ μεταλάβῃ τὸ πέμπτον μέρος τῶν ψήφων, χιλίας ἀποτίνειν, κἂν μὴ ἐπεξίῃ ⟨γ'⟩, ὦ Θεοκρίνη, χιλίας ἑτέρας, ἵνα μήτε συκοφαντῇ μηδείς*, Harpokr. s.v. *ἐάν τις γραψάμενος μὴ μεταλάβῃ τὸ πέμπτον μέρος τῶν ψήφων, ὀφλισκάνει χιλίας καὶ πρόσεστιν ἀτιμία τις. Λυσίας ἐν τῷ ὑπὲρ τοῦ κατὰ τῶν ῥητόρων νόμου διείλεκται περὶ τούτων καὶ Θεόφραστος ἐν τοῖς περὶ τῶν νόμων*, *Lex. Cant.* s.v. *πρόστιμον ἔκειτο τῷ μὴ μεταλαβόντι τὸ πέμπτον μέρος τῶν ψήφων, ὡς Θεόφραστος ἐν πέμπτῳ περὶ νόμων· ἐν δὲ τοῖς δημοσίοις ἀγῶσιν ἐζημιοῦντο χιλίαις καὶ πρόσεστί τις ἀτιμία, ὥστε μὴ ἐξεῖναι μήτε γράψασθαι παρανόμων μήτε φαίνειν μήτε ἐφηγεῖσθαι· ἐὰν δέ τις γραψάμενος μὴ ἐπεξέλθῃ, ὁμοίως*. Lipsius, *AR* 449, Bo. Sm. ii. 56 f. take the view that one kind of partial *ἀτιμία* was loss of the right to bring a *γραφή*; Paoli, *St. Dir.* 322 ff., denies this. See also pp. 103 ff. Other kinds of partial *ἀτιμία*, such as loss of the right to be a member of the boule, to address the ekklesia, to enter the Agora, to sail to the Hellespont or to Ionia (enumerated in Andok. 1 *Myst.* 75 f.), do not concern us here.

[3] Dem. 21 *Meid.* 47, 24 *Timokr.* 63, 59 *Neair.* 16, 52, Aischin. 1 *Timarch.* 32.

minors nor women were qualified to make a will, nor could one whose judgement had been clouded by madness, senility, drugs, sickness, undue influence of women, force, or restriction of liberty. We should not however conclude that there was any written law by which these disabilities invalidated other acts than making a will, since Hypereides argues in one passage that a contract arrived at under duress should be regarded as invalid only on the analogy of the law referring to wills.[1]

A male Athenian came of age probably at the end of his seventeenth year.[2] Until he reached that age he had to be represented in all legal relations by his father or, if he were dead, by his guardian.[3] An Athenian woman, on the other hand, remained under tutelage all her life under rules set out in the section on guardianship (vol. i, pp. 108 ff.). Claims or charges against a woman were made to her in person, although it was for her *κύριος* to conduct her case in court.[4] Lipsius maintains that the same was true of claims or charges against a minor;[5] but he advances no evidence for this, and it would seem more likely that in their case the summons had to be delivered to the *κύριος* himself.

The effect of metic status on a man's or woman's juristic position has been fully discussed in vol. i, pp. 193 ff. (see also p. 10 of this volume). For freedmen and freedwomen see vol. i, pp. 184 ff.; for slaves, vol. i, pp. 166 ff., 177 ff. The position of foreigners other than metics depended on the treaty relations between their home cities and Athens.

Various subdivisions of the body politic, such as tribes and demes, phratries and *γένη*, could sue and be sued in the courts, as could free associations, such as *ἔρανοι*, *θίασοι*, and *ὀργεῶνες*.[6]

[1] Hyper. 5 *Athenog.* 17.

[2] Conceivably eighteenth (so Ar. *Ath. Pol.* 42. 1), but Dem. 27 *Aphob.* i suggests that Demosthenes ceased to be under tutelage while still seventeen; cf. R. Sealey, *CR* 7 (1957) 195 ff.

[3] See vol. i, pp. 73, 108.

[4] Lipsius, *AR* 790 f., gives the following examples: the *γραφὴ ξενίας* against Neaira, the *γραφαὶ ἀσεβείας* against Aspasia and against Phryne, the *δίκη βουλεύσεως* against the stepmother (Ant. 1 *Stepmother*), the *δίκη φόνου* in Ant. 3 *2nd Tetr.* Cf. schol. Aristoph. *Knights* 969 *ὥσπερ ἐν ταῖς εἰσαγωγαῖς τῶν ἐγκλημάτων κηρύττειν εἰώθασιν, ἐπειδὰν γυναικὶ ἐπιφέρηται ἔγκλημα. οὕτω γὰρ προκαλεῖσθαι εἰώθασιν ἐν τῷ δικαστηρίῳ, ἡ δεῖνα καὶ ὁ κύριος, τουτέστιν ὁ ἀνήρ.*

[5] Lipsius, *AR* 790 f.

[6] Ar. *Ath. Pol.* 42. 1 (in a *δοκιμασία*, if the deme reject a man's application to be enrolled in the deme on the ground that he is not free, the man has an appeal to a dikastery and the demesmen choose five of their number to sustain their rejection

As we have seen above (pp. 76 f.), one of the privileges or duties of the full citizen at Athens was to act as prosecutor in all those suits which for one reason or another had been placed by the legislator in the category of γραφαί. In this he was performing the function of a public prosecutor. We have also seen that in certain limited ways it was the duty of one or another magistrate to initiate action at law for the preservation of law and order (pp. 6 f.).

§ 4. *Initiating procedure*

In the three special types of procedure known as ἀπαγωγή, ἔνδειξις, and ἐφήγησις no summons was needed. The distinguishing mark of the wrongs with which they dealt was that the perpetrators were discovered *flagrante delicto* or had acted so openly that the only point at issue could be the nature of the penalty to be inflicted. The procedures were therefore abnormally summary; they are discussed on pp. 221 ff. The initiation of a δίκη φόνου also had many peculiarities.[1] We are here concerned with the rules which obtained in other δίκαι and in γραφαί.

A plaintiff or prosecutor in one of these suits had to summon the defendant to appear before the relevant magistrate on a stated day; he declared what his plaint was, and was accompanied by one or two witnesses. The verb for this act was προσκαλεῖσθαι or καλεῖσθαι, the act πρόσκλησις or κλῆσις, the witnesses κλητῆρες and their activity κλητεύειν. The names of the witnesses might be added to the document handed to the magistrate, though this was not obligatory. Their participation in the summons on the other hand was necessary to guard against a possible denial by the defendant if he failed to appear and judgement was then given against him by default; indeed to secure such a judgement the law prescribed that the plaintiff must produce these witnesses, and they laid themselves open to a γραφὴ ψευδοκλητείας if the defendant could prove that they had given false evidence.[2]

before the court), Isai. 12 *Euphil.* 11, Dem. 59 *Neair.* 60, D.H. *Dein.* 11. For corporate bodies as owners see vol. i, pp. 241 f.; the scepticism expressed there (p. 242, n. 1) of the view that ownership by such bodies did not imply recognition of them as juristic persons could have been put more strongly.

[1] MacDowell, *Homicide* 22 ff.

[2] Lipsius, *AR* 446 f., Berneker, *RE* s.v. ψευδοκλητείας γραφή. See also p. 198.

Notice had to be served on the defendant himself. If he could not be met with in public, it was perhaps sufficient to make an announcement in front of his house; it is very unlikely that it was permitted to enter a house for this purpose.[1] We do not know what the rule was when the defendant was not in Athens, but in serious cases of *εἰσαγγελίαι* specially appointed summoners with the name of *κλητῆρες* could be sent to deliver a summons, as happened to Alkibiades after the mutilation of the Hermai.[2]

The summons stated the charge or claim[3] and named a day for the appearance before the magistrate, though this day did not apparently have to be agreed with the magistrate in advance. There were however some suits which could only be brought on certain days of the month; thus a *γραφὴ ξενίας* could only be brought on the last day of a month, as could also a suit for debt or for adultery.[4] It is probable that a summons could not be made on a feast day nor on unlucky days (*ἡμέραι ἀποφράδες*).[5] Certain suits could not be initiated at certain times. *δίκαι ἐμπορικαί* could not be brought during six months of the year: according to the single text which bears on the matter, the months allowed were the winter months, Boedromion to Mounichion; but Paoli has convincingly argued that it is so unlikely *a priori* that these suits should have been limited to precisely those months when foreign litigants, whether plaintiff or defendant, were not likely to be in Athens, that the passage should be emended to give the summer months, from Mounichion to Boedromion.[6] As we saw in the section on succession (vol. i, pp. 158 f.), suits in succession cases could not be brought in the last month of the year, since it was necessary that they should be completed under the same archon as the one with whom they had been initiated. For a similar reason *δίκαι φόνου* could not be admitted by a basileus after the ninth month of the year, since he had to

[1] Dem. 49 *Timoth.* 19 refers to a witness *προσκληθεὶς ἀπὸ τῆς οἰκίας* (*οὐ γὰρ ἦν φανερός*). For the sanctity of a man's house cf. Dem. 47 *Euerg.* 60.

[2] Thuc. 6. 61.

[3] Aristoph. *Clouds* 1224, *Wasps* 1407, 1418.

[4] Krateros, *F.Gr.H.* 342 F 4 *ἐὰν δέ τις ἐξ ἀμφοῖν ξένοιν γεγονὼς φρατρίζῃ, διώκειν εἶναι τῷ βουλομένῳ Ἀθηναίων, οἷς δίκαι εἰσί· λαγχάνειν δὲ τῇ ἕνῃ καὶ νέᾳ πρὸς τοὺς ναυτοδίκας*, Aristoph. *Clouds* 1131 ff., 1178 ff., 1222, Men. fr. 512 Kock.

[5] Dem. 24 *Timokr.* 29, Lucian *Pseudol.* 12; Lipsius, *AR* 160 f.

[6] Dem. 33 *Apatour.* 23 *αἱ δὲ λήξεις τοῖς ἐμπόροις τῶν δικῶν ἔμμηνοί εἰσιν ἀπὸ τοῦ βοηδρομιῶνος μέχρι τοῦ μουνιχιῶνος*. Paoli, *St. Proc.* 177 ff., Gernet, *DSGA* 184, n. 3, *Dem.* i. 141, n. 2.

conduct preliminaries in three successive months and introduce the case in a fourth month, and he could not pass the suit on to the next basileus.[1] The summons had to be made at least four days before the day on which the appearance before the magistrate was required.[2]

Where the defendant was a metic or foreigner, the plaintiff could take him by force before the proper magistrate and could then exact sureties for his appearance in court.[3] A citizen defendant on the other hand could, even in case of murder (with the possible exception of parricide), either not appear or go into voluntary exile after the first speech in defence.[4]

εἰσαγγελίαι κακώσεως ὀρφανῶν, etc., followed the rules for *γραφαί* (see vol. i, pp. 117 f.). In *εἰσαγγελίαι* which derived from the ekklesia the boule in its *προβούλευμα* laid down whether the accused should be arrested or should have to provide sureties for his appearance, though in serious treason cases even the provision of sureties was not allowed and the accused had to remain in custody until trial (see p. 56). Where the accused was absent from Athens, the summons was in writing.[5]

If a man was held in custody, a law of Timokrates imposed on the Eleven the duty of bringing him before a court within thirty days of his arrest if within that period his case had not been reported to the thesmothetai; we may assume that the thesmothetai had to do the same in cases which were duly reported to them.[6] We may perhaps assume a similar rule in cases which originated in *μήνυσις*.

Cases of *φάσις* of whatever kind followed the rules for *γραφαί*.

[1] So at least we are told in Ant. 6 *Chor.* 42. The statement seems however to be based rather on custom than on a written provision, and it may be that there was nothing in the law compelling the basileus to bring the suit forward in these circumstances, rather than a law which forbade him; cf. MacDowell, *Homicide* 34 ff., Gernet, *DSGA* 115, n. 5.

[2] That this was a general rule can be fairly deduced from the fact that this is the interval prescribed when the archon proceeds against a man in certain cases (Dem. 43 *Makart.* 75 *προσκαλεσάμενος πρόπεμπτα*) and that in Aristoph. *Clouds* 1131 ff. Strepsiades is summoned four days before the last day to appear on the last day of the month. Cf. Plut. *Mor.* 833 f *ἐπειδὰν αἱ κλήσεις ἐξήκωσιν*, Aischin. 1 *Timarch.* 35.

[3] Isok. 17 *Trapez.* 12, Dem. 32 *Zenoth.* 29.

[4] Ant. 5 *Her.* 13, Dem. 23 *Aristokr.* 69, Poll. 8. 117 *μετὰ δὲ τὸν πρότερον λόγον ἐξῆν φυγεῖν, πλὴν εἴ τις γονέας εἴη ἀπεκτονώς.*

[5] The *πινάκιον* in Dem. 8 *Chers.* 28 is not the charge, as schol. ad loc. and Harpokr. s.v. *πινάκια* assumed, but a written summons. Alkibiades' summons (Thuc. 6. 61) was presumably in writing.

[6] Dem. 24 *Timokr.* 63 (quoted on p. 56, n. 4).

In ἀπογραφαί and in most διαδικασίαι, particularly those concerning heiresses and inheritances, since there was normally in them no plaintiff and no defendant, there could be no summons, but in the κυρία ἐκκλησία of each prytany a list of public confiscations and of inheritances and heiresses which were to be adjudicated upon was read out.[1]

The next, but distinct, step in the normal procedure was the actual reception of the case by the appropriate magistrate.[2] The plaintiff presented a statement of his accusation or claim, which indicated what type of suit it fell under.[3] The plaintiff is said λαγχάνειν δίκην with the genitive either of the kind of wrong done (βλάβης, φόνου) or the thing claimed (κλήρου).[4] The word λῆξις besides its more restricted sense of a claim to an inheritance, could be used of any claim, whether in a δίκη or a γραφή,[5] and the word γραφή could be used of the claim in a δίκη.[6] The word ἔγκλημα in its technical sense was confined to a claim in a private suit.[7] The claim or indictment was originally made orally and reduced to writing by an official; it was not until well on in the fourth century (possibly in 378/7) that oral gave way to written pleadings, probably at the same time as evidence ceased to be given orally and was recorded in writing at the ἀνάκρισις.[8] The technical term for handing in the written claim was ἀποφέρειν τὴν γραφὴν πρὸς τὸν ἄρχοντα.[9]

There is some controversy as to what exactly is implied by the phrase λαγχάνειν δίκην. The clause of a law quoted in Dem. 46

[1] Ar. *Ath. Pol.* 43. 4. For πρόσκλησις exceptionally in inheritance cases see vol. i, pp. 161, 214.

[2] e.g. Lys. 6 *Andok.* 11 προσεκαλέσατο δίκην ἀσεβείας πρὸς τὸν βασιλέα καὶ ἔλαχεν.

[3] e.g. Aischin. 1 *Timarch.* 13 ὁ νόμος . . . κατ' αὐτοῦ μὲν τοῦ παιδὸς οὐκ ἐᾷ γραφὴν εἶναι, κατὰ δὲ τοῦ μισθώσαντος καὶ τοῦ μισθωσαμένου, τοῦ μὲν ὅτι ἐξεμίσθωσε, τοῦ δὲ ὅτι, φησίν, ἐμισθώσατο.

[4] λαγχάνειν λῆξιν κλήρου or λαγχάνειν κλήρου is used when a man other than the *suus heres* enters his claim either to an inheritance or to the hand of an heiress with the archon in the absence of other claimants (Isai. 3 *Pyrrh.* 2, 32, 43). On the other hand the phrase is λαγχάνειν δίκην κλήρου where a man is making claim to an inheritance or the hand of an heiress when these are already occupied by another (Isai. 11 *Hagn.* 13).

[5] For λῆξις of a γραφή see Dem. 24 *Timokr.* 83, 39 *Boiot.* i. 17, 58 *Theokr.* 32.

[6] Dem. 27 *Aphob.* i. 12, D.H. *Dein.* 3.

[7] Lipsius, *AR* 817.

[8] G. M. Calhoun, *TAPA* 50 (1919) 177 ff., showed that there was no allusion to written pleadings in the forensic speeches of Antiphon, Andokides, Lysias, and Isokrates. Cf. F. D. Harvey, *RÉG* 79 (1966), 593 f.

[9] Dem. 23 *Aristokr.* 5. 27 *Aphob.* i. 12, 58 *Theokr.* 32, Aischin. 3 *Ktes.* 217.

Steph. ii necessarily implies that the archon had to decide by lot in what order or on what days suits concerning inheritances or heiresses were to have their ἀνάκρισις (not their hearing in chief, for if that were meant there would have been no object in excluding the last month of the official year).[1] Thus the phrase λαγχάνειν δίκην (which is the correlate of κληροῦν in that clause) means, not to get a day for the hearing allotted to one, but to apply for a hearing.[2] The paredroi of the archons and the secretaries of the various boards were empowered to receive the written plaints, but probably this was the limit of their authority (but on the paredroi see pp. 11 f.).[3]

It is not clear what exact powers a magistrate had when he was presented with a written plaint. We can conjecture that, if the defendant did not put in an appearance, the magistrate had to satisfy himself, by hearing the witnesses, that he had been duly summoned, and that if he was not so satisfied he could refuse to go further on the ground that the suit would be οὐκ εἰσαγώγιμος.[4] In such a case it was presumably still open to the plaintiff to remedy the defect by summoning the defendant for a future occasion. If on the other hand the magistrate was satisfied that the defendant had been summoned, he presumably took the next appropriate step in the procedure in his absence. This might be the reference of the case to a public arbitrator, and we do not know exactly what disadvantages the defendant would then suffer through having defaulted at the first hearing before the magistrate. Or the case might be set down for hearing by a dikastery; before this hearing however there would have intervened the ἀνάκρισις (see next section), and again we cannot be sure what would have been the position of a defaulting defendant in relation to that. All we can say is first that it is very unlikely that the magistrate could condemn him by default before the ἀνάκρισις, and second that, before the case actually came into court,

[1] Dem. 46 *Steph.* ii. 22 κληροῦν δὲ τὸν ἄρχοντα κλήρων καὶ ἐπικλήρων, ὅσοι εἰσὶ μῆνες, πλὴν τοῦ σκιροφοριῶνος.

[2] Lipsius, *AR* 817 f., Gernet, *DSGA* 115. Gernet argues that this 'allotment' applied equally to suits that were going to be considered by public arbitrators with those which were subject to ἀνάκρισις.

[3] Dem. 58 *Theokr.* 32 (paredros of the archon), 8 (secretary of the overseers of the market).

[4] Dem. 53 *Nikostr.* 15, *An. Bekk.* (*Λέξ. Ῥητ.*) 199. 14 ff.; Lipsius, *AR* 819. We cannot be quite clear about the circumstances in which the archon summoned the parties to the ἀνάκρισις in Dem. 58 *Theokr.* 8; Lipsius, *AR* 823, n. 71.

a defendant who wished to challenge the allegation that he had been duly summoned could do so by way of a παραγραφή (see pp. 106 ff.) alleging that the δίκη was ἀπρόσκλητος.[1]

Let us now suppose the more normal case where the defendant did appear. It is no doubt formally correct to state, as most scholars do, that the magistrate had, in some circumstances at least, the right to refuse a case without further reference to a court. This is conclusively shown by the fact that a magistrate could be charged at his εὔθυνα (and possibly at the ἐπιχειροτονία held each prytany)[2] for wrongful admission of a suit. An obvious case would have been one where the magistrate approached was not the one charged with that particular procedure in the written law. On similar grounds we are told of a basileus who refused to accept a murder charge because it was preferred too late in the year for its completion while he was still in office and, he claimed, the law forbade him to entertain it; he was bitterly criticized for his action by the prosecutor, but the latter did not attack him for it at his εὔθυνα.[3] In another recorded case the Eleven required the plaintiff to add the words ἐπ' αὐτοφώρῳ to an indictment by way of ἀπαγωγή, and the implication is that, had he not done so, the Eleven could have refused to entertain his complaint.[4] Again in a claim for an estate a litigant is required by the magistrate to alter his plea, and there is the same implication here.[5] Another reason for refusing a suit might have been the incapacity of either the plaintiff or the defendant to be heard.

It is however an over-simplification to state that the magistrate had the right to refuse in cases where the complaint was manifestly ill-founded.[6] We cannot suppose that the plaintiff would invariably have agreed with the magistrate on what was self-evident, and whereas an aggrieved defendant could always challenge the magistrate's decision to accept the case by way of

[1] Dem. 53 *Nikostr.* 15, *An. Bekk.* (*Λέξ. Ῥητ.*) 199. 14 ff. Cf. Berneker, *RE* s.v. πρόσκλησις 851; but the passages referring to a δίκη ἀπρόσκλητος which he cites from Dem. 21 *Meid.* 87, 92 must be used with caution, since they refer to an action against an arbitrator for malfeasance in his office and this was a special procedure.

[2] Ar. *Ath. Pol.* 43. 4.

[3] See p. 87, n. 1.

[4] Lys. 13 *Agorat.* 86.

[5] Isai. 10 *Aristarch.* 2.

[6] Thus Lipsius, *AR* 845 ('in solchen Fällen, in denen die Unzulässigkeit der Klage unzweifelhaft war'), Bo. Sm. ii. 75, n. 2 ('if *for good and sufficient reasons* it was not deemed εἰσαγώγιμος'; my italics). See too, equally unsatisfactory, Calhoun, *CP* 14 (1919) 338 ff., especially 346.

παραγραφή, it seems at first sight that the plaintiff was in this respect at the mercy of the magistrate; for it is clear that the right to arraign the magistrate either at his εὔθυνα or at the ἐπιχειροτονία, though some protection, is not the same as the right to have the issue of whether the suit is *prima facie* admissible taken out of the hands of the magistrate. We can only suppose that the threat of proceedings by way of εὔθυνα or ἐπιχειροτονία had the effect of making magistrates lean heavily in the direction of allowing suit and relying on the παραγραφή to correct errors of laxity in this respect. There is nothing to suggest that, where the court decided that in fact a case was not εἰσαγώγιμος, any liability attached to the magistrate who had come to the conclusion that *prima facie* it was. The whole matter is discussed more fully below (pp. 105 f.) in connection with παραγραφή and similar pleas.

If a plaintiff's plea was accepted by a magistrate, it was published in the form approved by the magistrate on whitened tablets in the Agora by the statues of the tribal ἐπώνυμοι. (Pleas entertained by the overseers of the market were published near their office in Peiraeus.) This happened whether it was a public or a private suit.[1] There is some reason to believe that the pleas, together with judgements of the courts, were eventually deposited in the state archives in the Metroon; the plea advanced against Sokrates was alleged to be on view there in the second century B.C.[2]

The Demosthenic corpus has provided us with three examples of duly accepted pleas. One of them, the plea of Aischines in his γραφὴ παρανόμων against Ktesiphon, inserted in Dem. 18 *Crown* 54 f., must be disregarded, since its genuineness is suspected on good grounds.[3] The other two however, Apollodoros' plea against Stephanos in a δίκη ψευδομαρτυρίων[4] and the partially preserved

[1] Aristoph. *Clouds* 770, Ant. 6 *Chor.* 41, Hesych. and Phot. s.v. σανίς. (Isok. 15 *Antid.* 237, though quoted by Lipsius, *AR* 820, n. 57, is not relevant here, since it refers to the publication of names of men convicted of various offences.)

[2] D.L. 2. 40. On archives see Paoli, *Studi Betti* (Milan, 1962) iii. 3 ff.

[3] J. G. Droysen, *Zeitschrift für die Altertumswissenschaft* (1839) 537 ff. (*Kleine Schriften* i. 95 ff.).

[4] Dem. 45 *Steph.* i. 46 Ἀπολλόδωρος Πασίωνος Ἀχαρνεὺς Στεφάνῳ Μενεκλέους Ἀχαρνεῖ ψευδομαρτυρίων, τίμημα τάλαντον. τὰ ψευδῆ μου κατεμαρτύρησε Στέφανος μαρτυρήσας τὰ ἐν τῷ γραμματείῳ γεγραμμένα. J. E. Kirchner, *De litis instrumentis quae exstant in Demosthenis quae fertur in Lacritum et priore adversus Stephanum orationibus* (Halle, 1883) 34 ff.

plea of Nikoboulos against Pantainetos,[1] are likely to be genuine. Dionysios has also preserved for us the plea of Deinarchos against Proxenos in a *δίκη βλάβης*.[2] As you would expect, the document gives the name of the plaintiff, the name of the defendant, the kind of suit and the amount claimed. There follows a short description of the wrong alleged. In Apollodoros' case an additional document gives a transcript of the evidence which Stephanos had given and which is the subject of this plea.[3] The text of the charge brought against Alkibiades in an *εἰσαγγελία* by Thessalos is given in Plutarch;[4] and there is a version of the charge brought by Meletos against Sokrates in Diogenes Laertios, though this is of doubtful authenticity.[5] Finally there is a parody of a charge *κλοπῆς* in the proceedings against the dog in Aristophanes *Wasps*.[6]

At this initial stage the defendant had to state his defence,[7] and both parties were instructed when to appear for the *ἀνάκρισις* and as to the payment of court dues in so far as these had not already been deposited by the plaintiff.[8] If the defendant was a foreigner, he was either imprisoned or had to furnish sureties. Certain special steps had to be taken at this juncture in cases of *ἀπαγωγή*, *ἔνδειξις*, and *ἐφήγησις*[9] and in homicide cases.[10]

Court dues were of three kinds. The most important were known as *πρυτανεῖα*. These probably derived their name from a very old Athenian court, the Prytaneion.[11] When payable, they

[1] Dem. 37 *Pant.* 22, 25, 26, 28, 29; Höck, *De Demosthenis adversus Pantaenetum oratione* (Berlin, 1878) 24 ff., Lipsius, *AR* 821, n. 64.

[2] D.H. *Dein.* 3 *Δείναρχος Σωστράτου Κορίνθιος Προξένῳ, ᾧ σύνειμι, βλάβης ταλάντων δύο. ἔβλαψέ με Πρόξενος ὑποδεξάμενος εἰς τὴν οἰκίαν τὴν ἑαυτοῦ τὴν ἐν ἀγρῷ, ὅτε πεφευγὼς Ἀθήνηθεν κατῄειν ἐκ Χαλκίδος, χρυσίου μὲν στατῆρας ὀγδοήκοντα καὶ διακοσίους καὶ πέντε, οὓς ἐκόμισα ἐκ Χαλκίδος εἰδότος Προξένου καὶ εἰσῆλθον ἔχων εἰς τὴν οἰκίαν αὐτοῦ, ἀργυρώματα δὲ οὐκ ἔλαττον εἴκοσι μνῶν ἄξια, ἐπιβουλεύσας τούτοις.*

[3] Dem. 45 *Steph.* i. 8.

[4] Plut. *Alk.* 22 *Θεσσαλὸς Κίμωνος Λακιάδης Ἀλκιβιάδην Κλεινίου Σκαμβωνίδην εἰσήγγειλεν ἀδικεῖν περὶ τὼ θεώ, ἀπομιμούμενον τὰ μυστήρια καὶ δεικνύοντα τοῖς αὑτοῦ ἑταίροις. . . .*

[5] D.L. 2. 40 *τάδε ἐγράψατο καὶ ἀντωμόσατο Μέλητος Μελήτου Πιτθεὺς Σωκράτει Σωφρονίσκου Ἀλωπεκῆθεν· ἀδικεῖ Σωκράτης, οὓς μὲν ἡ πόλις νομίζει θεοὺς οὐ νομίζων, ἕτερα δὲ καινὰ δαιμόνια εἰσηγούμενος· ἀδικεῖ δὲ καὶ τοὺς νέους διαφθείρων. τίμημα θάνατος.*

[6] Aristoph. *Wasps* 894 ff. *ἐγράψατο Κύων Κυδαθηναιεὺς Λάβητ' Αἰξωνέα τὸν τυρὸν ἀδικεῖν ὅτι μόνος κατήσθιεν τὸν Σικελικόν. τίμημα κλῳὸς σύκινος.*

[7] Dem. 42 *Phain.* 17, 45 *Steph.* i. 46.

[8] Aristoph. *Clouds* 1136, 1180.

[9] See pp. 221 ff.

[10] MacDowell, *Homicide* 22 ff.

[11] See pp. 42 f.

were payable by both plaintiff and defendant. If the plaintiff did not produce them at once, he was non-suited. We do not know the rule if the defendant did not pay up, but it has been conjectured that the plaintiff could pay for him and he would have to pay up if he lost the case. Both fees went to the state towards the dikasts' pay, but the losing party had to reimburse his opponent for his fee.[1] The amount of the fee was related to the value of the matter in dispute: for things worth between 100 and 1,000 drachmai each party paid three drachmai; for those over 1,000 thirty each; for things worth less than 100 drachmai no fee was payable.[2]

We cannot define precisely those cases where *πρυτανεῖα* were payable,[3] but broadly speaking it seems to have been those where the plaintiff was seeking primarily his own interest. These included actions for debt,[4] a *δίκη βλάβης*,[5] and a cross-action in a *δίκη αἰκείας*;[6] we are specifically told that a *δίκη αἰκείας* itself did not involve the payment of *πρυτανεῖα*.[7] A suggested, though unsatisfactory, explanation for the penalty on the cross-action only is that it was designed to discourage frivolous litigation; to quote Lipsius, 'if a counter-plea rests on the same ground as the plea in chief, it raises the presumption of bad faith or frivolousness on the one side or the other'.[8] But it is hard to see why a cross-action implies a greater degree of bad faith on one side

[1] Poll. 8. 38 *τὰ μὲν πρυτανεῖα ὡρισμένα, ὅ τι ἔδει καταβαλεῖν πρὸ τῆς δίκης τὸν διώκοντα καὶ τὸν διωκόμενον· εἰ δὲ μή, διέγραφον τὴν δίκην οἱ εἰσαγωγεῖς. ὁ δ' ἡττηθεὶς ἀπεδίδου τὸ παρ' ἀμφοτέρων δοθέν, ἐλάμβανον δ' αὐτὸ οἱ δικασταί.* But *πρὸ τῆς δίκης* must be wrong as applied to the defendant, who could not have been allowed to hold up the case by refusing to pay.

[2] Poll. 8. 38 *καὶ οἱ μὲν ἀπὸ ἑκατὸν δραχμῶν ἄχρι χιλίων δικαζόμενοι τρεῖς δραχμὰς κατετίθεντο, οἱ δὲ ἀπὸ χιλίων [μέχρι μυρίων] τριάκοντα*, Isok. 18 *Kallim.* 3 and 12, Dem. 47 *Euerg.* 64. Böckh, *Staatsh.* i. 416, conjectures that for sums over 10,000 drachmai the fees went up in proportion. This however was a deduction from a doubtful reading in the text of Pollux, where *μέχρι μυρίων* is interpolated. Those who thought that the fee was one-tenth of the *τίμημα* were making a false equation of the *πρυτανεῖα* with the *παρακαταβολή*.

[3] The passage in Ps.-Xen. *Ath. Pol.* 1. 16 which alleges, doubtless with some exaggeration, that during the first Athenian empire dikastic pay was furnished out of the *πρυτανεῖα* paid in Athens by the allies (cf. also Aristoph. *Wasps* 659) is good evidence for the general theme that Athens used her power to force many suits into the courts at Athens, but is of no use in determining what kind of suits entailed *πρυτανεῖα*.

[4] Aristoph. *Clouds* 1136, etc.

[5] Isok. 18 *Kallim.* 3, 12.

[6] Dem. 47 *Euerg.* 64.

[7] Isok. 20 *Loch.* 2, where *παρακαταβολῆς* has the general sense of 'court fees', not its technical sense.

[8] Lipsius, *AR* 826.

or the other than the simple denial of the claim or charge. We cannot in truth determine why the *δίκη αἰκείας*, if not met by a counter-plea, incurred no *πρυτανεῖα*.[1]

In public suits involving the interests of the state alone there were no *πρυτανεῖα*. But it is significant that in at least one kind of public case, the *φάσις* which controlled the number of olive trees a man could cut down, where a convicted defendant had to pay for every tree over the limit 100 drachmai to the state and 100 to the prosecutor, the latter had to pay *πρυτανεῖα* calculated on that part of the penalty which he was due to receive in case of a conviction.[2]

A second kind of court fee was known as *παράστασις*. This was payable in a large class of public suits (the majority of those which were not liable for *πρυτανεῖα*) and was paid by the plaintiff alone.[3] We do not know what the scale of these fees was, nor whether they were refunded to the plaintiff in case of conviction.[4]

The third kind of court fee was the *παρακαταβολή*. This was a kind of penalty to discourage vexatious litigation, and is therefore considered in the section dealing with penalties (pp. 179 ff.).

§ 5. *ἀνάκρισις*

At a date which had been fixed when the plaintiff reported his claim or charge to the proper magistrate[5] both parties appeared before that magistrate.[6] Our information on the exact procedure at the *ἀνάκρισις* is scanty, since it took place at the stage before the speech-making which provides us with the bulk of our

[1] See also pp. 131 f.

[2] Dem. 43 *Makart.* 71.

[3] Ar. *Ath. Pol.* 59. 3 εἰσὶ δὲ καὶ γραφαὶ πρὸς αὐτοὺς ὧν παράστασις τίθεται, ξενίας καὶ δωροξενίας, ἄν τις δῶρα δοὺς ἀποφύγῃ τὴν ξενίαν, καὶ συκοφαντίας καὶ δώρων καὶ ψευδεγγραφῆς καὶ ψευδοκλητείας καὶ βουλεύσεως καὶ ἀγραφίου καὶ μοιχείας (there is no reason to suppose that this list is exhaustive; cf. p. 15, n. 2), Phot. s.v. παρακατάστασις· . . . κατεβάλλετο δὲ καὶ τοῖς θεσμοθέταις ἐπί τισι γραφαῖς, Andok. 1 *Myst.* 120, Isai. 3 *Pyrrh.* 47, Harpokr. s.v. παράστασις; Lipsius, *AR* 72, 827 f., Bu. Sw. 1097.

[4] For the fee paid to public arbitrators see p. 67.

[5] In certain kinds of διαδικασίαι there was no πρόσκλησις, and therefore the date for the ἀνάκρισις must have been fixed otherwise. We can only conjecture that it was done by some form of public notice.

[6] On ἀνάκρισις see especially Lipsius, *AR* 829 ff., Bo. Sm. i. 283 ff., Lämmli, *Prozeß.* 74 ff., Gernet, *DSGA* 115 ff., N. J. Pantazopoulos, *Festschrift Koschaker* (Weimar, 1939) iii. 204 ff., Wolff, *Traditio* 4 (1946) 67 ff. (*Beitr.* 60 ff.), *Paragraphe* 120, 127.

evidence. We can however be sure that it embraced questions put to the litigants by the magistrate and by each other, as its name implies, and that there might be adjournments of the procedure to enable one or other litigant to furnish correct answers to these questions.[1] It is much more difficult to define precisely what the aim of this questioning might be, and in general what the purpose of the whole procedure was and what powers were therein reserved to the presiding magistrate. A parallel, though one to be used with caution, is that with the Roman procedure *in iure*. In both cases the aim in very general terms was to define the issue juristically in such a way that a straight condemnation or acquittal of the defendant could be pronounced, in Rome by the *iudex*, in Athens by the dikastery.

The questions in Isai. 6 *Philokt.* 12 were put by the plaintiff in a *δίκη ψευδομαρτυρίων*, and were designed to elicit the exact relationship alleged to exist between two boys on whose behalf an estate was being claimed and the *de cuius*. It is to be noted that the archon orders the defendants to answer the question, though his power must be regarded as a pale reflection of the Roman magistrate's *imperium*. A more difficult, though still more important, case occurs in Isai. 10 *Aristarch.* 2. The speaker there is claiming the estate of Aristarchos I through his mother, who was Aristarchos I's daughter. Aristarchos I had had a son, Kyronides, but he had been adopted by his maternal grandfather and had therefore left Aristarchos' house. Kyronides married and had two sons, Xenainetos and Aristarchos II. The latter was posthumously adopted as son of Aristarchos I, and thus became heir to his property; when he died he left it by will to his brother Xenainetos. The speaker claimed that all these transactions were invalid, since his mother was entitled to succeed to her father, Aristarchos I, and he through her; but, and here is the point, he was compelled at the *ἀνάκρισις* to describe his mother as sister of Aristarchos II, and this was very damaging to his case, which depended on the contention that in fact Kyronides, and therefore his son Aristarchos II, had left the house of Aristarchos I. Here then we have the archon—for it must be his fiat which

[1] Isai. 6 *Philokt.* 12, 10 *Aristarch.* 2, Xen. *Symp.* 5. 2, Harpokr. s.v. *ἀνάκρισις*. The verb used of the magistrate is *ἀνακρίνειν* in the active (Dem. 48 *Olymp.* 31, Isai. 5 *Dikaiog.* 32, Ar. *Ath. Pol.* 56. 6), of the litigants *ἀνακρίνεσθαι* in the middle (Dem. 21 *Meid.* 103, 53 *Nikostr.* 14, 17), of the case *ἀνακρίνεσθαι* in the passive (Dem. 48 *Olymp.* 23).

'compelled' the speaker to use this description of his mother—empowered to insist on a point damaging to a litigant's case.[1] But we should not overstress this: it did not prevent the speaker arguing that in truth his mother was not legally the sister of Aristarchos II; in other words, it was left to the dikastery to override the archon's ruling in this case. Under the Roman formulary system the *iudex* would certainly not have had any such latitude.

There must however have been cases, especially in the sphere of succession, where the archon had perforce to take a decision on facts with legal significance, for in a *διαδικασία* where there were a number of claimants of different degrees of relationship to the *de cuius* we know that there might be a corresponding number of voting urns (*καδίσκοι*) each of which would be common to those who bore the same relationship; the allotting of the litigants to the several urns must in the last resort have rested with the magistrate at the *ἀνάκρισις*, though there may well have been some means unknown to us of challenging his decision in a court.[2] This function of the archon in the *ἀνάκρισις* of succession cases incidentally makes it difficult to believe, as most scholars do, that in the famous case of Hagnias' inheritance Theopompos managed to get away with a claim based on a flagrant misdescription of his relationship to the *de cuius*.[3]

For the sort of question put in other kinds of case at the *ἀνάκρισις* we are left to conjecture. Bonner and Smith (i. 289) have the following plausible suggestions: 'Was the plaintiff eligible to appear in court? Was the defendant qualified to answer the charge or the claim? If the defendant failed to appear, had he been duly summoned? Were the documents—plaint or indictment—properly drawn? Was the matter at issue actionable? Was the proper form of action chosen? Did the magistrate have jurisdiction in the case? Was the action brought at the proper time according to law? Was the matter *res judicata*?' The object of the exercise was to determine first whether there was an

[1] Isai. 10 *Aristarch.* 2 *ἠνάγκασμαι μὲν οὖν, ὦ ἄνδρες, διὰ τὸ μὴ δύνασθαι δίκην παρ' αὐτῶν λαβεῖν, τὴν μητέρα τὴν ἐμὴν ἐν τῇ ἀνακρίσει Ἀριστάρχου εἶναι ἀδελφὴν προσγράψασθαι.*

[2] Isai. 11 *Hagn.* 21 *τοῖς δὲ κατὰ ταὐτὰ ἀμφισβητοῦσιν εἷς τίθεται καδίσκος, οὗ οὐκ ἂν ἦν τὸν μὲν ἡττᾶσθαι τὸν δὲ νικᾶν, ἀλλ' ὁμοίως ἀμφοτέροις ἦν ὁ αὐτὸς κίνδυνος*, Dem. 43 *Makart.* 10.

[3] Vol. i, p. 143, n. 1; cf. now Lacey, *Family* 246, n. 82.

issue to be put to a dikastery (whether the case was εἰσαγώγιμος), and second how exactly the question was to be framed. Some, if not all, of these questions must have arisen at the preliminary stage when the plaintiff made his first approach to the magistrate.

One point of serious controversy is what amount of evidence had to be produced by the litigants at the ἀνάκρισις. At one time the prevailing view was that the procedure followed in arbitration cases on appeal, where all the evidence given before the arbitrator was filed and on appeal to a dikastery litigants were restricted to that evidence, applied to other cases, so that all the evidence that a litigant wished to use had to be produced by him at the ἀνάκρισις. A more recent, and better, view is that the procedure in arbitration was peculiar to it, and that where there was no reference to an arbitrator all that was required of litigants at the ἀνάκρισις was evidence to satisfy the magistrate that their answers to the kind of questions suggested above were *prima facie* correct; it would have been perfectly open to the litigants to vary this evidence or introduce new evidence at the hearing in chief.[1] The argument for this second view is mainly negative: the procedure of sealing all the evidence up in a casket is never mentioned except in connection with cases where it is known there had been an arbitration; the positive cases where a litigant appears to produce a piece of new evidence do not amount to much.[2] There is however a good reason why the rule should have been different for arbitration cases: in them the arbitrator had given a decision which one of the two parties had declined to accept; natural justice required that the dikastery in pronouncing on the same case should do so only on the evidence which had been before the arbitrator. No such consideration applied in other cases. There is also the probability that written

[1] Bonner, *Evidence* 48 ff., Lipsius, *AR* 838, Bo. Sm. i. 283 ff., Lämmli, *Prozeß.* 75 ff., A. P. Dorjahn, *TAPA* 66 (1935) 274 ff., *CP* 36 (1941) 182 ff.

[2] In Plut. *Aristeid.* 25 Kallias, observing that his prosecutors were making an impression on the jury by denigrating his treatment of his kinsman Aristeides, called on Aristeides to give evidence that he had refused financial aid from Kallias; but (as Lämmli, *Prozeß.* 107, points out) this may have been an exception made in favour of a hard-pressed defendant. In Isok. 18 *Kallim.* 52 ff. in a homicide case the allegedly dead person was produced alive by the defence not at the ἀνάκρισις but at the hearing in chief; again this is an obviously exceptional case, and it would be absurd to suppose that in the interests of a procedural rule the Athenians would have allowed a man to be condemned for the manslaughter of a person who was demonstrably alive.

evidence and pleadings did not become mandatory until 378/7 B.C. (see p. 99), and until that happened there can have been no such restricting rule.

We should not however press this negative conclusion too far. The fragmentary nature of our evidence on what actually took place at an ἀνάκρισις makes it impossible to decide whether the questions in it were strictly limited to the legal points as outlined by Bonner and Smith (see p. 96),[1] or whether by being spread wider they could be used to uncover an opponent's proposed method of attack or defence.[2] Whatever the rule was, we may safely conjecture that its enforcement would have varied considerably in accordance with the views of the individual magistrates, since it must have rested with them whether an answer was to be mandatory or not.[3]

At first procedure at the ἀνάκρισις was probably oral. In the forensic speeches of Antiphon, Andokides, Lysias, and Isokrates amid a studied variety of terms for the opening of an action there is none that can be construed as alluding to the handing in of written pleas by the litigants, and this can hardly be an accident.[4] By the time of Demosthenes however language is regularly used which implies the handing in of written pleas as an element in the initial procedure.[5] A plausible date for the introduction of this

[1] Leisi, *Zeuge* 83 f., Bo. Sm. i. 291 ('there is no indication that a litigant ever discovered anything at the *anakrisis* regarding his opponent's proposed plan of conducting his case').

[2] Lämmli, *Prozeß.* 84 ff., basing himself mainly on the law in Dem. 46 *Steph.* ii. 10 (τοῖν ἀντιδίκοιν ἐπάναγκες εἶναι ἀποκρίνασθαι ἀλλήλοις τὸ ἐρωτώμενον, μαρτυρεῖν δὲ μή), a law which is to be taken seriously and not (with Latte, *HR* 16, n. 27) brushed aside as an archaic survival, holds that the ἀνάκρισις gave litigants some chance of seeing into their opponents' cards; for they could put questions to them which the opponents had to answer, though they were not forced to furnish evidence on the points raised.

[3] For an example of a litigant taking advantage of an answer (presumably in an ἀνάκρισις) to change his tactics see Isai. fr. 1 Th.; but we cannot tell there what the aim of the questioning had been. In Isai. 6 *Philokt.* 12 the questions were clearly related to the issue whether the case was εἰσαγώγιμος. The exact bearing on this issue of the questioning at an ἀνάκρισις recorded in Dem. 53 *Nikostr.* 22 is not clear, and the same is true of Dem. 47 *Euerg.* 10, though both passages suggest that the questioning might be pretty wide (Lipsius, *AR* 838). See also Isai. 6 *Philokt.* 16, where answers to an abortive interrogation are recorded and read out.

[4] G. M. Calhoun, *TAPA* 50 (1919) 177 ff.

[5] γραφὰς ἀποφέρειν in Dem. 19 *Embassy* 257, 23 *Aristokr.* 5, 27 *Aphob.* i. 12 (in a private suit). Writing is referred to in Dem. 29 *Aphob.* iii. 30 (not a speech to be used lightly as evidence, but a fair guide on a point like this), 32 *Zenoth.* 4, 36 *For Phorm.* 20.

new rule is the archonship of Nausinikos, 378/7 B.C., when it is likely that two other changes in judicial procedure were initiated, the rule that evidence had to be written and some change in the method of selecting jury panels (see p. 241). The plea of the plaintiff was answered by a counter-plea in writing put in by the defendant.[1]

At some point in the *ἀνάκρισις* both parties had to take an oath. A general discussion of the part played by oaths in Athenian judicial procedure is reserved for the section on methods of proof (pp. 150 ff.). Here it must suffice to say that in very early days oaths, sometimes described as evidentiary oaths, were the normal way of settling disputes, parallel to trial by ordeal. One or both parties would swear to the truth of their contentions; if one did not swear, the issue was decided in favour of the other; if both swore, it was clear that one was perjured, but it was left to the gods to adjust any wrong which resulted if his cause prevailed.[2] It was as a relic of this primitive procedure that both litigants were required to take an oath at the *ἀνάκρισις*. The terminology was confused. Pollux (8. 55) says that the oath sworn by the plaintiff that his plaint was true (*ἦ μὴν ἀληθῆ κατηγορεῖν*) was *προωμοσία*, and the oath of the defendant that he was doing no wrong (*ἦ μὴν μὴ ἀδικεῖν*) was *ἀντωμοσία*. The word *προωμοσία* however does not appear elsewhere, and the corresponding words in the Suda are *διωμοσία* and *ἀντωμοσία* (s.vv.). In the orators the tendency is for the word *ἀντωμοσία* to be used of the oath of either party at the *ἀνάκρισις* (as well as being used in other senses).[3] These oaths seem to have been specifically to the truth of the pleas in the documents handed in, rather than oaths that

[1] Dem. 45 *Steph.* i. 46, 87. This use of the word *ἀντιγραφή* must be distinguished from its other uses (see p. 131, n. 3).

[2] Bo. Sm. i. 27 f., 49 ff., 173 ff., ii. 145 ff., Latte, *HR* 19 ff., Gernet, *Plat.* p. cxlv. *An. Bekk.* (*Λέξ. Ῥητ.*) 242. 19 ff. *δοξασταί· κριταί εἰσιν οἱ διαγινώσκοντες, πότερος εὐορκεῖ τῶν κρινομένων. κελεύει γὰρ Σόλων τὸν ἐγκαλούμενον, ἐπειδὰν μήτε συμβόλαια ἔχῃ μήτε μάρτυρας, ὀμνύναι, καὶ τὸν εὐθύνοντα δὲ ὁμοίως*: this probably means that Solon introduced a rule by which the magistrate could require both parties to take an oath that their pleadings were true (cf. Bo. Sm. ii. 161). The grammarian has falsely deduced, probably from some passage similar to Ant. 5 *Her.* 94, that there were special officers called *δοξασταί*; there is no reason however to doubt the reference to a law of Solon.

[3] Isok. 16 *Chariot* 2, Isai. 3 *Pyrrh.* 6, 5 *Dikaiog.* 1, 16, 9 *Astyph.* 1, 34, Harpokr. s.v. *ἀντωμοσία*, *An. Bekk.* (*Λέξ. Ῥητ.*) 200. 16 ff. The form *διωμοσία* is specially connected with homicide and, as always, the procedure in homicide cases has peculiarities; cf. MacDowell, *Homicide* 90 ff.

everything the litigant was going to say would be true. Even so the taking of them did imply that one or other of the litigants was perjured, and it was this consideration which led Plato to exclude them from his state in the *Laws*.[1] There is no good foundation for the view that there were circumstances in which one or other party could evade this preliminary oath.[2]

In a διαδικασία, where there was no plaintiff or defendant, the contestants had none the less to state their respective claims in documents called ἀντιγραφαί[3] and swear to the truth of what was stated.[4]

If the defendant wished to plead that for some reason or another the action did not lie, which might be his only answer to the plaintiff or might be in addition to rebuttal of the facts alleged against him, he incorporated this point in his document before the exchange of oaths,[5] and thereon, from 401 B.C. onwards at least, this plea became a separate issue on which a dikastery had to pronounce before there could be a judgement on the main issue. This preliminary procedure was called παραγραφή, and there is controversy on the degree to which it was separated from the trial of the main issue; there is a theory that in principle

[1] Plato, *Laws* 948 d ἐν γὰρ λήξεσιν δικῶν τοὺς μετὰ νοῦ τιθεμένους νόμους ἐξαιρεῖν χρὴ τοὺς ὅρκους τῶν ἀντιδικούντων ἑκατέρων, καὶ τὸν λαγχάνοντά τῳ τινα δίκην τὰ μὲν ἐγκλήματα γράφειν, ὅρκον δὲ μὴ ἐπομνύναι, καὶ τὸν φεύγοντα κατὰ ταὐτὰ τὴν ἄρνησιν γράψαντα παραδοῦναι τοῖς ἄρχουσιν ἀνώμοτον. δεινὸν γάρ που, δικῶν γ' ἐν πόλει πολλῶν γενομένων, εὖ εἰδέναι σμικροῦ δεῖν τοὺς ἡμίσεις αὐτῶν ἐπιωρκηκότας.

[2] M. H. Hudtwalcker, *Über die öffentlichen und Privat-Schiedsrichter — Diäteten — in Athen* (Jena, 1812) 76, n. 17, argued this from Isai. 11 *Hagn.* 6; MSL 825, n. 178, urged that all that Theopompos is saying there is that certain facts had not been covered in his opponent's sworn statement which should have been covered, not that there had been no sworn statement at all. Lipsius, *AR* 833, n. 16, following K. Mederle, *De iurisiurandi in lite Attica decem oratorum aetate usu* (Munich, 1902) 12 f., has an equally possible reply to Hudtwalcker, that Theopompos is not referring to the ἀνάκρισις in this passage, but to a challenge offered and refused in the course of the trial. The other passage cited to show the possibility of evading the oath is Ant. 5 *Her.* 11; but the speaker there is merely underlining the fact that his opponent had not brought against him a straightforward homicide charge, which involved a particularly solemn oath.

[3] Isai. 6 *Philokt.* 52, 11 *Hagn.* 17, Dem. 44 *Leoch.* 39, 48 *Olymp.* 31, Harpokr. s.v. ἀντιγραφή.

[4] Dem. 43 *Makart.* 3 γένει μὲν ὡς ἐγγυτέρω τις εἴη αὐτῶν τῆς γυναικός, οὐδ' ἐπεχείρησεν οὐδεὶς ἀντομόσαι.

[5] Isai. 5 *Dikaiog.* 16 μελλόντων δ' ἡμῶν ἀντόμνυσθαι διεμαρτύρησε Λεωχάρης οὑτοσὶ μὴ ἐπίδικον εἶναι τὸν κλῆρον ἡμῖν. This is a διαδικασία in an inheritance suit, but we may perhaps safely assume that the same procedure would have applied *mutatis mutandis* in δίκαι and γραφαί.

the trial in such circumstances was indivisible and was conducted at one hearing before the same jurors. This theory will have to be examined in detail when we come to deal with special pleas (see pp. 106 ff.). We may perhaps presume that a defendant who had not appeared at the preliminary stage but did appear at the *ἀνάκρισις* waived his right to plead that he had not been summoned.[1]

A peculiar and somewhat archaic form of procedure for dealing with the question whether an issue was actionable was that known as *διαμαρτυρία*. This again will come up for discussion in the section on special pleas. All that need be said here is that in certain cases, primarily inheritance cases, but also certain *γραφαί*, a litigant could himself make or procure from some witness a formal statement either that the suit was or that it was not *εἰσαγώγιμος*. In such a case his opponent could bring against whoever made the statement a *δίκη ψευδομαρτυρίων*, and this, like a *παραγραφή*, had to be passed upon before the main issue was tried. If the statement was not challenged in this way, then if it had proceeded from the plaintiff the main issue came on for immediate trial, if it had proceeded from the defendant he was acquitted without further trial.[2]

When there was no plea that the case was not *εἰσαγώγιμος* or such plea had been rejected, where the suit was a private one and the value of the plaintiff's claim exceeded ten drachmai, it would in many cases be referred by the magistrate to a public arbitrator. (For the types of cases so qualified see pp. 19 f.) Part of the proceedings before the arbitrator must have covered ground which in other suits was covered by the *ἀνάκρισις*. In some glimpses which we get of actual arbitrations we can detect the arbitrator doing the same sort of things as the archon is seen doing at the *ἀνάκρισις* in the cases of the estates of Philoktemon and Aristarchos (see pp. 95 f.).[3] Evidence given before the arbitrator could neither be changed nor added to at the hearing

[1] So Berneker, *RE* s.v. *πρόσκλησις* 851, but it is a presumption.

[2] Paoli, *St. Proc.* 101 ff., 143 ff., 170 ff., argues against the view that *διαμαρτυρία* was a special case of *παραγραφή*. On the other side Wolff, *Paragraphe* 125, n. 43, holds that the differences between the two procedures were merely external. See too Gernet, *DSGA* 86, Lämmli, *Prozeß.* 146 ff.

[3] Dem. 21 *Meid.* 84 *ὑπωμοσίαι καὶ παραγραφαί*, 47 *Euerg.* 45 *ὁ μὲν Θεόφημος παρεγράφετο καὶ ὑπώμνυτο*. Here *παραγραφή* has nothing to do with the technical use of the word for a plea that the suit was not *εἰσαγώγιμος*; see p. 108, n. 1.

in chief.[1] This meant that the arbitrator's role in conducting a kind of ἀνάκρισις differed from that of the magistrate in an ἀνάκρισις proper, since there is no ground for supposing that evidence given before the latter could not be altered or added to when the trial itself came along (see p. 97). This difference would have been of considerable importance if, as Calhoun argued,[2] an arbitrator could of his own motion decline a παραγραφή, since it would have put the litigant who raised a παραγραφή at the arbitration at a greater disadvantage than one who did so at a magistrate's ἀνάκρισις. It is however not easy to see how in practice the issues proper to be discussed in a παραγραφή could have been left as such to an arbitrator. Once the idea of a παραγραφή as a procedure for settling in advance certain legal issues was accepted, it is difficult to see how these issues can have been left unsettled when a case was remitted to arbitration.[3]

An ἀνάκρισις could be adjourned from day to day. Thus in the Philoktemon case one party procured an adjournment to procure some evidence from Lemnos,[4] and there is reference to 'the first ἀνάκρισις' in the Nikostratos case.[5] The adjournments by agreement of the parties referred to in Dem. 42 *Phain.* 13 probably included adjournments of the ἀνάκρισις. We must suppose that it lay within the magistrate's discretion what adjournments he would allow.

If the prosecutor or plaintiff failed to appear at the ἀνάκρισις, judgement went to the defendant and, if the case was a γραφή, the prosecutor was fined 1,000 drachmai (see p. 83). If the defendant failed to appear at the ἀνάκρισις, he lost his case.[6]

[1] Dem. 39 *Boiot.* i. 17 *ταῦτα δ' εἰ μὴ σεσημασμένων ἤδη συνέβη τῶν ἐχίνων, κἂν μάρτυρας ὑμῖν παρεσχόμην* (that this was an arbitrated case is highly probable, though not certain; the assumption of Gernet, *Dem.* ii. 13, n. 2, that it is seems to rest on a circular argument), Ar. *Ath. Pol.* 53. 3.

[2] Calhoun, *CP* 14 (1919) 22 ff.

[3] Wolff, *Paragraphe* 134 f., questions Calhoun's hypothesis that a παραγραφή could be laid before a public arbitrator so long as he had not given a decision; in Dem. 47 *Euerg.* 45, though the word παρεγράφετο is used, there is nothing in the context or the whole story to suggest any possible ground for a technical παραγραφή. Bo. Sm. ii. 92 ff. agree with Calhoun. Steinwenter, *Streit.* 62, believes that one object of the law on arbitration was to save magistrates' time by relieving them of the ἀνάκρισις.

[4] Isai. 6 *Philokt.* 13.

[5] Dem. 53 *Nikostr.* 22.

[6] Ant. 5 *Her.* 13 is hardly conclusive as to this, as it refers to a homicide charge and the speaker is an alien. Dem. 32 *Zenoth.* 26 f. is equally inconclusive, since we cannot be sure whether Protos was condemned by default at the ἀνάκρισις or at a trial. But the statement may stand on *a priori* grounds.

We find a plaintiff withdrawing a case from a public arbitrator,[1] and there are recorded cases where suits were actually withdrawn from the jurors, on one occasion even after they had voted.[2] *A fortiori* private suits, at least, could be withdrawn by the plaintiff at the *ἀνάκρισις* stage. For this purpose the *δίκη φόνου* did not count as a private suit, since Demosthenes was fined by the Areopagos for abandoning a prosecution of Demomeles for *τραῦμα ἐκ προνοίας*.[3]

On the other hand a prosecutor was not permitted to drop a charge in a *γραφή*;[4] if he did, he was fined 1,000 drachmai (see p. 83). There is an apparent exception to this rule when Apollodoros alleges that he had been willing to withdraw his *γραφὴ ξενίας* against Neaira if his opponent, Stephanos, was willing to hand over for examination under torture some slaves who might have testified that the children alleged in the indictment to be Neaira's were in fact not hers.[5] Had this fact been established, it would have entirely undermined Apollodoros' case, since it could have been argued that Neaira was living with Stephanos simply as a courtesan and not as purporting to be able to give birth to children who would be Athenian citizens. It may be that where such a challenge was issued it was in the power of the magistrate to allow it to proceed with the understanding that the prosecutor could then withdraw without penalty. But perhaps we should not

[1] Dem. 52 *Kallip.* 14 *λαχὼν δὲ παρὰ μὲν τοῦ διαιτητοῦ ἀνείλετο τὸ γραμματεῖον, προὐκαλέσατο δ' αὐτὸν ἐπιτρέψαι Λυσιθείδῃ.*

[2] Isok. 18 *Kallim.* 39 *ἔτι καὶ νῦν ἔξεστιν αὐτῷ, πρὶν ἀποπειραθῆναι τῆς ὑμετέρας γνώμης, ἀφέντι τὴν δίκην ἀπηλλάχθαι πάντων τῶν πραγμάτων*, Isai. 5 *Dikaiog.* 31, Dem. 34 *Ag. Phorm.* 18, 37 *Pant.* 39 ff. In Isai. 5 *Dikaiog.* 17 a compromise was reached even after the votes had been cast, but before they had been counted. Dem. 48 *Olymp.* 3 implies that a suit could be withdrawn from the jury by consent of the parties at the last moment. Wolff, *Paragraphe* 111, regards the conclusion as doubtful, but quotes only the Isokrates passage.

[3] Aischin. 2 *Embassy* 93 *πρότερον δ' ὑπέμεινας τὴν ἐπιβολὴν τῆς βουλῆς τῆς ἐξ Ἀρείου πάγου, οὐκ ἐπεξιὼν τῇ τοῦ τραύματος γραφῇ, ἣν ἐγράψω Δημομέλην τὸν Παιανιέα.* Here the *γραφή* is perhaps the charge, not the type of action.

[4] Dem. 58 *Theokr.* 20 expresses the principle involved: *οὐ γὰρ ἐὰν Κτησικλῆς ὁ μέτοικος συγχωρήσῃ τούτῳ, πονηρὸς πονηρῷ, μὴ παραδοθῆναι τοῖς πράκτορσιν τὸν προσοφλόντα κατὰ τὸν νόμον, διὰ τοῦτο δεῖ τὴν πόλιν ἀπεστερῆσθαι τῶν ἐκ τῶν νόμων ἐπικειμένων ζημιῶν, ἀλλὰ προσήκει τοὺς ἀντιδίκους ὑπὲρ μὲν τῶν ἰδίων, ὅπως ἂν αὐτοὺς πείθωσιν, διοικεῖσθαι πρὸς ἀλλήλους, ὑπὲρ δὲ τῶν πρὸς τὸ δημόσιον, ὅπως ἂν οἱ νόμοι κελεύωσιν.*

[5] Dem. 59 *Neair.* 121 *καὶ ἐὰν φαίνηται ἐκ τῆς βασάνου γήμας Στέφανος οὑτοσὶ ἀστὴν γυναῖκα καὶ ὄντες αὐτῷ οἱ παῖδες οὗτοι ἐξ ἑτέρας γυναικὸς ἀστῆς καὶ μὴ Νεαίρας, ἤθελον ἀφίστασθαι τοῦ ἀγῶνος καὶ μὴ εἰσιέναι τὴν γραφὴν ταύτην.*

lay too much stress on a hypothetical promise.[1] On the other hand we may perhaps conclude from the fact that Theokrines withdrew from a prosecution in an *εἰσαγγελία κακώσεως ὀρφανοῦ* without any apparent penalty[2] that the rule did not apply in such cases; this would be logical, since we know that prosecutors in those cases were not penalized if they failed to secure one-fifth of the votes (vol. i, p. 118), and if there had been the penalty for withdrawing no prosecutor in his senses would have withdrawn. We find mention of other cases where public suits were withdrawn by composition, sometimes paid for, with the accused.[3] In fact this practice became sufficiently common to attract a regular terminology, recorded in Poll. 8. 143, of which the most important word was *καθυφίημι*, with much the same sense as the Latin *praevarico*.[4] We can safely reject the statement of Pollux that there was a *δίκη καθυφέσεως* available against prosecutors who behaved in this way;[5] in any case such a suit would surely have been a *γραφή*. But it is not easy to see where such action ceased to be merely something which was regarded as slightly disreputable and became definitely actionable, or in other words to be quite sure what powers a magistrate had to remove a cause from the list and thus free the prosecutor from liability. Here again there was a technical term, *διαγράφω* for the magistrate and *διαγράφομαι* for the prosecutor; and the fact that this word is used (once at least) of the prosecutor in a *γραφή* suggests that there were ways in which the operation

[1] Lipsius, *AR* 843, n. 55; but note that the *πρόκλησις* was not, as he there asserts, a challenge to produce evidence of Neaira's citizenship.

[2] Dem. 58 *Theokr.* 32 *προσκαλεσάμενος τὸν Πολύευκτον ἀποφέρει γραφὴν κατ' αὐτοῦ κακώσεως πρὸς τὸν ἄρχοντα καὶ δίδωσι τὴν λῆξιν Μνησαρχίδῃ τῷ παρέδρῳ· λαβὼν δὲ διακοσίας δραχμὰς παρὰ τοῦ Πολυεύκτου, καὶ τὰ δεινὰ ταῦτ' ἀποδόμενος μικροῦ λήμματος ἐφ' οἷς τῷ πατρὶ ἐτιμήσατο δέκα ταλάντων, ἀπηλλάγη καὶ τὴν γραφὴν ἀνείλετο προδοὺς τὸν ὀρφανόν.*

[3] In Dem. 59 *Neair.* 53 Phrastor, having laid a *γραφή* against Stephanos with the thesmothetai for having given the daughter of a foreign woman away in marriage to an Athenian citizen by *ἐγγύη*, withdraws the *γραφή* in return for Stephanos' withdrawing a *δίκη σίτου* against him and renouncing a dowry. A similar situation is described ibid. 68 f. In Lys. 6 *Andok.* 12 a *γραφή ἀσεβείας* is withdrawn on payment of money by the accused. In Dem. 21 *Meid.* 39 accusations are not pursued, but we cannot specify at what stage of the proceedings.

[4] Dem. 21 *Meid.* 151, 23 *Aristokr.* 96, 58 *Theokr.* 6, 12, 34; of the thesmothetes in 21 *Meid.* 39.

[5] For the possibility that the *δίκη καθυφέσεως* of Poll. 8. 143 had a quite different aim, the protection of those who had been defrauded by a breach of trust, see Lipsius, *AR* 773, n. 363.

could be carried through so as to immunize the defaulting prosecutor.[1]

There may have been exceptional cases where an ἀνάκρισις could have been reasonably dispensed with. Lipsius suggests that this happened when the ekklesia appointed commissioners (ζητηταί) to carry out special investigations;[2] he assumes that these commissioners had ἡγεμονία of an extraordinary court, but on this see p. 35. On other special occasions the people deputed the task of a preliminary inquiry to the Areopagos; the report of that body (ἀπόφασις) was laid before the ekklesia, who then appointed accusers to argue the case before a dikastery.[3] The examination by the Areopagos clearly dispensed with the need for an ἀνάκρισις.

§ 6. *Special pleas*

(i) *Introduction*

As we have seen, one purpose of the procedure up to and including the ἀνάκρισις was to determine whether the action initiated by the plaintiff was maintainable (εἰσαγώγιμος) or not. A magistrate had the power to decline to introduce a case, and so far as we can tell a plaintiff who was thus non-suited had no redress save to attack the magistrate at his εὔθυνα, which did not help him in the specific matter on which he was suing. We can assume fairly safely that only in the most obvious cases would a magistrate have refused out of hand to introduce a suit, cases where for example the plaintiff was demonstrably not entitled to plead or had chosen the wrong magistrate. In other cases, where the issue could reasonably be in doubt, the procedure differed at different epochs, and at least one important change took place within our period, the period of the orators.[4]

[1] In Dem. 48 *Olymp.* 26 the archon διέγραψε τὴν ἀμφισβήτησιν (this was a private suit). In 58 *Theokr.* 8 Theokrines, having received money, allowed a φάσις to be διαγραφῆναι just when the magistrates were going to open the ἀνάκρισις. In 20 *Lept.* 145 a prosecutor in a γραφή, under suasion from the defendant, διεγράψατο. In Isai. 5 *Dikaiog.* 17 ἡ λῆξις τοῦ κλήρου διεγράφη when a witness was put forward that the estate was not claimable by law, and the suit had to be postponed till the δίκη ψευδομαρτυρίων had been settled. In Lys. 17 δημ. ἀδ. 5 the middle (if the emendation is accepted) is used of a defendant getting a suit taken out of a list. Cf. Harpokr. s.v. διαγράψασθαι.

[2] Lipsius, *AR* 988 (addition to p. 844).

[3] This was how the Harpalos scandal was dealt with: Dein. 1 *Dem.* 51, 58, 2 *Aristogeit.* 6, Hyper. 1 *Dem.* 38.

[4] On this topic see Wilamowitz, *A. und A.* ii. 368 ff., Lipsius, *AR* 845 ff., Paoli, *St. Proc.* 77 ff., Bo. Sm. ii. 75 ff., Gernet, *RHD* 6 (1927) 5 ff. (*DSGA* 83 ff.),

When the magistrates were the sole judicial organ (pp. 1 ff.), this problem did not arise; a magistrate's decision on the particular issue before him was taken in the light of all the facts before him, including the facts bearing on the admissibility of the plea or charge, the capacity of the litigants, and so forth. In the early days of the heliaia and the dikasteries, when they were acting simply as courts of appeal from magistrates' decisions, we have no clue as to the kind of issues that were raised on appeal, but it is safe to conjecture that these would have embraced, as well as questions of fact, the sort of questions of law that later became the subject of a *παραγραφή*. We are however very much in the dark about procedure during the latter half of the fifth century, a period during which the magistrate's role was no longer to give a decision from which the litigants could appeal, but merely to conduct the *ἀνάκρισις* and preside at the trial, while on the other hand the system of *παραγραφαί* which prevailed in the fourth century had not been devised.

(ii) *παραγραφή*

Amid the controversy which surrounds the institution of the *παραγραφή* one point stands clear of controversy. There was a law proposed by Archinos and passed in 403/2 B.C. which marked an epoch in the development of the *παραγραφή*. We have not the text of the law; only a reference to it in Isokrates' speech against Kallimachos, delivered not long after the law had been passed.[1] According to the speaker the aim of the law had been to bolster

Lämmli, *Prozeß.* 146 ff. (with review by A. Biscardi in *Riv. Fil.* 68 (1940) 131 f.), Calhoun, *CP* 13 (1918) 169 ff., 14 (1919) 20 ff., 338 ff., W. Hellebrand, *RE* s.v. *παραγραφή*, A. Biscardi in *Novissimo Digesto Italiano* s.v. 'Giudizi paragrafici', E. Schönbauer, *AAW* (1964) 203 ff., Wolff, *Paragraphe.*

[1] Isok. 18 *Kallim.* 1 ff. *εἰ μὲν καὶ ἄλλοι τινὲς ἦσαν ἠγωνισμένοι τοιαύτην παραγραφήν, ἀπ' αὐτοῦ τοῦ πράγματος ἠρχόμην ἂν τοὺς λόγους ποιεῖσθαι· νῦν δ' ἀνάγκη περὶ τοῦ νόμου πρῶτον εἰπεῖν καθ' ὃν εἰσεληλύθαμεν, ἵν' ἐπιστάμενοι περὶ ὧν ἀμφισβητοῦμεν τὴν ψῆφον φέρητε, καὶ μηδεὶς ὑμῶν θαυμάσῃ διότι φεύγων τὴν δίκην πρότερος λέγω τοῦ διώκοντος. ἐπειδὴ γὰρ ἐκ Πειραιέως κατελθόντες ἐνίους ἑωρᾶτε τῶν πολιτῶν συκοφαντεῖν ὡρμημένους καὶ τὰς συνθήκας λύειν ἐπιχειροῦντας, βουλόμενοι τούτους τε παῦσαι καὶ τοῖς ἄλλοις ἐπιδεῖξαι ὅτι οὐκ ἀναγκασθέντες ἐποιήσασθ' αὐτὰς ἀλλ' ἡγούμενοι τῇ πόλει συμφέρειν, εἰπόντος Ἀρχίνου νόμον ἔθεσθε, ἄν τις δικάζηται παρὰ τοὺς ὅρκους, ἐξεῖναι τῷ φεύγοντι παραγράψασθαι, τοὺς δ' ἄρχοντας περὶ τούτου πρῶτον εἰσάγειν, λέγειν δὲ πρότερον τὸν παραγραψάμενον, ὁπότερος δ' ἂν ἡττηθῇ, τὴν ἐπωβελίαν ὀφείλειν, ἵν' οἱ τολμῶντες μνησικακεῖν μὴ μόνον ἐπιορκοῦντες ἐξελέγχοιντο μηδὲ τὴν παρὰ τῶν θεῶν τιμωρίαν ὑπομένοιεν ἀλλὰ καὶ παραχρῆμα ζημιοῖντο.*

up the amnesty arrived at after the overthrow of the Thirty and the restoration of the democracy. It laid down that, if anyone brought suit contrary to the oaths sworn at that time, the defendant should be allowed to enter a plea that the action was barred (παραγράψασθαι). The magistrate had then to put this plea before a court, and the defendant spoke first. Whichever litigant lost on this plea had to pay a fine of one-sixth of the value of the claim (ἐπωβελία).[1] The first paragraph of the speech makes it clear that procedurally there was something novel and in need of explanation when the defendant, as this speaker was, spoke first at a preliminary hearing, or, as some would prefer to phrase it, at a preliminary stage of a single hearing. So far Isokrates. We may safely go one step further and assume that, if the defendant won, that was the end of the proceedings and the plaintiff was fined one-sixth for having initiated them; whereas, if the plaintiff won, the main issue was tried and, whichever side won, the defendant had to pay the ἐπωβελία to the state. (This assumes that the ἐπωβελία was imposed on the losing party, however small the majority vote; on this see p. 184.)

There is disagreement among scholars as to the degree of novelty entailed by Archinos' law. On one view, the παραγραφή already existed, and the only new thing was the reversal of the order in which the litigants addressed the court.[2] This view is based largely on the opening words of Isok. 18 *Kallim.* (p. 106, n. 1); it is argued that the phrase τοιαύτην παραγραφήν implies that it is only this particular type of παραγραφή which was new. A better view is that the emphasis in this phrase rests rather on παραγραφήν than on τοιαύτην ('if there were any others who had fought a παραγραφή, as this is', rather than 'such a παραγραφή' as opposed to another kind), and that Archinos' law for the first time set up a specific form of procedure for deputing to a court as a separate issue the question whether a suit was maintainable in those cases where the defendant pleaded the amnesty; at this stage of the proceedings the defendant spoke first.[3]

Our ancient sources for the working of παραγραφαί in the fourth century are abundant. We have nine speeches delivered

[1] For ἐπωβελία cf. Isok. 18 *Kallim.* 35, 37, and see pp. 183 ff.

[2] So Calhoun, *CP* 13 (1918) 170, H. Hommel, *BPW* 44 (1924) 541, Steinwenter, *Streit.* 136, n. 4, Bo. Sm. ii. 78.

[3] Gernet, *DSGA* 84, n. 6, Wolff, *Paragraphe* 88.

either to support or to overthrow a *παραγραφή*, namely Isok. 18 *Kallim.* (about 402 B.C.), Lys. 23 *Pankl.* (roughly the same date), Dem. 32–8 *Zenoth.*, *Apatour.*, *Ag. Phorm.*, *Lakrit.*, *For Phorm.*, *Pant.*, *Nausim.*[1] There are also two rather full statements about the matter in the lexicographers.[2] In the light of this relative wealth of evidence it is surprising, though true, that the exact functioning and purpose of the institution remain something of a mystery. Paoli's study *L'inscindibilità del processo in diritto attico*, published in 1933,[3] opened a controversy to which Wolff's *Die attische Paragraphe* (1966) is the latest and most effective contribution. Paoli's main contention, as the title of his study suggests, was that, though an issue raised by *παραγραφή* had to be determined in advance of the main issue and in determining it the order of speaking was reversed, this was only the first phase of a single debate and the consideration of the main issue followed immediately before the same jury. Biscardi, who followed Paoli closely, even suggested that there might have been no second exchange of speeches after the decision of the *παραγραφή* if that were against the defendant.[4] This view is based principally on the fact, which is not contested, that speakers, whether for or against a *παραγραφή*, by no means limit themselves to the issue raised by the *παραγραφή*, but bring in arguments for or against

[1] Wolff, *Paragraphe* 8, n. 5, 135, is probably right to maintain, against Calhoun, *CP* 14 (1919) 22 ff., and Hellebrand, *RE* s.v. *παραγραφή* 1173, that in Dem. 21 *Meid.* 84, 47 *Euerg.* 39, 45 *παραγράφεσθαι* (*παραγραφή*), appearing in each case joined to *ὑπόμνυσθαι* (*ὑπωμοσία*), is not used in the strict technical sense, but means to advance under oath (seemingly before a public arbitrator) grounds for postponing a decision. See Poll. 8. 60, *Lex. Cant.* s.v. *μὴ οὖσα δίκη*; MSL 910, Lipsius, *AR* 836.

[2] Poll. 8. 57 *παραγραφὴ δ' ἦν ἡ αὐτὴ καὶ διαμαρτυρία, ὅταν τις μὴ εἰσαγώγιμον λέγῃ εἶναι τὴν δίκην ἢ ὡς κεκριμένος ἢ διαίτης γεγενημένης ἢ ὡς ἀφειμένος, ἢ ὡς τῶν χρόνων ἐξηκόντων ἐν οἷς ἔδει κρίνεσθαι . . . οἷον οὐκ εἰσαγγελίας ἀλλὰ παρανόμων, οὐ δημοσίᾳ ἀλλ' ἰδίᾳ, ἢ ὡς οὐ παρὰ τούτοις κρίνεσθαι δέον, οἷον οὐκ ἐν Ἀρείῳ πάγῳ ἀλλ' ἐπὶ Παλλαδίῳ. ἄγραπτος δὲ δίκη ἐκαλεῖτο ἡ ὑπὸ τῆς παραγραφῆς ἀναιρεθεῖσα καὶ διαγραφεῖσα*, Phot. (and Suda) s.v. *παραγραφή· ὅταν λέγῃ τις ὅτι τὸ πρᾶγμα, περὶ οὗ τὸ ἔγκλημά ἐστιν, εἰσήχθη πρότερον εἰς δικαστήριον, καὶ γεγένηται περὶ αὐτοῦ γνῶσις. καὶ διὰ τοῦτό φησι μὴ δεῖν ἔτι περὶ αὐτοῦ συνίστασθαι κρίσιν· μάλιστα δὲ τοὺς νόμους ἀναγινώσκειν τοῖς δικασταῖς, οἳ πλεονάκις δικάζεσθαι περὶ τῶν αὐτῶν οὐ συγχωροῦσι. λέγει δὲ περὶ αὐτοῦ τοῦ πράγματος ἅμα τοῖς δικασταῖς παραδεικνύς, ὡς οἱ πάλαι δικάσαντες καὶ δικαίως καὶ κατὰ τοὺς νόμους ψηφίσαντες. καὶ τοῦτό ἐστι παραγραφή. καὶ ἐπ' ἐκείνῃ τῇ δίκῃ, περὶ ἧς οὐδὲν ὥρισται παρὰ τοῖς νόμοις, οὐδὲ ἔνεστιν αὐτὴν ὁ εἰσάξων, ὥσπερ καὶ τὰς ἄλλας δίκας· τῶν γὰρ ἄλλων δικῶν προστέτακται ἑκάστῳ τῶν ἐν ταῖς ἀρχαῖς εἰσάγειν τινά. παραγράφεσθαι οὖν ἐφεῖται καὶ τοῖς τοσοῦτόν τι ἐγκαλουμένοις, περὶ οὗ οὐ νενομοθέτηται.*

[3] Paoli, *St. Proc.* 77 ff.

[4] Biscardi, *Nov. Dig. It.* s.v. 'Giudizi paragrafici'.

the substantive claim of the plaintiff. Wolff is right to ask what possible reason there could have been for the complete reversal of the order of speaking for the hearing in chief which this view implies, and he seeks to show, with success on the whole, that Paoli has built too much on the fact that speakers did not confine themselves strictly to the issue of the *παραγραφή*.

Taking first speeches of plaintiffs in *παραγραφαί* which have survived,[1] we should expect to find in them a full discussion of the main issue in addition to the issue raised by the *παραγραφή*, since it was manifest that this might be their only opportunity of bringing the former to the notice of the jurors. Nevertheless it can be shown that the speaker's eye is always fixed on the target of convincing the jury that they must reject the *παραγραφή*, and arguments on the principal issue are subordinated to that aim.[2]

Thus in Dem. 34 *Ag. Phorm.* Phormion borrowed 2,000 drachmai from Chrysippos on bottomry for a voyage to Bosporos and back (*ἀμφοτερόπλουν*). On arrival in the Crimea he found conditions unfavourable for trade, and allowed the ship's captain, Lampis, to start back without a return cargo. Lampis suffered shipwreck shortly after starting, though he personally got back to Athens safely, where he told the foregoing story to Chrysippos. When later Phormion himself reappeared in Athens, Chrysippos, accompanied by Lampis, summoned him to meet a claim for repayment of the loan; the process must have been a *δίκη*

[1] Lys. 23 *Pankl.* is not relevant here, since it alone of all the speeches in question does not at any point enter on the merits of the main issue. Ox. Pap. 27. 2464 is a fragment, it seems, of a speech by a plaintiff in a *παραγραφή*. The precise circumstances are largely conjectural, and the editor's reconstruction is not satisfactory. What is clear is that the speaker had sued Demeas in connection with the estate of his grandfather, Demostratos, that he sued him as his quondam guardian, and that Demeas had countered with a *παραγραφή*. We do not know what the basis of the *παραγραφή* was, and the editor does not speculate on this, but only on what defence Demeas might have made to the claims of the speaker. It seems possible that he was alleging that the action did not lie on the ground that he had not been properly constituted guardian: col. iii. 41 ff. *οὐ γὰρ δικαίαν τ[ὴν κ]ατ[ά]στασίν φησιν αὐτῷ γεγονέναι Δημέας*. In any case the speaker recognizes that the first point on which the jurors had to vote was whether the suit was or was not *εἰσαγώγιμος*: col. iii. 11 ff. *καὶ γὰρ ἂν εἴη ἄτοπον εἰ ἐπιτρόπους μὲν καθίστατε τοῖς ὀρφανοῖς ἵνα μηδ' ὑφ' ἑνὸς ἀδικῶνται καὶ ἔχωσι τοὺς βοηθήσοντας, ὑπ' αὐτῶν δὲ τῶν ἐπιτρόπων ἀδικουμένων μὴ εἰσαγώγιμον εἶναι ψηφίζ[ο]ισθε τὴ[ν] δίκ[ην]*.

[2] J. M. Kelly, *Z* 84 (1967) 403, finds it hard to believe that in these speeches the original plaintiff would not have made more explicit reference to the fact that a verdict against him at the *παραγραφή* would preclude him altogether from developing his full case against the defendant, if this was actually so.

ἐμπορική, and it is to be noted in passing that both litigants were foreigners (1, 50). Phormion countered with a *παραγραφή*, the terms of which were read out in court (17), but are not preserved in our text; what we are told is that it specifically did not say that Phormion had repaid the loan to Lampis. Positively the speaker indicates (3) that the ground was that there was no longer any *συμβόλαιον* between the parties, and we may perhaps conjecture that the *παραγραφή* alleged that this was so because there was a *σωθείσης τῆς νεώς* clause in the loan agreement[1] and the sinking of the ship meant that the *συμβόλαιον* on which a *δίκη ἐμπορική* could be based no longer existed.[2] (To qualify for such a suit there had to be a *συμβόλαιον* for imports to and exports from Athens.[3]) After the *παραγραφή* had been entered, but before the case came into court, the whole issue was put before a private arbitrator at the instance of Phormion, and during the hearings by the arbitrator Lampis went back on his previous statements and alleged that Phormion had repaid the whole sum due to Chrysippos to him, Lampis, in Bosporos. The arbitrator however declined to give a ruling on the case and remitted it to the court (21); we should assume that this meant the reinstatement of the *παραγραφή* based on the *σωθείσης τῆς νεώς* condition, with no mention of the alleged repayment to Lampis.[4] If this reconstruction of the case is on the right lines, it can be plausibly argued that Phormion's purpose at this stage was to keep the main issue out of court by maintaining that the action did not lie because the ship had been wrecked. He would thus have been dispensed from proving, what it might have been difficult to prove, that he had repaid the loan to Lampis. Lampis might have felt reluctant to stick to this story in court, since it might have rendered him liable to be sued by Chrysippos. It was in the interest of Chrysippos, on the other hand, to bring out the apparent inconsistency of Phormion's two lines of defence, and

[1] Dem. 34 *Ag. Phorm.* 33 λέγει δὲ ὡς ἡ συγγραφὴ σωθείσης τῆς νεὼς αὐτὸν ἀποδοῦναι κελεύει τὰ χρήματα.

[2] Wolff, *Paragraphe* 64, suggests that the phrase at the end of 3 (πεποιηκέναι γὰρ οὐδὲν ἔξω τῶν ἐν τῇ συγγραφῇ γεγραμμένων), which is very difficult to understand, is a deliberate misinterpretation of the aim of the *παραγραφή*. Kelly, *Z* 84 (1967) 403, disagrees.

[3] Dem. 32 *Zenoth.* 1, 33 *Apatour.* 1, 34 *Ag. Phorm.* 42.

[4] Some scholars, e.g. E. Ziebarth, *Eine Handelsrede aus der Zeit des Demosthenes* (Heidelberg, 1936) 21, have supposed that there was a wholly new beginning to the process after the breakdown of the arbitration; but Wolff, *Paragraphe* 64, n. 86, is right to insist that at that point the original process once more took its course.

in so doing to confuse the minds of the jurors as to the exact point at issue in the *παραγραφή*.[1] On Chrysippos' view, the ship was not travelling at his risk, and the wreck was therefore irrelevant. There is nothing in all this to weaken the view that the issue raised by the *παραγραφή* was treated quite separately from the main issue.

The other speech of a plaintiff in a *παραγραφή* is Dem. 35 *Lakrit.* An Athenian, Androkles, had made a bottomry loan to two Phaselites, Artemon and Apollodoros, brothers of Lakritos, for a voyage to and from the Black Sea. The text of the contract (*συγγραφή*) is given (10 ff.), and is now generally accepted as genuine. Lakritos is not mentioned either in the loan clauses or in the executive clause. Artemon died without repaying the loan, and Androkles brought what was no doubt a *δίκη ἐμπορική* against Lakritos, as heir to Artemon, for the sum. Lakritos countered with a *παραγραφή*, the basis of which seems to have been that, though he had at first acted as heir to Artemon, he had eventually renounced the succession, and that therefore there did not exist between him and Androkles that *συμβόλαιον* which was needed to form a legitimate basis for a *δίκη ἐμπορική*.[2] The issue at the *παραγραφή* was a simple one of law. It seems to have been a principle of the Athenian law of succession that the estate only, and not the heir, was liable for the debts of the *de cuius* (see vol. i, p. 127, however, which takes a different view). The question here is whether this principle meant that any act on the part of the heir which indicated his readiness to take was irrevocable, or whether he could change his mind and renounce if he found the debts more than balanced the assets. Androkles wishes the court to accept the former rule, and states it shortly.[3] In spite of this short reference (there was in fact little else to say on the subject)

[1] Wolff, *Paragraphe* 71. On the following pages Wolff discusses the possibility that Chrysippos was himself confused on the true juristic significance of the *παραγραφή*, but leans to the view that the account is confused designedly.

[2] Demisch, *Schuldenerb.* 18, and Paoli, *St. Dir.* 101, are probably wrong in deducing from 44 ff. that there was a second ground for the *παραγραφή*, viz. that Lakritos was not an *ἔμπορος*. In those paragraphs Androkles is probably trying to cover up the fact that it would have been theoretically possible for him to bring a *δίκη βλάβης* against Lakritos before the polemarch if, as is probable, Lakritos was a metic. Cf. Wolff, *Paragraphe* 75, n. 101, 79.

[3] Dem. 35 *Lakrit.* 4 *οὐκ ἂν ἔχοντος τούτου δεῖξαι νόμον ὅστις αὐτῷ δίδωσιν ἐξουσίαν ἔχειν μὲν τὰ τοῦ ἀδελφοῦ καὶ διῳκηκέναι ὅπως ἐδόκει αὐτῷ, μὴ ἀποδοῦναι δὲ τὰ ἀλλότρια χρήματα, ἀλλὰ λέγειν νῦν ὅτι οὐκ ἔστιν κληρονόμος, ἀλλ' ἀφίσταται τῶν ἐκείνου.*

the whole speech makes it clear that it was of vital importance for the plaintiff to get the case to the further stage of *εὐθυδικία*, and for the defendant to prevent this. This was a matter of the burden of proof, since at the *εὐθυδικία* the defendant would have to deal in detail with the *συγγραφή* and the difficulties of proving that its terms had been carried out, but at the stage of the *παραγραφή* he need not; the contrary suggestion[1] is mere rhetoric. Again there is nothing in the speech to prevent our believing that the issue immediately to be decided was whether suit lay against Lakritos or not.

The same picture emerges when we look at the speeches of defendants in *παραγραφαί*. In the case with which Dem. 33 *Apatour.* is concerned Apatourios, a Byzantine trader, had some rather unsatisfactory dealings with a fellow Byzantine, Parmenon, leading to a suit for damages by him against Apatourios and a counter-claim by Apatourios. These issues were submitted under terms laid down in a document to three arbitrators; it was common ground to the parties that this document had been lost. Parmenon then had to leave Athens; and one of the three arbitrators, in defiance of the agreement (so the speaker alleges), pronounced against Parmenon in his absence. According to Apatourios the speaker had gone surety for Parmenon's carrying out the award, and when it was not carried out he sued the speaker for the amount due. The speaker on the other hand maintained that it was a certain Archippos and not he who had undertaken this suretyship, and that therefore there did not exist between himself and Apatourios that *συμβόλαιον* which was needed to form the basis of a *δίκη ἐμπορική*.[2] He states emphatically that his main task is to establish the *παραγραφή*,[3] and the

[1] Dem. 35 *Lakrit.* 43 *κελεύσατε αὐτὸν διδάξαι ὑμᾶς, ἢ ὡς τὰ χρήματα οὐκ ἔλαβον παρ' ἡμῶν, ἢ ὡς λαβόντες ἀποδεδώκασιν, ἢ ὅτι τὰς ναυτικὰς συγγραφὰς οὐ δεῖ κυρίας εἶναι, ἢ ὡς δεῖ ἄλλο τι χρήσασθαι τοῖς χρήμασιν ἢ ἐφ' οἷς ἔλαβον κατὰ τὴν συγγραφήν.*

[2] Dem. 33 *Apatour.* 2 *τοῖς δὲ περὶ τῶν μὴ γενομένων συμβολαίων εἰς κρίσιν καθισταμένοις ἐπὶ τὴν παραγραφὴν καταφεύγειν ἔδωκεν ὁ νόμος,* 3 *ὅσα μὲν ἐμοὶ καὶ τούτῳ ἐγένετο συμβόλαια, πάντων ἀπαλλαγῆς καὶ ἀφέσεως γενομένης, ἄλλου δὲ συμβολαίου οὐκ ὄντος ἐμοὶ πρὸς τοῦτον, οὔτε ναυτικοῦ οὔτ' ἐγγείου, παρεγραψάμην τὴν δίκην μὴ εἰσαγώγιμον εἶναι κατὰ τοὺς νόμους τουτουσί.* When he speaks of *ἀπαλλαγή* and *ἄφεσις* of all *συμβόλαια*, he is not being strictly relevant, since there had on his own showing been no release of the *συμβόλαιον* on which Apatourios was relying; this, in the view of the speaker, had in fact never existed.

[3] Dem. 33 *Apatour.* 35 *ὅτι μὲν οὖν ἐγὼ μὲν ὀρθῶς τὴν παραγραφὴν πεποίημαι, Ἀπατούριος δὲ τὰ ψευδῆ ἐγκέκληκε καὶ παρὰ τοὺς νόμους τὴν λῆξιν πεποίηται, ἐκ πολλῶν οἶμαι ἐπιδεδεῖχθαι τοῦτο ὑμῖν.*

reason is not far to seek. If it came to *εὐθυδικία*, he would have been hampered by two difficulties in evidence. In the first place the absence of the document would have fallen more to his disadvantage than to Apatourios', since on it alone rested the assertion that the arbitration had to be that of a majority of the three arbitrators (15). In the second place he would have to prove that Archippos alone stood surety for the carrying out of the award; but it is significant that Archippos is not put forward by him as witness to this fact, which suggests that, if put to it, he would have found it hard to prove. Wolff does not go too far in saying that in his position the speaker must have regarded the rejection of his *παραγραφή* as virtually the loss of the whole case.[1] Incidentally this explains why he expressly says that he will make no use of the law on prescription, which laid down that *ἐγγύαι* were to be *ἐπέτειοι*, but will only mention it as showing that he had not in fact been guarantor, otherwise Apatourios would have sued him earlier.[2] He is scrupulously avoiding the least hint that he could have been himself a guarantor.

A second speech in this group is Dem. 32 *Zenoth.* The plaintiff was Zenothemis, probably a Massaliot; the defendant Demon, an Athenian. The suit was probably a *δίκη ἐμπορική* in the shape of a *δίκη ἐξούλης*.[3] Either Demon had lent a certain Protos money on a bottomry loan for a voyage to and from Syracuse, or Protos was his agent for buying corn in Syracuse for import to Athens. According to Demon's story, Protos had purchased corn in Sicily and loaded it on a ship sailed and owned by Hegestratos, also probably a Massaliot. After an eventful voyage, the details

[1] Wolff, *Paragraphe* 33.

[2] Dem. 33 *Apatour.* 27 *λαβὲ δή μοι καὶ τὸν νόμον, ὃς κελεύει τὰς ἐγγύας ἐπετείους εἶναι. καὶ οὐκ ἰσχυρίζομαι τῷ νόμῳ, ὡς οὐ δεῖ με δίκην δοῦναι εἰ ἠγγυησάμην, ἀλλὰ μάρτυρά μοί φημι τὸν νόμον εἶναι τοῦ μὴ ἐγγυήσασθαι καὶ αὐτὸν τοῦτον· ἐδεδίκαστο γὰρ ἄν μοι τῆς ἐγγύης ἐν τῷ χρόνῳ τῷ ἐν τῷ νόμῳ γεγραμμένῳ.*

[3] It is most unsafe to be dogmatic on the type of suit; see vol. i, p. 219, n. 3. Wolff, *Paragraphe* 35, n. 32, complains that Meyer-Laurin, *Ges. Bill.* 8, n. 29, describes Zenothemis as possessor, which he was not; but we must keep distinct in our minds Zenothemis' suit against Protos, in which it would probably be right to describe Protos and not Zenothemis as possessor, and the present suit against Demon, in which, as a result of the decision against Protos in the former case, Zenothemis was probably the possessor. On the other hand Meyer-Laurin may have been wrong in asserting that a *δίκη ἐξούλης* is essentially a suit brought against a resisting possessor by someone carrying out an execution on the property; in Paoli's schema in *Studi Albertoni* ii (Padua, 1937) 313 ff. (on which see Harrison, vol. i, p. 313, case (*d*)), if A possesses a thing and B *ἐξάγει*, A should yield the thing but bring a *δίκη ἐξούλης* against B.

of which are graphically described by Demon, the ship arrived at Peiraeus. Hegestratos had been drowned *en route*, but when Protos wished to unload the corn Zenothemis interposed with the assertion that he and Hegestratos had borrowed money on the security of corn which they had loaded on board the ship. Demon's version of this was that Zenothemis and Hegestratos had transmitted the borrowed money to Massalia, had put no corn on board, and had made an abortive attempt to sink the ship, which had led to the drowning of Hegestratos. When the ship finally arrived at Peiraeus, Protos asserted his right to the corn by means of *ἐξαγωγή*. Zenothemis refused to cede possession to him, and insisted that Demon should carry out the *ἐξαγωγή*;[1] and this in the end was what happened, though for a time Protos continued to express his desire to carry out the *ἐξαγωγή* (19). Eventually Protos disappeared from the scene, and Zenothemis procured against him a court judgement by default on a claim which Demon, perhaps intentionally, leaves obscure.[2] The disappearance of Protos was a serious blow to Demon, since his evidence would have been of the utmost importance to his case. He interposed a *παραγραφή*, which seems to have been based on the assertion that there was no *συμβόλαιον* or *συγγραφή* between him and Zenothemis; this is shown by the latter's statement of claim, the gist of which he quotes. He goes on to say that from this speech of his the jury will both learn that the suit is not maintainable and will see Zenothemis' whole plot and his wickedness.[3] This last phrase seems to confirm Paoli's thesis that *παραγραφή* and action are one; and the very large part of the speech

[1] Dem. 32 *Zenoth.* 17 *ἐξῆγεν αὐτὸν Πρῶτος καὶ ὁ κοινωνὸς τοῦ Πρώτου, Φέρτατος· οὑτοσὶ δ' οὐκ ἐξήγετο, οὐδ' ἂν ἔφη διαρρήδην ὑπ' οὐδενὸς ἐξαχθῆναι, εἰ μὴ αὐτὸν ἐγὼ ἐξάξω.*

[2] From what is said at 27, it might have been a *δίκη βλάβης*, based on alleged behaviour of Protos during the voyage. The motives of the parties at this point are conjectural. Zenothemis probably did not wish Protos as his opponent in the *δίκη ἐξούλης* on the corn because a judgement against him would have been less likely to be profitable than one against a man of substance who was also an Athenian. Protos had an interest in procuring the corn quickly for sale in Athens, but when the price fell this interest waned (according to Demon at 25), and he was probably bought off cheaply by Zenothemis under the threat of another action.

[3] Dem. 32 *Zenoth.* 2 *τουτῳὶ τοίνυν Ζηνοθέμιδι πρὸς μὲν ἐμὲ ὅτι οὐδὲν ἦν συμβόλαιον οὐδὲ συγγραφή, καὐτὸς ὁμολογεῖ ἐν τῷ ἐγκλήματι· δανεῖσαι δέ φησιν Ἡγεστράτῳ ναυκλήρῳ, τούτου δ' ἀπολομένου ἐν τῷ πελάγει, ἡμᾶς τὸ ναῦλον σφετερίσασθαι· τουτὶ τὸ ἔγκλημ' ἐστίν. ἐκ δὴ τοῦ αὐτοῦ λόγου τήν τε δίκην οὐκ εἰσαγώγιμον οὖσαν μαθήσεσθε, καὶ τὴν ὅλην ἐπιβουλὴν καὶ πονηρίαν τουτουὶ τοῦ ἀνθρώπου ὄψεσθε.*

which is devoted to a detailed description of what happened on the voyage tends at first sight in the same direction, since much of this is irrelevant to the question whether there was or was not a *συμβόλαιον* between Zenothemis and Demon.[1] On a closer view this impression fades. Demon's emphatic assertion, with the reading out both of his *παραγραφή* and of the law of *παραγραφή* (23 f.), and his rather clumsy attempt to make something out of the requirement that the *δίκη ἐμπορική* lay only in connection with imports to Athens, with the childish play on the word *εἰσαγώγιμος* (22), indicate that he is concerned at the moment exclusively with the decision whether the suit is maintainable or not. The seemingly irrelevant details he gives are simply designed to undermine the credibility and respectability of Zenothemis. As we have seen was the case with the speaker against Apatourios, if it came to *εὐθυδικία* he was going to be at a grave disadvantage in the matter of proof: Protos had decamped, and Zenothemis could rely on a *συγγραφή* the genuineness of which Demon can make only a feeble effort to discredit. We must believe that, if Demon had lost on the *παραγραφή*, he would have still been able to argue the issue of fraud and the non-existence of the alleged *συγγραφή* at the *εὐθυδικία*, though his prospects of success might have been bleak.

In Dem. 37 *Pant.* Nikoboulos had been sued by a *δίκη βλάβης* by Pantainetos.[2] It appears further that he had been sued under a *νόμος μεταλλικός* (35). Nikoboulos had pleaded in the first place that Pantainetos had given him release and discharge, which were grounds for a *παραγραφή*.[3] He had also pleaded that

[1] Demon may well have been taking advantage of an ambiguity in the use of *συμβόλαιον*. One use was for what we should call contract, but strictly, when this is meant, the epithet *ἑκούσιον* should be attached; there could be a *συμβόλαιον ἀκούσιον*, a liability arising out of tort rather than contract, if we may use a perhaps dangerous modern term. Ar. *Nik. Eth.* 1130^{b} ff. elaborates a distinction between *ἑκούσια* and *ἀκούσια συναλλάγματα* ('involvement' seems a good neutral translation for *συνάλλαγμα*); cf. 1164^{b} and A. R. W. Harrison, *JHS* 77 (1957) 45 f., Wolff, *Paragraphe* 44, n. 56. Wolff is probably right in saying that for this procedural purpose the original and proper meaning of *συμβόλαιον* was 'relationship of liability' whether arising out of tort or contract, and that Demon is here improperly trying to narrow it to 'contract'.

[2] In 22 ff. we have the text, genuine it is believed, of Pantainetos' claim, which begins *ἔβλαψέ με Νικόβουλος*.

[3] Dem. 37 *Pant.* 1 *δεδωκότων, ὦ ἄνδρες δικασταί, τῶν νόμων παραγράψασθαι περὶ ὧν ἄν τις ἀφεὶς καὶ ἀπαλλάξας δικάζηται, γεγενημένων ἀμφοτέρων μοι τούτων πρὸς Πανταίνετον τουτονί, παρεγραψάμην, ὡς ἠκούσατ' ἀρτίως, μὴ εἰσαγώγιμον εἶναι τὴν δίκην.*

Pantainetos' claim contained many delictual charges against him which, though they might be maintainable in some other court, did not belong to a suit brought before the thesmothetai under the *νόμος μεταλλικός*; this plea was struck out by the magistrate, which however did not prevent Nikoboulos from enlarging upon it in his speech (34). He states the main ground for his *παραγραφή* succinctly (18), and after the reading of the law governing this type of *παραγραφή* drives home his point.[1] He then proceeds to go into the merits of the substantive case, on the ground (expressed in 21) that he does not wish to evade the main issues by a procedural device. He has already stated (1) that, if he had not entered the special plea, his failure to do so might have been used at the *εὐθυδικία* as evidence that he did not trust in his contention that there had been *ἄφεσις* and *ἀπαλλαγή*. Here again there is nothing to suggest that the principal aim of the speech was to persuade the jury on the merits of the substantive case rather than on the special plea.

In two other speeches, Dem. 36 *For Phorm.* and 38 *Nausim.*, *ἄφεσις* and *ἀπαλλαγή*, and secondarily prescription, are the grounds advanced for the *παραγραφή*. Phormion was defendant in a *δίκη βλάβης*[2] brought against him by Pasion's son, Apollodoros. Apollodoros had charged Phormion with embezzling a capital sum (*ἀφορμή*) due to him out of the estate of his father, Pasion. The sum he claimed was twenty talents; the claim arose probably out of a sum of eleven talents which appeared in a document as being owed by Pasion to the bank which was leased by Pasion to Phormion and later became a part of the estate which Pasion left to his two sons, Apollodoros and Pasikles.[3] Apollodoros alleged that the document was a forgery, and that in fact Pasion

[1] Dem. 37 *Pant.* 19 ἀκούετ', ὦ ἄνδρες δικασταί, τοῦ νόμου λέγοντος ἄντικρυς, ὧν ἂν ἀφῇ καὶ ἀπαλλάξῃ τις, μηκέτι τὰς δίκας εἶναι. καὶ μὴν ὅτι γ' ἀμφότερ' ἐστὶ πεπραγμένα ταῦτα τούτῳ πρὸς ἡμᾶς, ἠκούσατε τῶν μαρτυριῶν.

[2] Gernet, *Dem.* i. 201 f., Wolff, *Eranion Maridakis* i (Athens, 1963) 93, n. 17. In Dem. 36 *For Phorm.* hyp. 2 it is called a *δίκη ἀφορμῆς*, an action for the restitution of capital, mentioned in Ar. *Ath. Pol.* 52. 2 among the *δίκαι ἔμμηνοι* in the jurisdiction of the eisagogeis; but monthly suits were not sent to arbitration, as this one was. (Lipsius, *AR* 725 f., argues for the *δίκη ἀφορμῆς*.)

[3] The 20 talents is either the original 11 talents with interest at 10 per cent for eight years, the time of Phormion's lease (Sandys, *Select Private Orations of Demosthenes* i[4], p. xxiv, Lipsius, *AR* 725, n. 181, Gernet, *Dem.* i. 201, n. 2), or, if this was a *δίκη βλάβης*, the sum allegedly embezzled with an added penalty of an equal sum (Wolff, *Paragraphe* 54, n. 71). On the nature of the contract see Wolff, *Eranion Maridakis* i. 91.

did not owe this sum but Phormion had somehow made away with it.[1] Phormion maintained that this sum was entered in the bank's books as a debt due by Pasion because this amount had been lent out on landed security from money deposited in the bank and, since Phormion at the time was not a citizen and could not therefore hold the land in case of foreclosure, Pasion was entered as the debtor. The *παραγραφή* is based on the facts that (1) Phormion had had from Apollodoros both a discharge from the lease under which he had taken on the management of the bank and on another occasion a discharge from a claim submitted to arbitration, and (2) the suit was statute-barred, since the events to which it related had taken place more than twenty years previously and there was a statutory limitation of five years. Although it was not easy to disentangle these issues from those which would have been raised in a *εὐθυδικία*, and therefore it may appear that the speaker is addressing himself equally to the latter as to the former, actually he emphasizes that his primary concern is whether the suit is maintainable.[2] He too may have adopted this tactic for reasons of ease of proof: he shows that he is in a strong position to prove *ἄφεσις* and *ἀπαλλαγή* (10, 16), whereas if this line of defence had been abandoned he would have had the difficult task of rebutting detailed charges about matters twenty years past. Moreover he could play on the known antipathy against Apollodoros' litigiousness, which he did with such success that Apollodoros lost the *παραγραφή* and was mulcted of the *ἐπωβελία*.[3]

[1] In Dem. 45 *Steph.* i. 33 f. (a speech which relates to another phase of this case) Apollodoros tries to represent the 11 talents as having been embezzled, and at the same time to suggest that the entry of them in the document as a debt due by Pasion proves the document to be a forgery, since it would have been gross incompetence to have had such a large debt outstanding; he glosses over the fact, emphasized by the speaker for Phormion, that this was a debt secured by hypothec.

[2] Dem. 36 *For Phorm.* 23 f. *ἃ τοίνυν ἤδη περὶ αὐτοῦ τοῦ μὴ εἰσαγώγιμον εἶναι τὴν δίκην δεῖ σκοπεῖν ὑμᾶς, ταῦτ' ἀναμνήσθητ' ἐκ τῶν εἰρημένων. ἡμεῖς γάρ, ὦ ἄνδρες Ἀθηναῖοι, γεγενημένου μὲν διαλογισμοῦ καὶ ἀφέσεως τῆς τραπέζης καὶ τοῦ ἀσπιδοπηγείου τῆς μισθώσεως, γεγενημένης δὲ διαίτης καὶ πάλιν πάντων ἀφέσεως, οὐκ ἐώντων τῶν νόμων δίκας ὧν ἂν ἀφῇ τις ἅπαξ λαγχάνειν, συκοφαντοῦντος τούτου καὶ παρὰ τοὺς νόμους δικαζομένου παρεγραψάμεθ' ἐκ τῶν νόμων μὴ εἶναι τὴν δίκην εἰσαγώγιμον. ἵν' οὖν εἰδῆθ' ὑπὲρ οὗ τὴν ψῆφον οἴσετε, τόν τε νόμον ὑμῖν τοῦτον ἀναγνώσεται καὶ τὰς μαρτυρίας ἐφεξῆς τῶν παρόντων, ὅτ' ἀφίει τῆς μισθώσεως καὶ τῶν ἄλλων ἁπάντων ἐγκλημάτων Ἀπολλόδωρος.*

[3] Dem. 45 *Steph.* i. 6 *προλαβὼν δέ μου ὥστε πρότερος λέγειν διὰ τὸ παραγραφὴν εἶναι καὶ μὴ εὐθυδικίᾳ εἰσιέναι, . . . οὕτω διέθηκε τοὺς δικαστάς, ὥστε φωνὴν μηδ' ἡντινοῦν ἐθέλειν ἀκούειν ἡμῶν· προσοφλὼν δὲ τὴν ἐπωβελίαν καὶ οὐδὲ λόγου τυχεῖν*

Dem. 38 *Nausim.* presents much the same picture. More than twenty years before the case came on, Aristaichmos, father of the speaker, and later Demaretos, who became his and his brother's guardian on Aristaichmos' death, were alleged, as guardians of Nausimachos and Xenopeithes, the plaintiffs in this suit, to have received money due to the two latter and not to have paid it over to them. Each of the two brought separate suits *βλάβης* against each of the four sons of Aristaichmos; this is the speech for one of the sons.[1] It is important to note that the suit was a *δίκη βλάβης*, not *ἐπιτροπῆς*, and that the plaintiffs alleged that the moneys had been collected from Hermonax after the guardianship had come to an end (9). The grounds for the *παραγραφή* were (1) that there had been release and discharge,[2] and (2) that suits by wards against their guardians were statute-barred after five years,[3] presumably from the time when the ward came of age.[4] It seems to be one aim of the speaker to question the payment of any sum by Hermonax either to Aristaichmos or to Demaretos. Had the matter come to *εὐθυδικία*, this would have been a main point to establish; and it would have presented formidable difficulties of proof, as is shown by the feebleness of his argument from probabilities (10 ff.). He is trying throughout to blur this issue, and to give the impression that the plaintiffs' claim is simply a warming-up of their original claim against Aristaichmos as guardian. Wolff seems right in his contention that the speech can only be properly understood on the assumption that it is directed solely to procuring a favourable verdict in the *παραγραφή*.[5]

ἀξιωθείς, ἀλλ' ὑβρισθεὶς ὡς οὐκ οἶδ' εἴ τις πώποτ' ἄλλος ἀνθρώπων, ἀπῄειν βαρέως, ὦ ἄνδρες Ἀθηναῖοι, καὶ χαλεπῶς φέρων. We may assume that Apollodoros' statement that he was not allowed a hearing is a piece of rhetoric.

[1] Dem. 38 *Nausim.* 2 *ὄντες γὰρ δύο τέτταρας εἰλήχασι δίκας ἡμῖν, τῶν αὐτῶν χρημάτων πάσας, τρισχιλίων ἑκάστην, βλάβης.* Wolff, *Eranion Maridakis* i. 97 f., conjectures that the plaintiffs maintained that the debt collected had been incorporated in the estate of Aristaichmos before its division among the four sons; each of the four sons was thereby guilty of withholding moneys due to each of Nausimachos and Xenopeithes.

[2] Dem. 38 *Nausim.* 1 *δεδωκότων, ὦ ἄνδρες δικασταί, τῶν νόμων παραγράψασθαι περὶ ὧν ἄν τις ἀφεὶς καὶ ἀπαλλάξας πάλιν δικάζηται, γεγενημένων ἀμφοτέρων τούτων τῷ πατρὶ πρὸς Ναυσίμαχον καὶ Ξενοπείθην τοὺς εἰληχότας ἡμῖν, παρεγραψάμεθα, ὥσπερ ἠκούσατ' ἀρτίως, μὴ εἰσαγώγιμον εἶναι τὴν δίκην.*

[3] Dem. 38 *Nausim.* 17 *βούλομαι καὶ τοῦτον ὑμῖν τὸν νόμον εἰπεῖν, ὅστις διαρρήδην λέγει, ἐὰν πέντ' ἔτη παρέλθῃ καὶ μὴ δικάσωνται, μηκέτ' εἶναι τοῖς ὀρφανοῖς δίκην περὶ τῶν ἐκ τῆς ἐπιτροπῆς ἐγκλημάτων.*

[4] Vol. i, p. 120, n. 6.

[5] Wolff, *Paragraphe* 61.

We can then say with some confidence that argument and voting on a *παραγραφή* were quite distinct from argument and voting on the issue of substance, and that when the *παραγραφή* was rejected a new hearing, quite possibly though not necessarily before a different jury, was opened.[1] It could of course happen that a defendant who lost his *παραγραφή*, recognizing that his case in the *εὐθυδικία* was hopeless, withdrew his defence; in such a case the *παραγραφή* would in fact amount to the trial of the case, but such an instance, if one could be established, would in no way support Paoli's contention that in principle process at law at Athens was indivisible. It may however have been the rule that, if the *παραγραφή* was turned down, no more *λαγχάνειν τὴν δίκην* was needed and the magistrate would bring the case without further ado before a court; in this limited sense Paoli's principle would stand.

Any *παραγραφή* without exception had to be grounded on some particular provision of a particular law.[2] Though the process of *παραγραφή* was probably initiated by the law of Archinos (see p. 107), there were by the end of our period several different laws laying down a variety of grounds for a *παραγραφή*. First there was a law which, among other grounds for barring a suit, specifically banned bringing suit on matters already settled.[3] The settlement might be either by release and discharge (*ἄφεσις* and

[1] Isok. 18 *Kallim.* 40 and Dem. 32 *Zenoth.* 13 at first might seem to suggest that in those two cases the same jurors would hear both the *παραγραφή* and *αὐτὸ τὸ πρᾶγμα* (Steinwenter, *Z* 54 (1934) 385). A closer study shows that in each case the argument is really directed to convincing the jurors that they must vote in favour of the *παραγραφή*.

[2] Dem. 32 *Zenoth.* 1 *οἱ νόμοι κελεύουσιν, ὦ ἄνδρες δικασταί, τὰς δίκας εἶναι τοῖς ναυκλήροις καὶ τοῖς ἐμπόροις τῶν Ἀθήναζε καὶ τῶν Ἀθήνηθεν συμβολαίων, καὶ περὶ ὧν ἂν ὦσι συγγραφαί· ἂν δέ τις παρὰ ταῦτα δικάζηται, μὴ εἰσαγώγιμον εἶναι τὴν δίκην*, 34 *Ag. Phorm.* 4 *οἱ μὲν οὖν νόμοι . . . ὑπὲρ μὲν τῶν μὴ γενομένων ὅλως συμβολαίων Ἀθήνησι μηδ' εἰς τὸ Ἀθηναίων ἐμπόριον παραγράφεσθαι δεδώκασιν, ἐὰν δέ τις γενέσθαι μὲν ὁμολογῇ, ἀμφισβητῇ δὲ ὡς πάντα πεποίηκεν τὰ συγκείμενα, ἀπολογεῖσθαι κελεύουσιν εὐθυδικίαν εἰσιόντα, οὐ κατηγορεῖν τοῦ διώκοντος*. Note the phrase at the end of the latter quotation which makes the defendant who pleads a *παραγραφή* into the accuser of the plaintiff.

[3] Dem. 20 *Lept.* 147 *οἱ νόμοι δ' οὐκ ἐῶσι δὶς πρὸς τὸν αὐτὸν περὶ τῶν αὐτῶν οὔτε δίκας οὔτ' εὐθύνας οὔτε διαδικασίαν οὔτ' ἄλλο τοιοῦτ' οὐδὲν εἶναι*, 36 *For Phorm.* 25 *τοῦ νόμου λέγοντος . . . τά τ' ἄλλ' ὧν μὴ εἶναι δίκας, καὶ ὅσα τις ἀφῆκεν ἢ ἀπήλλαξεν*, 38 *Nausim.* 5 *τοῦ νόμου σαφῶς λέγοντος ἕκαστα, ὧν μὴ εἶναι δίκας· ὧν ἕν ἐστιν . . . περὶ ὧν ἄν τις ἀφῇ καὶ ἀπαλλάξῃ, μὴ δικάζεσθαι*, 24 *Timokr.* 54 *ὅσων δίκη πρότερον ἐγένετο ἢ εὔθυνα ἢ διαδικασία περί του ἐν δικαστηρίῳ, ἢ ἰδίᾳ ἢ δημοσίᾳ, ἢ τὸ δημόσιον ἀπέδοτο, μὴ εἰσάγειν περὶ τούτων εἰς τὸ δικαστήριον μηδ' ἐπιψηφίζειν τῶν ἀρχόντων μηδένα, μηδὲ κατηγορεῖν ἐώντων ἃ οὐκ ἐῶσιν οἱ νόμοι*, Poll. 8. 57 (quoted on p. 108, n. 2).

ἀπαλλαγή) or by a previous δίκη. There is some doubt what exactly constituted a bar by previous δίκη. The usual view has been that it meant a judgement given in a previous suit. Wolff however has argued that it meant rather the bringing of a suit, since for him the technical meaning of δίκη is not 'judgement' but 'the procedural act of one who makes a claim'.[1] Settlement of a case by arbitration, whether public or private, when the decision was accepted by both parties, barred suit on the same issue.[2] Payment of a sum owed was probably not in itself a ground for παραγραφή, but only a payment acknowledged by a formal release from the creditor. This explains why plaintiffs were eager to get such cases to εὐθυδικία, where burden of proof that the debt had been paid rested on the defendant.[3]

A second ground for παραγραφή was prescription.[4] In Dem. 36 *For Phorm.* 25 the speaker, having dealt with ἄφεσις and ἀπαλλαγή, cites another law which he calls τὸν τῆς προθεσμίας νόμον. It is doubtful whether there was a single law of prescription; rather there were different laws for different cases.[5] In this case it was probably a five-year period from the end of a wardship in which a δίκη ἐπιτροπῆς had to be brought.[6]

[1] Wolff, *Paragraphe* 90, n. 8: the meaning of δίκη is 'nicht "Urteil", sondern zuvörderst "rechtsverwirklichender Zugriff"'. Wolff gives bibliography on the topic; note especially Partsch, *GB* 195, and now D. Liebs, *Z* 84 (1967) 121 f. The point is more important than it might at first seem; for, though Wolff argues that the condition would not be realized unless and until the case had come before a dikastery ('der Prozeß rechtshängig sein mußte') and this would normally mean that a judgement on it had been given, we have cases where the issue is withdrawn from the jury before a decision has been reached (see p. 103), and on Wolff's view this would bar a subsequent action on the same plea.

[2] Isok. 18 *Kallim.* 11 οὐκ εἰσαγώγιμος ἦν ἡ δίκη διαίτης γεγενημένης, Dem. 21 *Meid.* 94 (a law on private arbitrators, perhaps not a genuine text), Poll. 8. 57 (quoted on p. 108, n. 2).

[3] Dem. 34 *Ag. Phorm.* 4 (quoted on p. 119, n. 2); Steinwenter, *Z* 54 (1934) 384, n. 7, Wolff, *Paragraphe* 93. This rule suited a system such as the Athenian, which did not recognize any obligation resting simply on a formal act which needed a cancelling formal act to release from the obligation.

[4] Contrary to the view of Calhoun, *CP* 14 (1919) 340, it was not the right or duty of the magistrate to refuse the claim of a plaintiff which on its face was prescribed; this could only be done by the defendant's entering a παραγραφή. So Bo. Sm. ii. 75, n. 2, followed by Wolff, *Eranion Maridakis* i (Athens, 1963) 101. Wolff rightly rejects the assertion of Gernet, *Dem.* iii. 11, that prescription could not be invoked alone as a ground for a παραγραφή; see Poll. 8. 57 (quoted on p. 108, n. 2).

[5] Wolff, *Eranion Maridakis* i. 87 ff.

[6] Dem. 38 *Nausim.* 17 (quoted on p. 118, n. 3); vol. i, p. 120, n. 6.

Thirdly there were claims which could not be prosecuted either because by their nature they were not deemed worthy of protection by legal process or because the plaintiff had chosen the wrong legal process. The most notable example of the second of these grounds is the alleged wrong use of the δίκη ἐμπορική: this was the main plea in the four cases dealt with by Dem. 32–5 (see pp. 109 ff.). The bar was laid down in a specific law or laws,[1] but we cannot be certain of the exact content or even of the number of such rules. We know for example that it was illegal to lend money on any ship which was not going to bring back corn or other privileged goods to Athens, and that no suit could be brought for the recovery of moneys so lent.[2] Wolff seems to be right in contending (especially from the language of Dem. 33 *Apatour.* 3) that some positive rule was needed to found a plea that an action was not properly a δίκη ἐμπορική, and that such a plea could not simply rest on the mere absence of conditions required for such a suit.

The law which prohibited suits on matters already settled included a ban on suits concerning property sold by the treasury (that is confiscated property).[3] In practice this meant that the buyer of such property could protect himself from actions in connection with the property by a παραγραφή.[4]

It seems probable *a priori* that a defendant who had not been summoned could ban a suit by a παραγραφή.[5]

Lastly we have a specific ban on suits in matters 'in regard to which there are no eisagogeis' (περὶ ὧν οὐκ εἰσὶν εἰσαγωγεῖς).[6] This is not the usual translation, which is rather that of the Loeb edition, 'charges brought before magistrates who have not due competence'. But Wolff should be followed in the former translation.[7] It entails the view that it was a bar to action if the plaintiff

[1] Dem. 34 *Ag. Phorm.* 4 (quoted on p. 119, n. 2), 32 *Zenoth.* 23, 33 *Apatour.* 3.

[2] Dem. 35 *Lakrit.* 51 ἀργύριον δὲ μὴ ἐξεῖναι ἐκδοῦναι Ἀθηναίων καὶ τῶν μετοίκων τῶν Ἀθήνησι μετοικούντων μηδενί, μηδὲ ὧν οὗτοι κύριοί εἰσιν, εἰς ναῦν ἥτις ἂν μὴ μέλλῃ ἄξειν σῖτον Ἀθήναζε. . . . ἐὰν δέ τις ἐκδῷ παρὰ ταῦτα, εἶναι τὴν φάσιν καὶ τὴν ἀπογραφὴν τοῦ ἀργυρίου πρὸς τοὺς ἐπιμελητάς, καθάπερ τῆς νεὼς καὶ τοῦ σίτου εἴρηται, κατὰ ταὐτά. καὶ δίκη αὐτῷ μὴ ἔστω περὶ τοῦ ἀργυρίου, ὃ ἂν ἐκδῷ ἄλλοσέ ποι ἢ Ἀθήναζε, μηδὲ ἀρχὴ εἰσαγέτω περὶ τούτου μηδεμία.

[3] Dem. 24 *Timokr.* 54 (quoted on p. 119, n. 3).

[4] The possessor in such a case was protected from forcible ejectment by the δίκη ἐξούλης; cf. vol. i, p. 218, n. 1.

[5] See pp. 89 f.

[6] Dem. 37 *Pant.* 33. That a single law is meant is shown by the words which follow: λέγε δ' αὐτοῖς τουτονὶ τὸν νόμον.

[7] Wolff, *Paragraphe* 97.

could not point to a δίκη allotted to a specific magistrate as its introducer.[1] It is possible that this clause could be used if the defendant wished to plead that he had been cited before the wrong magistrate, though it would seem more likely that such cases would have been settled between the parties and the magistrate before the matter came to trial.[2] The more likely use of this ground of παραγραφή would have been perhaps to allow new forms of action to arise where plaintiffs succeeded in winning the παραγραφή. In such cases the courts would have been performing much the same function as did the praetors at Rome. This is however pure speculation, as no such cases have been preserved.[3]

It is clear that the particular grounds for παραγραφαί were added to the statute book over the years; in fact one of the principal grounds in our sources, wrong use of the δίκη ἐμπορική, cannot date before the middle of the fourth century, when this type of suit originated.[4] We should probably not deduce from the phrase τοῦ νόμου λέγοντος ἕκαστα, ὧν μὴ εἶναι δίκας that there was in the end one comprehensive law.[5] If we are right in this, we may further suppose that it was no mere accident that the Athenians did not draw together the rules governing παραγραφαί into a single law, but that their failure to do so illustrates

[1] εἰσαγωγεῖς in this context has this sense, and does not refer to the college of eisagogeis: Wolff, *Paragraphe* 97, n. 25.

[2] Except perhaps where the status of one or other party was relevant. A citizen defendant might perhaps use this plea if cited before the polemarch, or if cited before any magistrate by a ξένος who had no entitlement to bring that particular type of suit.

[3] But cf. Phot. and Suda s.v. παραγραφή (quoted on p. 108, n. 2). Dem. 37 *Pant.* 34 ff. (immediately following the passage just discussed) suggests how this might have happened. Nikoboulos entered a plea that Pantainetos was accusing him of αἴκεια, ὕβρις, βίαια, and even πρὸς ἐπικλήρους ἀδικήματα in a δίκη μεταλλική, and that for none of these wrongs were the thesmothetai introducers. He was made to strike out this plea by the magistrate. What Nikoboulos seems to have been arguing was that, given the plaints of Pantainetos were as he alleged, though they were each maintainable in themselves, there was no εἰσαγωγεύς for them when lumped together as a δίκη μεταλλική. The magistrate, in making him strike the plea out, may have done so on the ground that, whatever Pantainetos said, his plaint was a δίκη βλάβης and this *was* maintainable as a δίκη μεταλλική.

[4] The δίκη ἐμπορική was apparently not in existence when Xen. *Poroi* 3. 3 was written (probably about 355 B.C.); it was in use when Dem. 7 *Hal.* 12 was delivered. See Gernet, *DSGA* 173.

[5] Dem. 36 *For Phorm.* 25, 38 *Nausim.* 5 (both quoted on p. 119, n. 3). The deduction is made by Paoli, *St. Proc.* 84, but convincingly negatived by Calhoun, *CP* 13 (1918) 174 f., Bo. Sm. ii. 90 f., Wolff, *Paragraphe* 101.

a fundamental point about the institution, namely that it was conceived not so much as a positive weapon of protection put as such into the defendant's hand, but as a negative one (*μὴ εἶναι δίκας*) which left it to the defendant to prove that the *δίκη* was not maintainable.[1]

Lack of evidence makes it difficult to be precise on the legal effects of a judgement in a *παραγραφή*. It seems likely that, if the *παραγραφή* was rejected and the issue came on for trial, the defendant was restricted to pleas on the merits and could not formally raise again the issues raised in the *παραγραφή*, though this would not have prevented speakers in fact continuing to argue them. If the *παραγραφή* was successful, it barred the plaintiff from further litigation on the same matter, where the *παραγραφή* had been based on previous settlement (either by a court or by express agreement of the two parties), on absence of statutory protection of the plaintiff's claim, on prescription, or on absence of a *συμβόλαιον* needed to qualify the suit as *ἐμπορική*. On the other hand the plaintiff could return to the attack if he could fit his plaint into a different mould, for example call his suit a *δίκη βλάβης* instead of suing under the executive clause in a contract; such a change might also involve suing before a different magistrate. Where, as in Lys. 23 *Pankl.*, the *παραγραφή* was based simply on the ground that the magistrate was not competent because of the status of the defendant, natural justice would have suggested that an unsuccessful plaintiff would have had the right to sue in the proper court; but it is possible that the law quoted in Dem. 24 *Timokr.* 54 (see p. 119, n. 3 and p. 120, n. 1) would have been used to bar such a suit.[2]

[1] Steinwenter, *Z* 54 (1934) 384, Wolff, *Paragraphe* 102 f. Wolff lays special stress on the phraseology in Dem. 36 *For Phorm.* 25 *ὧν ἂν ἅπαξ γένηται δίκη, μηκέτ' ἐξεῖναι δικάζεσθαι*, 37 *Pant.* 19 *τοῦ νόμου λέγοντος ἄντικρυς, ὧν ἂν ἀφῇ καὶ ἀπαλλάξῃ τις, μηκέτι τὰς δίκας εἶναι*, and for the rules on prescription a similar phrase in 38 *Nausim.* 18 *τοῦ νόμου λέγοντος ἄντικρυς, ἐὰν μὴ πέντ' ἐτῶν δικάσωνται, μηκέτ' εἶναι δίκην*.

[2] Wolff, *Paragraphe* 145, n. 12, points out that the Zenothemis case (Dem. 32) raises an interesting problem here. If Zenothemis was a *ξένος*, the loss of this *παραγραφή* would have meant that he could not sue further, since (so the argument seems to go) he could only bring a *δίκη ἐμπορική*. If on the other hand he was a metic, could he not formally at least bring a *δίκη ἐξούλης* before the polemarch? But such a suit would have had to rest on the same delictual *συμβόλαιον* the absence of which was pleaded by Zenothemis' opponent as the ground of his *παραγραφή*. We simply cannot say whether in a subsequent action Zenothemis would have been able to plead that this decision barred only a *δίκη ἐμπορική*.

It is a mistake to equate the παραγραφή with the Roman *exceptio*.[1] The decision in that is simply a negative condition for condemnation of the defendant, and it says nothing as to the claim set out in the *intentio*; but the decision in the παραγραφή declares positively that the δίκη is οὐκ εἰσαγώγιμος.

(iii) διαμαρτυρία

A quite different method of raising issues of jurisdiction and the like in isolation from the merits was the διαμαρτυρία. A good deal of study has been devoted recently to this institution, and it is generally held that its origins go back to a distant past compared with those of the παραγραφή.[2] Our evidence for the procedure is relatively good.[3]

There are two cases reported from the end of the fifth century. In one a defendant, who was being sued for 10,000 drachmai, put forward one to depose (μάρτυς) that the suit was not maintainable as the matter had been settled by arbitration; the defendant finally withdrew this defence, but we should assume that it was

[1] This is suggested by Gernet, *DSGA* 86, n. 4, rebutted by Wolff, *Paragraphe* 10.

[2] Leisi, *Zeuge* 28 ff., Calhoun, *CP* 13 (1918) 169 ff., Gernet, *RHD* 6 (1927) 5 ff. (*DSGA* 83 ff.), Paoli, *St. Proc.* 143 ff., Bo. Sm. ii. 82 ff., Lämmli, *Prozeß.* 146 ff., Wolff, *Paragraphe* 106 ff. A different view of the origin and significance of the διαμαρτυρία is taken by E. Schönbauer, *AAW* (1964) 208, 217 ff.

[3] Isok. 18 *Kallim.* 11 f. and Lys. 23 *Pankl.* 13 f. are important evidence for the procedure at the end of the fifth century. It figures prominently in three surviving speeches of Isaios (2 *Menekl.*, 3 *Pyrrh.*, 6 *Philokt.*) and one of Demosthenes (44 *Leoch.*), and there are important references in Isai. 5 *Dikaiog.* 16 f., 7 *Apollod.* 3. See also Harpokr. s.v. διαμαρτυρία καὶ διαμαρτυρεῖν· τρόπος τις ἦν παραγραφῆς ἡ διαμαρτυρία· πρὸ γὰρ τοῦ εἰσαχθῆναι τὴν δίκην εἰς τὸ δικαστήριον ἐξῆν τῷ βουλομένῳ διαμαρτυρῆσαι ὡς εἰσαγώγιμός ἐστιν ἡ δίκη ἢ οὐκ εἰσαγώγιμος. διαφέρει δὲ τῆς παραγραφῆς τῷ τὴν διαμαρτυρίαν γίνεσθαι οὐ μόνον ὑπὸ τῶν φευγόντων, ἀλλὰ καὶ ὑπὸ τῶν διωκόντων. καὶ πρότερόν γε τῷ διώκοντι ἦν προβάλλεσθαί τινα μαρτυροῦντα εἰσαγώγιμον εἶναι τὴν δίκην, καὶ περὶ τούτου πρότερον ἐγίνετο ἡ κρίσις πρὸς αὐτὸν τὸν διαμαρτυρήσαντα, οὐ πρὸς τὸν ἐξ ἀρχῆς δικαζόμενον· εἰ δὲ μὴ προβάλοιτο μάρτυρα ὁ διώκων, τότε ἐξῆν τῷ φεύγοντι προσαγαγεῖν τινα μαρτυροῦντα μὴ εἰσαγώγιμον εἶναι τὴν δίκην, καὶ πάλιν πρὸς τὸν διαμαρτυρήσαντα ὁ ἀγὼν ἐγίνετο. ἐπεσκήπτοντο δὲ ψευδομαρτυρίων καὶ ταῖς διαμαρτυρίαις, ὥσπερ ταῖς μαρτυρίαις· Λυσίας ἐν τῇ πρὸς Ἀριστόδημον διαμαρτυρίᾳ, εἰ γνήσιος ὁ λόγος. Ἰσαῖος δ' ἐν τῷ πρὸς Πύθωνα ἀποστασίου φησὶν ὅτι οὐχ οἷόν τε διαμαρτυρεῖν ξένους· Ὑπερείδης δ' ἐν τῷ κατ' Ἀρισταγόρας ἀπροστασίου β' φησὶν ὡς οἱ νόμοι κελεύουσι διαμαρτυρεῖν ἐπὶ ταῖς γραφαῖς ταῖς τοῦ ἀπροστασίου τὸν βουλόμενον ὁμοίως τῶν ξένων καὶ τῶν ἐπιχωρίων. μήποτ' οὖν ἐν μὲν ταῖς τοῦ ἀποστασίου δίκαις κεκώλυνται διαμαρτυρεῖν οἱ ξένοι, ἐν δὲ ταῖς τοῦ ἀπροστασίου οὐ κεκώλυνται. Δείναρχος μέντοι τὸ διαμαρτυρῆσαι τέθεικεν οὐκ ἐπὶ τοῦ μαρτυρήσαντος αὐτοῦ, ἀλλ' ἐπὶ τοῦ παρασχόντος τινὰ διαμαρτυρήσαντα ἐν τῇ διαμαρτυρίᾳ περὶ τοῦ μὴ ἐπίδικον εἶναι τὴν Ἀριστοφῶντος θυγατέρα. οὗτος δὲ ὁ ῥήτωρ ἐν τῷ κατὰ Ἡδύλης καὶ τὸν τρόπον διαγράφει τῆς διαμαρτυρίας.

a feasible one.[1] In the other a defendant was cited before the polemarch, but alleged that as a Plataian he should not have been cited before the polemarch; it was deposed against him that he was not a Plataian and, although he opposed the *διαμαρτυρία* (*ἐπισκηψάμενος*), he did not follow this up by prosecuting the witness; the case therefore came on, and he was condemned.[2]

The principal use of the procedure, and one which predominated in the fourth century, was in succession cases; this has been briefly discussed in vol. i, pp. 156 ff. Certain claimants to an estate (the direct male—or, in the absence of males, female—descendants of the *de cuius*, or those adopted *inter vivos*) had the right of immediate entry (*ἐμβάτευσις*). Anyone who wished to challenge such a claim had to do so either by himself entering, in which case he might be met by a *δίκη ἐξούλης* involving a penalty in case of defeat, or by applying to the archon for *ἐπιδικασία*. The putative son or adoptive son could then, if he chose, answer by *διαμαρτυρία*, a solemn declaration either by himself or by another that the estate was not adjudicable. It seems that he did this at some stage before the exchange of oaths at the *ἀνάκρισις* (p. 100). The effect of this declaration was to annul the *λῆξις τοῦ κλήρου*.[3]

Gernet is probably right in his thesis that the fifth and fourth century procedure was a survival of a much older procedure which was in some respects quite different in its purpose.[4] There

[1] Isok. 18 *Kallim.* 11 f. *λαγχάνει μοι δίκην μυρίων δραχμῶν. προβαλλομένου δ' ἐμοῦ μάρτυρα ὡς οὐκ εἰσαγώγιμος ἦν ἡ δίκη διαίτης γεγενημένης, ἐκείνῳ μὲν οὐκ ἐπεξῆλθεν, εἰδὼς ὅτι, εἰ μὴ μεταλάβοι τὸ πέμπτον μέρος τῶν ψήφων, τὴν ἐπωβελίαν ὀφλήσει, πείσας δὲ τὴν ἀρχὴν πάλιν τὴν αὐτὴν δίκην ἐγράψατο, ὡς ἐν τοῖς πρυτανείοις μόνον κινδυνεύσων.*

[2] Lys. 23 *Pankl.* 13 f. *ἐν τῇ ἀντωμοσίᾳ γὰρ τῆς δίκης ἣν αὐτῷ ἔλαχεν Ἀριστόδικος οὑτοσί, ἀμφισβητῶν μὴ πρὸς τὸν πολέμαρχον εἶναί οἱ τὰς δίκας διεμαρτυρήθη μὴ Πλαταιεὺς εἶναι. ἐπισκηψάμενος δὲ τῷ μάρτυρι οὐκ ἐπεξῆλθεν, ἀλλ' εἴασε καταδικάσασθαι αὑτοῦ τὸν Ἀριστόδικον.* The passage does not imply, as Calhoun, *CP* 14 (1919) 348 ff., and Hommel, *BPW* 27 (1927) 342 f., would have it, a revisionary procedure grounded on an obscurity in the facts. Cf. Paoli, *St. Proc.* 152, Wolff, *Paragraphe* 131, n. 56.

[3] Isai. 5 *Dikaiog.* 16 f. *ἔδοξέ τε ἡμῖν λαχεῖν τοῦ κλήρου κατ' ἀγχιστείαν, καὶ ἐλάχομεν τοῦ μέρους ἕκαστος. μελλόντων δ' ἡμῶν ἀντόμνυσθαι διεμαρτύρησε Λεωχάρης οὑτοσὶ μὴ ἐπίδικον εἶναι τὸν κλῆρον ἡμῖν. ἐπισκηψαμένων δ' ἡμῶν ἡ μὲν λῆξις τοῦ κλήρου διεγράφη, ἡ δὲ τῶν ψευδομαρτυρίων δίκη εἰσῄει.* As Gernet, *DSGA* 83, n. 3, explains, this text is inexact in its implication that the *λῆξις* was annulled by the *ἐπίσκηψις*; it is clear that it was the *διαμαρτυρία* which annulled it. Isok. 18 *Kallim.* 12 *πάλιν τὴν αὐτὴν δίκην ἐγράψατο* shows that the original *λῆξις* had been annulled. Cf. also Lämmli, *Prozeß.* 151, Berneker, *RE* s.v. *ψευδομαρτυρίων δίκη* 1372 f.

[4] Gernet, *DSGA* 83 ff.

are anomalies in the fourth-century institution. On the one hand the declaration is sometimes starkly negative in form, consisting in the bare formula 'the estate is not adjudicable',[1] with the implication that this bare assertion has the power to inhibit the process of ἐπιδικασία. On other occasions the declaration contains positive elements, as that there is someone who is seised of the estate,[2] or that there is a fact which tends to the confirmation of a man's claim to enter,[3] or that statements made by the other claimant are untrue.[4] It is argued that this anomaly can best be explained by supposing that originally the διαμαρτυρία was an oath taken by what in England was known as a 'compurgator' (in Germany 'Eideshelfer'). This was a purely ritual or procedural act with definite procedural effects which were not related to the question whether what had been affirmed was true or not. In the Athenian system the effect was either to justify an act of self-help by the party supported by the compurgator (that is, take it out of the class of delictual acts) or to inhibit an act of self-help by an opponent (that is, give such an act a delictual character).[5] By the late fifth century what had been a formal act had become an element in a reasoned judicial process. The compurgator is now a witness who vouches for the truth of what is said in his deposition. He can be challenged by ἐπίσκηψις and

[1] Isai. 5 *Dikaiog.* 16 (quoted on p. 125, n. 3), 6 *Philokt.* 4, 59.

[2] Isai. 6 *Philokt.* 10, 17, 58.

[3] Dem. 44 *Leoch.* 54. If we are right to assume that the speaker is quoting the actual words of the written deposition, it asserted that Archiades (the *de cuius*) had left behind γνήσιοι υἱοί, but the claim was on behalf of a great-great-grandson of Archiades' sister and was based on a series of alleged posthumous adoptions. The case is significant on another count: in the succeeding paragraph the speaker alleges that this deposition is invalid because it must be based on hearsay, and hearsay evidence was ruled out in Athenian law.

[4] Isai. 6 *Philokt.* 62: the διαμαρτυρία seems to have contained affirmations (1) that the estate was not adjudicable because sons of Euktemon were in existence, (2) that Philoktemon had not made a will; it is conjecturally reconstructed by Schoemann ad loc. (quoted by Wyse ad loc.). On this and the Leochares case see vol. i, pp. 139 ff. It we are to believe the speaker in Isai. 6 *Philokt.* 52, διαμαρτυρία was appropriate when A was claiming the estate as one adopted by will by the *de cuius* and B asserted that the *de cuius* was not entitled to make a will. The passage is putting a hypothetical case, and the whole of the speech is bedevilled by the fact that the estate in question is Euktemon's whereas the speaker is making out a claim for an alleged adopted son of Philoktemon; Philoktemon was a son of Euktemon who had predeceased him by ten years.

[5] Gernet, *DSGA* 83 ff., Bo. Sm. ii. 174 ff. Note that there is no direct evidence for διαμαρτυρία being used in this sense, nor indeed for the existence of anything like compurgators at Athens.

is liable to prosecution thereafter by a δίκη ψευδομαρτυρίων.[1] The decisive procedural effect of this deposition is underlined by the fact that the claimant on whose behalf it was made had to produce at once the παρακαταβολή (a deposit of one-tenth of the estimated value of the estate, on which see vol. i, p. 158), which he forfeited if he lost the case.[2] A further anomaly was that in the fourth century there was often only one witness (who could be the claimant himself, in spite of the general rule that a man could not give evidence on his own behalf), though there might be several.[3] All in all, by the fourth century the institution had become somewhat bastardized, if one accepts Gernet's account.

There are two conflicting explanations of the fact that the διαμαρτυρία survived almost exclusively in succession cases. On one view, while the παραγραφή was limited to the particular matter in dispute (its result, if the defendant prevailed, was simply that that particular suit was excluded: μὴ εἰσαγώγιμον εἶναι τὴν δίκην), a διαμαρτυρία on the other hand, if not overset by a successful δίκη ψευδομαρτυρίων 'established a title that effectually barred, not only other present claims, but also those that might be set up in the future'.[4] This is an attractively simple view, but it fails to explain either of the fifth-century cases cited above. Another, and perhaps preferable, view is that the διαμαρτυρία was in origin directed to inhibiting (or for that matter demanding) extra-judicial coercive action by a magistrate. What is implied by the coercive action of a magistrate can be seen by

[1] According to Ar. *Pol.* 1274^b5 ff. Charondas invented the δίκη ψευδομαρτυρίων 'for he invented the ἐπίσκηψις': this shows that Aristotle at least did not regard the δίκη ψευδομαρτυρίων as very old. On ἐπίσκηψις see pp. 192 f.

[2] Isai. 6 *Philokt.* 12 (cf. 4), Dem. 44 *Leoch.* 42. As Gernet, *DSGA* 89, n. 4, points out, the speaker in the latter case is guilty of sophistry in suggesting that the deposition was false on the face of it.

[3] If the witnesses had been simply probative, to multiply them would have been obviously desirable. There is a single witness in Isok. 18 *Kallim.* 11, Lys. 23 *Pankl.* 13 f., Isai. 2 *Menekl.* 2, 5 *Dikaiog.* 16, 6 *Philokt.* 4 (here the single witness was Androkles, who himself at some stage put in a claim to the estate; this claim was, it would appear, inconsistent with the statement in his deposition that Euktemon had legitimate sons still living). The claimant himself is the witness in Dem. 44 *Leoch.* (see especially 42); cf. Harpokr. s.v. διαμαρτυρία (quoted on p. 124, n. 3). In Isai. 7 *Apollod.* 3 the speaker, suggesting a hypothetical use of the procedure, uses the plural (the emendation μάρτυρα is arbitrary): ἐγὼ δ' εἰ μὲν ἑώρων ὑμᾶς μᾶλλον ἀποδεχομένους τὰς διαμαρτυρίας ἢ τὰς εὐθυδικίας, κἂν μάρτυρας προὐβαλόμην μὴ ἐπίδικον εἶναι τὸν κλῆρον.

[4] Calhoun, *CP* 13 (1918) 177, Hommel, *BPW* 44 (1924) 542 f., Steinwenter, *Streit.* 87, n. 2.

looking at the role of the magistrate in pre-Solonian days, as pictured for example by Wolff (see pp. 70 ff.). This role was to allow self-help to the aggrieved party, or to forbid it. The two deponents in the fifth-century cases had this in common: they both implied some direct action by the magistrate with regard to the next step in the case. In the Isokrates case it is implied that the giving of this statement at the *ἀνάκρισις* prevented the immediate reference of the case to a dikastery. In the Lysias case the deponent prevented such a delay. Thus in form the *διαμαρτυρία* acted directly upon the magistrate's power as *ἡγεμών*, and the paramountcy of the dikastery as dispenser of all important judicial decisions was preserved only by means of the *δίκη ψευδομαρτυρίων*. The *παραγραφή* procedure tended towards minimizing this anomaly: the defendant had to state in writing at the *ἀνάκρισις* grounds for alleging that the suit was not maintainable, and these grounds were added to by statute from time to time. On this second view, the reason why the *διαμαρτυρία* held its own in succession cases was that there the archon had powers which were distinct in origin from his power as *ἡγεμών* of a court. In the *ἐπιδικασία* of an estate or an heiress some scholars think that the archon acted, not as the *ἡγεμών* (even fictitiously) of a dikastery, but by virtue of an administrative power exemplified by his duty to look after orphans, heiresses, and *οἶκοι* left masterless (*ἐξερημούμενοι*). In succession cases therefore the deponent was parrying a different weapon in the archon's rather antiquated armoury, and this explains why in those cases alone *διαμαρτυρία* survived side by side with *παραγραφή*.[1]

We shall be concerned elsewhere with the *δίκη ψευδομαρτυρίων* as a general remedy against perjury (see pp. 192 ff.); here we are only concerned with its function when brought against one who had made a *διαμαρτυρία*. We are fortunate in having several speeches delivered in such cases, namely Isai. 2 *Menekl.*, 3 *Pyrrh.*, 6 *Philokt.*, Dem. 44 *Leoch.* There were also a number of lost

[1] Vol. i, p. 159, n. 5 came down mildly in favour of the view that even in *ἐπιδικασία* the archon was acting technically as *ἡγεμών* of a dikastery. It is probably better to accept the view of Wolff, *Paragraphe* 128 with n. 52, that the *ἐπιδικάζειν* of the magistrate was in no sense a 'judgement', the vestigial remains of an originally much wider 'judicial' competence of magistrates. His *ἐπιδικάζειν* decree was an official act, resting on coercive powers, enabling the applicant to enter upon the estate or to take the heiress as wife. This decree did not have the binding force of a judgement; if it had, it would have barred a future *διαδικασία* on the estate, but this it did not do.

speeches.[1] The important, and controversial, issue is what was the precise effect of the verdict in such a case. As we shall see, there is some doubt whether in the ordinary suit for perjury a conviction, in addition to the damages payable to the plaintiff, involved some alteration in the judgement of the suit in which the perjured evidence had been given; the probability is that it did not (see pp. 193 ff.). In the cases we are now considering the main case had not been decided, and the problem is what was the effect of a verdict in the *δίκη ψευδομαρτυρίων* on the further conduct of that case.

There is general agreement that if the defendant was acquitted the plaintiff thereby lost his claim to the estate or to the hand of the heiress. If he was convicted on the other hand there is a doubt. Paoli argues that this judgement too settled the main issue, this time in favour of the man claiming the estate or heiress.[2] Wolff on the other hand is firmly of the view that a conviction in the *δίκη ψευδομαρτυρίων* did nothing more than bar the defendant from using the line of defence set out in the *διαμαρτυρία*; the main issue would still be heard separately.[3] Although he throws some legitimate doubt on the conclusiveness of Paoli's arguments, he hardly faces one difficult question: the man who

[1] Lysias *διαμαρτυρία πρὸς τὴν Ἀριστοδήμου γραφήν* (a unique reference to a *γραφή* in this context; what *γραφή* was it?), *ὑπὲρ Εὐκρίτου*, *πρὸς Κλεινίαν*, Deinarchos *ὡς οὐδὲ εἰσὶν ἐπίδικοι αἱ Ἀριστοφῶντος θυγατέρες*, *περὶ τοῦ Εὐίππου κλήρου πρὸς Χάρητα* (D.H. *Dein.* 12).

[2] Paoli, *St. Proc.* 165 ff. He relies mainly on Isai. 3 *Pyrrh.* and Dem. 44 *Leoch.* In Isai. 3 *Pyrrh.* 5 it is clearly implied that the conviction of Xenokles (who had deposed that Pyrrhos' estate was not adjudicable, since he was survived by Phile, his legitimate daughter) in a *δίκη ψευδομαρτυρίων* had entailed the rejection of Phile's claim; but the wording would not be wholly incompatible with a formal trial of the main issue separately. Dem. 44 *Leoch.* is almost certainly a speech in a *δίκη ψευδομαρτυρίων* (see para. 42); yet at 7 we find *ἔστιν γὰρ ὁ μὲν ἀγὼν οὑτοσὶ κλήρου διαδικασία*, and at 14 (a point not made by Paoli) the speaker says that the essentials about which the dikasts have sworn they will vote are contained in the law assigning inheritances to the nearest male kin, but by definition this law would not apply unless and until the deposition of Leochares had been rejected by an adverse verdict in the *δίκη ψευδομαρτυρίων*. Gernet, *DSGA* 89, takes this view of the Leochares case, but changes his mind in *Dem.* ii. 129, where he says that a conviction would have meant simply damages payable to the plaintiff (it is not easy to see how 59, which he cites in n. 3, proves this), and that he would have had to proceed then to a *διαδικασία* to secure the estate, where he might find the same adversary against him.

[3] Wolff, *Paragraphe* 130 f. The agnosticism expressed in vol. i, p. 157, n. 2, still seems justified; but reference should have been made there to Berneker, *RE* s.v. *ψευδομαρτυρίων δίκη* 1374, who disagrees with Paoli.

advanced a διαμαρτυρία surely thereby committed himself to a particular line of argument, for example that Phile was the legitimate daughter of Pyrrhos. What issue was there left to try if the jury rejected that assertion? Or was it theoretically possible for the deponent to change his ground within the same suit as it were and plead, say, that there was a will in his or her favour? This seems at least unlikely, and therefore in this sphere Paoli may still be right in claiming that the trial of the διαμαρτυρία issue was the trial of the main issue as well. The rule might have applied here and not in παραγραφαί because here there was one simple fact on which the defence was based, and if that fact was not established there could be nothing else for the defendant to fall back on; not on a will, for example, since his plea had been that Phile was a legitimate daughter and the existence of such a one ruled out the validity of any will which did not dispose of her hand to an adopted son. On the other hand a man who pleaded that there was no συμβόλαιον binding him to the plaintiff could quite consistently, if that plea was ruled out by an adverse verdict in a παραγραφή, argue that the document alleged to bind him was capable of other interpretations than those put upon it by the plaintiff. His παραγραφή did not assert one single fact, the rejection of which *ipso facto* invalidated his whole defence. It is true that there could be διαμαρτυρίαι that were not plain single statements (see p. 126) and were therefore hard to distinguish from παραγραφαί. Perhaps a compromise is possible: in the cases where the διαμαρτυρία asserted one single fact, the existence of a legitimate son, the trial of the δίκη ψευδομαρτυρίων was recognized *de facto* as conclusive, though there may have been formally a second verdict; but in other cases a second and genuine trial took place.

There seems to have been a certain feeling—probably it was not much more—that there was something slightly evasive in employing the διαμαρτυρία. Dem. 44 *Leoch.* 57 ff. reads like a commonplace designed to suggest that a διαμαρτυρία is suspect because it deprives the courts of decision in matters which they should properly decide.[1] Even if this is a factitious point, invented

[1] The passage also suggests surprisingly that the only justifiable use of the procedure might be to compel a hearing which was being denied (end of 57); that is, its use as in Lys. 23 *Pankl.* 13 f. This use had apparently become obsolete in the fourth century. See also Isai. 6 *Philokt.* 4, 52, 7 *Apollod.* 3 (quoted on p. 127, n. 3).

by orators to discredit their clients' opponents, the fact that it could even plausibly be made does show that it was not necessary for a *suus heres* to use this procedure; he could allow the case to go forward by εὐθυδικία, and this course might have the attraction that if he pursued it he did not need to make the παρακαταβολή. If he did use it, on the other hand, and his opponent proceeded to the δίκη ψευδομαρτυρίων against him and failed to secure one-fifth of the votes, the opponent suffered ἐπωβελία; he himself would have to pay the ἐπωβελία if he failed to get a fifth of the votes.

(iv) ἀντιγραφή

A defendant, besides being able simply to deny the claim or charge (εὐθυδικία) or to plead that the action did not lie (by παραγραφή or διαμαρτυρία), might wish to enter a counter-claim or counter-charge. For this the verb was ἀντιπροσκαλεῖσθαι[1] or ἀντιλαγχάνειν[2] and the noun ἀντιγραφή.[3]

Our principal evidence for this procedure is Dem. 47 *Euerg.*, a speech certainly not by Demosthenes but possibly to be grouped with the speeches dealing with the affairs of Apollodoros, son of Pasion. The speaker was involved in a fracas with Theophemos when trying to seize a gage in execution of a judgement previously given in his favour. He brought a δίκη αἰκείας against Theophemos, a suit available against one who had struck the first blow in a mêlée; Theophemos initiated a counter-claim, asserting that the speaker had struck the first blow. As a result of this counter-claim the suit became as it were two, each being submitted to a different arbitrator.[4] The arbitration of the case in which Theophemos was plaintiff went in his favour; it was

[1] Dem. 47 *Euerg.* 45.

[2] Dem. 40 *Boiot.* ii. 3.

[3] ἀντιγραφή has three meanings set out in Poll. 8. 58. (1) The answer (in writing after perhaps 378/7 B.C.) of the defendant to the plaintiff's claim or charge (Dem. 45 *Steph.* i. 46, 87); see p. 99. (2) A synonym (used only at the end of the fifth century) of παραγραφή (Lys. 23 *Pankl.* 5, 10). (3) Notice of a counter-claim or counter-charge (Dem. 42 *Phain.* 17). The third of these is the meaning which now concerns us. For a fourth sense see p. 182. The use of ἀντιγράψασθαι in Aischin. 1 *Timarch.* 119 for an ἐπαγγελία δοκιμασίας seems untechnical.

[4] Dem. 47 *Euerg.* 45 προσεκαλεσάμην αὐτὸν καὶ ἔλαχον αὐτῷ δίκην τῆς αἰκείας. ἀντιπροσκαλεσαμένου δὲ κἀκείνου ἐμὲ καὶ διαιτητῶν ἐχόντων τὰς δίκας, ἐπειδὴ ἡ ἀπόφασις ἦν τῆς δίκης, ὁ μὲν Θεόφημος παρεγράφετο καὶ ὑπώμνυτο, ἐγὼ δὲ πιστεύων ἐμαυτῷ μηδὲν ἀδικεῖν εἰσῄειν εἰς ὑμᾶς. The plural διαιτητῶν must mean that there were two arbitrators (Lipsius, *AR* 861, n. 51).

appealed by the speaker of this speech, and the verdict was again in favour of Theophemos. In the suit in which the speaker was plaintiff Theophemos spun out the arbitration, so that the suit was still pending when this speech was delivered.[1] It is difficult to imagine how the procedure of the speaker's suit could work out in the light of the verdict given in favour of Theophemos in the other suit. It would surely have been absurd if the speaker had been awarded damages against Theophemos in relation to exactly the same incident for which damages had been awarded to Theophemos against the speaker. If on the other hand the two trials were concerned with different incidents, there seems no reason why the suits should not have been separate from the very start, with the speaker plaintiff in one and Theophemos in the other. Perhaps the explanation is that the speaker is bringing an action for perjury against two of Theophemos' witnesses in his suit, and a verdict adverse to Theophemos in this suit might have rendered a verdict reversing that in the previous suit rational.

A more difficult case is that of Mantitheos in Dem. 40 *Boiot.* ii. He agreed to the equal division of his father's estate between himself and two half-brothers, save that he claimed that his mother's dowry of one talent should have been paid over to him before the division into three parts took place. He is now suing for this dowry; and Boiotos has put in a counter-claim, not now, as he had previously done, for the dowry of his own mother, Plangon, but for some miscellaneous unspecified things.[2]

Another not very clear case is Dem. 41 *Spoud.* The speaker is the husband of the elder daughter of Polyeuktos, and is suing Spoudias, married to Polyeuktos' younger daughter, for part of his wife's dowry, which he alleges is due to him out of Polyeuktos' estate, and for a number of other things. Spoudias has not only

[1] Dem. 47 *Euerg.* 8 *τῆς αἰκείας . . . ἐφ' ᾗ ἐγὼ διώκω δίκῃ τὸν Θεόφημον* shows that the suit was still pending; cf. 10.

[2] Dem. 40 *Boiot.* ii. 3 *ἀποστεροῦμαι δὲ τὴν προῖκα τῆς ἐμαυτοῦ μητρός, περὶ ἧς νυνὶ δικάζομαι, αὐτὸς μὲν τούτοις δίκας ὑπὲρ ὧν ἐνεκάλουν μοι πάντων δεδωκώς, πλὴν εἴ τινα νῦν ἕνεκα τῆς δίκης ταύτης ἀντειλήχασίν μοι συκοφαντοῦντες.* Gernet, *Dem.* ii. 29, holds that Boiotos' counter-claim was for his mother's dowry. Lipsius, *AR* 863, n. 55, argued from Dem. 40 *Boiot.* ii. 55 that Boiotos could not have been claiming that at this stage, since the speaker there asserts that, whereas he cannot renew his claim for his mother's dowry if the present suit goes against him, the same does not apply to Boiotos; therefore Plangon's dowry cannot have been at issue here. Gernet, *Dem.* ii. 48, n. 3, perhaps rather cavalierly, dismisses this argument of Mantitheos as chicanery.

rebutted this claim, but has made a counter-claim for sums or objects due to him out of the estate. The two issues would be tried separately, for the speaker complains (12 f.) that Spoudias is bringing into argument now matters which he will have an opportunity of raising at a later date.

Finally in Dem. 33 *Apatour.* we find Parmenon, in the course of an action (probably a δίκη βλάβης) against Apatourios, challenging him to an oath on certain issues. Apatourios accepted the challenge, but later, in order to evade it, he brought a counter-claim against Parmenon. Although the two issues were sufficiently close to be submitted to private arbitration under one agreement, the orator's words show that they were regarded as two δίκαι, which presumably meant that, if the arbitration failed, the issues would go before separate juries, or the same jury on two occasions.[1]

The evidence is too fragmentary to allow us to see clearly the detail of this procedure, and in particular to say how the effects of a judgement in a counter-claim differed from what they would have been if the issue had been raised in isolation. One difference, though this is pure conjecture, must surely have been that, whichever issue was tried first (and we seem to have no evidence as to which issue was normally tried first), neither side could plead *res iudicata* to block the hearing of the other issue. Less conjectural is the rule that ἐπωβελία might be (or perhaps always was) incurred in a counter-action.[2]

§ 7. *Evidence*

(i) *Introduction*

Aristotle divides means of persuasion into those which can be produced by art (the art of the orator) and those which cannot (πίστεις ἔντεχνοι and ἄτεχνοι);[3] we are concerned only with the latter. In a later passage he lists five kinds of πίστεις ἄτεχνοι: laws, witnesses, agreements, tortures, and oaths.[4] We can work with these kinds, taking laws to include decrees of the boule or

[1] Dem. 33 *Apatour.* 14 ἐνεστηκυιῶν δ' αὐτοῖς τῶν δικῶν πεισθέντες ὑπὸ τῶν παρόντων εἰς ἐπιτροπὴν ἔρχονται. Wolff, *Freiburger Rechts- und Staatswissenschaftliche Abhandlungen* 27 (1967) 178.

[2] For ἐπωβελία see pp. 183 ff.

[3] Ar. *Rhet.* 1355^{b}35.

[4] Ar. *Rhet.* 1375^{a}24 f. νόμοι, μάρτυρες, συνθῆκαι, βάσανοι, ὅρκοι. On the whole topic see Bonner, *Evidence*, Leisi, *Zeuge*, Bo. Sm. ii. 117 ff., Latte, *RE* s.v. 'Martyria'.

ekklesia and agreements to include other kinds of document; but we should add a sixth, namely challenges (προκλήσεις). Expert evidence by such witnesses as doctors hardly formed a special category.[1]

(ii) *Laws and decrees*

We may find it strange that laws and decrees should be classed as evidence; we regard evidence as directed towards establishing the facts, while laws and decrees constitute the framework of rules under which the facts have to be subsumed. But in the Athenian courts of the fourth century there was no sharp distinction between decisions on law and on facts. Both were ultimately in the hands of the dikasts, and there was no judge experienced in the law whose task it was, with the help of advocates likewise experienced, to explicate the rules (of which laws would be the leading constituent) which should govern the decision on the facts. It was inevitable therefore that the litigant should have the duty of laying before the court any law or decree relevant to his case, whether he were plaintiff or defendant, and that the laws thus cited should come to be regarded as on all fours with evidence in convincing the dikasts to vote in his favour.

The litigant might simply quote from the law in the text of his speech, as for example Hypereides does with the law of εἰσαγγελία in 3 *Euxen.* 7 f. But the usual procedure, at least after the first quarter of the fourth century, was for the law or decree, or its relevant sections, to be written down and read out at the trial by the clerk of the court. During the period when all evidence was still oral[2] there must have been considerable laxity in the citation of laws, and we cannot tell what control a litigant (and by implication the court) had over the accuracy or strict relevance of his opponent's citations. This uncertainty would have been enhanced by the fact that until the end of the fifth century there was probably no recognized state archive containing the official

[1] In Dem. 54 *Kon.* 10 f. no particular emphasis is laid upon the evidence of the surgeon, as distinct from the bystanders, as to the character of the hurt suffered by the plaintiff, and we look in vain for expert medical evidence in Lys. 24 *Invalid* 14, Dem. 47 *Euerg.* 67.

[2] Oral evidence was replaced by written depositions probably in 378/7 B.C. See discussion with full reference to authorities and modern arguments in Bo. Sm. i. 357 ff.

copies of the laws,[1] with the result that it could be plausibly alleged against Nikomachos, an official concerned with a kind of codification of the law in the last decade of the fifth century, that he was handing out contradictory laws to opposing litigants for use in the courts.[2] Some improvement in this respect must have come from the initiation of a state archive in the Metroon, and from the rule that evidence (including laws to be cited) was to be in the form of written depositions read out by the clerk at the trial. But we must bear in mind that even thereafter the dikasts themselves would have had to rely on remembering the texts which had been read out[3] and that, in those cases which had not been before public arbitrators, there was nothing to prevent a litigant from producing at the trial evidence (again presumably including laws) which he had not mentioned at the ἀνάκρισις (see p. 97). There was, however, the threat of the death penalty against one who cited a non-existent law.[4]

Dem. 18 *Crown* has many examples of decrees, whether of the Athenian ekklesia or of other states, cited as evidence, as well as letters of Philip both to Athens and to other states.[5] There might be citations from the documents of officials, such as the lists of those liable to trierarchies or the books of customs officers.[6] Decisions in previous cases were not cited, unless they were points decided in an arbitration relevant to the case in hand.[7]

(iii) *Private documents*

These included contracts, wills, and such private documents as the ledgers of bankers. If a party wished to use such a document in evidence, but did not hold either it or a copy of it, he could make formal application (πρόκλησις) either to his opponent or to a third party to produce it and allow him to take a copy.[8] He would take witnesses with him when he made his demand, and

[1] Harrison, *JHS* 75 (1955) 26 ff.

[2] Lys. 30 *Nikom.* 3. For fraud in this sphere see Calhoun, *CP* 9 (1914) 140 ff.

[3] The men of that period were probably less dependent than we on the written word for memorizing a text.

[4] Dem. 26 *Aristogeit.* ii. 24.

[5] Hyper. 5 *Athenog.* 33 cites a decree of Troizen.

[6] Dem. 18 *Crown* 106, 34 *Ag. Phorm.* 7.

[7] As in Dem. 36 *For Phorm.* 16, 59 *Neair.* 47. For the possibility of an archive of previous decisions see Paoli, *Studi Betti* (Milan, 1962) iii. 3 ff.

[8] Dem. 49 *Timoth.* 43.

might summon his opponent to be present if the demand was of a third party.[1] He might also challenge his opponent to pronounce immediately on the genuineness of the document in question.[2] It is a matter of doubt whether the δίκη εἰς ἐμφανῶν κατάστασιν was available to force compliance with a demand to produce any document a litigant wanted, or could only be used when the document was the immediate subject of the suit, such as a will or a contract.[3]

Other kinds of challenge, to which it was usual to summon witnesses, were sometimes recorded in documents. For example, when there was a πρόκλησις εἰς βάσανον, it was provident to record the exact circumstances against the eventuality that the opponent either declined the challenge or, having accepted it, failed to carry it out.[4] Although to refuse such a challenge entailed no direct juristic consequences, orators knew how to make the most of it to their clients' advantage.[5]

(iv) *Witnesses*

We are here concerned solely with witnesses and their evidence in court cases;[6] the function of witnesses in various legal or quasi-legal acts such as marriage and wills is touched upon in the discussion of these acts.[7]

We begin with a controversial point. The prevailing view is that giving evidence to a court was a privilege restricted to free males of age; as an exception to the rule, slaves and women could give evidence against (but not on behalf of) one accused of homicide. MacDowell has argued persuasively that the evidence does not allow us to decide whether the exception held or not, that is whether slaves and women were or were not permitted to give evidence in homicide cases.[8] In other cases, however, Isai. 12 *Euphil.* 5 and Dem. 57 *Euboul.* 67 both suggest that if women's evidence was needed it would be given either by or only with the

[1] Dem. 48 *Olymp.* 48.

[2] Dem. 45 *Steph.* i. 8 ff.

[3] Vol. i, p. 209, n. 2.

[4] The technical term for proving such a challenge in evidence was πρόκλησιν μαρτυρεῖν (Dem. 45 *Steph.* i. 15, 46 *Steph.* ii. 11).

[5] Dem. 45 *Steph.* i. 8 ff., 46 *Steph.* ii. 4 ff., 48 *Olymp.* 49 f.

[6] Bonner, *Evidence* and Leisi, *Zeuge* remain indispensable. See also Bo. Sm. ii. 117 ff., Pringsheim, *RIDA* 6 (1951) 161 ff.

[7] See vol. i, index s.v. 'witnesses'.

[8] MacDowell, *Homicide* 102 ff.; cf. vol. i, p. 170.

permission of their *κύριοι*. According to the Isaios passage a woman could stop her *κύριος* giving in her name evidence of which she did not approve.[1] It is not easy to see what difference it made that the evidence was technically given by the *κύριος*, at least from the period when all evidence was in writing; before that time one can understand that there might have been social objections to women's appearing publicly in court. The view that the restriction applied also to minors seems to rest merely on analogy with women. Slaves' evidence is considered in the section on tortures (pp. 147 ff.).

A man who had come of age could give evidence about facts during his minority,[2] as could a freedman about facts which had occurred while he was still a slave.[3]

There seems no doubt that loss of citizenship involved incapacity to give evidence in court.[4] On the other hand foreigners certainly gave evidence both in private and in public suits.[5]

There is in all this an unresolved paradox. The incapacity of certain persons to give evidence must sometimes have spelt substantial denial of justice to litigants. The rule may have arisen from an irrational feeling that this class of persons (slaves, women, minors, or those deprived of citizenship) could not be trusted to speak the truth; or it may have been a survival from the days when witnesses were rather compurgators than people who assisted the court to arrive at the truth.[6] If a witness was in essence a compurgator, the right to be one was understandably a privilege; it was unavoidable bad luck for a litigant if a potential compurgator was thus disqualified.

A litigant could not give evidence in support of his own case,[7] but a man who was going to speak as a litigant's advocate

[1] Isai. 12 *Euphil.* 5 *οὐκ ἄν ποτε, ὦ ἄνδρες δικασταί, τοὺς ἑαυτῶν ἄνδρας αἱ ἀδελφαὶ μαρτυρεῖν εἴασαν καὶ ἐπέτρεψαν.* Bo. Sm. ii. 131 ('Normally the evidence of a woman *could* be presented by her *κύριος*': my italics) is unhelpful. Lacey, *Family* 174, does not distinguish sufficiently between oaths taken by women and unsworn testimony.

[2] Dem. 49 *Timoth.* 42. As Leisi, *Zeuge* 12, points out, this would suggest that a minor was held to be incapable, not of noticing the facts, but of giving a true account of what he had noticed.

[3] Dem. 49 *Timoth.* 17, 33, 55.

[4] Dem. 21 *Meid.* 95, 59 *Neair.* 26 f., Hyper. 4 *Phil.* 12.

[5] Private suits: Dem. 35 *Lakrit.* 14, 20, 23, 33 f., Hyper. 5 *Athenog.* 33. Public: Dem. 19 *Embassy* 146, 25 *Aristogeit.* i. 62, Aischin. 2 *Embassy* 155.

[6] For the possibility of the compurgator in early Athens see p. 126.

[7] Dem. 46 *Steph.* ii. 9 *μαρτυρεῖν γὰρ οἱ νόμοι οὐκ ἐῶσιν αὐτὸν αὑτῷ οὔτ' ἐπὶ ταῖς γραφαῖς οὔτ' ἐπὶ ταῖς δίκαις οὔτ' ἐν ταῖς εὐθύναις*, 40 *Boiot.* ii. 58.

(συνήγορος) could first give evidence on his behalf.[1] As we have seen (p. 127), in spite of this rule a man might make a διαμαρτυρία on his own behalf.

We cannot tell what, if any, precautions were taken to see that one who had given evidence for either party did not sit on the jury, or what provisions there were for ensuring that a witness required in one case was not called upon for jury service in another; but there surely were such. On the other hand orators could and did make general appeals to jurors to their personal recollection of matters in issue.[2]

An Athenian court had no power corresponding to the modern *sub poena* to compel a witness to appear before it. Litigants however had ways of compelling a reluctant witness to give evidence for them, though there is some doubt about the exact details of the procedure. A man could not compel his opponent to give evidence, though he could require him to answer questions.[3] We have several examples of such questioning.[4] On the other hand relationship to a litigant probably did not confer immunity against being called to give evidence in favour of his opponent;[5] nor could a reluctant witness escape on the ground that he might incriminate himself.[6] But a man who had been twice convicted of false evidence could not be compelled to give evidence; this was because a third conviction would render him liable to total ἀτιμία.[7] This again was a rule which might have

[1] Isai. 12 *Euphil.* 4, Aischin. 2 *Embassy* 170; Leisi, *Zeuge* 36 f.

[2] Andok. 1 *Myst.* 37, 69, Lys. 10 *Theomn.* i. 1, 12 *Ag. Erat.* 74, Dem. 21 *Meid.* 18, 47 *Euerg.* 44; Leisi, *Zeuge* 34 ff.

[3] Dem. 46 *Steph.* ii. 10 τοῖν ἀντιδίκοιν ἐπάναγκες εἶναι ἀποκρίνασθαι ἀλλήλοις τὸ ἐρωτώμενον, μαρτυρεῖν δὲ μή, Plato, *Apol.* 25 d.

[4] Lys. 12 *Ag. Erat.* 25, 13 *Agorat.* 30, 32, 22 *Corn-dealers* 5, Isai. 11 *Hagn.* 5; Latte, *HR* 16, n. 27. Leisi, *Zeuge* 41, supposes on *a priori* grounds that in such ἐρωτήσεις the water-clock was not stopped; he explains Dem. 57 *Euboul.* 61 by supposing that the evidence the speaker seeks to extract from his opponents would be by way of ἐρωτήσεις and hence will be in the speaker's time.

[5] The only evidence seems to be Dem. 29 *Aphob.* iii. 15, 20, which would tend to show that Aisios could have been forced to give evidence against his brother Aphobos, and Aphobos against his uncle Demon; for doubts as to the reliability of this speech as a source see vol. i, p. 105, n. 5. There is no hint that wives could not give evidence against their husbands, though one cannot imagine their doing so, at least while they were in their husbands' κυριεία (cf. vol. i, p. 30).

[6] Aischin. 1 *Timarch.* 45, 98; for testimony incriminating the witness Dem. 58 *Theokr.* 35, 59 *Neair.* 28, Aischin. 1 *Timarch.* 115.

[7] Hyper. 4 *Phil.* 12 τοῖς τῶν ψευδομαρτυρίων δὶς ἡλωκόσιν δεδώκατε ὑμεῖς τὸ τρίτον μὴ μαρτυρεῖν μηδ' οἷς ἂν παραγένωνται, ἵνα μηδενὶ τῶν πολιτῶν ᾖ τὸ ὑμέτερον πλῆθος αἴτιον τοῦ ἠτιμῶσθαι, ἀλλ' αὐτὸς αὑτῷ, ἂν μὴ παύηται τὰ ψευδῆ μαρτυρῶν.

borne hardly upon a litigant who needed such a man's evidence. It seems probable that witnesses could not be forced to give evidence in homicide cases; it is certainly surprising that no witnesses are called for the prosecution in Ant. 1 *Stepmother*, but this may have been because the prosecutor could not find a voluntary witness. One peculiarity of evidence in homicide cases was that the witness had to take an oath not merely that what he said was true but that the accused had or had not killed. With such a rule, not in itself very rational, it would have been even more irrational to compel a reluctant witness.[1]

In the normal case a litigant would secure evidence from volunteers, and a passage from Isaios shows that a wise man would provide against possible litigation by having friends present as witnesses of any act which might need the support of witnesses in court later.[2] Where the situation was unforeseen, the wise man called on the bystanders as witnesses. In both cases he had to draft, either in advance or fairly soon after the event, a written document to which the witnesses were prepared to assent when it was produced either at the trial or, if it was a case for arbitration, before the arbitrator. It would have been the duty of the litigant, not any state official, to secure that the said witnesses did actually attend at the trial or arbitration to acknowledge their testimony.

More interesting is the case where an important or vital witness was unwilling to give evidence or, having promised to, failed to attend at the required hearing. Lykourgos has a passage reflecting on the need which sometimes arose to force reluctant witnesses to appear in court and to acknowledge the evidence in the depositions.[3] The passage envisages either failure of the witness to appear or failure, if he did appear, either to acknowledge the deposition or to take an oath of rejection. We have concrete instances of bystanders and also of unfriendly witnesses

[1] Leisi, *Zeuge* 38 f., Gernet, *Ant.* 36 f., MacDowell, *Homicide* 101.

[2] Isai. 3 *Pyrrh.* 19 *ἴστε γὰρ πάντες ὡς ὅταν μὲν ἐπὶ προδήλους πράξεις ἴωμεν, ἃς δεῖ μετὰ μαρτύρων γενέσθαι, τοὺς οἰκειοτάτους καὶ οἷς ἂν τυγχάνωμεν χρώμενοι μάλιστα, τούτους παραλαμβάνειν εἰώθαμεν ἐπὶ τὰς πράξεις τὰς τοιαύτας, τῶν δὲ ἀδήλων καὶ ἐξαίφνης γιγνομένων τοὺς προστυχόντας ἕκαστοι μάρτυρας ποιούμεθα.* The whole passage is important as an account of how evidence was normally collected.

[3] Lykourg. *Leokr.* 20. When the orator says 'If the witnesses do neither [neither acknowledge their evidence nor take an oath of disclaimer], we will summons them (*κλητεύσομεν*)', he must mean 'we will claim that they are liable to the fine for such double failure'.

being roped in.[1] The details of the procedure are not clear. There were three ways in which a litigant could bring pressure to bear on an unwilling witness. The most direct was described by the verb *κλητεύω*, used of the litigant, or *ἐκκλητεύω*, used of the herald.[2] The litigant challenged the witness to acknowledge the deposition or to take an oath of disclaimer; if he did neither of these things, the litigant would 'summons' him (*κλητεύσω*), and would call upon the herald to make public that he had been summonsed (*ἐκκλήτευε*). Although in the passage cited above from Lykourgos and in Dem. 58 *Theokr.* 7 the litigant begs the jury to help him in making the reluctant witness come up to scratch, this seems mere rhetoric, and it is unlikely that any vote was put to the jury on the matter, though they may have been able to indicate their displeasure against a reluctant witness by some informal means. Rather, the failure of the witness was punished automatically with a fine of 1,000 drachmai as soon as the litigant made his formal summons, and solemn publicity was given to the fine by the herald's announcement.[3] The fine went to the state, probably even when the case was a private one.[4]

[1] See Aristoph. *Clouds* 494 ff. for bystanders in a case of assault. In Dem. 57 *Euboul.* 14 the litigant wished evidence about proceedings at a meeting of demesmen which had been prolonged into the night. He had not taken the precaution of ensuring that some of his friends should be present; he therefore wrote out what he alleged happened, and administered this document to be acknowledged by witnesses hostile to his cause. Apparently they accepted it. In Isai. 9 *Astyph.* 18 the speaker was trying to discredit a will of Astyphilos in favour of the son of Kleon. One of his points was that Astyphilos' father had died as the result of blows received in a fight with Kleon's father, but the only witness to this fight he could furnish was one Hierokles, who had produced the allegedly forged will. He therefore administered a deposition describing the affray to Hierokles, though he was sure he would disclaim it by oath, which is what happened. See Wyse's note ad loc. (though note that he commits himself to the view that no new evidence could be produced at the trial). The usefulness of such a move to a litigant, who would usually know when a witness was likely to refuse, may have been parallel to the modern trick of getting a witness to say something which is then ordered to be stricken from the record.

[2] Dem. 59 *Neair.* 28 *τὸν δ' Ἵππαρχον αὐτὸν ὑμῖν καλῶ, καὶ ἀναγκάσω μαρτυρεῖν ἢ ἐξόμνυσθαι κατὰ τὸν νόμον, ἢ κλητεύσω αὐτόν*, Aischin. 2 *Embassy* 68 *κάλει δέ μοι Ἀμύντορα Ἑρχιέα, καὶ ἐκκλήτευε, ἐὰν μὴ θέλῃ δευρὶ παρεῖναι.*

[3] Aischin. 1 *Timarch.* 46 *ἐὰν δὲ προαιρῆται ἐκκλητευθῆναι μᾶλλον ἢ τἀληθῆ μαρτυρεῖν, ὑμεῖς τὸ ὅλον πρᾶγμα συνίδετε. εἰ γὰρ ὁ μὲν πράξας αἰσχυνεῖται καὶ προαιρήσεται χιλίας μᾶλλον δραχμὰς ἀποτεῖσαι τῷ δημοσίῳ, ὥστε μὴ δεῖξαι τὸ πρόσωπον τὸ ἑαυτοῦ ὑμῖν* . . . Leisi, *Zeuge* 54 ff., Lipsius, *AR* 880, Bo. Sm. ii. 138. It is not clear what Gernet, *Dem.* i. 262, has in mind when he describes this procedure as 'moyen de contrainte par voix de héraut et après autorisation du tribunal'.

[4] In only one case where *κλητεύειν* is used or implied was the suit a private one,

If a litigant made use of this immediate sanction, we must suppose that he was precluded from any further remedy against the witness and had to be content with the feeling of satisfied revenge.[1] If however he held his hand (and we must suppose that this was left in his discretion), he could bring one of two private actions against the recalcitrant witness. He could bring a *δίκη λιπομαρτυρίου* against him. Our only direct evidence for this suit is in Dem. 49 *Timoth.* According to the rather confused account[2] of the speaker, Apollodoros, he needed the evidence of a certain Antiphanes in a debt case against Timotheos. Antiphanes had frequently said he would give this evidence, but on the day fixed for the arbitration of this suit (*ἡ κυρία*), although summoned, he failed to appear (*ἔλιπε τὴν μαρτυρίαν*), having been suborned by Timotheos. Apollodoros 'deposited the drachma of the *λιπομαρτυρίου* according to the law'; but the arbitrator did not give the case against him (this might be either Antiphanes[3] or Timotheos[4]), but went off having given his decision late at night in favour of Timotheos. 'At the present time', Apollodoros goes on, 'I have filed against Antiphanes a private suit *βλάβης* because he neither gave evidence for me nor took an oath of disclaimer as the law demands; and I demand that he now mount the tribune and tell you on oath that he lent Timotheos one thousand drachmai' and so forth. We can dismiss the last demand as mere rodomontade,[5] but we must try to make something out of the earlier sentences. The most plausible, but far from certain, explanation is that the deposit of one drachma was a court fee[6] for bringing the charge of *λιπομαρτυρίου* against the witness, and that it was at the

Dem. 32 *Zenoth.* 30. The other six are Aischin. 1 *Timarch.* 46, 2 *Embassy* 68, Dem. 19 *Embassy* 176, 198, 58 *Theokr.* 7, 42, 59 *Neair.* 28, Lykourg. *Leokr.* 20.

[1] So Bonner, *Evidence* 42 f., Leisi, *Zeuge* 49, Bo. Sm. ii. 139, as against MSL 497; Lipsius, *AR* 880 f. tacitly accepts the view of Leisi and Bonner. In the absence of direct evidence either view is *a priori*.

[2] Dem. 49 *Timoth.* 19 f. *τοῦ μὲν γὰρ μαρτυρίαν με ἐμβαλέσθαι πρὸς τὸν διαιτητὴν παρεκρούσατο, φάσκων ἀεί μοι μαρτυρήσειν εἰς τὴν κυρίαν· ἐπειδὴ δὲ ἡ δίαιτα ἦν, προσκληθεὶς ἀπὸ τῆς οἰκίας (οὐ γὰρ ἦν φανερός), ἔλιπε τὴν μαρτυρίαν πεισθεὶς ὑπὸ τούτου. τιθέντος δέ μου αὐτῷ τὴν δραχμὴν τοῦ λιπομαρτυρίου κατὰ τὸν νόμον, ὁ διαιτητὴς οὐ κατεδιῄτα, ἀλλ' ἀπιὼν ᾤχετο ἀποδιαιτήσας τούτου τὴν δίαιταν, ἑσπέρας ἤδη οὔσης. νυνὶ δὲ τῷ Ἀντιφάνει εἴληχα βλάβης ἰδίαν δίκην, ὅτι μοι οὔτ' ἐμαρτύρησεν οὔτ' ἐξωμόσατο κατὰ τὸν νόμον. καὶ ἀξιῶ αὐτὸν ἀναβάντα εἰπεῖν ἐναντίον ὑμῶν διομοσάμενον, πρῶτον μὲν εἰ ἐδάνεισε Τιμοθέῳ* . . .

[3] So Lipsius, *AR* 785, Bo. Sm. ii. 140.

[4] So Gernet, *Dem.* iii. 19.

[5] So Bo. Sm. ii. 140, Lämmli, *Prozeß.* 103, n. 1.

[6] Poll. 8. 39 for a *παράστασις* of one drachma.

discretion of the arbitrator to pronounce the fine against the witness;[1] he did not do so, and as a result neither was the witness fined nor was his refusal to give evidence recorded in the documents which were to be put into the casket and thus furnish the evidence for the trial of the case if it were appealed.[2] It is the latter point which really concerns Apollodoros, since he is trying to explain away the fact that evidence from one very material witness is missing from the dossier. According to his own statement he had still the chance of recovering damages from Antiphanes by means of a *δίκη βλάβης*, but we may perhaps assume that that suit would not have been heard until the case against Timotheos was finished, since the verdict on the latter would necessarily affect the amount of damages he could reasonably claim.[3]

This brings us on to the *δίκη βλάβης*. The passage from Dem. 49 *Timoth.* is our only evidence from the orators for this suit in this connection,[4] and we are therefore driven back on speculation in deciding whether the action was in principle based on breach of contract (not giving evidence after having undertaken to do so) or was delictual and directed against anyone who resisted a statutory duty to give evidence (or take an oath of disclaimer) when requested by a litigant to do so.[5] Although Pringsheim has shown

[1] On the translation of Lipsius and Bo. Sm. (p. 141 n. 3 above) his refusal to do this is expressed in the words *ὁ διαιτητὴς οὐ κατεδιῄτα.*

[2] Gernet, *Dem.* iii. 19, n. 2, doubts whether the expression *τοῦ λιπομαρτυρίου* necessarily entails that there was a *δίκη* so named. For him the deposit of one drachma is the formal notice of intention to bring an action (parallel to *ἐπίσκηψις* as formal notice of a future *δίκη ψευδομαρτυρίων*). He seems to imply, though he does not say, that the effect should have been (at least if Apollodoros' statement of the situation was correct) that proceedings on the main case were postponed until the *δίκη βλάβης* was decided. This is the view of Lipsius, *AR* 784. Would this mean that a possible issue of the *δίκη βλάβης* was an instruction to the witness to give his evidence? If we could accept Dem. 29 *Aphob.* iii. 20 as reliable evidence, the arbitrator could order a witness to give evidence or take the oath. Does Apollodoros mean by *οὐ κατεδιῄτα* 'did not order him to', an order which would have implied a fine of 1,000 drachmai if he refused?

[3] The *δίκη βλάβης* must have been an *ἄγων τιμητός*. If the rule was as suggested in the text, the estimation procedure must have been held over till after the decision of the main case; and this might suggest that the *ἀνάκρισις* of such a *δίκη βλάβης* had to await that event also.

[4] But Plato, *Laws* 937 a may be based on an Athenian law: *ὁ δ' εἰς μαρτυρίαν κληθείς, μὴ ἀπαντῶν δὲ τῷ καλεσαμένῳ, τῆς βλάβης ὑπόδικος ἔστω κατὰ νόμον.* Dem. 29 *Aphob.* iii. 15 confirms that a reluctant witness could be forced to give evidence through fear of a *δίκη*; but this speech is suspect as a source.

[5] Lipsius, *AR* 659, assumes that the claim was contractual, as against Bo. Sm. ii. 143, Pringsheim, *GLS* 53. The treatment of the three methods by Bo. Sm. is not satisfactory.

that there is no certain instance of a δίκη βλάβης being used for a simple breach of contract, it would be a circular argument to say that the phrase δίκη βλάβης applied to a suit proves *ipso facto* that that suit was non-contractual. Nevertheless it seems on general grounds to be probable that this particular action was delictual.

Tentatively we may sum up the position thus. If a witness was reluctant, the litigant could call upon him to give evidence or take an oath of disclaimer. If and when the matter was before an arbitrator, the litigant could issue a summons (κλητεύειν), in which case the arbitrator would make formal record of the fact and the record would go into the casket; presumably the fine against the witness would stand, though he may have had some redress unknown to us for getting it reversed. Alternatively the litigant could give notice that he was going to proceed against the witness by a δίκη λιπομαρτυρίου (possibly a δίκη βλάβης). If he chose this course, the arbitrator could at his discretion (or perhaps was strictly bound to) postpone his own decision on the main issue until the trial of the δίκη λιπομαρτυρίου was completed. But he could ignore this notice and give a decision, as the arbitrator in the Timotheos case did. This of course had the damaging effect on the litigant that strictly he could not bring that particular issue before the dikasts by way of evidence at all. In cases where there was no arbitration the procedure was simpler. As we have seen, there was in such cases no rule that all evidence had to be produced before the magistrate at the ἀνάκρισις. The litigant had still the choice between κλητεύειν and a suit for damages against the recalcitrant witness. But it seems unlikely that, if he chose the latter, the condemnation of the witness would involve the reversal of his own condemnation in the main suit, though this has sometimes been supposed on the analogy of the effects of a δίκη ψευδομαρτυριῶν.[1]

Another controversial matter is the nature and effect of the oath of disclaimer.[2] According to Pollux the oath of disclaimer

[1] Leisi, *Zeuge* 52, believes that a sentence in either suit might be either for money damages or for an instruction to the witness to conform to the challenge; which of the two would have depended on the τίμησις of the plaintiff and the defendant. For the possibility of a new trial see pp. 193 ff.

[2] The procedure is referred to directly or indirectly in Isai. 9 *Astyph.* 18, Aischin. 1 *Timarch.* 47, 67, 69, Dem. 29 *Aphob.* iii. 15, 18, 20, 45 *Steph.* i. 58 ff., 49 *Timoth.* 20, 58 *Theokr.* 7, 59 *Neair.* 28, Ar. *Ath. Pol.* 55. 5; cf. Plato, *Laws* 936 e. The word is

simply stated that the witness had not been present or knew nothing of the matter.[1] This statement should probably be accepted at its face value; but some scholars have supposed on *a priori* grounds that it must have been open to a witness to state that the matter was quite otherwise than as stated in the deposition. Rationality certainly demanded such a rule, since the skilful drafting of a deposition must often have made it impossible for a witness either to accept it or to take the oath of disclaimer. Nevertheless, if the witness to fact was the survivor of the compurgator (see p. 137), this might explain the irrationality of requiring of every witness that he must take a stand either for the litigant, by giving the evidence that he was asking him to give, or against him by the oath of disclaimer. A passage in Aischines shows a litigant drafting depositions with an eye to the likelihood of their being acceptable to the witness.[2] Probably the rule was that the witness had no other choice, but must either accept or reject the deposition drawn up by the litigant who was challenging him.[3] Such a rule might obviously be harsh upon a witness; for, although there was no penal action against false evidence as such, there was an action for damages arising out of false evidence, the *δίκη ψευδομαρτυρίων*, to which the witness might be liable on the basis of the evidence in the deposition or of his oath of disclaimer. There is one piece of evidence which might suggest that a witness could bring a *δίκη βλάβης* against a litigant who wrongfully put him in this position: according to Dem. 29 *Aphob.* iii. 16, Demosthenes might have been sued by Aisios for having compelled him to give false evidence against his brother, Aphobos.[4] Unfortunately this speech is suspect; but the sentence

usually *ἐξομνύναι*; in Aischin. 1 *Timarch.* 67, Plato, *Laws* 936 e it is *ἀπομνύναι*. In only three of the recorded cases did the witness choose the oath of disclaimer: Isai. 9 *Astyph.* 18, Aischin. 1 *Timarch.* 67, Dem. 45 *Steph.* i. 60. Cf. Leisi, *Zeuge* 67 ff., Lipsius, *AR* 878 f., Bo. Sm. ii. 137.

[1] Poll. 8. 37 *ἔδει δὲ αὐτὸν ἢ μαρτυρεῖν ἢ ἐξομόσασθαι ὡς οὐκ εἰδείη ἢ μὴ παρείη*, 55 *ἐξώμνυντο δὲ καὶ οἱ κληθέντες μάρτυρες, εἰ φάσκοιεν μηδὲν ἐπίστασθαι τούτων ἐφ' ἃ ἐκαλοῦντο.*

[2] Aischin. 1 *Timarch.* 67 *οὐκοῦν καὶ αὐτὸν ὑμῖν καλῶ τὸν Ἡγήσανδρον. γέγραφα δ' αὐτῷ μαρτυρίαν κοσμιωτέραν μὲν ἢ κατ' ἐκεῖνον, μικρῷ δὲ σαφεστέραν ἢ τῷ Μισγόλᾳ. οὐκ ἀγνοῶ δ' ὅτι ἀπομεῖται καὶ ἐπιορκήσει.* Dem. 54 *Kon.* 26 has another instance of a litigant composing depositions in the hope of getting a witness to accept them.

[3] So Lipsius, *AR* 879, n. 51, against Leisi, *Zeuge* 89. Wyse, *Isai.* 638, takes the same view as Lipsius.

[4] Dem. 29 *Aphob.* iii. 16 *οὐκ ἂν ἡσυχίαν ἦγεν, ἀλλὰ δίκην ἄν μοι βλάβης ἔλαχεν, εἰ ψευδομαρτυρίων ὑπόδικον αὐτὸν ἐποίουν κατὰ τἀδελφοῦ οὐ προσῆκον.*

has some residual value, since it is perhaps unlikely that the inventor of the speech, if it is a forgery, conjured this suit out of his head.[1] Evidence collected in advance by the litigant would have been written out on a whitened board in a way which made it difficult to amend the text.[2]

Hearsay evidence was ruled out by law.[3] But there was a specific exception in favour of evidence of what a dead man was alleged to have said.[4] It seems probable that such evidence could itself be challenged by a *δίκη ψευδομαρτυρίων*, but the only point then put to test would have been whether the living witness had in fact heard the dead witness so testify, not whether the latter could have been in a position to say what was attributed to him.[5] There is recorded a possible breach of the rule, when evidence was produced by a plaintiff that the defendant's wife had acknowledged the seals on a will to be genuine; whether the sex of the witness was relevant here we cannot say.[6] Another doubtful case occurs in Dem. 34 *Ag. Phorm.* 11, 46: a vital point there is whether Lampis was or was not paid a sum of money in

[1] Lipsius, *AR* 659, supposes that the charge would have been that of having read out in court evidence without the will or knowledge of the alleged witness; cf. Leisi, *Zeuge* 52. Bo. Sm. ii. 144 point out (so too Gernet, *Dem.* i. 76, n. 1) that the plain rules of the court would have made this impossible, and they discredit this statement as mere rhetoric. But, if we can assume that the speech is, if not genuine, at least well invented, this will not do. Demosthenes is trying to show that the evidence attributed by him to Aisios in the original suit, which was to the same effect as that of Phanos now on trial, had really been given by him, though he is now declining to give the same evidence; he would, Demosthenes says, either have taken the oath of disclaimer at that trial or have brought a *δίκη βλάβης* subsequently against Demosthenes for making him perjure himself. The only sense that can be given to the passage, if genuine, is that a witness could sue for being forced into an impossible dilemma by a litigant's challenge.

[2] Dem. 46 *Steph.* ii. 11: on the other hand, evidence given in answer to a *πρόκλησις* was taken down on a wax tablet to facilitate amendment.

[3] Dem. 57 *Euboul.* 4 *οὐδὲ μαρτυρεῖν ἀκοὴν ἐῶσιν οἱ νόμοι, οὐδ' ἐπὶ τοῖς πάνυ φαύλοις ἐγκλήμασιν*, 46 *Steph.* ii. 7 (quoted on p. 146, n. 4). On the whole subject see Bonner, *Evidence* 20 ff.

[4] Dem. 46 *Steph.* ii. 7 (quoted on p. 146, n. 4). The same rule seems to be referred to in Dem. 44 *Leoch.* 55, but the passage has to be emended to make sense. Evidence by hearsay of a dead man is given in Isai. 8 *Kir.* 13 f., Dem. 43 *Makart.* 36 f., 42 ff.; in the absence of an official register evidence like this about kinship was particularly important.

[5] Lipsius, *AR* 886, n. 81, quoting Schömann, *Berl. Jahrb.* (1827) 1392.

[6] Dem. 41 *Spoud.* 24 *καί μοι λαβὲ τὴν μαρτυρίαν ὡς ὡμολογεῖτο τότε τὰ σημεῖα τῶν γραμμάτων ὑπὸ τῆς τούτου γυναικός*. Lys. 32 *Diogeit.* 18 (*pace* Bo. Sm. ii. 131, n. 1) is not relevant here, since it is not certain that the woman in question did not in fact give evidence.

the Crimea; he shifted his ground during the case, but the speaker is allowed to produce evidence of third parties as to what Lampis said to him at an earlier stage.[1]

Another important and necessary exception to the rule against hearsay evidence allowed evidence to be taken from a qualified witness who for reasons of health or absence abroad could not appear in court to confirm the deposition. The technical term for such evidence was *ἐκμαρτυρία*. The deposition was put in writing to the witness in the presence of another witness or witnesses, and these latter appeared in court to authenticate the deposition.[2] We have in Dem. 35 *Lakrit.* 20 and 33 f. the texts of a number of depositions of absent witnesses. They contain in each case the names and depositions of the absent witnesses, followed by a deposition that the preceding depositions were as stated, with the names of those attesting this last deposition. The probability is that these documents are genuine, though this has been contested.[3]

If false witness was alleged when there had been an *ἐκμαρτυρία*, suit was brought against the original witness if he acknowledged that he had given the evidence; if he denied this, against those who had confirmed that he had given it. In either case the same objection (*ἐπίσκηψις*) by the aggrieved litigant served.[4] Analogy would suggest that one to whom evidence had been falsely attributed in an *ἐκμαρτυρία* would have had a *δίκη βλάβης*

[1] This may be an exception proving the rule. Lampis, as the agent of Phormion, was almost a party to the suit, and it might have been held in this case legitimate to take independent evidence of what he had said about receiving money alleged to have been paid to him in discharge of a debt. Aischin. 2 *Embassy* 155 is hardly an exception; witnesses are there called in to confirm that Aristophanes had told them the same story about Demosthenes as he told Aischines, but Aristophanes himself gives evidence.

[2] Isai. 3 *Pyrrh.* 20 f. *παρὰ δὲ τῶν ἀσθενούντων ἢ τῶν ἀποδημεῖν μελλόντων ὅταν τις ἐκμαρτυρίαν ποιῆται, τοὺς ἐπιεικεστάτους τῶν πολιτῶν καὶ τοὺς ἡμῖν γνωριμωτάτους ἕκαστος ἡμῶν παρακαλεῖ μάλιστα, καὶ οὐ μεθ' ἑνὸς οὐδὲ μετὰ δυοῖν, ἀλλ' ὡς ἂν μετὰ πλείστων δυνώμεθα τὰς ἐκμαρτυρίας πάντες ποιούμεθα*, Dem. 46 *Steph.* ii. 7 (quoted in n. 4 below), Aischin. 2 *Embassy* 19, Dein. fr. lx; Calhoun, *CP* 9 (1914) 140.

[3] For the authenticity of the documents Lipsius, *AR* 887, n. 84, following Drerup, *NJ* Supp. 24 (1898) 319; similarly Gernet, *Dem.* i. 191, n. 3.

[4] Dem. 46 *Steph.* ii. 7 *ἀκοὴν δ' οὐκ ἐῶσι* (sc. *οἱ νόμοι*) *ζῶντος μαρτυρεῖν, ἀλλὰ τεθνεῶτος, τῶν δὲ ἀδυνάτων καὶ ὑπερορίων ἐκμαρτυρίαν γεγραμμένην ἐν τῷ γραμματείῳ· καὶ ἀπὸ τῆς αὐτῆς ἐπισκήψεως τήν τε μαρτυρίαν καὶ ἐκμαρτυρίαν ἀγωνίζεσθαι ἅμα, ἵν' ἐὰν μὲν ἀναδέχηται ὁ ἐκμαρτυρήσας, ἐκεῖνος ὑπόδικος ᾖ τῶν ψευδομαρτυρίων, ἐὰν δὲ μὴ ἀναδέχηται, οἱ μαρτυρήσαντες τὴν ἐκμαρτυρίαν*. Isai. 3 *Pyrrh.* 18 gives an example of an absentee witness who refused to acknowledge evidence attributed to him.

both against those who confirmed the deposition in the ἐκμαρτυρία and against the litigant who initiated it. Likewise there must have been an action available against the witness who falsely repudiated evidence attributed to him.

(v) *Tortures*

One of the darker rules of evidence at Athens was that the evidence of slaves was not admitted save when given under torture—dark not only as cruelty, but as irrational. The rule may have arisen from the antiquated concept of the right to give evidence as a privilege (see p. 137). Slaves had obviously to be excluded from this privilege; yet there was the pragmatic point that evidence of slaves was often very material for litigants. Torture must therefore be applied to the slave as a mark of the fact that he was not in himself a free agent entitled to support one side or the other. The orators distinguish *βάσανοι* from *μαρτυρίαι*,[1] and there was a commonplace to the effect that evidence given by a slave under torture was more reliable than evidence given by a free man. Orators even went so far as to assert that, while evidence of free men had sometimes been successfully impugned, this had never happened with evidence given under torture.[2] That this was mere rhetoric seems to be indicated by two facts. If it suited his book, an orator was quite capable of arguing the contrary—that evidence extracted under torture was suspect, since it depended on the strength or weakness of the slave whether he would say what was wanted of him or stick to some original statement which did not seem agreeable to the litigant putting him to the torture.[3] Secondly, although there are in the orators many instances of challenges either offering or demanding a slave for torture, there is no single instance where such a challenge was accepted and carried through; naturally in such cases the challenger was expecting the slave to say what he, the challenger, wanted, but it is straining credulity to believe that in all surviving cases the truth was so plainly on the challenger's side that his opponent recognized the

[1] Lys. 7 *Sacr. Ol.* 37, Dem. 30 *Onet.* i. 36, Hyper. fr. 5 J.

[2] Isai. 8 *Kir.* 12, repeated almost verbatim in Dem. 30 *Onet.* i. 37. Cf. Ant. 1 *Stepmother* 8, 6 *Chor.* 25, Isok. 17 *Trapez.* 54, Lykourg. *Leokr.* 29, Dem. 47 *Euerg.* 8.

[3] Ant. 5 *Her.* 31 ff., 40, Lys. 5 *Kall.* 3 ff., Dem. 37 *Pant.* 41. Ar. *Rhet.* $1376^{b}31$ ff. spells out the rhetorical possibilities of taking either line.

hopelessness of acceding to the challenge. If the average Athenian really believed that a slave could be normally expected to speak the truth under torture, surely at least one case would have survived where a challenge actually produced a piece of evidence.[1]

Besides being given under torture, a slave's evidence to be valid had to be given with the consent of both parties. Thus a litigant who wished to use evidence from a slave had to issue a challenge (πρόκλησις) to his opponent, either requiring him to hand over one of his slaves for torture or offering for torture one of his own slaves.[2] A litigant could also challenge his opponent to accept the evidence under torture of the slave of a third party, undertaking when he did so to procure the consent of the third party.[3] Any of these challenges would normally be given in the presence of witnesses,[4] and its acceptance constituted a contract between the parties, for the performance of which there might even be sureties. In such a case the terms would have been drafted in advance by the litigant; they would then be acknowledged and sealed.[5] In all cases the πρόκλησις must have contained, set out in writing, the points which were to be put to the slave,[6] the manner in which the torture was to be conducted,[7] and the person who was to conduct it. This was normally an official called the βασανιστής, but it could be one of the parties.[8] If either party did not stand by the contract which resulted if and

[1] In Isok. 17 *Trapez.* 15 f. and Dem. 37 *Pant.* 42, the only two cases where a challenge was at first accepted, the matter fell through because the litigants could not agree on the terms of the challenge. In Dem. 47 *Euerg.* 5 the reality of the challenge itself is in question. J. W. Headlam, *CR* 7 (1893) 1 ff., 8 (1894) 136 f., explained the irrationalities of βάσανοι by the supposition that they were a survival of a kind of trial by ordeal, and argued that it was a condition of any challenge to βάσανος that if it was accepted the whole case was decided by the result; thus *ex hypothesi* we could have no recorded case in a forensic speech. Against this argument Lipsius, *AR* 889, n. 91.

[2] ἐξαιτεῖν is used of demanding a slave for torture, παραδιδόναι or ἐκδιδόναι of offering or surrendering one, παραλαμβάνειν of accepting one offered: Lys. 7 *Sacr. Ol.* 36 f.

[3] Ant. 6 *Chor.* 23. It is true, as Bo. Sm. ii. 126 say, that the whole proceeding there described was extra-judicial; nevertheless it must have been a possible result of what was done that the challenge became evidence in a court case.

[4] Lys. 7 *Sacr. Ol.* 34, Dem. 45 *Steph.* i. 61, 54 *Kon.* 28, 59 *Neair.* 123.

[5] Dem. 37 *Pant.* 42.

[6] Ant. 1 *Stepmother* 10, Dem. 59 *Neair.* 124. The latter passage gives the text, probably genuine, of a πρόκλησις, the only one we have; it is not (*pace* Berneker, *RE* s.v. πρόσκλησις 852) a πρόσκλησις.

[7] Dem. 45 *Steph.* i. 61.

[8] Ant. 1 *Stepmother* 10, Isok. 17 *Trapez.* 15, Dem. 37 *Pant.* 40, 42.

when a πρόκλησις had been accepted, we must assume that an action (δίκη βλάβης perhaps) lay against the transgressor. On the other hand the litigant who declined a challenge had nothing to fear except the capital that could be made by his opponent out of his refusal.[1] This is why challenges became a separate category of proofs (see p. 153). The challenged party could weaken the effect of the challenge by making a counter-challenge relating to the same matter, demanding for example that the torture should be conducted in a different manner from that set out in the challenge.[2]

A challenge could be issued at any time while a case was before an arbitrator; but it seems unlikely that, if a case had been appealed from an arbitrator, any challenge could be made which had not been before the arbitrator.[3] We cannot say what, if any, time limit was fixed after which challenges were banned in non-arbitrational cases. It has been suggested that they could be issued right up to the beginning of the hearing or even, with the consent of the dikasts, at the hearing itself, but the evidence is inconclusive.[4]

A challenge could be issued in anticipation of a suit about to be brought, or with a view to preventing the bringing of one.[5] There were also instances of a challenge issuing in an agreed compromise, by which the evidence of the slave would determine the

[1] Ant. 1 *Stepmother* 11, 5 *Her.* 38, 6 *Chor.* 27, Lys. 4 *Wound* 12, Dem. 49 *Timoth.* 58.

[2] Dem. 37 *Pant.* 43, 53 *Nikostr.* 22 ff. Lys. 4 *Wound* 15 (*pace* Lipsius, *AR* 892, n. 104) does not describe a counter-challenge, but a challenge relating to different slaves, though admittedly about the same subject-matter.

[3] In Dem. 54 *Kon.* 27 a litigant issued a challenge at the very last moment, when the arbitrator was about to seal up the evidence. If subsequent challenges had been allowed, it would have run counter to the spirit of the rule that no new evidence could be admitted at the hearing of the appeal from an arbitrator's decision.

[4] Lipsius, *AR* 892, n. 106, concludes from Dem. 47 *Euerg.* 17 that a πρόκλησις could take place at the moment when the dikasts were assembling to hear the case. As Lämmli, *Prozeß.* 105, points out, this was a δίκη αἰκείας, there had been an arbitration, and it is therefore probable that we have here a piece of mere rhetoric (as indeed Lipsius himself suggests at *AR* 836); but it is still possible that the orator was building on a procedure which would have been in order had there been no arbitration. Aischines, in 2 *Embassy* 126, offers slaves for torture at the hearing in the presence of the dikasts, if Demosthenes and the dikasts themselves agree. This again is probably mere rhetoric; Dem. 45 *Steph.* i. 16 says it is not possible to put to the torture in the presence of the dikasts (Gernet, *DSGA* 112, n. 2, and *Dem.* ii. 159, n. 1, asks 'Impossibilité matérielle ou interdiction légale?'). But Lämmli, *Prozeß.* 105, is reluctant to admit that Aischines would have, even rhetorically, offered to do something plainly impossible.

[5] Ant. 6 *Chor.* 23, Isai. 6 *Philokt.* 42.

issue between the parties.[1] If a man extracted by torture from his own slave information incriminating a third party, such information could not be used, unless of course the slave was offered to and accepted by the opponent for torture.[2] Evidence could be sought under torture from a public slave; if the challenge was accepted, the examination was in the presence of members of the boule or of the Eleven.[3]

In exceptional cases of public danger magistrates could compel masters to surrender their slaves for examination under torture,[4] while on the other hand masters sometimes succeeded in evading the examination of one of their slaves by declaring the slave to be free.[5] Foreigners who were free men could be examined under torture for reasons of state, but citizens were specifically made immune from torture by a decree of uncertain date.[6]

(vi) *Oaths*

Witnesses in Athenian trials were not sworn as a matter of course, but they might take an oath either as the result of a challenge by one of the litigants or voluntarily to render their statements more persuasive.[7] In earlier times oaths had played

[1] Dem. 37 *Pant.* 40: if the slave, who belonged to the speaker, gave evidence in favour of Pantainetos, the issue was to be settled in his favour; if not, in the speaker's; and in the latter case the named *βασανιστής*, Mnesikles, was to assess the damage done in the torture to the slave. 59 *Neair.* 124: it is noteworthy here that the *πρόκλησις* is to Stephanos, although the suit is against Neaira.

[2] Ant. 5 *Her.* 29 ff. gives the case of a slave who under torture allegedly gave information incriminating the speaker. The slave was then done away with by the speaker's opponents, and he rightly complains that this made it impossible for him to proceed by way of challenge. There is some evidence of what was said and how the examination was conducted; but, if he had been present, he might have caused the slave to alter what he said by continuing the torture for a longer time.

[3] Dem. 53 *Nikostr.* 23.

[4] Andok. 1 *Myst.* 22, 64; Jones, *LLTG* 141 ff., MacDowell, *Mysteries* 79.

[5] Lys. 4 *Wound* 14, Isok. 17 *Trapez.* 14, Dem. 49 *Timoth.* 55. In the last case the frustrated litigant tries, but in vain, to get the witness, who has been declared to be free, to give evidence as a free man.

[6] Andok. 1 *Myst.* 43, Lys. 13 *Agorat.* 27, 59. The date of Skamandrios is uncertain; cf. T. J. Cadoux, *JHS* 68 (1948) 113, MacDowell, *Mysteries* 92 f. J. Schreiner, *De corpore iuris Atheniensium* (Bonn, 1913) 64, argues that he was not an archon.

[7] Isai. 9 *Astyph.* 24: 'I think he would gladly take an oath, if one were to proffer it to him'. 12 *Euphil.* 9: 'the mother of Euphiletos, whom they admit to be a citizen, was ready to take an oath before the arbitrator'; later the speaker says that he is prepared to take an oath. Aischin. 2 *Embassy* 156: *τῶν μὲν μαρτύρων διομνυμένων*. Dem. 45 *Steph.* i. 58: 'when I had left the presence of the arbitrator to administer the oath to (*ἐξορκώσαιμι*) a witness'. 52 *Kallip.* 28: 'if he wishes to put him on oath

a much more prominent role in litigation, and a grammarian records a law of Solon which laid down that, where neither party could produce either contract or witness to establish his case, the parties had to take an oath (the so-called evidentiary oath) as to the truth of their case, and the court had to decide on that basis.[1] It is a survival of this degree of importance attached to an oath when an oath taken by the mother of two boys determined a case which was being brought by the boys against their father that they should be recognized as legitimate; the case was before an arbitrator at the time, and the woman took the oath at the Delphinion.[2] There is one other similar case: the mother of Euphiletos took an oath as to his paternity before an arbitrator; she too swore at the Delphinion.[3] But in this case the mother's evidence seems to have been one among a number of others, and not absolutely decisive as in the other case.

A litigant might combine in one challenge the offer of an oath to be taken by a witness of his own together with the same oath to be taken by a named witness of his opponent. Thus one speaker, trying to prove that his opponent has blocked a water-course, proffers an oath to a fact to be sworn both by his own mother and by his opponent's mother.[4] Conversely, when one litigant had offered evidence on oath, his opponent might offer himself to make a statement on oath.[5]

As will have been seen from the above-cited passages, statements given or to be given under oath in this form might be made either by the litigants themselves or by witnesses on their behalf.

(ἐξορκῶσαι), he will be forced to confirm (πίστιν ἐπιθεῖναι) whatever he bids him to'. 54 *Kon.* 26: before an arbitrator, 'leading our witnesses to the stone and putting them to the oath (ἐξορκοῦντες)'. 57 *Euboul.* 22, 39, 44, 56 of testimony given on oath to the kinship of the litigant with a view to establishing his citizen status; Gernet, *Mélanges Desrousseaux* (Paris, 1937) 174, suggests that these oaths are parallel to the διωμοσία in a homicide case, survivals of compurgation. ὅρκον διδόναι is to offer an oath, ὅρκον δέχεσθαι to accept an offer. The passages quoted suffice to show that an oath was not something normally attached to evidence, but that it gave the evidence special force.

[1] *An. Bekk.* (Λέξ. Ῥητ.) 242. 19 ff.; see p. 99, n. 2. Bonner, *Evidence* 75 f., argues *a priori* that, if an evidentiary oath was to be brought as evidence before a court, it had to be taken by a person competent to give ordinary evidence.

[2] Dem. 39 *Boiot.* i. 3 f., 40 *Boiot.* ii. 10 f. On this case see vol. i, p. 79, n. 1.

[3] Isai. 12 *Euphil.* 9.

[4] Dem. 55 *Kallikl.* 27. In 23 f. the facts referred to in the challenge are related as what the speaker had heard from his mother.

[5] Dem. 49 *Timoth.* 65 (before an arbitrator), 54 *Kon.* 40.

Such statements are to be distinguished from ordinary evidence by the oath attached to them and by the fact that no such statement could be made except with the agreement of both parties, though the procedure of challenge meant that a litigant could get the content of what his adversary was unwilling to have evidenced under oath before the attention of the dikasts (see the section on challenges, p. 153).[1] It is rather a circular argument to state[2] that the only way a woman's evidence could be brought before a court was by challenge to an oath, since the incapacity of women to give evidence in the normal way is not certain (see pp. 136 f.); but if women were so incapacitated, this was a way round the incapacity, though it was available only with the consent of the other party to the suit.

There is some doubt as to the precise legal effects of a refusal to take an oath when proffered. In Lipsius' view this entailed nothing more than the rhetorical advantage conceded to the litigant who had proffered the oath.[3] Gernet has rightly made a distinction between the effect of a challenge when it was made at an arbitration and when it was made in any other connection.[4] For him, in the former case the refusal to take an oath proffered amounts to conceding the case, and conversely to take the oath means to win the case; on the other hand, when the matter is not before an arbitrator, refusal to take the oath or taking it is one among other pieces of evidence which has to be weighed up by the dikasts.[5]

When an oath was proffered with the aim of arriving at a compromise, acceptance of the challenge might be accompanied by a real guarantee, a deposit of money to be forfeit if the oath was not in the end taken.[6]

[1] In this respect the case in Dem. 55 *Kallikl.* 27 is particularly illuminating; see also 49 *Timoth.* 65. No citations have been made from Dem. 29 *Aphob.* iii, for reasons already stated (vol. i, p. 105, n. 5); Lipsius, *AR* 897, incautiously makes free use of that speech.

[2] As does Lipsius, *AR* 897.

[3] Lipsius, *AR* 898, Latte, *HR* 27.

[4] Gernet, *DSGA* 110 f.

[5] In the hypothetical case put in Dem. 52 *Kallip.* 15 f., had Pasion declined the oath, he would *ipso facto* have been condemned by the arbitrator (see p. 66, n. 2). In Dem. 59 *Neair.* 60 Phrastor was non-suited in an action against his *γένος* when he refused to swear before an arbitrator to the paternity of his son. Cf. Dem. 39 *Boiot.* i. 3 f., 40 *Boiot.* ii. 10 f. If we were permitted to use it, Dem. 29 *Aphob.* iii. 51 ff. would afford a contrast; a challenge has been refused, but that has not been decisive; as Lipsius, *AR* 898, n. 137, puts it, this refusal, coupled with Demosthenes' readiness to take an oath, is used to create prejudice against his opponent.

[6] Dem. 33 *Apatour.* 13.

When an oath was taken by a litigant without the formality of challenge, it had not the same strictly evidential value, but merely served to give some rhetorical colour to the statement he was making.[1]

(vii) *Challenges*

Challenges merit a brief mention as a separate category. It is true that one kind of challenge led either to evidence given by a slave under torture or to evidence given under oath by free men or women, and we have considered challenges under those heads. But even this kind of challenge might issue in simple negation, and in such a case the challenge and its refusal became evidence. And we find quite a different kind of challenge, the challenge either to fulfil an obligation[2] or to accept fulfilment of it.[3] Such a challenge was evidence and admitted as such. So we find Aristotle listing *προκλήσεις* with *μαρτυρίαι* and *νόμοι* as documents which had to be sealed up in the casket when a case was appealed from an arbitrator's decision, and in Dem. 47 *Euerg.* false *προκλήσεις* are classed with false witness and illegal evidence as grounds for a *δίκη ψευδομαρτυρίων*.[4]

(viii) '*Real*' *evidence*

The Athenians do not seem to have attached much importance to real objects as pieces of evidence, and in particular they paid little attention to the physical side of documents, such as the

[1] Isai. 11 *Hagn.* 6, Dem. 54 *Kon.* 40 f.

[2] Isok. 17 *Trapez.* 51, Lys. fr. 16 Th., Dem. 37 *Pant.* 12, 48 *Olymp.* 34, 56 *Dionysod.* 40.

[3] Dem. 50 *Polykl.* 31 ff.

[4] Ar. *Ath. Pol.* 53. 2, Dem. 47 *Euerg.* 1. Lipsius, *AR* 867, denies that challenges were a separate category of evidence, but does not refer to these two passages. In Dem. 45 *Steph.* i. 15 f. Apollodoros suggests that the purpose of *προκλήσεις* was to allow evidence to be used from slaves, who could not physically be (or perhaps were legally banned from being; cf. p. 149, n. 4) examined under torture in the presence of the dikasts, or from witnesses abroad. As Lipsius, *AR* 867, n. 3, points out, this is a one-sided view; Apollodoros uses it to deduce *a priori* that Phormion would not have been likely to challenge him, as Stephanos had alleged, when neither of these factors was present. Lipsius however seems to ignore the fact that the archon had evidently in fact allowed this *πρόκλησις* to figure in the evidence. (It is hard to see what Lipsius means by characterizing the definition in Poll. 8. 62 as too narrow; it seems too wide.)

materials of the document, the seals on it, or the handwriting.[1] But there is one instance at least where the bodily presence and appearance of an elderly slave is used to mark the absurdity of the story that the old man had violently dispossessed Pantainetos.[2] In the law of homicide we may suppose that the inanimate objects or animals which might be subject to the charge of homicide (see pp. 42 f.) would have been put in evidence, but this is mere conjecture.

§ 8. *Hearing in chief*

When the ἀνάκρισις was completed, it was the duty of the magistrate as ἡγεμών to introduce the case (and if necessary any παραγραφή that was appropriate) to the court (εἰσάγειν εἰς τὸ δικαστήριον). In the fifth century, when the jurors were assigned to a particular court under a particular magistrate for the year, the magistrate decided on what day the trial was to take place. But after the rearrangements described on pp. 44 ff. the thesmothetai fixed the dates (see p. 13, n. 2). We cannot tell on what principle they did this, but there were two kinds of case in which they were bound by rule. δίκαι ἔμμηνοι, monthly suits, had to be heard within a month; we are not exactly informed from what day the period began to run.[3] If a man brought a γραφὴ ὕβρεως against another, the thesmothetai had to introduce the case within thirty days from the day when he brought the γραφή, unless public business prevented it.[4] We may perhaps generalize from this that the time in any δίκη ἔμμηνος began to run from the day the suit was brought before the magistrate. It is possible, but

[1] In Dem. 33 *Apatour.* 17 the only test of authenticity seems to be the slave amanuensis recognizing his own hand. In Isok. 17 *Trapez.* 23 ff. there is no hint of testing a suspected document by objective tests. Calhoun, *CP* 9 (1914) 143.

[2] Dem. 37 *Pant.* 44.

[3] On monthly suits see pp. 21 ff. and Gernet, *DSGA* 173 ff.

[4] Dem. 21 *Meid.* 47 οἱ δὲ θεσμοθέται εἰσαγόντων εἰς τὴν ἡλιαίαν τριάκοντα ἡμερῶν ἀφ' ἧς ἂν γραφῇ, ἐὰν μή τι δημόσιον κωλύῃ. According to a law of Timokrates (Dem. 24 *Timokr.* 63), if it is genuine, when a man had been committed to prison by the boule in an εἰσαγγελία for future trial, the Eleven were obliged to bring his case into court within thirty days (presumably dating from the decree of the boule), if the secretary of the prytany failed to report the case to the thesmothetai. It is not clear here whether 'introduce' means 'see that the thesmothetai introduce' by a brachylogy, or whether in such a case the Eleven themselves acted as ἡγεμών of the court.

not certain, that in all cases, including even these, the statutory thirty days could be ignored if both parties agreed.[1]

One of the parties could secure adjournment without agreement with the other in case of illness or enforced absence from Attica. He did this by an evidentiary oath declaring the reason for his absence. The other party could put in a counter-oath that his opponent was not thus prevented from appearing. After hearing argument on either side the court decided either to grant the adjournment or to give judgement in favour of the litigant who was present.[2] We cannot say for certain how a case which had been thus adjourned was reinstated; it is at least possible that this was left to the initiative of the party which had opposed the adjournment.[3] Where an adjournment was by agreement between the parties, we may suppose that they agreed on a date for the postponed hearing. In ways not entirely clear to us postponements could lead to scandalous prolongation of actions. Demosthenes claims to have secured judgement against Meidias in a *δίκη κακηγορίας*, and when he could not secure payment to have brought a *δίκη ἐξούλης* against him, but even at the time of this speech (the speech against Meidias) not yet to have been able to get the case heard; on this showing that was a period of some sixteen years.[4] By some means or other Aristaichmos, guardian of Nausimachos and Xenopeithes, was able to fend off a suit on the guardianship so that, according to the son Aristaichmos, a compromise of the case was agreed eight years after the two

[1] This is the implication at first sight of Dem. 42 *Phain.* 13. But, as Gernet, *Dem.* ii. 82, n. 2, remarks, the thirty days there referred to is more probably a statutory interval between a judgement and the day when the mulcted defendant became *ὑπερήμερος* (cf. Dem. 47 *Euerg.* 49 ff.) than that between the bringing of a suit and its hearing.

[2] Dem. 48 *Olymp.* 25 f., 58 *Theokr.* 43, Hyper. fr. 202 J., Harpokr. s.v. *ὑπωμοσία*, Poll. 8. 81 (to plead absence in Skyros became a comic joke); Lipsius, *AR* 901 f., Partsch, *GB* 219, n. 2, Bo. Sm. ii. 164, Berneker, *RE* s.v. *παλινδικία* 125.

[3] According to the speaker of Dem. 58 *Theokr.* 43, Theokrines brought a *γραφὴ παρανόμων* against Demosthenes, someone swore an affidavit that Demosthenes was sick, and Theokrines neither entered a counter-affidavit at the time nor subsequently proceeded against him: *οὐθ' ὕστερον ἐπήγγελκεν* (*ἐπήγγειλεν* A: *num εἰσήγγειλεν?* Gernet). Whatever the reading, and whatever precise procedure it hides, some further action by Theokrines seems to have been required to reinstate the action.

[4] Dem. 21 *Meid.* 81. The speech was published about 347/6. The incident out of which the original suit arose took place in 364/3. In the spurious document purporting to give the evidence on the point (82) the period given is eight years; it was certainly more than that.

wards had come of age.[1] Most notable of all, Aischines prevented Demosthenes receiving the crown voted to him on the motion of Ktesiphon by indicting the latter through a γραφὴ παρανόμων; this happened while Philip was still alive (before the middle of 336 B.C.), but the suit did not come on until the archonship of Aristophon (331/0 B.C.).[2]

If the cases to be heard were private, the magistrate indicated on a board the order in which they would be taken on that particular day. The number taken on any given day would have varied according to the importance of the issues, but was probably four on the average. Only one public case could be heard on one day.[3]

In Aristotle's day the magistrate, who had had allotted to him by the elaborate procedure described in *Ath. Pol.* 64 ff. the jurors to sit with him for the day, selected by lot from among their number ten dikasts, one from each tribe. Of these one was put in charge of the water-clock and four in charge of the voting urns, to ensure that there was no chicanery with either of these. The other five had to supervise the receipt of dikastic pay at the end of the sitting.[4] The magistrate then called on the herald to announce the business and summon the parties,[5] and on the clerk to read out the charge or claim and the defendant's answer.[6]

If the picture given of the judicial process in early Athens (pp. 69 ff.) is on the right lines, it would be entirely consonant with it that the parties to a suit should plead their own case. They with their attendant supporters (the witnesses) were engaged in a contest (ἀγών); the judges (the jury) awarded victory to the more impressive performer. It is not certain whether this fact ever expressed itself in a definite rule of law, a rule laying down that a litigant (or his or her κύριος) and he alone must conduct his case in court.[7] Whatever the law had been or was *stricto sensu* in

[1] Dem. 38 *Nausim.* 6; cf. vol. i, p. 120, n. 6.

[2] Aischin. 3 *Ktes.* 219 (ἔτι Φιλίππου ζῶντος), D.H. *Ep. Amm.* 1. 12; Schaefer, *Demosthenes und seine Zeit* iii. 84, n. 2, 224, n. 1. In the second of those notes Schaefer gives further references which confirm that there was this gap. While unable to suggest how the adjournment was worked, he gives reasons for thinking that neither party was eager to bring the trial on.

[3] See p. 47, n. 4.

[4] Ar. *Ath. Pol.* 66. 2 f.

[5] καλεῖν τὴν δίκην (γραφήν) in Dem. 37 *Pant.* 42, 58 *Theokr.* 43; εἰσκαλεῖν τὸν ἀγῶνα in Ar. *Ath. Pol.* 67. 1.

[6] Aristoph. *Wasps* 894, Aischin. 1 *Timarch.* 2.

[7] As asserted by Lipsius, *AR* 905. He points out that the only direct evidence for such a rule of law is Quintilian 2. 15. 30 'tum maxime (at the time of the trial of Sokrates) scribere litigatoribus quae illi pro se ipsi dicerent erat moris, atque ita

the fourth century, it is quite clear that litigants at that time could make use of two kinds of professional aid in presenting their case, the speech-writer (λογογράφος) and the pleader (συνήγορος).[1]

Writing of speeches by professionals for delivery by the litigant himself began towards the end of the fifth century. There is no reason to doubt the substantial accuracy of the statement attributed to 'some people' by Pseudo-Plutarch that Antiphon was the first to write speeches for litigants.[2] We can infer that the help thus given to litigants was not restricted to writing out a speech for them, but extended to giving them advice on the whole strategy of litigation. Thucydides tells us that Antiphon's advice to prospective litigants was highly valued,[3] and in the *Clouds* one of the assets which Strepsiades will acquire from a legal education will be the money he will get from those who come to consult him on legal business and counter-pleas.[4] In Theophrastos a litigant who has come off splendidly in court nevertheless criticizes his speech-writer for having missed many telling points.[5] But the most significant example occurs in Dem. 58 *Theokr.*, where a metic, Ktesikles, who is described as a λογογράφος, acts as intermediary in legal bargaining between two parties.[6] One of the best-known of logographers was Isaios, himself possibly a metic,[7] who, to judge by his surviving speeches, specialized in matters concerning the law of the family. Isokrates certainly wrote forensic speeches for others early in his career, though he later disclaims this activity in a passage which confirms the

iuri quo non licebat pro altero agere fraus adhibebatur.' Lavency, *Logographie* 113 ff., argues cogently that, taken in its whole context, this passage does not justify the assumption of a law specifically requiring a litigant to conduct his own case; Quintilian has turned what was no doubt a strong dictate of custom, that a man should appear in court to conduct his own case, into a rule of law (*ius*).

[1] Bo. Sm. ii. 7 ff., Lavency, *Logographie* 68 ff.

[2] Plut. *Mor.* 832 c καί τινας λόγους τοῖς δεομένοις τῶν πολιτῶν συνέγραφεν εἰς τοὺς ἐν τοῖς δικαστηρίοις ἀγῶνας, πρῶτος ἐπὶ τοῦτο τραπείς, ὥσπερ τινές φασιν. In a papyrus fragment perhaps attributable to Antiphon (fr. 1a Th.) he says that he has been accused of writing speeches for others for money.

[3] Thuc. 8. 68. 1 τοὺς μέντοι ἀγωνιζομένους καὶ ἐν δικαστηρίῳ καὶ ἐν δήμῳ πλεῖστα εἷς ἀνήρ, ὅστις ξυμβουλεύσαιτό τι, δυνάμενος ὠφελεῖν.

[4] Aristoph. *Clouds* 466 ff.

[5] Theophr. *Char.* 17. 8 δίκην νικήσας καὶ λαβὼν πάσας τὰς ψήφους ἐγκαλεῖν τῷ γράψαντι τὸν λόγον, ὡς πολλὰ παραλελοιπότι τῶν δικαίων.

[6] Dem. 58 *Theokr.* 19 διοικησαμένου πρὸς Κτησικλέα τὸν λογογράφον, ὃς ἦν ἐπὶ τοῖς τῶν ἀντιδίκων πράγμασιν.

[7] D.H. *Isai.* 1, Harpokr. s.v. Ἰσαῖος.

importance of such speech-writing for private litigation.[1] Several of the speeches in the Demosthenic corpus were logographer's speeches.

Akin to the speech-writer was the advocate (*συνήγορος*), who spoke in his own person on behalf of a litigant. Originally he was a man who was ready for reasons of family or friendly relations to speak in court on a litigant's behalf, and in theory this is what he remained.[2] He could become almost the equivalent of a witness to good character, while remaining immune from a possible *δίκη ψευδομαρτυρίων*.[3] Right back in 489 B.C. the great Miltiades had friends to plead for him after the Parian débâcle, since he was too sick to conduct his own case.[4] In 343 B.C. Philokrates, being ill, called on Demosthenes to be his advocate.[5] In 356 B.C. Isokrates for the same reason deputed his defence in a case of *ἀντίδοσις* to his son-in-law, Aphareus.[6] These however were exceptional cases of sickness, and it was not easy to get the courts to agree to the conduct of a case by a man's advocate in the man's absence, as Olympiodoros found to his cost.[7] Phormion, the guardian of the notorious Apollodoros, was defended, in the suit brought against him by his ward, in a speech written by Demosthenes and delivered by an advocate.[8] Phormion was an

[1] Isokrates' six forensic speeches are 16–21, *Chariot*, *Trapez.*, *Kallim.*, *Aigin.*, *Loch.*, *Euth.* In 15 *Antid.* 36, talking of speeches in the courts, he says *οὐδ' οὕτω φανήσομαι περὶ τοὺς λόγους τοὺς τοιούτους γεγενημένος*, a rather vague phrase, which however is hardly compatible with his having written six such speeches. In the following paragraphs he describes the activities of speech-writers who live on the legal relationships between Athenians and the litigation arising out of them: *τοὺς μὲν τοίνυν ἀπὸ τῶν συμβολαίων τῶν ὑμετέρων ζῶντας καὶ τῆς περὶ ταῦτα πραγματείας ἴδοιτ' ἂν μόνον οὐκ ἐν τοῖς δικαστηρίοις οἰκοῦντας* (38). 15 *Antid.* is a fictitious forensic speech written in 354/3 B.C. when Isokrates was eighty-two (9).

[2] In Andok. 1 *Myst.* 150 we find reference to a litigant's fellow tribesmen chosen to act as his advocates (*συνδικεῖν*), cf. Dem. 23 *Aristokr.* 206, Hyper. 3 *Euxen.* 12; in Lys. 5 *Kall.* 1 a friend of the family; Lykourg. fr. 93 Bl. *δεῖ φίλοις καὶ τοῖς οἰκείοις βοηθεῖν ἄχρι τοῦ μὴ ἐπιορκεῖν*. Calhoun, *Clubs* 85 ff.; Lavency, *Logographie* 84, n. 1 for the words *συνήγορος* and *σύνδικος*.

[3] Latte, *RE* s.v. 'Synegoros' 1353. Aischin. 1 *Timarch.* 193, Dem. 21 *Meid.* 190 illustrate how much a matter of course it was that a litigant should have the support of *συνήγοροι*. Aischin. 2 *Embassy* 170 shows that a *συνήγορος* was not liable for anything he said *qua συνήγορος*; this may also be deduced somewhat less certainly from Isai. 12 *Euphil.* 4. (Isok. 12 *Panath.* 4 has no relevance here, *pace* Latte, *RE* s.v. 'Synegoros' 1354, Lavency, *Logographie* 90, n. 1.)

[4] Hdt. 6. 136. Miltiades was present on a couch.

[5] Aischin. 2 *Embassy* 14.

[6] Plut. *Mor.* 839 C.

[7] Dem. 48 *Olymp.* 25.

[8] Dem. 36 *For Phorm.* 1.

enfranchised slave, whose Greek was deficient; he must have uttered a few words, and the advocate then took over.[1]

Two rules seem fairly well established. Speeches made by advocates, as distinguished from statements by witnesses, must have counted against the time allowed to litigants which was measured by the water-clock. This rule is never stated in so many words, but it is highly probable *a priori*, and is perhaps implied in at least one remark in a speech.[2] It is also probable that by the strict letter of the law the advocate could not be paid,[3] though a remark of Demosthenes suggests that this law, if it existed, was evaded.[4] In order to preserve ostensible conformity with this rule, it was a commonplace for an advocate to stress either his close ties with the litigant for whom he was appearing or his personal grudge against the opposing litigant.[5]

A third possible rule was that the court had to give leave for an advocate to speak. We certainly find a number of instances where the litigant begs the leave of the court,[6] but this may have been more a matter of tact than conformity to an absolute rule. Perhaps their immunity from suits for false witness implies that they must have had the leave of the court to speak as advocates.

There must have been great variation in the proportion of time which advocates took up in different cases. In Dem. 36 *For Phorm.* the litigant himself spoke only a few words. In 59 *Neair.* the first sixteen paragraphs are spoken by the plaintiff, Theomnestos, and then Apollodoros takes over as advocate.

During the closing years of the fifth century the political clubs (ἑταιρεῖαι) provided mutual aid in the law-courts in the form of

[1] Lavency, *Logographie* 26 ff., has a useful table of all surviving speeches by λογογράφοι or συνήγοροι.

[2] Dein. 1 *Dem.* 114 παραδίδωμι τὸ ὕδωρ τοῖς ἄλλοις κατηγόροις. All that this implies strictly is that when, as in this case, a number of accusers were speaking as συνήγοροι the time allowed to them was a whole, so that when one came to the end of his speech he would naturally speak of handing on the water to the others. Lavency, *Logographie* 87, n. 7.

[3] Dem. 46 *Steph.* ii. 26 ἐάν τις . . . συνήγορος ὢν λαμβάνῃ χρήματα ἐπὶ ταῖς δίκαις ταῖς ἰδίαις ἢ δημοσίαις, τούτων εἶναι τὰς γραφὰς πρὸς τοὺς θεσμοθέτας. On the question of the genuineness of this law see Lavency, *Logographie* 91 ff.

[4] Dem. 21 *Meid.* 112 states as one advantage of the rich in litigation that they can call on the services of advocates. Cf. Dem. 51 *Trier. Cr.* 16, Lykourg. *Leokr.* 138.

[5] Isok. 21 *Euth.* 1, Lys. 14 *Alk.* i. 1 ff., 15 *Alk.* ii. 12, fr. 78 Th., Isai. 4 *Nikostr.* 1, 6 *Philokt.* 1, Dem. 22 *Androt.* 1, 59 *Neair.* 16.

[6] Dem. 34 *Ag. Phorm.* 52, 59 *Neair.* 14, Aischin. 2 *Embassy* 170, Hyper. 2 *Lyk.* 20.

skilled speakers (as well as witnesses), and the practice continued in the fourth century.[1]

In important political cases there could be a number of speakers for the prosecution. For example, Dem. 22 *Androt.* was written for delivery by Diodoros speaking second (after Euktemon) in a γραφὴ παρανόμων against Androtion in 355/4 B.C.; and in 353/2 B.C. Diodoros spoke first against Timokrates (Dem. 24 *Timokr.*) in a γραφὴ νόμον μὴ ἐπιτήδειον θεῖναι, being followed by Euktemon. It is not certain whether in such cases one of the accusers alone stood as initiator, and therefore alone bore the brunt of a fine if not more than a fifth of the votes were for condemnation, or whether they shared this liability. In this respect we must distinguish clearly between γραφαί brought by ὁ βουλόμενος on the one hand and εἰσαγγελίαι and ἀποφάσεις on the other; in the latter, accusers might have been officially appointed by the ekklesia or boule.[2] In private suits there could be more than one plaintiff or defendant, and we must suppose that then they shared equally between them the gains or losses of the suit.[3]

In some suits each party was only allowed to speak once (though that one occasion could be divided among a number of speakers), and there was then no opportunity for the litigant who had the first turn (usually the plaintiff) to reply to the arguments of him who had the second (usually the defendant). Sometimes however there were λόγοι πρότεροι and λόγοι ὕστεροι (the latter

[1] Thuc. 8. 54. 4, Lys. 8 *Coass.* 18, Isai. fr. 22 Th., Dem. 21 *Meid.* 139, 39 *Boiot.* i. 2, 40 *Boiot.* ii. 9, 58 *Theokr.* 42; Calhoun, *Clubs* ch. iii. Lipsius, *AR* 909, n. 33, says that in the passages from Dem. 39 and 40 ἐργαστήριον συκοφαντῶν has nothing to do with ἑταιρεῖαι; he does not say why.

[2] Kahrstedt, *Mag.* 223 f., *Staatsg.* 305 f., seeks to show that there was always only one accuser, though he might have the aid of one or more συνήγοροι or σύνδικοι; where these were elected by state organs, the state was the one accuser. Kahrstedt quotes as examples Dein. 1 *Dem.* 51, 2 *Aristogeit.* 6, Hyper. 1 *Dem.* 38, Plut. *Mor.* 846 c. This suits εἰσαγγελίαι and ἀποφάσεις, but hardly γραφαί, where there could not have been an official accuser. σύνδικοι were normally appointed to defend a law attacked in a γραφὴ παρανόμων (Dem. 20 *Lept.* 146, 152, 24 *Timokr.* 23).

[3] Dem. 34 *Ag. Phorm.* is spoken by Chrysippos and a partner, perhaps his brother (Gernet, *Dem.* i. 150, n. 1). In Dem. 38 *Nausim.* two brothers, Nausimachos and Xenopeithes, are suing the four sons of their guardian, now deceased, for moneys claimed to be due to them under the guardianship. Each of the two plaintiffs sued each of the four defendants for thirty mnai, a total sum of four talents. The speaker in this παραγραφή is one of the guardian's sons. It seems that the suit was taken as a single suit, and the time was allotted to the speakers accordingly. Dem. 47 *Euerg.* is a suit for false witness against two defendants, who had given evidence in favour of a relative at an arbitration arising out of a δίκη αἰκείας; so far as we can see they were joint defendants.

to be distinguished from the speeches of συνήγοροι, who had to speak immediately after their principals). Thus in homicide cases accuser and accused each had two speeches, in that order.[1] In each of two private suits of Demosthenes, the δίκη ἐπιτροπῆς against Aphobos and the δίκη ἐξούλης against Onetor, we have his first and his second speech; and the speaker in Dem. 48 *Olymp.* 51 refers to the first and second of his opponent's speeches in a δίκη βλάβης. In a διαδικασία concerning an inheritance the archon made provision for water for the second speech.[2] Probably in public suits no second speeches were allowed.[3]

The hearing of any case which came before a dikastery had to be completed in one day.[4] To achieve this it was necessary to limit the time allowed to either party (or in a διαδικασία to each of the several parties) to present their case. This was done by the device of the water-clock and the allotment to each party of a certain quantity of water, a device already employed in the time of Aristophanes.[5] Only one public suit could be heard on any single day;[6] such a day was divided into three parts, one of which was allotted to the prosecution, one to the defence, and the third to the assessment of the penalty if the defendant was convicted.[7] A case brought on such a day was sometimes described as πρὸς διαμεμετρημένην τὴν ἡμέραν.[8]

[1] Each of Antiphon's three *Tetralogies* consists of four speeches on homicide, composed on that pattern, and, though there is scepticism about their attribution to Antiphon, it is on the whole probable that they mirror Athenian law in a general way. (So MacDowell, *Homicide* 80, 114. K. J. Maidment, *Minor Attic Orators* i. 46 is less dogmatic: 'the writer of the *Tetralogies* was acquainted with Attic law.') But Ant. 6 *Chor.* 14 is conclusive: the defendant in a homicide case says that his accuser can refute any point he likes in his (the accuser's) second speech. Cf. Ant. 5 *Her.* 13, Dem. 23 *Aristokr.* 69.

[2] Dem. 43 *Makart.* 8 ἐξ ἀνάγκης γὰρ ἦν, ὦ ἄνδρες δικασταί, τῷ ἄρχοντι ἀμφορέα ἑκάστῳ ἐγχέαι τῶν ἀμφισβητούντων, καὶ τρεῖς χοᾶς τῷ ὑστέρῳ λόγῳ. According to Ar. *Ath. Pol.* 67. 2 there were certain διαδικασίαι in which only one speech for each litigant was allowed.

[3] Dem. 19 *Embassy* 213.

[4] There seems no direct evidence for this statement, and indeed it has been argued from some passages that, at least at the end of the fifth century, the hearing of a case might extend over more than one day. But Lipsius, *AR* 912, n. 41, rightly urges that, although Ant. 6 *Chor.* 22 f. is good evidence that the same jurors sat in a particular court on two successive days, it is clear from 37 that there were different defendants on the two days.

[5] Aristoph. *Ach.* 693, *Wasps* 93, 856. Exceptionally pleaders in εἰσαγγελίαι κακώσεως were not limited in time, ἄνευ ὕδατος (Harpokr. s.v. κακώσεως); we do not know how completion of these cases within the day was secured.

[6] Ar. *Ath. Pol.* 67. 1.

[7] Aischin. 3 *Ktes.* 197, Ar. *Ath. Pol.* 67. 3, Harpokr. s.v. διαμεμετρημένη ἡμέρα.

[8] Dem. 19 *Embassy* 120, 53 *Nikostr.* 17, Ar. *Ath. Pol.* 67. 3. 'A day measured

In the mid fourth century we learn that the defence in a public suit was allowed 11 amphoreis (132 choes) of water.[1] In Aristotle's day the time allowed for speeches in private cases differed according to the value of the matter at issue. If the value was over 5,000 drachmai, each party was allotted 10 choes for its first and 3 for its second speech; for values between 1,000 and 5,000 drachmai the respective figures were 7 and 2; for values less than 1,000, 5 and 2; and for those *διαδικασίαι* where only one speech was allowed to each party 6 choes were allotted.[2] These times were calculated as for a day in midwinter,[3] when daylight in Athens lasted approximately nine and a half hours.[4] In private cases at least (possibly in them alone) time taken to read out evidence did not count against the time allowed for speeches; hence the common instruction to the official to stop the flow of water. Presumably this rule applied if the jurors asked, as they were entitled to do, that the evidence should be read out again.[5]

Inherent in this exact division of time was the rule that a litigant could not intervene or interrupt during his opponent's speech, though his opponent might allow, or even ask, him to do so.[6] A litigant could ask his opponent to answer a specific question (presumably in the asker's time), and he had to reply.[7]

Some passages from the orators and elsewhere show that an

through' was one for which the water-clock measurement was continuous throughout the sitting. In the first passage cited above Demosthenes in effect is saying that Aischines was prepared on occasion to speak for a third of a sitting.

[1] So Photiades, Ἀθηνᾶ 16 (1904) 20, deduces from Aischin. 2 *Embassy* 126 and schol. ad loc. But Lipsius, *AR* 915, believes the 11 amphoreis covered one whole day's speaking.

[2] Ar. *Ath. Pol.* 67. 2 and Sandys's notes ad loc. According to Dem. 43 *Makart.* 8 (quoted on p. 161, n. 2) in a διαδικασία on inheritance each claimant was allotted one amphoreus for his first speech and three choes for his second.

[3] Ar. *Ath. Pol.* 67. 4, Harpokr. s.v. διαμεμετρημένη ἡμέρα.

[4] For various attempts to deduce the lengths of time corresponding to these figures see Sandys's edition of Ar. *Ath. Pol.*, pp. xcii and 257 ff., and earlier literature there cited. See also S. Young, *Hesperia* 8 (1939) 274 ff. Comparisons between one period and another must be used with caution, since obviously a difference in the perforations in the clock will produce differing times for the same quantity of water; this seems to be ignored by Lipsius, *AR* 915.

[5] Aischin. 3 *Ktes.* 192.

[6] Andok. 1 *Myst.* 26, 55, Lys. 20 *Polystr.* 11, Aischin. 2 *Embassy* 59, Dem. 18 *Crown* 139, 19 *Embassy* 57, 50 *Polykl.* 2, 57 *Euboul.* 61.

[7] See p. 138, nn. 3 and 4.

orator could not always count on a patient hearing from the jury.[1] As we have seen (p. 46), jurors may have been directed where to sit in a way which avoided the forming of groups which could act as claques.

The rules which governed the withdrawal of suits once they had been begun, rules which differed for private and for public suits, have been discussed above (pp. 103 ff.). According to a grammarian, portents put an end to proceedings;[2] but we do not know either what the exact portent had to be or what arrangements were made for taking the case up again.

According to Aristotle, the parties in private suits swore to keep to the point in their speeches.[3] The reason for this can hardly have been to ensure that the business was concluded in the time allowed;[4] that objective was secured by use of the water-clock. Perhaps it was an archaic survival from a time when the water-clock had not yet been devised. The rule as applied in homicide courts had perhaps a more solemn tinge because of the communal implications of decisions there, but it is difficult to see in what way the rule itself was different in homicide and in other cases.[5]

Appeals to the emotions of the jurors were considerably less bridled than would be tolerated in most modern courts. A litigant would try to impress the court by getting a number of supporters (*παράκλητοι*) simply to appear beside him, without speaking or giving evidence.[6] The practice of appealing to the compassion of juries by parading wife and children is noted by orators and

[1] Aristoph. *Wasps* 622, Dem. 57 *Euboul.* 1, Lykourg. *Leokr.* 52, Isok. 15 *Antid.* 272 (no less significant for being a speech for an imaginary occasion).

[2] Poll. 8. 124 *ἀνίσταντο δὲ τὰ δικαστήρια, εἰ γένοιτο διοσημεῖα· ἐξηγηταὶ δ' ἐκαλοῦντο οἱ τὰ περὶ τῶν διοσημείων καὶ τὰ τῶν ἄλλων ἱερῶν διδάσκοντες.* This suggests that the exegetai decided whether a significant portent had occurred. Aristoph. *Ach.* 169 can hardly be used to prove that the exegetai did not always need to be called on (*pace* Bu. Sw. 1161, n. 1); comic passages can rarely be used to establish *ex silentio* a point like this.

[3] Ar. *Ath. Pol.* 67. 1 *δ[ιο]μνύ[ουσι]ν οἱ ἀντίδικοι εἰς αὐτὸ τὸ πρᾶγμα ἐρεῖν.*

[4] As Lipsius, *AR* 918, supposes.

[5] Lys. 3 *Sim.* 46, Ant. 6 *Chor.* 9, Ar. *Rhet.* 1354^a22; MacDowell, *Homicide* 43 f. Lipsius, *AR* 918, thinks there must have been a specific law relating to homicide cases, but does not suggest what it could have been. Lipsius, *AR* 919, n. 68, suggests that the rule had been applied to private suits only recently when Ar. *Ath. Pol.* was written, and this explains why it is referred to comparatively rarely in Demosthenes' private speeches. Special attention to the point in Dem. 57 *Euboul.* 7, 33, 59, 63, 66 (about 345 B.C.).

[6] Dem. 19 *Embassy* 1.

satirized by Aristophanes;[1] and, if we are to believe the speaker of the speech against Timotheos, that statesman owed his acquittal in an εἰσαγγελία in part to the appearance by his side of two princes from northern Greece.[2]

After the parties had finished speaking, the herald called on the jurors to cast their votes.[3] Although there is no direct evidence, Athens was probably one of those cities referred to by Aristotle where discussion between jurors on their verdict was discouraged.[4]

The method of voting differed at different periods, and also in accordance with the type of case. There must at all periods have been a different method for δίκαι and γραφαί on the one hand and for διαδικασίαι on the other, since in the former there were normally two litigants only, defendant and plaintiff (or prosecutor), while in the latter there might be more than two.

For the former type there were, according to Aristotle, two urns (ἀμφορεῖς or καδίσκοι), one of bronze, the other of wood. The bronze urn was the one that 'counted' (κύριος), the wood the one that 'did not count' (ἄκυρος). Each juror had two voting pebbles (discs with axes), one with the axis bored through (ψῆφος τετρυπημένη), the other with the axis solid (πλήρης). The bored disc was for the litigant who spoke first (normally the plaintiff), the solid for him who spoke second (normally the defendant). Care was taken that each juror should get one and only one of each type of disc. The dikast, holding his two discs between thumb and finger by their axes, so that no one could see which was which, placed the disc favouring the litigant whom he supported in the bronze urn, which was so constructed that only one pebble could be put in at a time, and the other disc in the wooden urn. When voting was complete, the discs were emptied out of the bronze urn and counted on a specially constructed counting board. The herald announced the number of votes for each litigant in that urn. The litigant with more votes won; if the votes were equal, the case went to the defendant (see p. 47, n. 3). When in ἀγῶνες

[1] Aristoph. *Wasps* 568 ff., 976 ff., Lys. 20 *Polystr.* 34, Dem. 21 *Meid.* 99, 186. Plato, *Apol.* 34 c deprecates such appeals.

[2] Dem. 49 *Timoth.* 10, where ἐξαιτουμένων, though strictly implying some kind of speech, probably does not in fact do so.

[3] Aischin. 1 *Timarch.* 79, Ar. *Ath. Pol.* 68. 2.

[4] Ar. *Pol.* 1268^{b}9 ff. τῶν νομοθετῶν οἱ πολλοὶ παρασκευάζουσιν ὅπως οἱ δικασταὶ μὴ κοινολογῶνται πρὸς ἀλλήλους.

τιμητοί the defendant was condemned and there was τίμησις, the second vote was conducted in the same way.[1]

At the end of the fifth century the method was different.[2] There were two urns, but one was for acquittal, the other for condemnation. Each juror had only one voting pebble, which he put into the appropriate urn.[3] It is difficult to see how with such a method secrecy was maintained, though passages in Lysias suggest that it was, nominally at least;[4] the suggestion that the urns were somehow kept out of sight of all but the voting dikast is not plausible.

We are less well informed on the method of voting in διαδικασίαι, since Aristotle does not distinguish it. We have therefore to rely on two passages which both refer to the famous case of the inheritance of Hagnias. That inheritance was the subject of a lawsuit more than once. On one occasion we know that there were five claimants and four voting urns;[5] and we are specifically told that, for example, two claimants who based their claims on being second cousins of the *de cuius* would have shared the same urn, and divided the inheritance in two between them if they secured the

[1] Ar. *Ath. Pol.* 68–9, Aischin. 1 *Timarch.* 79.

[2] A difficulty is raised by Lykourg. *Leokr.* 149 χρὴ νομίζειν . . . δυοῖν καδίσκοιν κειμένοιν τὸν μὲν προδοσίας, τὸν δὲ σωτηρίας εἶναι. It is contemporary with Aristotle, and yet at first sight suggests that the voting is as it was in the fifth century, with one urn for acquittal and the other for condemnation. As it seems unlikely that the two methods operated contemporaneously, Lykourgos may be saying that the κύριος καδίσκος will be the urn of safety (the safety of the state) if it proves to contain more condemning than acquitting votes, while the ἄκυρος καδίσκος will be the urn of betrayal if *it* proves to have a majority of condemning votes. So Lipsius, *AR* 926, n. 98, following Sauppe, *De Atheniensium ratione suffragia in iudiciis ferendi* (Göttingen, 1883). See also Schömann, *Opuscula* i. 260 ff., Wyse, *Isai.* 423 ff. Wyse argues that there is no need to interpret Isai. 5 *Dikaiog.* 17 as entailing the old fifth-century method of voting; on the other side Lipsius, *AR* 926, n. 98, Bu. Sw. 1164, n. 3.

[3] Aisch. *Agam.* 816 f. (with Fraenkel's note), Phrynichos com. 32, Aristoph. *Wasps* 987 ff.

[4] Lys. 13 *Agorat.* 37 contrasts voting under the Thirty, where votes were laid openly upon two tables, with voting by the use of urns, implying that the latter preserved secrecy. Lys. 12 *Ag. Erat.* 91 says: 'Do not think your vote will be secret; your verdict will be known to the whole state': the obvious sense is that, though the individual votes will not be known, the sum total will be.

[5] Dem. 43 *Makart.* 10 καδίσκων τεττάρων τεθέντων κατὰ τὸν νόμον, εἰκότως οἶμαι οἱ δικασταὶ ἐξηπατήθησαν. . . . καὶ αἱ ψῆφοι ὀλίγαις πάνυ ἐγένοντο πλείους, ἢ τρισὶν ἢ τέτταρσιν, ἐν τῷ Θεοπόμπου καδίσκῳ ἢ ἐν τῷ τῆς γυναικός. See Wyse, *Isai.* 673, for speculation as to who the five claimants were and how they were divided between the urns. Lipsius, *AR* 926, maintains that the last sentence suggests one pebble only for each dikast; but it is surely easy to understand by αἱ ψῆφοι here the κύριαι ψῆφοι.

majority of the votes cast.[1] We get no hint of how in such a case the secrecy of the ballot can have been secured; but it is possible that each juror had one bored pebble, which he put into the appropriate urn, and enough unbored pebbles to enable him to put one into each of the other urns.

If the suit was an ἀγὼν τιμητός and judgement had gone against the defendant, there had to follow the process of estimation (see pp. 80 ff.). This was not concerned solely with estimation of penalties, but also in contractual cases with the estimation of the sum due from the defendant. Each litigant had made during the preliminary stages of the suit an estimation of the sum due should judgement go against the defendant. When that happened, each litigant was granted an equal time for his speech championing his own estimate. The total amount of time was very short, relative to the time allowed for the main speeches: about one-fourteenth of the time allowed for the least important among the private cases.[2] Several passages in the orators show that it was open to a plaintiff to concede to a defendant a lowering of the penalty, as estimated by him, right up to the moment when the vote was about to be taken.[3] But it is quite clear that, in Aristotle's day at least, the dikasts had to opt for one or the other estimate and could not impose any compromise between the two.[4]

There was at least one type of case, the γραφὴ κλοπῆς, where the statute laid down that, over and above restitution of the stolen property plus a fine of double the estimated value of it, the convicted defendant might be condemned to five days in the stocks, if the court so decided.[5] Probably the last penalty was

[1] Isai. 11 *Hagn.* 21.

[2] According to Ar. *Ath. Pol.* 69. 2, half of one chous for each side. (7 choes were allowed for speeches on each side in private suits involving less than 1,000 drachmai.) Modern estimates of the actual time represented by half of one chous vary between 2 minutes and 42 seconds.

[3] Dem. 53 *Nikostr.* 18 (Apollodoros as plaintiff had originally put in a τίμησις of death, but agreed with the defendant to reduce it to one talent), 58 *Theokr.* 70, 59 *Neair.* 6.

[4] Ar. *Ath. Pol.* 69. 2. In *Pol.* 1268^{a-b} Aristotle tells us that Hippodamos, in an ideal constitution, laid down that for determining penalties dikasts should vote not by pebbles but by tablets, on which they could record a compromise sentence. Aristotle objects on pragmatic grounds: how to quantify a large number of differing votes?

[5] Dem. 24 *Timokr.* 105 ὅ τι ἄν τις ἀπολέσῃ, ἐὰν μὲν αὐτὸ λάβῃ, τὴν διπλασίαν καταδικάζειν, ἐὰν δὲ μή, τὴν διπλασίαν πρὸς τοῖς ἐπαιτίοις. δεδέσθαι δ' ἐν τῇ ποδοκάκκῃ

only imposed if the prosecutor (ὁ βουλόμενος) so moved. When this occurred, it would have necessitated three votes: the first on the guilt or innocence of the accused; the second, if he was judged guilty, on the value of the thing at issue, as between the estimates of the prosecutor and the accused; the third, if the prosecutor so moved, on whether the accused should or should not spend five days in the stocks.

There is a more difficult type of case alluded to by Aristotle, where a man who had acted as a dikast when he was not legally entitled to was convicted in an ἔνδειξις. The dikasts imposed on him the penalty, either monetary or corporal, which they thought fit; the defendant remained in prison till he had paid any monetary fine imposed.[1] We are quite in the dark how the penalty was fixed in such a case, but it was probably again by process of τίμησις and ἀντιτίμησις.[2]

No need for further estimation or for decision by the court arose in those cases where the law prescribed a penalty payable to the state equal to the sum awarded to the plaintiff.[3] These

τὸν πόδα πένθ' ἡμέρας καὶ νύκτας ἴσας, ἐὰν προστιμήσῃ ἡ ἡλιαία. προστιμᾶσθαι δὲ τὸν βουλόμενον, ὅταν περὶ τοῦ τιμήματος ᾖ. 24 *Timokr.* 39 is not relevant here, since that passage refers to provision for release from any kind of incarceration for public debt through furnishing of sureties.

[1] Ar. *Ath. Pol.* 63. 3 ἐὰν δέ τις δικάζῃ οἷς μὴ ἔξεστιν, ἐνδείκνυται καὶ εἰς τὸ δικαστήριον εἰσάγεται· ἐὰν δ' ἁλῷ, προστιμῶσιν αὐτῷ οἱ δικασταὶ ὅ τι ἂν δοκῇ ἄξιος εἶναι παθεῖν ἢ ἀποτεῖσαι. ἐὰν δὲ ἀργυρίου τιμηθῇ, δεῖ αὐτὸν δεδέσθαι, ἕως ἂν ἐκτείσῃ τό τε πρότερον ὄφλημα ἐφ' ᾧ ἐνεδείχθη καὶ ὅ τι ἂν αὐτῷ προστιμήσῃ τὸ δικαστήριον. This passage is not clear, since it does not keep distinct the various items which would disqualify a dikast, being under thirty years of age, being in debt to the treasury, or being ἄτιμος. For defaulters convicted under the first and third heads the dikastery had simply to determine the penalty (normally though not necessarily monetary). But where a man was convicted of serving while in debt to the treasury, one must ask whether payment of the outstanding debt was imposed by statute on a convicted man and the court's only discretion was whether a further penalty should be added (this is suggested by the words προστιμῶσιν and τὸ πρότερον ὄφλημα ἐφ' ᾧ ἐνεδείχθη), or whether, less probably, this payment itself was subject to the process of estimation, so that the court could in principle accept a total payment of less than the amount of the original debt due to the treasury. Note that according to Aristotle the incarceration of a convicted defendant till he had discharged any monetary obligation was mandatory and not, as Lipsius, *AR* 255, n. 52, seems to suggest, at the discretion of the court. Dem. 21 *Meid.* 182 records a case where a court imposed the death penalty on a dikast who sat while in debt to the treasury.

[2] This statement is based on silence: there is no hint in any ancient source that a dikastery could itself decide on a penalty except by some such device.

[3] *Pace* Lipsius, *AR* 255, the imposition of a fine payable to the state in these cases was not at the discretion of the court, but the liability to the fine and its amount followed automatically on the award against the defendant.

were the δίκαι βιαίων,[1] ἐξαιρέσεως,[2] and ἐξούλης.[3] Similarly in those δίκαι βλάβης in which there was a penalty over and above compensation (a penalty payable not to the state but to the plaintiff) no separate procedure was needed beyond that of τίμησις and ἀντιτίμησις.[4]

The judgements, whether single or multiple, were announced by the presiding magistrate and recorded in writing. The record was deposited in the state archive.[5]

§ 9. *Penalties*

(i) *Introduction*

Something has already been said on penalties in connection with the classification of suits, whether into δίκαι and γραφαί, into δίκαι πρός τινα and δίκαι κατά τινος, or into ἀγῶνες τιμητοί and ἀτίμητοι (pp. 74 ff.).[6] Here we are considering problems of punishment over the whole range of judicial actions.

Penalties might either affect the person (σῶμα) of the convicted defendant or his property (χρήματα), and this twofold division of penalties is reflected in the phrase ὅ τι χρὴ παθεῖν ἢ ἀποτεῖσαι. There were four types of penalty which affected the person, namely death, imprisonment, exile, and diminution of personal status (ἀτιμία).[7] Penalties affecting the property of the defendant might range from a small fine to confiscation of his entire estate.

It has been said that being sold into slavery was a penalty which could be inflicted only on foreigners or metics, and not on

[1] Dem. 21 *Meid.* 44, Harpokr. s.v. βιαίων.

[2] Dem. 58 *Theokr.* 19, where the τίμημα is an estimated penalty for wrongful detention, half of it payable to the wronged party and half to the state; vol. i, p. 221.

[3] Dem. 21 *Meid.* 44, Ox. Pap. 221, col. 14, line 12, Harpokr. s.v. ἐξούλης; vol. i, p. 312.

[4] Dem. 21 *Meid.* 43 οἱ περὶ τῆς βλάβης οὗτοι νόμοι πάντες . . ., ἂν μὲν ἑκὼν βλάψῃ, διπλοῦν, ἂν δ' ἄκων, ἁπλοῦν τὸ βλάβος κελεύουσιν ἐκτίνειν. We need not assume a separate decision by the court as to whether the act was voluntary or involuntary. This decision would have been implicit in the estimation procedure.

[5] Paoli, *Studi Betti* (Milan, 1962) iii. 3 ff.

[6] On punishment in general see K. Latte, *Hermes* 66 (1931) 30 ff., 129 ff. (Berneker, *ZGR* 263 ff.). Lipsius, *AR* 930 ff., does not succeed in the admittedly extremely difficult task of disentangling problems of punishment from their connection with types of action.

[7] Ar. *Ath. Pol.* 67. 5 (which cannot be restored with quite the confidence expressed by Lipsius, *AR* 930, n. 1) δ̣ι̣[αιρ]εῖται δ' [ἡ ἡμ]έ[ρ]α ἐπὶ τοῖς [. . . . . ἀγώ]νω[ν ὅ]σοις πρόσεστι δεσμ[ὸς ἢ θάνατος ἢ φυγὴ ἢ ἀτ]ιμία ἢ δήμευσις χρημάτ[ων, καὶ οὐ κεῖται ἐν τοῖς νό]μ̣ο̣ι̣ς [ὅ] τι χρὴ παθεῖν ἢ ἀποτεῖσαι.

citizens.[1] This seems to be an argument from silence: selling into slavery is mentioned as a penalty only for offences which *ex hypothesi* could not be committed by a citizen, such as masquerading as a citizen, or (being a foreigner) entering into a permanent union with an Athenian, or (being a metic) failing to pay the μετοίκιον or failing to acquire a προστάτης.[2] There is no doubt that a court, under the general direction to determine what a convicted defendant should suffer or pay, could impose the death penalty on a citizen; it would seem illogical that it should have been precluded from imposing the less extreme penalty of being sold into slavery. On the other hand, early in their constitutional history the Athenians had ruled out enslavement for debt, and there was undoubtedly a sentiment against one Athenian becoming the master of another. This sentiment may have been strong enough to prevent the imposition of slavery as a penalty on an Athenian citizen in practice, without its being formally illegal for a court to impose it.

(ii) ἀτιμία

The words ἄτιμος and ἀτιμία do not unfortunately carry an unambiguous sense in a juridical context.[3] There were in fact two distinct types of ἀτιμία in the fourth century, one being a survival from early times, the other being the normal type. The primitive type can best be described by the word 'outlawry'. It entailed not merely the loss of all the rights of a citizen, but the loss of all rights whatever, so that in theory such an ἄτιμος could be put to death by anyone without the killer's being liable to any charge, though in practice in the fourth century the procedure

[1] Thus too dogmatically vol. i, p. 165 (following Lipsius, *AR* 930). It should have been stated there that a father (or brother) who caught his daughter (or sister) in the act of fornication could sell her, according to Plut. *Solon* 23; cf. vol. i, p. 73, n. 2.

[2] It may, but need not necessarily, be significant that two laws cited in Dem. 59 *Neair.* laid down that a foreign man or woman convicted of forming a permanent union with an Athenian woman or man was to be sold together with his property (16 πεπράσθω καὶ αὐτὸς καὶ ἡ οὐσία αὐτοῦ), whereas a man convicted of giving a foreign woman in marriage to an Athenian representing her as related to him was to be ἄτιμος and his goods were to be confiscated (52 ἄτιμος ἔστω, καὶ ἡ οὐσία αὐτοῦ δημοσία ἔστω). Such a man would normally be a citizen, and it may be that the phrase ἄτιμος ἔστω rather than πεπράσθω is used for that reason and means that he could not be sold into slavery. Vol. i, pp. 26 ff.

[3] On ἀτιμία as a penalty Paoli, *St. Dir.* 304 ff., has been closely followed.

was for ὁ βουλόμενος to hand the outlaw over to the thesmothetai to be dealt with by ἀπαγωγή.[1] ἀτιμία is to be taken in the sense of outlawry when any or all of the following qualifications are attached to it: (1) total confiscation of property, (2) extension of the ἀτιμία to the whole family (γένος)[2] of the ἄτιμος, (3) permanent exile from the state (ἀειφυγία), (4) the eventual penalty of death. In effect ἀτιμία in this sense and condemnation to death are interchangeable.[3]

In certain types of case we can see evidence for a transition from the imposition of outlawry as a penalty to the infliction of a fine. According to a law cited by Demosthenes a man convicted of giving or receiving bribes ἐπὶ βλάβῃ τοῦ δήμου was to be outlawed (ἄτιμος ἔστω καὶ παῖδες καὶ τὰ ἐκείνου),[4] whereas for Deinarchos a trial for corruption is an ἀγὼν τιμητός,[5] and Andokides implies a fine as penalty for this offence.[6] Again, Demosthenes tells us that there was an 'ancient law' that specified death as the penalty for 'deceiving the people';[7] but we know that even as far back as the time of the great Miltiades that statesman was condemned to a heavy fine on conviction for that very offence.[8] Again, a man might have been sentenced among other things to keep away from holy places on pain of death;[9] yet if he was caught violating this ban, the court had to decide ὅ τι χρὴ παθεῖν ἢ ἀποτεῖσαι.[10]

[1] For ἀπαγωγή applied to outlaws see for example Lykourg. *Leokr.* 121 τῶν ἐν τῷ πολέμῳ μεταστάντων εἰς Δεκέλειαν κατέγνωσαν, καὶ ἐψηφίσαντο, ἐάν τις αὐτῶν ἐπανιὼν ἁλίσκηται, ἀπαγαγεῖν Ἀθηναίων τὸν βουλόμενον πρὸς τοὺς θεσμοθέτας, παραλαβόντας δὲ παραδοῦναι τῷ ἐπὶ τοῦ ὀρύγματος. Probably any man who had the right of ἔφεσις could, if thus arrested, have his case heard before a dikastery, but it would then be an ἀγὼν ἀτίμητος involving death if he was condemned, nor would he be able to evade the penalty by going into exile before judgement.

[2] The γένος will be wider than simply descendants: ἀτιμία for public debtors extended to descendants until the debt was paid.

[3] In Dem. 21 *Meid.* 43 τοὺς μὲν ἐκ προνοίας ἀποκτιννύντας θανάτῳ καὶ ἀειφυγίᾳ καὶ δημεύσει τῶν ὑπαρχόντων ζημιοῦσι the three penalties are not alternative but coincidental. In Dem. 23 *Aristokr.* 37 the ἀνδροφόνος is specifically not Ἀθηναῖος, which shows that the sentence of death pronounced against him had also deprived him of his citizenship.

[4] Dem. 21 *Meid.* 113.

[5] Dein. 1 *Dem.* 60 περὶ δὲ τῶν δωροδοκούντων δύο μόνον τιμήματα πεποιήκασιν, ἢ θάνατον . . . ἢ δεκαπλοῦν τοῦ ἐξ ἀρχῆς λήμματος τὸ τίμημα τῶν δώρων. We must assume that the procedure took the usual form of estimation by the prosecutor and the defendant, between which the court had to choose.

[6] Andok. 1 *Myst.* 74.

[7] Dem. 20 *Lept.* 135 ἔστιν ὑμῖν νόμος ἀρχαῖος . . . ἄν τις ὑποσχόμενός τι τὸν δῆμον ἐξαπατήσῃ, κρίνειν, κἂν ἁλῷ, θανάτῳ ζημιοῦν.

[8] Hdt. 6. 136.

[9] Andok. 1 *Myst.* 33.

[10] Dem. 24 *Timokr.* 105.

There is clear evidence that side by side with this extreme kind of *ἀτιμία*, which we call 'outlawry', there was a kind which meant exclusion from the Agora, and therewith from all procedural protection of his rights as a citizen (though not loss of the rights themselves), a ban on addressing the ekklesia and boule, and exclusion from holy places and participation in public rites.[1] This we may call normal *ἀτιμία* and this (and not outlawry) is meant when for example Andokides uses the term *παντάπασιν ἄτιμοι* or Demosthenes the term *ἄτιμος καθάπαξ*.[2] Orators distinguish between those who are *ἄτιμοι* in this normal sense and those who have been outlawed.[3] A man who was *ἄτιμος* in this sense could remain in Attica and go about his business, provided he observed the restrictions laid down.

Normal *ἀτιμία* was the penalty laid down by law for certain delicts. It might also attach to a man automatically without his ever being arraigned in a court.[4] Thus certain modes of life or behaviour rendered a man *ἄτιμος* even though he had not been convicted of them in a court. We learn from a passage in Aischines that the law governing a certain form of *δοκιμασία* to which orators might be liable (on *ἐπαγγελία δοκιμασίας* see p. 204) laid down that 'notorious evil livers should not be allowed to address the people', and the orator goes on to specify some of those who were thus disqualified: those who had maltreated their parents, who had failed in their military duties, who had been guilty of homosexual offences, or who had squandered their patrimony.[5]

[1] Lys. 6 *Andok.* 24 *προσεψηφίσασθε ὑμεῖς αὐτὸν εἴργεσθαι τῆς ἀγορᾶς καὶ τῶν ἱερῶν, ὥστε μηδ' ἀδικούμενον ὑπὸ τῶν ἐχθρῶν δύνασθαι δίκην λαβεῖν.* Of Straton, whom Meidias had arraigned as public arbitrator and who had been judged *ἄτιμος*, Dem. 21 *Meid.* 95 says *πολίτης ὢν . . . ἕστηκε νυνὶ σιωπῇ, οὐ μόνον τῶν ἄλλων ἀγαθῶν τῶν κοινῶν ἀπεστερημένος, ἀλλὰ καὶ τοῦ φθέγξασθαι ἢ ὀδύρασθαι· καὶ οὐδ' εἰ δίκαι' ἢ ἄδικα πέπονθεν, οὐδὲ ταῦτ' ἔξεστιν αὐτῷ πρὸς ὑμᾶς εἰπεῖν.* See vol. i, p. 236, for the effect on ownership. Latte (Berneker, *ZGR* 309) aptly calls this type of *ἀτιμία* 'eine "Abspaltung" der alten Friedlosigkeit'.

[2] Andok. 1 *Myst.* 75, Dem. 21 *Meid.* 32. So Paoli, *St. Dir.* 316, n. 2; but H. Swoboda, *Z* 26 (1905) 154, holds that phrases like these imply outlawry.

[3] Andok. 1 *Myst.* 80 *κατὰ μὲν τὸ ψήφισμα τουτὶ τοὺς ἀτίμους ἐπιτίμους ἐποιήσατε· τοὺς δὲ φεύγοντας οὔτε Πατροκλείδης εἶπε κατιέναι οὔθ' ὑμεῖς ἐψηφίσασθε*, 107 and 109 *τούς τε φεύγοντας καταδέξασθαι καὶ τοὺς ἀτίμους ἐπιτίμους ποιῆσαι*, Dem. 9 *Phil.* iii. 43 f. *ἐχθρὸν αὐτῶν ἀνέγραψαν καὶ τῶν συμμάχων αὐτὸν καὶ γένος, καὶ ἀτίμους. τοῦτο δ' ἐστὶν οὐχ ἣν οὑτωσί τις ἂν φήσειεν ἀτιμίαν.*

[4] Paoli, *St. Dir.* 330 ff., suggests that there were two categories of persons subject to normal *ἀτιμία*, the 'incensurati' and the 'pregiudicati', and that the summary procedure of *ἀπαγωγή* was permitted against the latter but not against the former.

[5] Aischin. 1 *Timarch.* 28 ff.

We know that most, if not all, these forms of misconduct rendered a man liable to a *γραφή*. But it seems clear that the disqualification did not have to await conviction in a *γραφή*; and in one case at least, prostitution for reward (*ἑταίρησις*), the penalty for the *γραφή* was fixed at death if the accused had exercised a function (here mentioned as that of archon) when disqualified.[1]

Then there were those who became *ἄτιμοι* automatically as an indirect result of proceedings in court. A man who was convicted three times in certain cases became *ἄτιμος* in addition to whatever penalty had been imposed by the court on the third occasion; these were the *γραφὴ παρανόμων*,[2] the *δίκη ψευδομαρτυρίων*,[3] and the *γραφὴ ἀργίας*.[4] Much the largest class of persons who were *ἄτιμοι* not by a decision of a court (or only indirectly so) were state debtors (*ὀφείλοντες τῷ δήμῳ* or *τῷ δημοσίῳ*).[5] Our sources sometimes speak carelessly as though *ἄτιμοι* and public debtors were two distinct classes of person;[6] more often they correctly place public debtors among those who are *ἄτιμοι*.[7] A man might become debtor to the state in a number of ways.[8] He might have bought something, mining rights for example, from the state;[9] he might be holding property of the state which was due to be returned;[10] he might have incurred a fine.[11] For this purpose those who were in arrears with payments of *εἰσφορά* seem to have been treated more leniently than other public debtors, and did not automatically fall into the class of *ὀφείλοντες τῷ δημοσίῳ* until a decision was taken to sell them up.[12]

[1] Aischin. 1 *Timarch.* 19 f. Similarly by a law of Solon referred to in Dem. 24 *Timokr.* 103 a man who had been *convicted* of maltreatment of parents and who intruded into the Agora was liable to imprisonment (though this may be not a penalty so much as remand in custody).

[2] See passages cited on p. 176, n. 2.

[3] Andok. 1 *Myst.* 74. Cf. p. 138.

[4] *Lex. Cant.* s.v. *ἀργίας δίκη· Λυσίας* (fr. 10 Th.) *ἐν τῷ κατὰ Ἀρίστωνός φησιν ὅτι Δράκων ἦν ὁ θεὶς τὸν νόμον, αὖθις δὲ καὶ Σόλων ἐχρήσατο, θάνατον οὐχ ὁρίσας ὥσπερ ἐκεῖνος, ἀλλ' ἀτιμίαν, ἐὰν τρὶς ἁλῷ τις, ἐὰν δ' ἅπαξ, ζημιοῦσθαι δραχμαῖς ἑκατόν.*

[5] On these see Schulthess, *RE* s.v. *ὀφείλοντες τῷ δημοσίῳ*.

[6] For example Andok. 1 *Myst.* 78, Dem. 58 *Theokr.* 45, Ar. *Ath. Pol.* 63. 3.

[7] Andok. 1 *Myst.* 73 ff., Dem. 22 *Androt.* 33 f., 43 *Makart.* 58.

[8] Böckh, *Staatsh.* i. 456 ff.

[9] Dem. 37 *Pant.* 22.

[10] Dem. 47 *Euerg.* 22.

[11] See p. 83 on a prosecutor in a public suit who either dropped the prosecution or failed to secure one-fifth of the votes.

[12] Böckh, *Staatsh.* i. 456, points out that the Athenians thought of the *εἰσφορά* as a tax falling rather on the property than on the person; hence this difference of treatment. Cf. Lys. 29 *Philokr.* 9, Dem. 22 *Androt.* 50 ff., especially 54 *εἴ τις ἔροιτ' αὐτόν, τὰς εἰσφορὰς πότερον τὰ κτήματ' ἢ τὰ σώματ' ὀφείλει, τὰ κτήματα φήσειεν ἄν.*

It is a debated point at what precise moment a state debtor became *ἄτιμος*. On one view this only occurred if he had not paid up by the ninth prytany of the year in which the debt was incurred.[1] At that time the names of those who owed outstanding debts to the state were publicly recorded, and, on this view, it was only that publication which made them *ὀφείλοντες τῷ δημοσίῳ* in the technical sense. There are two important references to this date in the orators. Andokides, in what purports to be a complete catalogue of classes of *ἄτιμοι*, starts with those who owe money to the treasury. There are two subdivisions of this class: (A) those convicted in a judicial process (*a*) at their *εὔθυνα* as magistrates, (*b*) in a *δίκη ἐξούλης*, (*c*) in a *γραφή*, (*d*) by a magistrate's imposition of a fine (*ἐπιβολή*); (B) those owing under a contract (*a*) having purchased the right to collect taxes and being in arrear with the purchase money, (*b*) having stood guarantor (for such payment in arrear?). 'For these', the orator says, 'payment was in the ninth prytany; failing payment the sum owed was doubled and the debtors' goods were sold.'[2] In Dem. 59 *Neair.* a defendant in a *γραφὴ παρανόμων* has been convicted (case (A)(*c*) above); the prosecutor's estimation of the penalty has been 15 talents, and the speaker states that if the jury accept this estimate and if the defendant has not paid up at the ninth prytany, his name will be posted up as that of a public debtor to the tune of 30 talents and his property sold.[3] In Ar. *Ath. Pol.* 47 the phrase occurs three times; each reference is to payments to public or sacred treasuries of rent or purchase money which became due in the ninth prytany.[4] On the view

[1] Kahrstedt, *Staatsg.* 113. A variant of this view takes the relevant date to be the ninth prytany reckoned from that in which the debt was incurred; but the phrase as it occurs in Dem. 24 *Timokr.* 40 surely means the ninth prytany of the year, and this may be allowed to determine its meaning in other similar contexts.

[2] Andok. 1 *Myst.* 73 *τούτοις ἡ μὲν ἔκτισις ἦν ἐπὶ τῆς ἐνάτης πρυτανείας· εἰ δὲ μή, διπλάσιον ὀφείλειν καὶ τὰ κτήματα αὐτῶν πεπρᾶσθαι.*

[3] Dem. 59 *Neair.* 7 *μὴ ἐκτεισθέντος δὲ τοῦ ὀφλήματος ἐπὶ τῆς ἐνάτης πρυτανείας, διπλοῦν ἔμελλεν ἔσεσθαι τὸ ὄφλημα καὶ ἐγγραφήσεσθαι Ἀπολλόδωρος τριάκοντα τάλαντα ὀφείλων τῷ δημοσίῳ· ἐγγεγραμμένου δὲ τῷ δημοσίῳ, ἀπογραφήσεσθαι ἔμελλεν ἡ ὑπάρχουσα οὐσία Ἀπολλοδώρῳ δημοσία εἶναι, πραθείσης δ' αὐτῆς* . . . Dem. 40 *Boiot.* ii. 22 shows that after such an enforced sale any excess of the proceeds over the debt was repayable to the debtor or his family.

[4] (1) The poletai kept a separate list of those whose payment for the right to collect taxes became due in the ninth prytany. (2) Annual instalments on the purchase of houses or land from the state became due in the ninth prytany. (3) Payment of rent for sacred land became due in the ninth prytany. According to *Ath. Pol.* 54. 2 a man convicted at his *εὔθυνα* of *ἀδικίου* (malpractice in office) had to pay the

which we are considering, none of the debtors in these categories became ἄτιμος until the ninth prytany. Some colour is lent to the view by the fact that the whole purpose of the Andokides passage is to list those who are ἄτιμοι, and, unless ἀτιμία supervened only in the ninth prytany, the sentence quoted above would be irrelevant.[1]

There are however strong arguments against this view and in favour of the view that a man became ἄτιμος from the moment when he was in arrear with a payment due to the public or a sacred treasury. If the payment was a fine, it became due from the moment it was imposed.[2] If it arose out of a contract, it might of course, but need not necessarily, become due in the ninth prytany. The argument is partly *a priori*: to defer sanctions for not paying until the ninth prytany would have been asking for dilatory payment, and in fact would have made nonsense of fixing a contractual date for payment earlier than the ninth prytany. But in one passage an orator positively states that the disabilities falling upon a state debtor did not have to await his inclusion on any official list of such debtors, but eventuated on the day the debt arose; and he quotes a law to that effect. This piece of positive evidence has been too cavalierly swept aside by the main propounder of the first view.[3] On this second view we are to

estimated amount of his defalcation to which the jury assented at his trial, and if he had not paid by the ninth prytany this amount was doubled: ἂν δ' ἀδικεῖν καταγνῶσιν, ἀδικίου τιμῶσιν, ἀποτίνεται δὲ τοῦθ' ἁπλοῦν ἐὰν πρὸ τῆς θ' πρυτανείας ἐκτείσῃ τις, εἰ δὲ μή, διπλοῦται.

[1] This is on the assumption that τούτοις in Andok. 1 *Myst.* 73 refers to all the classes of ἄτιμοι hitherto mentioned. Linguistically it could refer only to the last class, those who had stood as sureties for money due to the state; but it is *a priori* unlikely that this provision applied exclusively to them.

[2] Böckh, *Staatsh.* i. 457, draws on the law quoted in Aischin. 1 *Timarch.* 16, which lays down that a man convicted in a γραφὴ ὕβρεως on whom a money fine has been imposed, if he cannot pay, is to be incarcerated for eleven days. A law quoted in Dem. 21 *Meid.* 47 has the slightly different rule that if a man has been convicted of ὕβρις against a free person he is to be incarcerated until he has paid. Böckh deduces from these two passages that after every such conviction the fine became due immediately and the defendant was incarcerated until he paid. The eleven days were the term after which, in these cases, the doubling of the penalty and the liability to selling up ensued. In other cases he supposes that this term was the ninth prytany, but that in those too the defendant might be incarcerated in the interim. It is not safe to rely too heavily on these two passages, since the laws quoted may not be genuine: Lipsius, *AR* 422, n. 8.

[3] Dem. 58 *Theokr.* 21 λέγε δὴ κἀκεῖνον τὸν νόμον τὸν ἀπ' ἐκείνης κελεύοντα τῆς ἡμέρας ὀφείλειν ἀφ' ἧς ἂν ὄφλῃ, ἐάν τε ἐγγεγραμμένος ᾖ, ἐάν τε μή, 49 τὸν νόμον, ὃς ὀφείλειν κελεύει ἀπ' ἐκείνης τῆς ἡμέρας, ἀφ' ἧς ἂν ὄφλῃ ἢ παραβῇ τὸν νόμον ἢ τὸ

suppose that a man became a state debtor in the technical sense immediately on his conviction in a court, or at the date set for payment if it was a contractual debt. From that moment, unless he paid up, he was ἄτιμος, and was liable to ἔνδειξις if he did any of those things which were banned for the ἄτιμοι.[1] It was only at the ninth prytany that he became liable to the doubling of his original debt, and only at that stage that he was publicly listed as a state debtor. Of course once his name was thus published it was much easier for a prosecutor to prove his liability. But it is wrong to conclude from this that being on the list was a necessary condition of being a state debtor in the technical sense.[2]

Liability for debts to the state or to the gods passed on death to the direct descendants of the defaulting debtor, and this extended to a public debtor's ἀτιμία (see vol. i, pp. 127 ff.). Sometimes ἀτιμία imposed as a sanction in a particular decree was made to descend to the children.[3]

This form of normal ἀτιμία fell also automatically upon any accuser in a γραφή or in an εἰσαγγελία (there were a few cases of εἰσαγγελία to which this rule did not apply)[4] who withdrew from the case or who secured less than one-fifth of the jurors' votes (see p. 83). We should reject the view sometimes put forward that there was a form of partial ἀτιμία for the accuser who withdrew or failed to secure one-fifth of the votes, namely incapacity to bring a public suit in future. The orators' language at times seems to imply this; but this is simply that they sometimes choose to underline that particular element in total ἀτιμία, incapacity to plead in the courts.[5] In fact it seems that such an accuser was

ψήφισμα. It is true that the last clause of the second quotation here is probably inaccurate (Kahrstedt, *Staatsg.* 113, n. 4); it is not likely that the debt was deemed to date from the commission of the act rather than conviction by the court. This however does not justify rejecting the clear and specific statement in the first sentence quoted.

[1] Dem. 58 *Theokr.* 14, 48.

[2] *Pace* Kahrstedt, *Staatsg.* 113, n. 4; there is nothing in Dem. 24 *Timokr.* 39 f., even if that were wholly reliable as evidence, to prove that debtors to the state were still ἐπίτιμοι until the ninth prytany. When the speaker in Dem. 25 *Aristogeit.* i. 70 describes the published list of state debtors as their ὅρος, he is simply saying that this list is of the same value as evidence of a debt to the state as would be a ὅρος on a piece of property as evidence of a private debt (see ibid. 69); it is quite wrong to argue that conversely no name on the list meant no debt.

[3] *IG* i². 45. 23.

[4] The rule did not apply to prosecutors in εἰσαγγελίαι κακώσεως of orphans and heiresses (vol. i, p. 118) or in a γραφὴ ἀσεβείας against one who had violated a sacred olive tree (Lys. 7 *Sacr. Ol.* 38).

[5] As in Dem. 22 *Androt.* 30, 33 f., 53 *Nikostr.* 1, 58 *Theokr.* 15, 45.

automatically liable to a fine of 1,000 drachmai,[1] that this made him technically *ὀφείλων τῷ δημοσίῳ*, and this in turn meant *ἀτιμία*. We may also reject the view that a *ῥήτωρ* who was thrice convicted in a *γραφὴ παρανόμων* suffered partial *ἀτιμία*, namely incapacity to propose a decree in future. None of the passages cited to support this view does in fact do so.[2] The rule most probably was that on the third conviction in a *γραφὴ παρανόμων* the jury fixed the penalty as in a normal *ἀγὼν τιμητός*, but there was added to it total *ἀτιμία* of the normal type.

There were however types of partial *ἀτιμία* which might be imposed by a court. They are referred to in the key passage in Andok. 1 *Myst.* 75 in the following terms: *ἄλλοι αὖ κατὰ προστάξεις, οἵτινες οὐ παντάπασιν ἄτιμοι ἦσαν ἀλλὰ μέρος τι αὐτῶν.*[3] As an example of the class Andokides gives the soldiers who stayed in Athens under the Four Hundred, who lost the right to speak in the ekklesia and to be members of the boule. Another form of partial *ἀτιμία* for which there is evidence was disqualification for holding a magistracy, though we cannot be certain for what wrongs this was a penalty prescribed by law.[4]

[1] Dem. 21 *Meid.* 47, 22 *Androt.* 26 f., 23 *Aristokr.* 80, 24 *Timokr.* 7, 53 *Nikostr.* 1, 58 *Theokr.* 6.

[2] Lipsius, *AR* 396, n. 81, cites Antiphanes 196 *πῶς γὰρ γένοιτ' ἄν, ὦ πάτερ, ῥήτωρ ἄφωνος, ἢν μὴ ἁλῷ τρὶς παρανόμων;* (So Kock. Cobet would read . . . *ἄφωνος; B. ἢν ἁλῷ τρὶς παρανόμων.* The argument is the same with either reading.) But silencing a *ῥήτωρ* would certainly involve more than banning him from proposing decrees and would embrace a ban on acting as public prosecutor; in other words this is a loose way of describing total *ἀτιμία*, as in the passages cited on p. 175, n. 5 above. In Hyper. 4 *Phil.* 11 f. there is the clear implication that a man convicted for a third time in a *γραφὴ παρανόμων* was in the same position as a man convicted three times in a *δίκη ψευδομαρτυρίων*, and, as we saw at p. 172, such a man was liable to total *ἀτιμία*. Dem. 51 *Trier. Cr.* 12 *τὸν μὲν εἰπόντα τι μὴ κατὰ τοὺς νόμους, ἐὰν ἁλῷ, τὸ τρίτον μέρος ἠτιμῶσθαι τοῦ σώματος* should probably be so punctuated and interpreted as meaning 'one who is convicted of speaking not according to the law (i.e. a *ῥήτωρ* who has proposed an illegal decree) may be penalized as to one-third of his rights as a citizen', i.e. may lose the right to be a magistrate, the three main rights of a citizen being *ἄρχειν*, *δικάζειν*, and *ἐκκλησιάζειν*. When Lipsius, *AR* 396, n. 81, says that to place the comma after *τρίτον* rather than after *ἁλῷ* is right in substance though formally unacceptable, he is right on the latter point but begs the question on the substance: Paoli, *St. Dir.* 325.

[3] Maidment, *Minor Attic Orators* i. 397, translates *κατὰ προστάξεις* 'curtailed in specified directions'; similarly MacDowell, *Mysteries* 107. Kahrstedt, *Staatsg.* 111, seems to imply, unnecessarily, that the specification was through a *ψήφισμα*.

[4] In Dem. 51 *Trier. Cr.* 12, as interpreted in n. 2 above, it is a prescribed penalty for conviction in a *γραφὴ παρανόμων*. We learn from Lys. 26 *Euandr.* 3 that Euandros had lost the right to hold a magistracy, though we are not told on what ground.

(iii) *Imprisonment*

Imprisonment may be used in a penal system in three different but connected ways. It may be used before trial to ensure the appearance of the defendant on the day (remand in custody). It may be used after conviction to ensure that the defendant pays up. It may be used as a punishment pure and simple. The first two uses, though both are amply vouched for in our sources, do not concern us here.[1]

It is sometimes erroneously alleged that the use of imprisonment as a penalty was quite exceptional in Athens.[2] There are statements in the orators and elsewhere which definitely imply that imprisonment was recognized as a normal penalty,[3] and there is evidence that this went back to the original code of Solon.[4] The fact that it could be imposed by a decision of the court in a private suit for theft (*δίκη κλοπῆς*) has led to the false generalization that it was never decreed except as an additional punishment.[5] In such a case certainly it was additional to the restitution of double the value of the stolen thing which the convicted thief had to make, though we do not know precisely how the court was moved to impose this extra penalty, that is to say whether it could impose it on its own motion or only if the plaintiff had so proposed. But when Plato makes Sokrates contemplate the possibility of estimating his penalty as imprisonment, he shows that this penalty could be arrived at by the normal process of estimation.[6]

[1] See Appendix G.

[2] As by Bu. Sw. 1109. But see Bo. Sm. ii. 275 and especially I. Barkan, *CP* 31 (1936) 338 ff.

[3] Dem. 24 *Timokr.* 146 *οὔτε γὰρ ἄν, ὦ ἄνδρες δικασταί,* (if you were to accept what Timokrates says) *τιμᾶν ἐξῆν ὑμῖν ὅ τι χρὴ παθεῖν ἢ ἀποτεῖσαι (ἐν γὰρ τῷ παθεῖν καὶ ὁ δεσμὸς ἔνι· οὐκ ἂν οὖν ἐξῆν δεσμοῦ τιμῆσαι),* 114 *εἰ δέ τις ἰδίαν δίκην κλοπῆς ἁλοίη, ὑπάρχειν μὲν αὐτῷ διπλάσιον ἀποτεῖσαι τὸ τιμηθέν, προστιμῆσαι δ' ἐξεῖναι τῷ δικαστηρίῳ πρὸς τῷ ἀργυρίῳ δεσμὸν τῷ κλέπτῃ, πένθ' ἡμέρας καὶ νύκτας ἴσας, ὅπως ὁρῷεν ἅπαντες αὐτὸν δεδεμένον,* Lys. 6 *Andok.* 21 ff.

[4] Lys. 10 *Theomn.* i. 15 f. *καί μοι ἀνάγνωθι τούτους τοὺς νόμους τοὺς Σόλωνος τοὺς παλαιούς. ΝΟΜΟΣ. δεδέσθαι δ' ἐν τῇ ποδοκάκκῃ ἡμέρας πέντε τὸν πόδα, ἐὰν [μὴ] προστιμήσῃ ἡ ἡλιαία.* The obsolete word *ποδοκάκκῃ* shows the law to be archaic.

[5] Gilbert, *Greek Constitutional Antiquities* 414.

[6] Plato, *Apol.* 37 b.

(iv) *Confiscation of property*

Confiscation of goods might be a method of execution, and will have to be discussed in that context (p. 186).[1] It was normally put into operation by the procedure known as ἀπογραφή (on which see pp. 211 ff.). It has been alleged that it could only be put into operation so, but this is by no means certain.[2] We are here concerned only with confiscation as a punishment.

Where the penalty of death was prescribed by law, it was common (some say universal) to prescribe confiscation of the guilty man's property as well. Thus for premeditated homicide the penalty was probably death and confiscation of property.[3] The same combination of penalties is found for crimes against the δῆμος or the πόλις,[4] crimes against the gods,[5] and warlike acts against an ally.[6] Sometimes confiscation is combined with ἀτιμία

[1] Paoli, *St. Dir.* 307, n. 1, distinguishes between δήμευσις which automatically accompanied outlawry and that which befell state debtors. The latter (*a*) could be wholly evaded by the debtor's paying off the debt, (*b*) though available against the total property of the debtor, was so only to the limit of his debt. This distinction, though in itself valid, is not exhaustive, as will be seen in what follows.

[2] Kahrstedt, *Staatsg.* 134, citing Ar. *Ath. Pol.* 47. 3: the poletai ἀναγράφουσι δὲ καὶ τὰ χωρία καὶ τὰς οἰκίας τἀπογραφέντα καὶ πραθέντα ἐν τῷ δικαστηρίῳ. Von Fritz and Kapp translate the last three words 'by order of a law court', Mathieu and Haussoulier 'par jugement'. This may imply that in every case there had to be a separate procedure (ἀπογραφή) over and above that in which the confiscation was originally decided; but it does not necessarily do so. Equally inconclusive are the other passages cited by Kahrstedt, Dem. 22 *Androt.* 54, 24 *Timokr.* 166, *IG* ii². 1631*c*. 350 ff. But cumulatively these passages do suggest that the normal procedure in confiscation was by way of ἀπογραφή.

[3] In Dem. 24 *Timokr.* 7 Diodoros says that, had he been convicted of parricide, οὐχ ὅτι τῶν ὄντων ἂν ἀπεστερήμην, ἀλλ' οὐδ' ἂν ἔζων. In Lys. 1 *Killing of Erat.* 50 Euphiletos, on trial for premeditated homicide, says ἐγὼ γὰρ νῦν καὶ περὶ τοῦ σώματος καὶ περὶ τῶν χρημάτων καὶ περὶ τῶν ἄλλων ἁπάντων κινδυνεύω. Here σώματος could mean 'civil rights', since Euphiletos would have been allowed to go into exile after his speech; but there is no hint that he intended to do this, and the word probably therefore means 'life'. It is certainly strange that in Ant. 2 *1st Tetr.* 2. 9 the speaker, speculating on what would happen if he were punished with death for the homicide of which he is accused, says that he will then bequeath to his children ἀνόσια ὀνείδη, a weak description for the disgrace and poverty as well. It is also strange that in Ar. *Ath. Pol.* 47. 2, where the poletai καὶ τὰς οὐσίας τῶν ἐξ Ἀρείου πάγου φευγόντων καὶ τῶν ἄλλων ἐναντίον τῆς βουλῆς πωλοῦσιν, those on whom capital punishment was imposed should be covered by the words τῶν ἄλλων. But MacDowell, *Homicide* 117, is right to urge against Glotz, *Solidarité* 515 ff., that the strange silence of these two passages cannot outweigh the evidence of those from Demosthenes and Lysias quoted above.

[4] Hdt. 6. 121, Xen. *Hell.* 1. 7. 20, 22, D.S. 13. 101. 7, Krateros, *F.Gr.H.* 342 F 17.

[5] Xen. *Hell.* 1. 7. 22, Poll. 10. 97.

[6] *IG* ii². 125 (Tod, *GHI* no. 154) 10 ff. (357/6 B.C.). This instance refutes the

as a sanction for the provisions of a particular decree or law.[1] Or it may be a penalty by itself, as for declining to take on a liturgy,[2] for acting as suppliant in favour of a man who owed money to the state as the result of a fine,[3] and exceptionally for not returning ship's gear, or even refusing to sell ship's gear privately owned, in a period of acute shortage.[4] It thus comes to be enumerated with death and *ἀτιμία* as one of the possible penalties which could be imposed.[5]

(v) παρακαταβολή

Certain penalties fell automatically upon plaintiffs who either failed to get a verdict or failed by a certain margin of votes. These penalties were a sanction intended to discourage frivolous litigation. They were of three kinds.

The first was that prosecutors in public suits who failed to secure one-fifth of the votes at the trial, or who abandoned the prosecution, were fined 1,000 drachmai and became *ἄτιμοι*. This has been discussed above (p. 83).

The second was known as *παρακαταβολή*. This word has a wider and a narrower sense. In the wider sense it is used to denote all deposits by litigants in advance of the hearing, whether technically they were *πρυτανεῖα*, *παραστάσεις*, or *παρακαταβολαί* in the narrower sense.[6] Here we are concerned with the narrower sense only.

παρακαταβολή in its narrower sense was a deposit related to the value of the matter at issue, which was forfeited by the litigant, either to the other litigant or to the state, if he failed to win the case, or in some instances if he failed to secure one-fifth of the

view of Glotz, *Solidarité* 522 ff., accepted by Gernet and Bizos, *Lys.* ii. 28, that there was no cumulation of the death penalty and confiscation of property after 403 B.C.

[1] *IG* i². 45. 23 f. against anyone who proposed to rescind the decree founding the colony of Brea, *IG* ii². 43 (Tod, *GHI* no. 123) 55 f. similarly with regard to the charter of the second Athenian confederacy, Dem. 59 *Neair.* 52 against one who had fraudulently given a *ξένη* in marriage to a citizen.

[2] Dem. 20 *Lept.* 40.

[3] Dem. 24 *Timokr.* 50.

[4] Dem. 47 *Euerg.* 44.

[5] Ar. *Ath. Pol.* 67. 5 (quoted on p. 168, n. 7); cf. Lys. 30 *Nikom.* 22.

[6] The word is used in the wider sense for example in Isok. 20 *Loch.* 2. In Dem. 37 *Pant.* 41 it is used for the deposit in a *δίκη βλάβης*: we know from Isok. 18 *Kallim.* 12 that in such a suit the only deposit was the *πρυτανεῖα*.

votes. According to Harpokration[1] this deposit fell to be paid in two broad categories of case: claims against the state for the return of property (or compensation for the loss of property) wrongfully included among property confiscated and sold by the state, and certain inheritance claims.

(a) Claims concerning confiscated property

When property confiscated by the state was put up for auction, there was a procedure by which anyone who wished to assert a claim on that property could put in an objection (*ἐνεπίσκηψις*: see pp. 215 ff.).[2] The issue was then tried by *διαδικασία*. The claimant, who should be looked on, exceptionally for a *διαδικασία*, as a plaintiff,[3] had to deposit before the issue was tried one-fifth of the value of his claim, which became forfeit to the state if he lost.[4]

[1] Harpokr. s.v. *παρακαταβολὴ καὶ παρακαταβάλλειν· οἱ ἀμφισβητοῦντες χρημάτων τινῶν δεδημευμένων πρὸς τὴν πόλιν καὶ οἱ περὶ κλήρων ἢ ἐπικλήρων πρὸς ἰδιώτας ἀντιδικοῦντες ἀργύριόν τι κατετίθεσαν· καὶ τούτου ἐχρῆν αὐτοὺς στέρεσθαι, εἰ τὴν δίκην ἡττηθεῖεν. ἐπὶ μὲν οὖν τῶν πρὸς τὸ δημόσιον ἀμφισβητήσεων δῆλόν ἐστιν ὅτι τὸ ε′ μέρος τοῦ ἀμφισβητουμένου κατετίθετο.*

[2] 'Assert a claim on' is intentionally stated rather vaguely. Lipsius, *AR* 464, describes such a claimant as 'der auf einen Teil eines konfiszierten Vermögens als sein Eigentum Anspruch erhebt'. The phrase 'als sein Eigentum' displeases Pringsheim, *GLS* 164, n. 2; he prefers a formulation which restricts objections to those based on debts secured on the property confiscated. No doubt Lipsius's wording is too narrow; Harpokr. s.v. *ἐνεπίσκημμα*, *An. Bekk.* (*Δικ. Ὀν.*) 189. 2 ff. speak only of property encumbered with debts. But (*pace* Pringsheim) Poll. 8. 61 does not restrict the procedure thus; he says *ἐνεπισκήψασθαι δ' ἦν, ὁπότε τις ἐν τοῖς δημευθεῖσιν ἑαυτῷ τι ὀφείλεσθαι ἢ προσήκειν λέγοι*, which would include claims other than those based on a secured debt. It would surely have been illogical to protect the rights of a creditor and not those of an owner whose property had for some reason become wrongly included in the property to be auctioned. So Beauchet iii. 716.

[3] Exceptionally, because in a *διαδικασία* there was normally neither plaintiff nor defendant. Lipsius, *AR* 934, n. 14, is right (against Partsch, *GB* 392) that the objector here is to be regarded as the plaintiff rather than the defendant.

[4] *Et. Mag.* 340. 37 ff. *ἐνεπίσκημμα καὶ ἐνεπισκήψασθαι καὶ ἐγγύης καταβολήν· καταδικασθέντων τινῶν δημοσιεύεσθαι τὰς οὐσίας, εἰ λέγοιέν τινες ὡς εἴησαν δανεισταὶ τῶν δημευομένων, ἀπογράφεσθαι τούτους ἐκέλευον, πότε καὶ πόσον ἐδάνεισαν ἀργύριον· ὅπερ ἔλεγον ἐνεπίσκημμα καὶ ἐνεπισκήψασθαι· εἰ μέντοι γε παρίστων ἐγγυητὰς τοῦ μὴ ἂν διαψεύσασθαι περὶ τοῦ δανείσματος οἱ δανείσαντες, τοῦτο ἐγγύης καταβολὴν ἔλεγον* (cf. Suda s.v. *ἐνεπισκήψασθαι*), Poll. 8. 39 *παρακαταβολὴ δ' ἦν ἐπὶ μὲν τῶν πρὸς τὸ δημόσιον ἀμφισβητημάτων τὸ πέμπτον, ἐπὶ δὲ τῶν ἰδιωτικῶν τὸ δέκατον*, 8. 61 (quoted in n. 2 above), Harpokr. s.v. *παρακαταβολή* (quoted in n. 1 above), *An. Bekk.* (*Λέξ. Ῥητ.*) 250. 14 ff. In Dem. 49 *Timoth.* 46 the hypothetical creditor of a man whose property had been confiscated by the state *ἐνεπισκηψάμενός γε οὔτ' ἂν παρακαταβολῆς ἠπόρησεν.*

It has been held that it is this forfeited deposit which is itemized under the description *ἐγγύης καταβολή* in one of the poletai records.[1] On this view, it was so described when the said sum had been paid by a third party on behalf of the intervener; the grammarians wrongly generalized from this, and suggested that the statutory deposit of a sum against failing in the suit was always equivalent to providing a suretor for that failure.[2] On another view, this phrase shows that it was possible to avoid paying down the deposit before the case opened, by providing a suretor who would pay up if the intervener lost his case; this was an alternative, not an addition, to the deposit of the actual sum of money.[3] Neither of these accounts explains how the deposit could be one-fifth of the purchase price, if by that is meant the price fetched at the auction, since *ex hypothesi* that price could not be known until the auction had taken place. Perhaps then this inscription should be left out of account here, and it may be that the fifth here described as *ἐγγύης καταβολή* is the same as the fifth part of the sale price mentioned in another poletai record under the name *προκαταβολή*.[4]

(*b*) *Inheritance claims*

The *παρακαταβολή* in inheritance cases was probably only exacted in the three following cases:[5]

1. When, in face of a *λῆξις*, a *διαμαρτυρία* was presented asserting *μὴ ἐπίδικον εἶναι τὸν κλῆρον*. Such a claimant, if his claim was

[1] *IG* ii². 1579. 8 ff. (*Λ*)*ευκόλοφος ἐξ Σαλα*[*μῖνος τάδε*] *ἀπέγ*(*ραψεν* Lipsius)· *Θεομένους Ξυπ*[*εταιῶνος οἰ*]*κίαν ἐν Σαλαμῖνι ἐ*[*ν* ....]*ι*, *ᾗι γείτων βορρᾶθ*[*εν* ...., *ν*]*οτόθεν δὲ Νικόδικ*[*ος· ἐπρίατο Σ*]*ωσίνομος Ἀριστονό*[*μου* ....]*ς· ἐγγύ*(*ης*) *καταβολ*(*ὴ*) 𐅄ΔΔΔ⊢⊢. In the margin [Η]ΗΗΗΔ *ἐπώ*(*νιον*) 𐅃⊢⊢⊢⊢. This probably means that the sum fetched was 410 drachmai, the *ἐγγύης καταβολή* was 82 drachmai (five per cent), and the *ἐπώνιον* 9 drachmai (just over two per cent).

[2] So MSL 815 f. (less clearly Lipsius, *AR* 934, n. 17), M. Fränkel in Böckh, *Staatsh.* ii. 81*, n. 569, referring to *Et. Mag.* and Suda (quoted on p. 180, n. 4).

[3] Partsch, *GB* 394: 'Diese Auffassung hätte ausserdem den Vorteil, auf die Quellen ein neues Licht zu werfen, die uns einerseits nur vom *παρακαταβάλλειν*, also von einer Barzahlung sprechen, und andererseits eine *ἐγγύη* als möglich annehmen.'

[4] *SEG* xii. 100. 35 ff. *ὠνητής*, *Λυσανίας Παλαθίωνος Λακι*(*άδης*) 𐅅𐅄ΔΔ𐅃· *τοῦτο τὴν προκαταβολὴν τὸ πέμπτον μέρος ἔχει ἡ πόλις καὶ τὰ ἐπώνια καὶ τὰ κηρύκεια.* This fifth is almost certainly the first of five annual payments, as laid down in Ar. *Ath. Pol.* 47. 3: Finley, *Land* 112 and *Studi Arangio-Ruiz* (Naples, 1953) iii. 478. Perhaps this first payment might have been called *ἐγγύη*.

[5] Paoli, *St. Proc.* 161; cf. vol. i, pp. 158 ff.

resisted, was technically the plaintiff; but his claim could only be contested by challenging him (or his witness) in a δίκη ψευδομαρτυρίων, in which he (or his witness) was the defendant. Presumably he lost the deposit if he was cast in the δίκη ψευδομαρτυρίων.[1]

2. When, in face of a λῆξις, the right to succeed as an adoptive son was asserted.[2]

3. When, in face of a previous assignment of an inheritance, a fresh ἐπιδικασία was set on foot by means of an ἀντιγραφή.[3]

If this is the correct account of the παρακαταβολή in inheritance cases, its object will have been to discourage the use of διαμαρτυρία in asserting a claim, to discourage claims by adopted children however asserted, and to discourage claims to an inheritance which had already been adjudged by ἐπιδικασία however asserted.

It must however be acknowledged that there is another possible view. According to this view, the παρακαταβολή was imposed on every litigant who became involved in an inheritance case which came to court.[4] Thus a legitimate son would have had to find a deposit of one-tenth of the value of the estate if his right to enter was challenged, or if he claimed (not by way of διαμαρτυρία) when some other claimant had asserted a right. The *a priori* objections to such a rule are strong; for it entails the belief that in all cases which came to court there was in effect a court fee of one-tenth of the value of the estate, since one or other party was bound to forfeit the παρακαταβολή.

The amount of the παρακαταβολή in inheritance cases was one-tenth of the value of the estate.[5] We do not know how this sum

[1] Isai. 6 *Philokt.* 12 (cf. 4).

[2] Dem. 44 *Leoch.* 34. This case, according to Paoli, *St. Proc.* 161 f., proves that an adopted son had always to make the deposit in a contested case, whether he proceeded by διαμαρτυρία or by εὐθυδικία.

[3] Dem. 43 *Makart.* 16. For ἀντιγραφή in this sense (which is additional to those set out on p. 131, n. 3) see Isai. 6 *Philokt.* 52, Dem. 44 *Leoch.* 39, 48 *Olymp.* 31, Harpokr. s.v. ἀντιγραφή.

[4] So for example Wyse, *Isai.* 374. He appears to suggest that the παρακαταβολή was payable by both litigants even where the holder of the estate had already been adjudged the heir. Lipsius, *AR* 935 f., believes that it was exacted from all litigants save those who either had already had an estate adjudged to them or had entered a claim before the herald made his announcement (Dem. 43 *Makart.* 5). This would seem a rather arbitrary advantage given to those who got their claims in before the herald's announcement.

[5] Poll. 8. 39 (quoted on p. 180, n. 4).

was calculated. It implies that for every estate which became the subject of litigation there might have been the necessity to fix its value in money. This is surprising when we remember that land was not in the modern sense a marketable commodity. But on the other hand we also know that for the purposes of dowries land had frequently to be valued.[1] One must suppose that here some process of τίμησις and ἀντιτίμησις took place. It has also been conjectured on *a priori* grounds that the deposit, if forfeit, was paid to the state. But it seems just as likely that it was payable to the other claimant or claimants. Its deterrent effect would have been the same either way, and payment to the private litigant would have been more apt to secure that the right sum was indeed exacted.

(vi) ἐπωβελία

The third kind of penalty falling automatically on an unsuccessful plaintiff was known as ἐπωβελία. In certain private suits such a plaintiff had to pay a fine of one-sixth of the value of the claim in issue. The fine was an obol for every drachma of the claim, and its name was derived from this. It was presumably calculated on the estimate put on the claim by the plaintiff, since *ex hypothesi*, the verdict having gone against him, there would have been no decision between his and the defendant's estimation of the claim.

The fine is vouched for in the following suits: δίκη ἐπιτροπῆς,[2] δίκη χρέως,[3] δίκη παραβάσεως συνθηκῶν (if indeed there was such a suit).[4] Some grammarians state that the fine was payable by an unsuccessful plaintiff in any monetary suit;[5] but this was certainly not true when Isok. 18 *Kallim.* was delivered, for it is specifically stated in that speech that as a plaintiff in a claim for 10,000 drachmai Kallimachos risked nothing more than the πρυτανεῖα.[6] It is a debated point whether ἐπωβελία fell to be paid

[1] Vol. i, pp. 296 ff.

[2] Dem. 27 *Aphob.* i. 67, 69, 28 *Aphob.* ii. 18, 31 *Onet.* ii. 14.

[3] Dem. 35 *Lakrit.* 46, 56 *Dionysod.* 4.

[4] Aischin. 1 *Timarch.* 163. Aischines is speaking of a hypothetical case of a plaintiff who had contracted for the services of a male prostitute. The passage hardly proves the existence of a suit for breach of contract as such.

[5] *An. Bekk.* (Λέξ. Ῥητ.) 255. 29 f. ἐπωβελία· ἐπιτίμιόν τι τοῦτό ἐστι τοῖς διώκουσι χρηματικήν τινα δίκην, ἂν μὴ ἕλωσιν, *Et. Mag.* 368. 48 ff., Suda s.v. ἐπωβελία.

[6] Isok. 18 *Kallim.* 12.

by an unsuccessful plaintiff in a *φάσις*. Pollux states that it did, but this may well be due to a confusion on his part.[1]

In addition to these suits for specific private wrongs *ἐπωβελία* was exacted in two categories of procedure irrespective of the precise matter in issue, namely *παραγραφαί* and *ἀντιγραφαί*; and here there is considerable difficulty in determining on whom and under what conditions it fell to be paid.

For *ἐπωβελία* in *παραγραφαί* we have the plain statement of the effect of the law of Archinos as reported in Isok. 18 *Kallim.* (see pp. 106 f.). According to this, whichever party lost had to pay the *ἐπωβελία*.[2] The rationale of this rule, if it was thus, would presumably have been that the losing party had caused misuse of the legal process, the plaintiff in the *παραγραφή* because he had used that procedure at all instead of facing a *εὐθυδικία*, the defendant because the verdict implied that, whatever the justice of his claim, he had gone the wrong way about seeking a remedy.[3]

Even more difficult is it to be certain of the rule as it applied to an *ἀντιγραφή* or counter-claim (on which see pp. 131 ff.). Taking the words of Pollux[4] strictly, the penalty fell only on the litigant who had instituted the cross-action (the original defendant); if the original plaintiff lost, he did not have to pay this penalty. But in Dem. 47 *Euerg.* 64 we seem to have a clear case of an original plaintiff who lost on the cross-action and had to pay the *ἐπωβελία*. If the rule was as Pollux states, the function of the *ἐπωβελία* will again here have been to discourage frivolous cross-actions. If on the other hand either litigant might have to pay, the only effect of the *ἐπωβελία* was to raise the stakes; such a rule might have been held to favour the rich against the poor litigant, and it is difficult to determine its aim. But this difficulty is mainly due to our uncertainty as to the exact nature of a cross-action and its relation to the original action.

[1] Poll. 8. 48 *καὶ τὸ μὲν τιμηθὲν ἐγίνετο τῶν ἀδικουμένων, εἰ καὶ ἄλλος ὑπὲρ αὐτῶν φήνειεν· ὁ δὲ μὴ μεταλαβὼν τὸ πέμπτον μέρος τῶν ψήφων τὴν ἐπωβελίαν προσωφλίσκανεν.* Rejected by A. W. Heffter, *Die Athenäische Gerichtsverfassung* (Köln, 1822) 190 f., M. Fränkel in Böckh, *Staatsh.* ii. 81*, n. 564, Lipsius, *AR* 937, n. 26.

[2] In Isok. 18 *Kallim.* 35 and 37 it is stated expressly that the *ἐπωβελία* will fall, if he loses, upon Kallimachos, who was the defendant in the *παραγραφή*, having been the plaintiff in the original suit.

[3] Hence the assimilation of Kallimachos' action to that of a sycophant in Isok. 18 *Kallim.* 37.

[4] Poll. 8. 58 *ἀντιγραφὴ δέ, ὅταν τις κρινόμενος ἀντικατηγορῇ. . . . ὁ δ' ἀντιγραψάμενος μὴ κρατήσας τὴν ἐπωβελίαν προσωφλίσκανεν.*

There is also controversy as to whether the ἐπωβελία was only incurred if the litigant concerned had failed to secure one-fifth of the votes (the rule in διαμαρτυρίαι according to Isok. 18 *Kallim.* 12) or if in some cases (the δίκη ἐπιτροπῆς for example) it fell on every unsuccessful plaintiff, however narrow the margin of votes. The former view is probably right.[1]

It seems clear that the ἐπωβελία was paid to the opposing litigant.[2]

§ 10. *Execution of judgement*

(i) *Introduction*

The rules for securing the execution of a judgement are obviously of prime importance for the efficiency of a judicial system. Unfortunately our evidence for these rules at Athens is less good than for other rules; naturally, since only rarely are the rules a matter for discussion or argument in court. It will be convenient to consider them separately in relation to public and to private suits.[3] Under each of these heads we need to consider separately again execution upon property and execution upon the person.

(ii) *Public suits*

The most serious acts of execution upon the person arising out of public suits were the death penalty and imprisonment. It was the function of the Eleven to carry these out (see pp. 17 f.). Presumably the names of the convicted men were passed to them by the ἡγεμών of the court. The heinousness of certain acts, such as sacrilege or treason, was sometimes underlined by the publication of the sentence on a στήλη; this was particularly appropriate when the convicted person had gone into exile in order to avoid the death penalty.[4] To increase the likelihood of execution of judgement in such cases a price might be set on the head of the

[1] See vol. i, p. 120, n. 4.

[2] Dem. 47 *Euerg.* 64, Harpokr. s.v. ἐπωβελία, *An. Bekk.* (*Λέξ. Ῥητ.*) 255. 33 f.

[3] Lipsius, *AR* 942 ff., Weiss, *GP* 451 ff. (with bibliographies in 455, n. 1, 495, n. 1), *RE* s.v. 'Katenechyrasia', *RE* Supp. 6 (1935) s.v. 'Exekution', Finley, *Land* 221, n. 1, Gernet, *Plat.* pp. cxlviii ff.

[4] Plut. *Mor.* 834 b, Andok. 1 *Myst.* 51, 78, Lykourg. *Leokr.* 117. Hence the term στηλίτης in Isok. 16 *Chariot* 9, Dem. 9 *Phil.* iii. 45.

exile.[1] When permanent exile (ἀειφυγία) had been imposed by a court (or self-imposed, when a convicted homicide evaded the death penalty by going into exile), the man so convicted ran the risk of summary execution if he was found in Attica; probably at one period he was at risk at the hands of anyone who found him, but by the fourth century the procedure of ἀπαγωγή or ἔνδειξις would have been followed.[2] Harbouring an exile rendered the host liable to the same penalty as had been laid upon his guest.[3]

The enforcement of the penalty of 'normal' ἀτιμία (on which see p. 171) did not arise unless and until the man in question performed some act which he was not entitled to perform because of his ἀτιμία. This probably rendered him liable to ἔνδειξις.[4] It is a conjecture, no more, that the name of such a man was removed from the deme list of citizens.[5]

For certain offences slavery might be imposed (see pp. 168 f.). The persons concerned would be sold; we may suppose that it was the duty of the poletai to conduct these sales, though this is firmly stated only for the sale of metics who had failed to pay the metics' tax.[6]

Confiscation of goods might be a method of executing a judgement already passed, or it might be a penalty in itself (see p. 178). In either case it was perhaps normal for the procedure of ἀπογραφή (on which see pp. 211 ff.) to be followed,[7] and then the man who initiated the ἀπογραφή probably procured the sale of the property by the poletai. In certain circumstances the demarch of the convicted man's deme was responsible for making an inventory of his property.[8] Only exceptionally were special state officials appointed to realize judicially confiscated property on behalf of the state (see pp. 34 f.).

[1] Thuc. 6. 60. 4, Lys. 6 *Andok.* 18.

[2] ἀπαγωγή in Lykourg. *Leokr.* 121 (quoted on p. 170, n. 1), ἔνδειξις in Lys. 6 *Andok.* 15.

[3] Dem. 50 *Polykl.* 49 *οἱ γὰρ νόμοι οὐκ ἐῶσιν ὑποδέχεσθαι τῶν φευγόντων οὐδένα, ἢ ἐν τοῖς αὐτοῖς κελεύουσιν ἐνέχεσθαι τὸν ὑποδεχόμενον τοὺς φεύγοντας*. Thuc. 1. 137. 2 implies that a law of this kind existed when Themistokles was in exile.

[4] Ar. *Ath. Pol.* 63. 3 *ἐὰν δέ τις δικάζῃ οἷς μὴ ἔξεστιν* (because ἄτιμος), *ἐνδείκνυται καὶ εἰς τὸ δικαστήριον εἰσάγεται*: in effect he has not committed an offence until he has wrongly exercised this right.

[5] Lipsius, *AR* 943, n. 6.

[6] Poll. 8. 99. Lipsius, *AR* 944, seems to go beyond the evidence when he says that selling into slavery always went hand in hand with confiscation of property.

[7] See p. 178, n. 2.

[8] Plut. *Mor.* 834 a, *An. Bekk.* (Λέξ. Ῥητ.) 199. 4 ff., 237. 8 ff., Harpokr. s.v. δήμαρχος (all quoted on p. 212, n. 2).

When a money fine had been imposed by a court, it was exacted by officials known as praktores (or, where tenths were due to Athena, by her treasurers). The ἡγεμών of the court which had imposed the fine had to communicate the amount of the fine and the name of the defendant to the praktores.[1] In some cases, where the court had imposed a fine payable to the state as well as compensation to the plaintiff, the plaintiff was responsible for posting up the fine.[2] For the publishing of the names of state debtors whose debts were outstanding at the ninth prytany see p. 173. In certain circumstances not easily defined a state debtor could be held in custody until payment.[3]

(iii) *Private suits*

Turning to the execution of judgements in private suits, the most important preliminary point to notice is that self-help remains basic to it (cf. p. 71). This can be seen in the survival of such expressions as συλᾶν, ἄγειν, and ἐφάπτεσθαι to express the action of a successful litigant asserting his adjudged right.[4] In many Greek cities this right of self-help meant that a judgement could be executed not only on the property but on the person of the debtor. This was the rule in Athens prior to Solon; but he abolished it, so far at least as private debts were concerned (see vol. i, p. 164).

In some cases Athenian law retained some traces of the old conception of vengeance. Thus, if a husband caught a man in the act of adultery with his wife and held the adulterer prisoner with a view to exacting a penalty from him, the alleged adulterer could bring an action against the husband; but if he lost he was handed over to the husband, who could do with him what he would in the presence of the court, short of wounding him with the sword (see vol. i, p. 33). This was a roundabout way of getting personal redress against an adulterer sanctioned by a court, and

[1] Dem. 43 *Makart.* 71 ὅτου δ' ἂν καταγνωσθῇ, ἐγγραφόντων οἱ ἄρχοντες, πρὸς οὓς ἂν ᾖ ἡ δίκη, τοῖς πράκτορσιν, ὃ τῷ δημοσίῳ γίγνεται· ⟨ὃ δὲ τῇ θεῷ γίγνεται⟩, τοῖς ταμίαις τῶν τῆς θεοῦ, Andok. 1 *Myst.* 77, Dem. 58 *Theokr.* 20, 48, Aischin. 1 *Timarch.* 35.

[2] Dem. 39 *Boiot.* i. 15, 53 *Nikostr.* 14, 58 *Theokr.* 19; Berneker, *RE* s.v. ψευδεγγραφῆς γραφή.

[3] See Appendix G.

[4] H. Swoboda, *Z* 26 (1905) 169, Partsch, *GB* 289 ff., Weiss, *GP* 497.

it is not clear how things went if the adulterer did not bring the *γραφή*. In homicide cases (which were technically still private cases even in the fourth century), where the penalty of death had been pronounced, the prosecutor was entitled to be present when execution was carried out by officers of the state, but that was all.[1] These were cases where judgement imposed or implied a penalty against the person. But there were also private cases in which the penalty imposed was simply monetary, but the plaintiff could proceed to personal execution against the defendant. In *δίκαι ἐμπορικαί* a convicted defendant had to remain in custody until he had paid the judgement debt,[2] and a plaintiff who incurred the *ἐπωβελία* was likewise subject to imprisonment until he had paid.[3] This rule may be connected with the fact that litigants in such suits might often be foreigners. Alternatively it may have been due to a recognition that Athens' very existence depended on maintaining corn imports, and this in turn depended on a vigorous trade and the confidence of foreign traders that their contracts could be enforced.

No doubt the most important aspect of execution of judgements in the day-to-day life of the Athenian was that relating to execution upon property after a conviction in a private suit. An object distrained upon, which might be either movable or immovable (there is no evidence that claims could be distrained upon), is an *ἐνέχυρον* and the verb is *ἐνεχυράζειν*; but the terminology is not always clear.[4]

When a private litigant secured judgement in his favour, if the judgement was for ownership of a thing, he would proceed to seize the thing. If it was an immovable, he would enter on it (*ἐμβατεύειν*). If it was a movable, it would often be before the court, and the litigant would simply need to lay hands on it (*ἐφάπτεσθαι*).[5] Resistance to either of these acts rendered the resister liable to the *δίκη ἐξούλης* with its penal element of a fine

[1] Dem. 23 *Aristokr.* 69 *τῷ δ'* (the accuser) *ἐπιδεῖν διδόντα δίκην ἔξεστιν, ἣν ἔταξ' ὁ νόμος, τὸν ἁλόντα, πέρα δ' οὐδὲν τούτου.*

[2] Dem. 33 *Apatour.* 1 *τοῖς ἀδικοῦσιν δεσμὸν ἔταξεν τοὐπιτίμιον, ἕως ἂν ἐκτείσωσιν ὅ τι ἂν αὐτῶν καταγνωσθῇ, ἵνα μηδεὶς ἀδικῇ μηδένα τῶν ἐμπόρων εἰκῇ.* Partsch, *GB* 301, emphasizes that this was an exception to the rule that in Athens the private creditor had no right to execution against the person of the debtor.

[3] Dem. 35 *Lakrit.* 46, 56 *Dionysod.* 4.

[4] See Appendix H.

[5] Vol. i, pp. 206 ff. Add to the literature there cited P. Jörs, *Z* 40 (1919) 77 ff., with a useful analysis of *ἐμβατεία*.

payable to the state, equivalent in value to that of the object in dispute. If the judgement was for money, we may presume that the successful plaintiff again could distrain on property of a defaulting defendant, though he would be accountable to the defendant for any excess in value of the thing seized over the amount of the judgement debt.[1]

There does not seem in all this to have been any idea of contempt of court, or of anything corresponding to a modern 'officer of the court'; and one may ask how was there not a vicious circle if a defendant proved recalcitrant, particularly if he was a more powerful or influential man than the plaintiff. The demarch of the defendant's deme played a part here; he was certainly called in when entry to a house for purposes of execution was necessary, and he may have been more widely accessible in this connection.[2] In an execution undertaken by a trierarch against his defaulting predecessor we find that he takes with him 'an officer from the magistrate' (the magistrate in question being an apostoleus), but we hear nothing further of this officer.[3] It is probably significant that in this same execution the plaintiff makes a formal statement that he is about to make seizure in accordance with the law.[4]

[1] Gernet, *Dem.* ii. 196 f., denies this. In his view, 'la prise de gages' was simply a way of forcing the will of the defaulting debtor. There is, he says (rightly), no evidence at this date that the gage had to be sold by the creditor who did not get satisfaction. According to Dem. 47 *Euerg.* 57, Theophemos forcibly seized goods in excess of the amount of the judgement in his favour: *τὰ πρόβατα ἔχετε πεντήκοντα [καὶ τὸν παῖδα] καὶ τὸν ποιμένα, πλείονος ἄξια ἢ κατεδικάσασθε.*

[2] Aristoph. *Clouds* 37 *δάκνει με δήμαρχός τις*, in the context of Strepsiades' debts, indicates that the demarch is likely to play a part in their collection. Schol. Aristoph. *Clouds* 37 *ἔδει οὖν τὸν δήμαρχον ἀγαγεῖν εἰς τοὺς οἴκους τοὺς ἐνεχυραζομένους*, Harpokr. s.v. *δήμαρχος· . . . ὅτι δὲ ἠνεχυρίαζον οἱ δήμαρχοι δηλοῖ Ἀριστοφάνης ἐν Σκηνὰς καταλαμβανούσαις* (Aristoph. fr. 484), *An. Bekk.* (*Λέξ. Ῥητ.*) 242. 16 ff. *δήμαρχοι· ἀρχή τις Ἀθήνησι τῶν τὰ ἐνέχυρα λαμβανόντων παρὰ τῶν ὑποχρέων, εἰ μὴ κατὰ καιρὸν ἀποδιδόναι τὸ χρέος.* Cf. Appendix H, p. 246. Dem. 57 *Euboul.* 63 refers to a demarch's activities in recovering debts due to the deme or to sacred treasuries. Beauchet iii. 226 ff., Schoeffer, *RE* s.v. 'Demarchoi', Bo. Sm. i. 321.

[3] Dem. 47 *Euerg.* 35 *λαβὼν παρὰ τῆς ἀρχῆς ὑπηρέτην ἦλθον ἐπὶ τὴν οἰκίαν τοῦ Θεοφήμου.* This was a part private, part public execution. Gernet, *Dem.* ii. 196, n. 1, states, perhaps too categorically, that the role of this officer was rather that of witness than that of executant. The whole speech illustrates the character and difficulties of execution in Athens.

[4] Dem. 47 *Euerg.* 37 *ἐνέχυρα ἔφην λήψεσθαι κατά τε τοὺς νόμους καὶ τὰ ψηφίσματα.* Gernet, *Dem.* ii. 213, n. 1, remarks that the speaker is acting on a judgement, but that the context shows that a defaulting trierarch was liable to distraint *ipso iure* by his succeeding trierarch. For other instances of formal statement see Rabel, *Z* 36 (1915) 348, Jörs, *Z* 40 (1919) 79.

A stated time was laid down within which a judgement debt had to be paid. Only thereafter was the debtor technically in arrear (ὑπερήμερος) and liable to the levying of distress. We do not know what this period was, nor whether it varied from case to case or with different types of action. But we do know that the litigants could by agreement vary the prescribed time limit.[1]

We may perhaps venture the judgement that the procedure as a whole was adequate for a city state based on a largely rural population, and that the special provisions in δίκαι ἐμπορικαί indicated where its inadequacies were liable to be felt. These difficulties were particularly apparent in relation to execution of judgements given in Athenian courts against citizens of the cities in her empire.[2]

§ 11. *Remedies against judgement*

(i) ἔφεσις

There is no doubt that the Athenians recognized as a principle that an issue once decided between parties should then be closed. This principle is enunciated by Demosthenes, and confirmed by the text of a law in another speech.[3] We have discussed above (pp. 119 f.) what precisely was meant by the bar on reopening a matter already adjudicated. We may assume that the rule was strictly observed in relation to those acquitted on a public charge, and it is only an apparent exception when a magistrate who has had his accounts passed by the logistai might be charged later during his εὔθυνα (see pp. 30 f.).

In private litigation the position is less clear-cut. We have discussed above (pp. 72 ff.) what was the result of a decision by an arbitrator in barring further proceedings, and noted the danger of importing into the story words like 'appeal' without trying to specify what precisely they might have meant to an Athenian. We saw there that, on the most probable view, the trial of a case that had already been before a public arbitrator is to be regarded not so much as an appeal, but as a totally new trial. The same may be said, *mutatis mutandis*, of cases referred to a dikastery by

[1] Dem. 47 *Euerg.* 49 προσελθὼν τῷ Θεοφήμῳ μελλούσης μοι ἤδη ἐξήκειν τῆς ὑπερημερίας, ἐδεήθην αὐτοῦ ἐπισχεῖν μοι ὀλίγον χρόνον.

[2] On these see G. E. M. de Ste Croix, *CQ* 11 (1961) 94 ff., 268 ff.

[3] Dem. 20 *Lept.* 147, 24 *Timokr.* 54 (both quoted on p. 119, n. 3).

the process of ἔφεσις against a magistrate's decision. As we saw above (p. 7), a magistrate might preside at the hearing of a case where he himself had imposed the fine which formed the issue before the court. This indicates how remote ἔφεσις from a magistrate's decision was from the modern concept of appeal.

When a man was excluded from a deme, a γένος, or a phratry, his exclusion, though not strictly a judgement, was a quasi-judicial act. It could be reversed by bringing suit against the demesmen (or γεννῆται or φράτερες) in the court of the thesmothetai. In some manner not wholly clear to us a public arbitrator might become involved in such a suit.[1] Again, we cannot be quite certain how ἔφεσις worked when an arbitrator was charged with malpractice. As the text of Ar. *Ath. Pol.* 53. 6 stands, he was impeached before his fellow arbitrators; conviction entailed ἀτιμία, but ἔφεσις was allowed. Whatever we think about the trial before his fellow arbitrators (see p. 68), we must suppose that ἔφεσις here meant the right to have the matter tried before a dikastery. In Aristotle's time the boule's δοκιμασία of the bouleutai for the succeeding year and of the nine archons was subject to ἔφεσις to a dikastery.[2] Finally, ἔφεσις could be applied in cases which came before the courts of allied cities in the Athenian empire. In the well-known Chalkis decree of *c.* 445 B.C. there is ἔφεσις to Athens in cases involving exile, death, or ἀτιμία.[3] This probably means that such cases were first tried in Chalkis, but that either party, if dissatisfied with the judgement, could get a case transferred to Athens.

Hitherto we have been considering only the use of ἔφεσις, which, for reasons stated above, is not wholly satisfactorily to be translated 'appeal'. We now turn to the possibilities of reversing an actual judgement in a dikastery; for, in spite of their regarding such a decision as absolute, the Athenians could not evade the fact that there were circumstances in which justice demanded that it should be possible to reopen an issue. For a new trial which resulted in such circumstances the technical substantive was ἀναδικία and the verb ἀναδικάζεσθαι, though we cannot say precisely how these words were used. The adjective ἀνάδικος occurs several times to describe legal judgements which had for

[1] Isai. 12 *Euphil.* 11, Dem. 59 *Neair.* 60; Wyse, *Isai.* 716. Cf. p. 20, n. 1.
[2] Ar. *Ath. Pol.* 45. 3. On δοκιμασία see pp. 200 ff.
[3] *IG* i². 39. 71 ff.; de Ste Croix, *CQ* 11 (1961) 271 f.

some reason or other become invalid.[1] We cannot make an exhaustive list of conditions which might produce this result, but that which looms largest in our sources is connected with the giving of false evidence.

(ii) *On grounds of false evidence*

In some circumstances a litigant who had lost his case and could convict one or more of his opponent's witnesses could have the case retried. (We are not here concerned with the challenging of a *διαμαρτυρία* by a *δίκη ψευδομαρτυρίων*, which is discussed on pp. 128 ff.)

We have to distinguish between the effect of the *ἐπίσκηψις* and of the judgement in the resulting *δίκη ψευδομαρτυρίων*. Technically *ἐπισκήπτεσθαι* means 'to give formal notice of an intention to prosecute a witness'.[2] Such notice could be given orally at any time during the giving of the evidence.[3] In Aristotle's day the herald asked litigants just before the casting of the votes whether they wished to make formal objection to the evidence, and no such objection could be made once the voting began.[4] It is a disputed matter whether this *ἐπίσκηψις* was in itself equal to an indictment for false evidence, or whether it had to be followed by a *λῆξις*. We may perhaps assume that Plato, *Laws* 937 b is following Athenian law (it does in one other important particular) in prescribing that an *ἐπίσκηψις* had to be recorded by the magistrate and filed with the documents pertaining to the case. It is to be noted that in this type of *ἐπίσκηψις* notice is given in close connection with, but before voting on, the judgement. The implication would seem to be that the effect on the minds of the

[1] *ἀνάδικος* occurs in Andok. 1 *Myst.* 88, Dem. 24 *Timokr.* 191, 40 *Boiot.* ii. 34, 39, 42, to describe a judgement which has become a nullity. According to Poll. 8. 24, Lysias used *ἀναδικία* and Isaios *ἀναδικάζεσθαι*. Harpokr. s.v. *ἀναδικάσασθαι· τὸ ἄνωθεν δικάσασθαι· οὕτως Ἰσαῖος. ἐντεῦθεν καὶ τὸ ἀνάδικοι κρίσεις, αἱ ἄνωθεν δικαζόμεναι, ὅταν ἁλῶσιν οἱ μάρτυρες ψευδομαρτυρίων*: this unsatisfactory entry implies that alleged false evidence was the only ground for a retrial, but we shall see later that that is not likely. Lipsius, *AR* 955 ff., Bo. Sm. ii. 232 ff., Lämmli, *Prozeß.* 129 ff., Berneker, *RE* s.v. *παλινδικία* and *ψευδομαρτυρίων δίκη*.

[2] On *ἐπίσκηψις* see Rentzsch, *ψευδομ.* 27 ff., Leisi, *Zeuge* 125 ff., Calhoun, *CP* 11 (1916) 365 ff., Berneker, *RE* s.v. *ψευδομαρτυρίων δίκη*.

[3] Dem. 48 *Olymp.* 31, 44 f.

[4] Ar. *Ath. Pol.* 68. 4 *ἐπειδὰν δὲ διαψηφίζεσθαι μέλλωσιν οἱ δικασταί, ὁ κῆρυξ ἀγορεύει πρῶτον, ἂν ἐπισκήπτωνται οἱ ἀντίδικοι ταῖς μαρτυρίαις. οὐ γὰρ ἔστιν ἐπισκήψασθαι ὅταν ἄρξωνται διαψηφίζεσθαι.*

jury was relevant. The litigants did not yet know which way judgement would go, but they had to indicate whether they intended to challenge their opponent's witnesses (and presumably to state in particular which). It is clear that this type of ἐπίσκηψις had at the instant nothing but a psychological effect—on the minds of the jury. Judgement would be passed, and if the objector did not carry his objection to a δίκη ψευδομαρτυρίων (as he very well might not do if judgement were in his favour) the legal effect of the ἐπίσκηψις was nil.[1]

ἐπίσκηψις was probably a necessary precondition for a subsequent δίκη ψευδομαρτυρίων.[2] Failure to register an objection might be cited as relevant evidence in subsequent litigation.[3] On the other hand we cannot say whether there was any check, and if so what it was, on promiscuous objections. Without these, it would have seemed improvident not to enter objections in all cases. ἐπίσκηψις may have been at least highly desirable for a practical reason. In any subsequent δίκη ψευδομαρτυρίων the proof of what the defendant had said would have been difficult without some official document. It was probably a function of the ἐπίσκηψις to provide the would-be prosecutor with that documentation.[4] We cannot therefore say why litigants did not as a matter of course enter an ἐπίσκηψις. Perhaps there was a fee which was only recoverable if they followed up with a successful δίκη ψευδομαρτυρίων.[5]

Turning now to the effects of a δίκη ψευδομαρτυρίων, we have to ask first whether there was any rule governing the number or character of the witnesses who had to be convicted in order to

[1] There is one important exception. If the judgement deprived the defendant of his status as a free man (that is, if it was death or enslavement), the ἐπίσκηψις procured a stay of execution, and the defendant was held in custody until the δίκη ψευδομαρτυρίων was heard. We know this for certain of a defendant convicted in a γραφὴ ξενίας (Dem. 24 *Timokr.* 131) and we may safely generalize from this. Lys. 19 *Prop. Arist.* 4 shows that the rule was different when that speech was written. Partsch, *GB* 300 f., Gernet and Bizos, *Lys.* ii. 41, n. 1.

[2] So Calhoun, *CP* 11 (1916) 376 ff., followed by Berneker, *RE* s.v. ψευδομαρτυρίων δίκη 1367. We have to accept the fact that such a rule bears very hardly on a litigant who only discovers after the trial evidence which shows that a witness was perjured. See Gernet, *DSGA* 87 ff., for the distinction between ἐπίσκηψις when applied in relation to διαμαρτυρία and its use in other connections.

[3] For example, Dem. 48 *Olymp.* 31, 44 f.

[4] Calhoun, *CP* 9 (1914) 140, n. 1, 11 (1916) 377, is right to argue that it is impossible to envisage a δίκη ψευδομαρτυρίων working without such documentation.

[5] This is suggested by Rentzsch, ψευδομ. 29 f.; Calhoun, *CP* 11 (1916) 386, dissents.

allow a reopening of the original case. Here the most probable view seems to be that what counted was the evidence attacked rather than the witnesses as persons. A view has been expressed that the conviction of a single witness empowered the litigant who had been defeated in the original case to have the case reopened.[1] This view is based on a passage in Isaios which hardly supports it.[2] On *a priori* grounds it would seem unlikely that the conviction of just one witness, who might be either a witness to a relatively unimportant part of the case or one among a number of witnesses to the same fact, should have been thought a sufficient ground for upsetting a previous verdict. On the other hand it is quite impossible to say what rule was adopted for determining when a *δίκη ψευδομαρτυρίων* justified the reopening of the original case. Plato in the *Laws* lays down that this should happen when over half the evidence given by the witnesses on the winning side has been successfully attacked, and a scholiast implies that this was an actual rule, perhaps in Athens.[3] It is not easy to see how such a quantitative requirement could have been carried out in practice, but it has been thought that some rule of this kind applied in Athens. Two suggestions, neither of them very plausible, have been made as to how this practical difficulty might have been overcome. One is that there had to be a separate procedure, a nullity suit, to determine whether the evidence discredited in the *δίκη ψευδομαρτυρίων* had been sufficiently decisive to justify reopening the case.[4] But there is no positive evidence for such a procedure, and it would surely have been needlessly complex.[5] Another suggestion is that the *ἡγεμών* of the court in

[1] H. Buermann, *NJ* 115 (1877) 586, Leisi, *Zeuge* 134, Bo. Sm. ii. 265 ff., Calhoun, *TAPA* 65 (1934) 86 (though Calhoun had rejected this view in *CP* 11 (1916) 391).

[2] Isai. 11 *Hagn.* 46 *κελεύει δ' ὁ νόμος, ἐὰν ἁλῷ τις τῶν ψευδομαρτυρίων, πάλιν ἐξ ἀρχῆς εἶναι περὶ αὐτῶν τὰς λήξεις.* Lipsius, *AR* 958, n. 11, rightly points out that *τις* in this context cannot be pressed to mean *εἷς*.

[3] Plato, *Laws* 937 c–d *ὁπόσων δ' ἂν μαρτυρίαι ἁλῶσιν δίκῃ, ψευδῆ δοξάντων μαρτυρεῖν καὶ τὴν νίκην τῷ ἑλόντι πεποιηκέναι, ἐὰν τῶν τοιούτων ὑπὲρ ἥμισυ μαρτυριῶν καταδικασθῶσίν τινες, τὴν κατὰ ταύτας ἁλοῦσαν δίκην ἀνάδικον γίγνεσθαι,* schol. ad loc. *ἀνάδικος κρίσις· εἰ ἑάλωσαν ἤτοι πάντες οἱ μάρτυρες ψευδομαρτυρίων ἢ ὑπερημίσεις, ἐκρίνετο ἄνωθεν ἡ δίκη. οὐκ ἐπὶ πάντων δὲ τῶν ἀγώνων ἐγίγνοντο ἀνάδικοι αἱ κρίσεις, ἀλλ', ὥς φησι Θεόφραστος ἐν ζʹ Νόμων, ἐπὶ μόνης ξενίας καὶ ψευδομαρτυρίων καὶ κλήρων.* We may perhaps deduce from the scholiast's citation of Theophrastos that he had some evidence outside Plato for the institution, though we cannot of course be certain that the reference was to Athens.

[4] Rentzsch, *ψευδομ.* 59 f.

[5] Lipsius, *AR* 956, n. 7, Calhoun, *CP* 11 (1916) 393.

which the original decision was taken could pronounce authoritatively on the matter.[1] But it would be surprising if such power had been left to a magistrate so late as the fourth century.[2] We must admit defeat here. We simply do not know the precise requirements for using a δίκη ψευδομαρτυρίων to reopen the original case.

The information we have suggests that proved false evidence was not a means of reopening any and every case. Theophrastos said, if the citation is accurate,[3] that judgements could be reversed only in suits against foreigners who had usurped citizen rights, suits against false evidence, and inheritance suits. Some scholars have argued that these suits were mentioned by Theophrastos simply *exempli gratia*, and that any judgement imposing the death penalty, sale into slavery, or full ἀτιμία could be thus reopened.[4] But this is to do violence to the words of Theophrastos, our only direct witness on the matter. It has been argued that the object of the rule was to protect the rights of a litigant who by reason of the false evidence was threatened with a loss for which there could be no assessable monetary compensation: loss of life, loss of citizen rights, or loss of family rights (remembering that inheritance was often a matter of much more than the material estate).[5] This may be so; but those who argue thus do not tackle the objection that impeachment of evidence by ἐπίσκηψις, and therefore by implication a charge by way of δίκη ψευδομαρτυρίων, was certainly not confined to impeachment of the witnesses for the prosecution. It might therefore be argued that defendants in suits such as these stood to lose just as much as they stood to gain by a rule which might invalidate an acquittal equally with a conviction. On *a priori* grounds one would have expected that, once the principle had been recognized that false evidence might have led to an unjust verdict, the range of cases to which the rule was applied would gradually have been extended. Certainly such an extension is provided for by Plato in the *Laws*.[6] But there is no evidence that the Athenians took this step forward in the classical period.[7]

[1] Lipsius, *AR* 960.

[2] Bo. Sm. ii. 268.

[3] Schol. Plato, *Laws* 937 d (quoted on p. 194, n. 3).

[4] Lipsius, *AR* 957; against this are Lämmli, *Prozeß*. 135, Berneker, *RE* s.v. ψευδομαρτυρίων δίκη 1371.

[5] MSL 979 ff., Berneker, loc. cit.

[6] Plato, *Laws* 937 c–d (quoted on p. 194, n. 3).

[7] In *IG* ii². 1258, an inscription of 324/3 B.C., Polyxenos is honoured by the Eikadies, a cult group, for having entered an ἐπίσκηψις against a witness. We do

It is highly improbable that proved false evidence in a trial before the Areopagos could lead to the reopening of the case. It is significant that if evidence given in such a trial was impugned by a *δίκη ψευδομαρτυρίων* the case was taken not in the court of the basileus, but in that of the thesmothetai.[1] It might seem strange that in homicide cases, where one would have expected the principle of protecting the defendant to have reigned *par excellence*, no *δίκη ἀνάδικος* should have been allowed. We can only surmise that the defendant's interests were held to be sufficiently protected by the facts that a homicide trial proper was preceded by three preliminary trials (*προδικασίαι*) in the three months preceding the trial proper, which much reduced the chance of a prosecutor's getting away with shaky evidence, and that all the evidence was given under solemn oath and the witnesses had to swear not only to the truth of what they said, but also to the guilt or innocence of the accused (see p. 139). There may be some rhetorical exaggeration when Demosthenes says that only in regard to the court of the Areopagos had no convicted defendant and no defeated prosecutor ever succeeded in showing that the judgement of the court had been unjust to him.[2] But he could not have used such words unless there had been a general confidence in the procedures before the Areopagos.

Although we have spoken primarily of the rights of the defendant, and these may have been in the forefront of the minds of those who devised these rules, we must suppose that a frustrated prosecutor had an equal right to challenge the defendant's evidence and by this means turn an acquittal into a conviction.

Evidence given before a public arbitrator raises special problems, but it seems probable that a challenge of it by way of a *δίκη*

not know what was at issue in the original suit in which the impeached evidence was given, and it has been argued (e.g. by Berneker, *RE* s.v. *ψευδομαρτυρίων δίκη* 1372) that a cult group was not likely to have been a litigant in a case under one of the three heads mentioned by Theophrastos. But they surely might have been litigant in a *δίκη ψευδομαρτυρίων*, and in fact might have been interested in the result of litigation in a suit in either of the other two categories, and therefore grateful to a man who by *ἐπίσκηψις* had had a case reopened. Lipsius, *AR* 771, n. 358.

[1] See p. 16, n. 5. Note that, if we accept MacDowell's account of the Kallimachos case in Isok. 18 *Kallim.* 51 ff. (on which see pp. 40 ff.), we have a *δίκη ψευδομαρτυρίων* brought by a successful defendant in a homicide case (a case of the alleged killing of a slave, heard at the Palladion); but this is *ex hypothesi* not an instance of a *δίκη ψευδομαρτυρίων* being used to reopen a case.

[2] Dem. 23 *Aristokr.* 66 *ἐνταυθοῖ μόνον οὐδεὶς πώποτ' οὔτε φεύγων ἁλοὺς οὔτε διώκων ἡττηθεὶς ἐξήλεγξεν ὡς ἀδίκως ἐδικάσθη τὰ κριθέντα.*

ψευδομαρτυρίων had no bearing on the binding force of the arbitrator's decision.[1] There is nothing in our sources to suggest that if an arbitrator's decision had been accepted by both parties either of them could subsequently have it overset by impeaching the evidence on which his decision had been given, though this does not rule out the possibility of a suit to recover damages from a perjurer. It is relevant here that an arbitrator's decision could never involve a litigant in death, enslavement, or *ἀτιμία*. If on the other hand an arbitrator's decision had been challenged by *ἔφεσις* and the case came before a jury, each litigant had full opportunity at the hearing in chief to impeach his opponent's witnesses. According to a scholiast on Demosthenes, if an arbitrator was convicted for malfeasance as arbitrator, the decision on which the charge against him was based was in danger of being invalidated.[2] We have no indication how this could be achieved by the aggrieved litigant.

(iii) *After judgement by default*

Another important ground for reopening a case was where judgement had been given by default and the unsuccessful litigant wished to plead an excuse for his default.[3] The plea might be either that the suit had been brought on before the lapse of time allowed for adjournment at a previous hearing (see p. 155), or that there was good ground for the litigant's non-appearance. The term for this was *τὴν ἔρημον δίκην ἀντιλαχεῖν* or *τὴν δίκην ἀντιλαχεῖν*.[4] If the default had been before an arbitrator the term was *τὴν μὴ οὖσαν ἀντιλαχεῖν*.

The procedure had to be set on foot within two months of the judgement which it sought to reverse. On the analogy of the similar procedure against an arbitrator's decision we may presume that the litigant took an oath that his default had been

[1] Rentzsch, *ψευδομ.* 39 f., Leisi, *Zeuge* 125, Lipsius, *AR* 782, Steinwenter, *Streit.* 73, n. 1.

[2] Schol. Dem. 21 *Meid.* 83 *κατεγνώσθη γὰρ Στράτων ὡς κακῶς διαιτήσας, καὶ κινδυνεύει καὶ ἡ δίαιτα δι' αὐτὸ ἄκυρος γενέσθαι.*

[3] Lipsius, *AR* 960 ff., Thalheim, *RE* s.v. *ἀντιλαγχάνειν*.

[4] Dem. 32 *Zenoth.* 27, Poll. 8. 61 *ἀντιλαχεῖν δὲ δίκην ἐξῆν, ὁπότε τις μὴ παρὼν ἐν δικαστηρίῳ κατακηρυχθεὶς καὶ μὴ ὑπακούων ἐρήμην ὄφλοι. ἀντιλαχεῖν δὲ δύο ἐντὸς μηνῶν ὑπῆρχεν. εἰ δὲ μὴ τοῦτο σχοίη, τὸ ἐγγεγραμμένον ὦφλε καὶ ἄτιμος ἦν.* The last phrase can of course refer only to judgements imposing fines payable to the state.

unavoidable.[1] The court would then decide whether or not the plea could be accepted. If it was rejected, the original judgement stood; the litigant who had raised the plea had to furnish sureties for the carrying out of that judgement (if we rely on analogy with the arbitration procedure). If it was accepted, the original case was tried *de novo*.[2]

It was a special case of this plea when a defendant wished to claim that he had not been duly summoned. Since it was laid down that a magistrate was not to admit a case without being satisfied that the defendant had been summoned, and since to satisfy him on this point the plaintiff had to furnish witnesses that the summons had been issued (see p. 85), the defendant who wished to make this plea had first to show that he had not been so summoned. It is usually supposed that he could only do this by bringing a successful action either against the witnesses to the summons (presumably all the witnesses) in a γραφὴ ψευδοκλητείας or against his opponent in a δίκη κακοτεχνιῶν.[3] If this is right (and it is difficult to see how else he could establish that he had in fact not been summoned), we still cannot be sure whether success in one or other of these suits automatically cancelled the judgement in the original suit, or whether the rule was that he had then within the period of two months from the judgement in the original suit to bring suit for the annulment of that judgement (τὴν ἔρημον δίκην ἀντιλαχεῖν). The latter alternative seems preferable;[4] but this question is, like many problems in relation to this action and the δίκη ψευδομαρτυρίων, bedevilled by the fact that the Athenians made no clear distinction between the cassatory effects of these suits and their function as actions for damages.[5] There would of course have inevitably been cases

[1] Poll. 8. 60 (referring to default before an arbitrator) ὑπομοσάμενος νόσον ἢ ἀποδημίαν.

[2] We should not assume, as does Lipsius, *AR* 961 f., that such a plea was always on behalf of a defendant. There would have been cases, though perhaps rarer, where judgement went against the plaintiff in default. We must presume that he too had a right to put forward this plea.

[3] So, categorically, Berneker, *RE* s.v. πρόσκλησις 851. There seems to be no direct evidence.

[4] It is accepted by Berneker, *RE* s.v. ψευδοκλητείας γραφή, as against Lipsius, *AR* 962.

[5] Note that ψευδοκλητεία was subject to a γραφή, ψευδομαρτύριον only to a δίκη. It is not plausible to argue, as some scholars have, that the former was in some way a more public wrong than the latter. The reason may be that the former wrong might cause a litigant against whom judgement by default had been given to lose

where the original judgement by default had been executed; in these cases a cassatory procedure was ineffective.

(iv) *Amnesty*

It goes without saying that from time to time the regime in power exercised the sovereign right of amnesty.[1] Here the Athenian democracy tried, with what success we do not know, to limit its own power of reprieve. There was a law which prohibited a proposal to the people to release an individual from ἀτιμία or from a debt to the state (such a proposal, if carried, was called a νόμος ἐπ' ἀνδρί), unless an indemnity (ἄδεια) had been obtained by a majority vote in an assembly with a quorum of six thousand voting secretly.[2]

his freedom of movement or even his free status. He would then need the intervention of ὁ βουλόμενος to get a hearing.

[1] Thus on the fall of the Thirty in 403 B.C. all judgements, whether in public or in private suits, given during their regime were annulled (Dem. 24 *Timokr.* 56).

[2] Dem. 24 *Timokr.* 45. The rule went back to the fifth century: Andok. 1 *Myst.* 77. For instances see Lipsius, *AR* 963 f.

III · SPECIAL PROCEDURES FOR PUBLIC WRONGS

§ 1. δοκιμασία

(i) *Introduction*

THIS topic really belongs to constitutional law. We are here only concerned with it in so far as it involved court proceedings.[1] It may be slightly misleading to treat the procedure under the head of public wrongs. As will appear, that part of the institution which concerns us, a judicial transaction before a dikastery, had two rather different aims. One was to allow one who had been rejected in some way at the first stage by the administrative act of a magistrate or public body to have the case reconsidered by a dikastery; here was redress for an individual who was being wronged by an organ of the state. The other aim was to secure to a dikastery the final decision whether a person was in some way legally disqualified to enter upon some particular status; here was a judicial sanction against a public wrong.

There were four types of δοκιμασία, in any one of which process before a dikastery might arise. These types were the examination of incoming magistrates, of orators, of epheboi, and of new citizens.[2]

[1] Koch, *RE* s.v. δοκιμασία, Lipsius, *AR* 269 ff., Bo. Sm. ii. 243 ff., Wade-Gery, *EGH* 194; for the historical development of the institution, Bu. Sw. 1072 f., Kahrstedt, *Mag.* 59 ff., Hignett, *HAC* 205 ff.

[2] The boule also carried out an annual δοκιμασία of cavalry, πρόδρομοι, and ἅμιπποι (Ar. *Ath. Pol.* 49. 1, Lys. 15 *Alk.* ii. 11), as also of invalids who were publicly supported (Ar. *Ath. Pol.* 49. 4, Harpokr. s.v. ἀδύνατοι). But there is no evidence that any appeal was allowed from their decisions in these matters. Aischin. 1 *Timarch.* 104, speaking of a disabled man, uses the phrase ἱκετηρίαν θέντος εἰς τὴν βουλὴν ὑπὲρ τοῦ μισθοῦ: on that occasion an abortive attempt was made to get the boule to reinstate a man's name on the list of invalids when it had been omitted for some reason which is not given; this is the reverse of the usual role of the boule, which was to scrutinize for illicit inclusions. Lys. 24 *Invalid*, if genuine, was delivered in the boule in defence of a man whose name it had been proposed to remove (Lipsius, *AR* 270, n. 4); for the case against authenticity see now M. D. Reeve, *CR* 18 (1968) 235. The Athenians could never quite make up their minds whether the boule was to be regarded as a magistracy and therefore needing the curb of the courts, or as a representative random selection of ordinary citizens and therefore exactly on all fours with a dikastery of five hundred.

(ii) *Magistrates*

Our sources for the δοκιμασία of magistrates are relatively good. Aristotle deals with it twice in the *Ath. Pol.* (45. 2 and 55. 2–4). Several speeches of Lysias were delivered at one stage or another of a δοκιμασία. 26 *Euandr.* is a speech delivered to the boule opposing the admission of Euandros to the archonship. 25 *Subv. Dem.* was probably spoken in a dikastery in defence of a man being opposed for office. 16 *Mantith.* was spoken in the boule in defence of Mantitheos, who was standing for an office or for the boule. 31 *Phil.* was spoken in the boule by an outgoing bouleutes opposing the entry of an incoming one. The grammarians tend rather to confuse the picture.[1]

The aim of the δοκιμασία was to establish that anyone about to take up office possessed all the legal qualifications for that post. It was not intended to be a scrutiny of a man's general competence for the post.[2] According to Aristotle all holders of ἀρχαί, whether elected by lot or by show of hands, had to pass the scrutiny.[3] Aischines says that the law specifically mentioned also anyone who was to be in charge of any state business for more than thirty days and anyone who was to preside over a court.[4]

Originally, Aristotle tells us (without indicating when the change took place), the boule conducted the δοκιμασία and its decision against an official was final; but in his day there was reference to a dikastery, with which the final decision lay.[5] The

[1] Harpokr. s.v. δοκιμασθείς, Poll. 8. 44, *An. Bekk.* (Λέξ. Ῥητ.) 235. 11 ff.

[2] When Lys. 13 *Agorat.* 10 says of Theramenes στρατηγὸν χειροτονηθέντα ἀπεδοκιμάσατε, οὐ νομίζοντες εὔνουν εἶναι τῷ πλήθει τῷ ὑμετέρῳ, he implies nothing about the legal basis of the δοκιμασία; we may be sure that speakers at either stage of the process would not confine themselves to the strictly legal qualifications, and hostile references to Theramenes' supposed enmity towards the δῆμος in a speech by his opponent at the δοκιμασία would have been ample reason for Lysias to assume that that had been the effective cause of his rejection. The statement in Lys. 16 *Mantith.* 9, ἐν δὲ ταῖς δοκιμασίαις δίκαιον εἶναι παντὸς τοῦ βίου λόγον διδόναι, should also not be taken too literally, but shows how pleaders might be expected to argue.

[3] Ar. *Ath. Pol.* 55. 2 πάντες γὰρ καὶ οἱ κληρωτοὶ καὶ οἱ χειροτονητοὶ δοκιμασθέντες ἄρχουσιν.

[4] Aischin. 3 *Ktes.* 14 f. "τὰς χειροτονητάς" φησιν (sc. ὁ νόμος) "ἀρχάς . . . καὶ τοὺς ἐπιστάτας" φησὶ "τῶν δημοσίων ἔργων . . . καὶ πάντας ὅσοι διαχειρίζουσί τι τῶν τῆς πόλεως πλέον ἢ τριάκονθ' ἡμέρας, καὶ ὅσοι λαμβάνουσιν ἡγεμονίας δικαστηρίων, . . . ἄρχειν δοκιμασθέντας ἐν τῷ δικαστηρίῳ", 29.

[5] Ar. *Ath. Pol.* 45. 3 δοκιμάζει δὲ (sc. ἡ βουλή) καὶ τοὺς βουλευτὰς τοὺς τὸν ὕστερον ἐνιαυτὸν βουλεύσοντας καὶ τοὺς ἐννέα ἄρχοντας. καὶ πρότερον μὲν ἦν ἀποδοκιμάσαι κυρία, νῦν δὲ τούτοις ἔφεσίς ἐστιν εἰς τὸ δικαστήριον, 55. 2 καὶ πρότερον μὲν οὐκ ἦρχεν

language used by Aristotle suggests that in this connection the function of the boule was looked on as parallel to the function of a magistrate at the *ἀνάκρισις*. Each man who was being scrutinized had to establish by way of witnesses the name and deme of his father, his father's father, his mother, and his mother's father, that he maintained the cult of Apollo Patroos and Zeus Herkeios and of his ancestors at their tomb, that he did his duty by his parents, paid his taxes, and had done the military service required of him. When these witnesses had been heard, the question was asked (by a herald perhaps) whether anyone wished to challenge the candidate; if someone came forward, speeches on either side were made and the boule voted by show of hands.[1] Aristotle fails us from here on, since he does not distinguish clearly between procedure before the boule and that before the dikastery. The boule might vote against the candidate. We might then suppose that it rested with the candidate whether he acquiesced or whether he demanded a hearing by a dikastery. Some scholars believe that by its very nature *ἔφεσις* implied a choice by the individual concerned (usually a litigant, here a candidate already selected for office), and that it was never something set on foot as routine by an official.[2] Though we

ὅντιν' ἀποδοκιμάσειεν ἡ βουλή, νῦν δ' ἔφεσίς ἐστιν εἰς τὸ δικαστήριον, καὶ τοῦτο κύριόν ἐστι τῆς δοκιμασίας. We are not concerned with the question whether magistrates other than the archons and bouleutai had to submit to the double procedure, first before the boule and then before a dikastery. That the archons had to do so at a relatively early period in Athenian history is shown by Dem. 20 *Lept.* 90, though we need not accept from that passage that the institution went literally back to Solon.

[1] Ar. *Ath. Pol.* 55. 3 f. *ἐπερωτῶσιν δ', ὅταν δοκιμάζωσιν, πρῶτον μὲν "τίς σοι πατὴρ καὶ πόθεν τῶν δήμων, καὶ τίς πατρὸς πατήρ, καὶ τίς μήτηρ, καὶ τίς μητρὸς πατὴρ καὶ πόθεν τῶν δήμων;" μετὰ δὲ ταῦτα, εἰ ἔστιν αὐτῷ Ἀπόλλων πατρῷος καὶ Ζεὺς ἑρκεῖος, καὶ ποῦ ταῦτα τὰ ἱερά ἐστιν, εἶτα ἠρία εἰ ἔστιν καὶ ποῦ ταῦτα, ἔπειτα γονέας εἰ εὖ ποιεῖ, καὶ τὰ τέλη <εἰ> τελεῖ, καὶ τὰς στρατείας εἰ ἐστράτευται. ταῦτα δ' ἀνερωτήσας "κάλει", φησίν, "τούτων τοὺς μάρτυρας." ἐπειδὰν δὲ παράσχηται τοὺς μάρτυρας, ἐπερωτᾷ "τούτου βούλεταί τις κατηγορεῖν;" κἂν μὲν ᾖ τις κατήγορος, δοὺς κατηγορίαν καὶ ἀπολογίαν οὕτω δίδωσιν ἐν μὲν τῇ βουλῇ τὴν ἐπιχειροτονίαν, ἐν δὲ τῷ δικαστηρίῳ τὴν ψῆφον· ἐὰν δὲ μηδεὶς βούληται κατηγορεῖν, εὐθὺς δίδωσι τὴν ψῆφον*, Dein. 2 *Aristogeit.* 17 (quoted on p. 203, n. 4).

[2] So Wade-Gery, *EGH* 194, disagreeing with Bo. Sm. ii. 244. But we might urge in favour of Bo. Sm. that, although formally the referring of the condemnation of a candidate to a dikastery depended on the decision of the candidate to have it referred, unless there was some sanction against irresponsible use of this right (and there is no evidence that there was) it would have been exercised as a matter of course; the original feature, the decision of the individual candidate, would thus have become obscured.

cannot argue very certainly from the use of the word ἔφεσις,[1] this seems *a priori* more likely than that every case should necessarily go to a dikastery; but, if so, it must be admitted that the dikastery would not always have been master of the decision.[2] On the other hand the boule might, in an opposed case, vote for the candidate. In that case it seems clear that the candidate still had to get over the second hurdle, the hearing of the case by a dikastery. This also happened if no one came forward to oppose the candidate. We may follow Aristotle here when he says that in former times the vote of the dikastery was in such cases a mere formality, but that in his day, in order to avoid corrupt silencing of possible opponents, a dikastery voted by ballot even when there had been no opposition.[3] This was the limiting case, where a dikastery took action only very remotely judicial in character, since no discussion had taken place on the issue and no specific charge was laid.

So much for the procedure for magistrates who had to submit to δοκιμασία both before the boule and before a dikastery. The boule's function seems to have been very close to the ἀνάκρισις of the ἡγεμών in other cases; and indeed a passage of Deinarchos, which gives in a similar, but slightly different, form the points on which the boule had to satisfy itself about the candidate, uses the word ἀνακρίνειν of the boule's function.[4] Magistrates other than the archons and bouleutai probably came before a dikastery without the previous hearing by the boule. Probably the same sort of questioning about qualifications was in their case undertaken at an ἀνάκρισις before the thesmothetai, and the thesmothetai then introduced each case to a dikastery. They may at one time have given their own decision on each case (with the same rules about ἔφεσις as applied to the boule), but they had certainly ceased to do this by the fourth century. The thesmothetai had also the duty of introducing to a dikastery those cases in which the boule had pronounced against candidates.[5]

[1] On the meaning of ἔφεσις see pp. 72 ff.

[2] κύριον in Ar. *Ath. Pol.* 55. 2 (quoted on p. 201, n. 5).

[3] Ar. *Ath. Pol.* 55. 4 καὶ πρότερον μὲν εἷς ἐνέβαλλε τὴν ψῆφον, νῦν δ' ἀνάγκη πάντας ἐστὶ διαψηφίζεσθαι περὶ αὐτῶν, ἵνα, ἄν τις πονηρὸς ὢν ἀπαλλάξῃ τοὺς κατηγόρους, ἐπὶ τοῖς δικασταῖς γένηται τοῦτον ἀποδοκιμάσαι.

[4] Dein. 2 *Aristogeit.* 17 ἀνακρίνοντες τοὺς τῶν κοινῶν τι μέλλοντας διοικεῖν, τίς ἐστι τὸν ἴδιον τρόπον, εἰ γονέας εὖ ποιεῖ, εἰ τὰς στρατείας ὑπὲρ τῆς πόλεως ἐστράτευται, εἰ ἱερὰ πατρῷ' ἔστιν, εἰ τὰ τέλη τελεῖ.

[5] Ar. *Ath. Pol.* 59. 4 εἰσάγουσιν δὲ καὶ τὰς δοκιμασίας ταῖς ἀρχαῖς ἁπάσαις καὶ τοὺς

(iii) *Orators*

While orators were not a closed class or profession, and any citizen, unless suffering from some specific disqualification, was entitled to address the ekklesia, there were these recognized disqualifications and anyone who addressed the ekklesia when suffering from one or other of them rendered himself liable to a *δοκιμασία*.[1] There was a law entitled *ὁ νόμος ὁ περὶ τῆς τῶν ῥητόρων δοκιμασίας*,[2] and we find some at least of its provisions in Aischin. 1 *Timarch.* 28 ff.[3]

The procedure was set on foot by a formal pronouncement in the ekklesia of an intention to proceed.[4] It has been conjectured that the objector had to take an oath that he would proceed with the objection. There are two analogous cases which are alleged to support this conjecture. Timotheos is alleged to have taken an oath in the ekklesia that he would bring a *γραφὴ ξενίας* against Iphikrates;[5] the motive was presumably to stop, temporarily at least, Iphikrates' mouth in the assembly. A more persuasive analogy is with the oath which a man might take in the boule or ekklesia that he intended to bring a *γραφὴ παρανόμων* against the proposer of a decree; the effect of such an oath was to suspend voting on the decree (or, if it had already been passed, to suspend its being put into effect) until the *γραφή* had been heard. We should be more inclined to accept the force of these analogies if it were certain that the effect of the *ἐπαγγελία δοκιμασίας* was that the orator named could not speak again until the *δοκιμασία* had been decided. Unfortunately our evidence does not enable us to say whether this was so or not.[6]

ἀπεψηφισμένους ὑπὸ τῶν δημοτῶν καὶ τὰς καταγνώσεις τὰς ἐκ τῆς βουλῆς. Evidence for other magistrates: paredroi, Ar. *Ath. Pol.* 56. 1; strategoi, Lys. 13 *Agorat.* 10, 15 *Alk.* ii. 2; taxiarchs, Dem. 40 *Boiot.* ii. 34; overseers of the market, Dein. 2 *Aristogeit.* 10; overseers of public works, Aischin. 3 *Ktes.* 14 f. (quoted on p. 201, n. 4); athlothetai, Ar. *Ath. Pol.* 60. 1.

1 For an early use of *ῥήτωρ* in a semi-juristic sense see *IG* i². 45. 21. For a similar use of *ῥήτωρ* in the *νόμος εἰσαγγελτικός* see p. 54.

2 Aischin. 1 *Timarch.* 186.

3 We depend almost entirely on Aischin. 1 *Timarch.* for our knowledge of the working of the procedure. The grammarians do not help, as they too were probably equally limited in their resources.

4 *ἐπαγγελία δοκιμασίας*: Aischin. 1 *Timarch.* 2, 32, 64, 81.

5 Dem. 49 *Timoth.* 66.

6 Koch, *RE* s.v. *δοκιμασία* 1273, believes that it was. Lipsius, *AR* 281, disagrees.

The charge was presented in writing,[1] probably to the thesmothetai as presiding magistrates.[2] One or more of the following four charges alleged against an orator were sufficient ground for a *δοκιμασία*: that he had not behaved dutifully towards his parents; that he had not served as he ought to have done in the army, or had thrown away his shield; that he had prostituted himself; that he had squandered an ancestral or inherited estate.[3] We need not suppose that Aischines has given an exhaustive list of every disqualifying factor mentioned in the law.[4]

A conviction in the court resulted in *ἀτιμία* for the defendant.[5] He was liable to *ἔνδειξις* if he thereafter addressed the ekklesia. It was therefore a milder remedy than action by *γραφή* for prostitution, for which the statutory penalty was death. Penalties in other cases would be by estimation, and might therefore be heavier or lighter than *ἀτιμία*. We may assume that there was the usual penalty on the prosecutor who withdrew or who failed to secure one-fifth of the votes.

(iv) *Epheboi*

An Athenian-born male became a fully qualified citizen only at the end of his seventeenth (conceivably eighteenth) year.[6] To enter into his rights he had to pass a *δοκιμασία*, and the technical

[1] Aischin. 1 *Timarch.* 119, 154 uses the word *ἀντιγράψασθαι* to describe the initiation of the procedure before the court.

[2] That the thesmothetai were the magistrates is deduced by analogy from the *δοκιμασία* of magistrates. When Dem. 22 *Androt.* 23 (cf. 29) uses the phrase *πρὸς τοὺς θεσμοθέτας . . . ἐπαγγέλλειν*, he is thinking primarily of the *γραφὴ ἑταιρήσεως* and uses the word *ἐπαγγέλλειν* by a rather inaccurate analogy from the *δοκιμασία* procedure, since the *ἐπαγγέλλειν* stage took place in the ekklesia.

[3] Aischin. 1 *Timarch.* 28 ff.

[4] Koch, *RE* s.v. *δοκιμασία* 1273, holds that it is exhaustive, since the orator introduces his enumeration with the question *τίνας δ' οὐκ ᾤετο δεῖν λέγειν;* which implies that he is going to give a complete list. But the immediately succeeding words are *τοὺς αἰσχρῶς βεβιωκότας* (on which Poll. 8. 45 *ἢ ἄλλως κακῶς βεβιωκότες* no doubt depends). This shows that he is really going to concentrate on those disqualifications relevant to his attack. As Lipsius, *AR* 280, points out, *λιποταξίου* and *ἀναυμαχίου* must have been equally disqualifying with throwing away one's shield. The statement of Dein. 1 *Dem.* 71, that an orator was required to own land in Attica and to have produced children, is at least suspect, and should not be so confidently accepted as it is in Lipsius, *AR* 273, n. 13; cf. vol. i, p. 19, n. 1.

[5] Aischin. 1 *Timarch.* 134, Dem. 19 *Embassy* 257, 284 show that the result of an adverse verdict against Timarchos in a case under this category was *ἀτιμία*.

[6] See p. 84, n. 2.

term for this was either simply δοκιμάζεσθαι or δοκιμάζεσθαι εἰς ἄνδρας or ἄνδρα εἶναι.[1]

In the first instance he had to get his name on to the citizen list (ληξιαρχικὸν γραμματεῖον). This list was kept by the demarch, and the demesmen voted on each candidate, taking an oath, first that he was of the required age and second that he was a free man and born 'according to the law'.[2] The boule had the task of reviewing the candidates' age, and if they deemed any not to have reached the required age his name was struck off for the time being and the demesmen were fined.[3] There is no evidence that there was in that case any appeal from the decision of the boule to a dikastery, either for the excluded candidate or for the fined demesmen, though we should rather have expected that there would have been. Nor is there evidence of the possibility of appeal for a candidate whom the demesmen rejected as not yet of age. If on the other hand they rejected a man as not ἐλεύθερος, he could have the matter referred to a dikastery. The deme had to elect from their number five accusers. If the candidate was rejected by the dikastery, he was sold as a slave by the state. If the verdict was in his favour, the demesmen had to enrol him.[4] Even if the word ἐλεύθερος is to be interpreted strictly here as 'free',[5] it is still highly probable that a man who was rejected not because he was of slave extraction but because either his father or his mother was not Athenian could have his case referred to a dikastery. Some

[1] e.g. Lys. 10 *Theomn.* i. 31, Isok. 7 *Areop.* 37, Dem. 27 *Aphob.* i. 5 respectively; for further instances see Lipsius, *AR* 283, n. 57, Kahrstedt, *Staatsg.* 71, n. 2.

[2] Ar. *Ath. Pol.* 42. 1 ὅταν δ' ἐγγράφωνται, διαψηφίζονται περὶ αὐτῶν ὀμόσαντες οἱ δημόται, πρῶτον μὲν εἰ δοκοῦσι γεγονέναι τὴν ἡλικίαν τὴν ἐκ τοῦ νόμου, κἂν μὴ δόξωσι, ἀπέρχονται πάλιν εἰς παῖδας, δεύτερον δ' εἰ ἐλεύθερός ἐστι καὶ γέγονε κατὰ τοὺς νόμους. The last three words probably mean ἐξ ἀμφοτέρων ἀστῶν (so Lipsius, *AR* 506, n. 26); Aristotle has just defined citizens as οἱ ἐξ ἀμφοτέρων γεγονότες ἀστῶν.

[3] Ar. *Ath. Pol.* 42. 2 μετὰ δὲ ταῦτα δοκιμάζει τοὺς ἐγγραφέντας ἡ βουλή, κἄν τις δόξῃ νεώτερος ὀκτωκαίδεκ' ἐτῶν εἶναι, ζημιοῖ τοὺς δημότας τοὺς ἐγγράψαντας. According to Aristoph. *Wasps* 578 one function of dikasts was παίδων δοκιμαζομένων αἰδοῖα θεᾶσθαι, but Ps.-Xen. *Ath. Pol.* 3. 4, describing the business of the democratic courts, uses the phrase ὀρφανοὺς δοκιμάσαι, which does not suggest that cases involving the age of those whose fathers were still living came before them.

[4] Ar. *Ath. Pol.* 42. 1 ἂν μὲν ἀποψηφίσωνται μὴ εἶναι ἐλεύθερον, ὁ μὲν ἐφίησιν εἰς τὸ δικαστήριον, οἱ δὲ δημόται κατηγόρους αἱροῦνται πέντε ἄνδρας ἐξ αὑτῶν, κἂν μὲν μὴ δόξῃ δικαίως ἐγγράφεσθαι, πωλεῖ τοῦτον ἡ πόλις· ἐὰν δὲ νικήσῃ, τοῖς δημόταις ἐπάναγκες ἐγγράφειν.

[5] Possibly this is one of the cases where ἐλεύθερος means 'a free man with full citizen rights'; see vol. i, p. 188.

scholars have argued that such a man, if convicted, would not have been sold into slavery; certainly the rule that he should be sold would have been a very severe sanction against frivolous reference to a court.

The procedure as a whole is closely analogous to that followed when for some reason or another there was, either generally or in a particular deme (for example, if the deme register was lost), a revision of the deme list (*διαψήφισις τῶν δημοτῶν*). Then too a rejected man could have his case referred to a dikastery.

(v) *New citizens*

The fourth type of *δοκιμασία* was of those on whom citizenship had been conferred by decree of the ekklesia, either individually or as members of a class. When the Athenians conferred citizenship on all Plataians in 427 B.C.,[1] any individual Plataian who wished to avail himself of this privilege had to establish in a *δοκιμασία* by a dikastery that he was indeed a Plataian and that he was a friend of Athens.[2] This however was a quite exceptional occasion; and the detailed account of the procedure for conferring citizenship given in Dem. 59 *Neair.* 88 ff. makes it clear that at that time (about 340 B.C.) there was no such *δοκιμασία* in a dikastery, but that the remedy against wrongful assumption of citizenship by this route was the bringing of a *γραφὴ παρανόμων* against the proposer of the decree conferring citizenship.[3] By the last quarter of the fourth century, however, inscriptions show that it was becoming normal procedure, when citizenship was conferred by decree, for the thesmothetai to refer the case for *δοκιμασία* to a dikastery.[4]

[1] Thuc. 3. 55. 3.

[2] Dem. 59 *Neair.* 105 *ὁρᾶτε, ὦ ἄνδρες Ἀθηναῖοι, ὡς καλῶς καὶ δικαίως ἔγραψεν ὁ ῥήτωρ ὑπὲρ τοῦ δήμου τοῦ Ἀθηναίων, καὶ ἠξίωσε τοὺς Πλαταιέας λαμβάνοντας τὴν δωρεὰν πρῶτον μὲν δοκιμασθῆναι ἐν τῷ δικαστηρίῳ κατ' ἄνδρα ἕκαστον, εἰ ἔστιν Πλαταιεὺς καὶ εἰ τῶν φίλων τῶν τῆς πόλεως.* It is to be noted that in the decree quoted in the previous paragraph of the speech there is no mention of this *δοκιμασία*.

[3] So Lipsius, *AR* 284 f., Bu. Sw. 945 f., arguing against the view of Fränkel, *Att. Geschw.* 35, that the procedure followed for the Plataians was normal throughout the period.

[4] *IG* ii². 398*b*. 3 ff. (*c.* 320/19 B.C.) *καὶ [τοὺς θεσμοθέτας δο]κιμάσαι τὴν πο[λιτείαν, ὅταν πρῶ]τον χρῶνται δι[καστηρίοις]*. Cf. *IG* ii². 717. 17, of about the same date.

§ 2. εὔθυνα

The word εὔθυνα had a very general sense of punishment imposed by decision of a court.[1] But it had also a specialized sense, the examination of a magistrate's conduct during his tenure of office. It is the latter sense of the word which concerns us here.[2]

The procedures which were devised at Athens to bring magistrates to account for their conduct in office are discussed in some detail in connection with the judicial functions of the various accounting officers (see pp. 28 ff.). What we have here to examine is the precise function of the dikasteries in this procedure. As with δοκιμασία, the institution in its entirety is the concern of the constitutional lawyer. But the part played by the courts is more clearly here than there concerned with the redress of a public wrong, the wrong of misconduct in office; this is brought out by the word εὔθυνα itself. Of course the institution also served to secure the accused magistrate reference to a dikastery from oppressive and arbitrary condemnation by other magistrates.

Magistrates were accountable in two sharply distinguishable ways. In the first place there was accountability for money. There was an assumption that any magistrate might in the course of his magistracy have public money in his hands, and for this he was accountable. If he had had no such dealings, he was required on laying down office to make a formal statement to that effect. This financial accountability itself had two phases. In each

[1] The best known example is in the Chalkis decree, *IG* i². 71. Cf. also passages cited in Lipsius, *AR* 288, n. 9, Bu. Sw. 1080, n. 2.

[2] On the institution in general see Lipsius, *AR* 286 ff., Boerner, *RE* s.v. εὔθυνα, Bu. Sw. 1076 ff., Kahrstedt, *Mag.* 165 ff. Two surviving speeches in the corpus Lysiacum were almost certainly delivered in εὔθυναι: 12 *Ag. Erat.* (on which see Wilamowitz, *A. und A.* ii. 218 ff.) and 20 *Polystr.* The latter Wilamowitz, *A. und A.* ii. 359 f., argued to be a speech in an εἰσαγγελία and to be rightly described in the heading δήμου καταλύσεως ἀπολογία. But Lipsius, *AR* 286, n. 1, rightly points out that, if that had been the case, the probable penalty would have been more severe than the heavy fine which is the utmost which the defence contemplates in paragraph 32. Gernet and Bizos, *Lys.* ii. 59 f., while accepting that this was not an εἰσαγγελία, are unwilling to admit that it was in a normal εὔθυνα, since Polystratos had, as the speech shows, already passed his εὔθυνα and it was certainly more than thirty (let alone three) days since he had laid down office; but they do not commit themselves to any other accepted procedure. Two other speeches of Lysias were probably delivered in εὔθυναι: 27 *Epikr.* and 21 ἀπολ. δωρ. (cf. Lipsius, *AR* 287, n. 2). These speeches are of limited value as evidence, since they date from a time when purely political considerations were likely to dictate even the forms of procedure. Dem. 19 *Embassy* and Aischin. 2 *Embassy* are also εὔθυνα speeches.

prytany a committee of the boule (named logistai) examined each magistrate's accounts, and it is probable that the boule could, if the committee was not satisfied, initiate proceedings in a dikastery against the offending magistrate. There is however no direct evidence for this, and we therefore have no idea what the sanctions were. In addition to these interim checks, the magistrates had to pass a financial check on laying down office, carried out by a quite distinct body of ten logistai. These logistai, after examining the accounts, brought them before a dikastery of 501 members. The logistai might themselves be satisfied, but they were bound to allow any citizen who wished to bring a plaint on the accounts, and a herald had to ask publicly whether any citizen wished to do so. Alternatively the logistai could prefer charges against the magistrate on the accounts. These might either be on the ground that the accounts did not square, or they might bring specific charges of embezzlement or receiving bribes, or more generally an improper use of public funds or property (the probable import of the *γραφὴ ἀδικίου*).[1]

The case for the prosecution was conducted either by a private citizen who had come forward in answer to the herald's proclamation or, if the logistai were bringing a charge, by synegoroi on their behalf. If the dikasts acquitted, that was the end of the matter.[2] If they condemned, there must have followed the estimation procedure to settle the amount of the embezzlement or of the bribe or, if the charge was *ἀδικίου*, the amount of the penalty. In every case, we must assume, the prosecutor and the defendant each proposed a figure and the court chose between them. If the charge was one of embezzlement or of bribery, the penalty was fixed by law at ten times the amount embezzled or received as a bribe, as thus determined by estimation. If the charge was *ἀδικίου*, the penalty was the simple amount as determined by estimation. According to Aristotle, if this last fine had not been paid by the ninth prytany it was doubled, but the tenfold penalty was not thus doubled.[3] We are not informed who received

[1] For all this see the evidence cited on pp. 28 f.

[2] Dem. 18 *Crown* 250 *τὰς εὐθύνας ἐπεσημαίνεσθε* (a purely metaphorical use of the verb).

[3] Ar. *Ath. Pol.* 54. 2 *κἂν μέν τινα κλέπτοντ' ἐξελέγξωσι, κλοπὴν οἱ δικασταὶ καταγιγνώσκουσι καὶ τὸ γνωσθὲν ἀποτίνεται δεκαπλοῦν· ἐὰν δέ τινα δῶρα λαβόντα ἐπιδείξωσιν καὶ καταγνῶσιν οἱ δικασταί, δώρων τιμῶσιν, ἀποτίνεται δὲ καὶ τοῦτο δεκαπλοῦν· ἂν δ' ἀδικεῖν καταγνῶσιν, ἀδικίου τιμῶσιν, ἀποτίνεται δὲ τοῦθ' ἁπλοῦν ἐὰν πρὸ*

the penalties imposed, but analogy would suggest that, if a private prosecutor acted, he would have received at least some part of the penalty.

It seems probable that where there were boards of officials each member of the board went through the procedure separately. There are certainly instances of generals submitting to *εὔθυνα* separately.[1] On the other hand there is at least one passage in Demosthenes which seems to imply that ambassadors engaged on the same embassy might have been required to go through the *εὔθυνα* as a body.[2]

The second, non-financial, *εὔθυνα* which all magistrates had to undergo was under the direction of special officials named *εὔθυνοι*, and the procedural pattern it followed is sketched in the description of the judicial function of those officers (pp. 30 f.). Here we need only stress the following points. If Aristotle's account can be trusted and if the reading *ἀν[ακρίνα]ς* in *Ath. Pol.* 48. 5 is correct,[3] the euthynos conducted a kind of *ἀνάκρισις* when a charge had been brought against a magistrate, but this differed in two respects from a normal magisterial *ἀνάκρισις*. The implication of Aristotle's words is that the case only went to a dikastery if the euthynos condemned. It is surprising to find an official left with the power of clearing a magistrate when a charge had been brought against him, and there is something slightly

τῆς θ' πρυτανείας ἐκτείσῃ τις, εἰ δὲ μή, διπλοῦται. τὸ ⟨δὲ⟩ δεκαπλοῦν οὐ διπλοῦται. This is the only unequivocal evidence for penalties under the procedure of *εὔθυνα*. The evidence from the orators which suggests that the penalty for embezzlement or bribery might be death is drawn from cases which might have been either ordinary *γραφαί* or *εἰσαγγελίαι*.

[1] Kahrstedt, *Mag.* 170 holds that individual members of boards were examined. He bases himself mainly on the evidence of *εὔθυναι* of individual generals. All the instances he gives at p. 165, n. 5, are not equally convincing; but sufficient are Paches in Plut. *Nik.* 6, Kimon in Ar. *Ath. Pol.* 27. 1, Timotheos in Dem. 49 *Timoth.* 25. Dem. 22 *Androt.* 38 f. implies a separate *εὔθυνα* for each member of the boule and Lys. 30 *Nikom.* 2 ff. for each of the *ἀναγραφεῖς τῶν νόμων*, but in either case the *εὔθυνα* referred to may be of the second (non-financial) kind.

[2] Lipsius, *AR* 292, is too dogmatic when he deduces from Dem. 19 *Embassy* 211 f. that the summons before the logistai and before the dikastery had to be issued to the board as a whole. The implication of the passage certainly is that, if one ambassador was to go through the procedure, all would have to. But it is very unsafe to deduce a general rule from the rule applying to ambassadors, who in any case were exceptional in that their office had no defined limit of time.

[3] Ar. *Ath. Pol.* 48. 5 *ὁ δὲ λαβὼν τοῦτο καὶ ἀν[ακρίνα]ς, ἐὰν μὲν καταγνῷ παραδίδωσιν τὰ μὲν ἴδια τοῖς δικασταῖς τοῖς κατὰ δήμ[ους τοῖς] τὴν φυλὴν ταύτην εἰσάγουσιν, τὰ δὲ δημόσια τοῖς θεσμοθέτα[ις ἀ]ναγράφει.*

disquieting in the fact that the *μέν* in the clause *ἐὰν μὲν καταγνῷ* has no answering *δέ*. The other difference is that the euthynos is not the introducing magistrate if the case goes further. It then goes either through the channel of the Forty if the charge is a private one, or to the thesmothetai if it is public. Another point to note is that the wording, if it reflects that of a law, is somewhat loose. There must have been very considerable latitude in determining what constituted a 'wrong' (*ἀδίκημα*) and whether it was a public or a private wrong.[1]

In certain respects the *εὔθυνα* of generals differed from that of other magistrates. These differences however are of more concern to the constitutional historian than to the jurist. The main point to bear in mind is that, although generals unlike most other magistrates could go on being re-elected year after year, they could not put off examination by either kind of *εὔθυνα* until they had ceased to be generals.[2] This meant that nothing comparable to the famous 'Rechtsfrage' raised by Julius Caesar's holding of the *imperium* could have occurred in Athens.

§ 3. *ἀπογραφή*

ἀπογραφή has a number of meanings, but here we are concerned with two only. It could mean an inventory of property belonging to one who was a public debtor, made and published with a view to securing execution upon it for satisfaction of the debt; and by transference it could denote the actual process by which such a debtor was arraigned before a court.[3]

[1] Ar. *Ath. Pol.* 48. 4 says that the prosecutor must write down *τὸ ἀδίκημ' ὅ τι ἂν ἐγκαλῇ*. The word *ἀδίκημα* is used in the oath of the euthynos of the deme Myrrhinous in *IG* ii². 1183. 9 ff.: *κ̣α̣ὶ ἐάν μ[ο]ι [δ]οκεῖ ἀδικεῖν κα[τευθ]υν[ῶ] α[ὐτ]οῦ [καὶ τιμήσ]ω οὗ [ἄ]ν μ[ο]ι [δ]ο̣κεῖ ἄξιον εἶναι τὸ ἀδί[κ]ημα.*

[2] It should be noted however that Nikomachos, a comparatively unimportant official as compared with a general, held the post of *ἀναγραφεὺς τῶν νόμων* and, if we are to believe Lys. 30 *Nikom.* 2 ff., managed to avoid a *εὔθυνα* for a period of four years. This was an exceptional office at an exceptional time, but it throws some suspicion on the effectiveness of the popular safeguard. Cf. Harrison, *JHS* 75 (1955) 29 f.

[3] *An. Bekk.* (*Λέξ. Ῥητ.*) 198. 31 ff. *ἀπογραφὴ καὶ ἀπογράψαι· ἀπογραφὴ γίνεται τῆς οὐσίας, ὅταν τις δημόσιόν τι εἶναι παρά τινι φάσκῃ, μὴ πριαμένῳ αὐτὸ παρὰ τῆς πόλεως· ἢ ὅταν δημεύηται τά τινος πρὸς τὰ ὀφλήματα, ἃ ὀφείλει εἰς τὸ δημόσιον. ἀπογραφὴ γὰρ τοῦτο γίνεται. σημαίνει δὲ καὶ ἄλλα ἡ λέξις*, Harpokr. s.v. *ἀπογραφή· ὅταν τις λέγῃ τινὰ ἔχειν τι τῶν τῆς πόλεως, ἀπογραφὴν ποιεῖται ὁ ἐναγόμενος, δηλῶν πόθεν ἔχει τὰ χρήματα καὶ πόσα ταῦτα εἴη. μήποτε δὲ καὶ εἶδός τι δίκης ἐστὶν ἡ ἀπογραφή· εἰ γὰρ ἀρνοῖτό τις μὴ ἔχειν, ἀπογραφῆς ἐκρίνετο ὡς οὐκ ὀρθῶς γεγενημένης*

This process was in many respects similar to that of a *γραφή*. Its aim was to ensure that property which had been confiscated by the state, or which might be so confiscated in order to secure payment of a debt to the state, was available for public sale by the poletai. The function of the court was to decide whether the property was or was not properly thus listed. The procedure was initiated by *ὁ ἀπογράψας* (the equivalent of *ὁ βουλόμενος* in a *γραφή*) and, if successful, he received three-quarters of the value of the property in issue. It was, looked at from one point of view, one means of ensuring the execution of court judgements, and it might have equally well been treated in the section dealing with execution (pp. 185 ff.).

It was characteristic of the Athenian democracy that no magistrate or public office was set up to secure this end. It was left to the initiative of the private citizen, who might be moved to act either from a personal grudge against the owner of the property or by the expectation of the three-quarters premium. The rights of the owner, as of third parties, were supposedly protected by the reference of the issue to a court; but in times of financial stress dikasts, whose pay depended on the solvency of the treasury, were not likely to be wholly unprejudiced in their judgements.

Lipsius posits two distinct procedures.[1] There might have been a decision by a court (or by the ekklesia) imposing confiscation on a man. In such a case the confiscation followed automatically. It was carried out by the demarch of the defendant's deme,[2] and

τῆς ἀπογραφῆς. Thalheim, *RE* s.v. *ἀπογραφή*, Lipsius, *AR* 299 ff., Finley, *Land* 280 f., nn. 23 and 28. The following surviving speeches are relevant. Speeches in defence in an *ἀπογραφή*: Lys. 9 *Soldier* (probably not by Lysias but, *pace* Lipsius, *AR* 299, n. 2, not late in the fourth century; Ktesikles in paragraph 6 is certainly not the archon of 334/3 B.C.), 18 *Prop. Nik. brother*, 19 *Prop. Arist.* Speeches by the prosecutor: Lys. 29 *Philokr.*, Dem. 53 *Nikostr.* (The *ἀπογραφή* recorded in Dem. 42 *Phain.* 16 was a plea handed in to the strategoi preparative to an *ἀντίδοσις*, and Lipsius, *AR* 301, n. 10, would even like to read there *γραφήν* for *ἀπογραφήν*.)

[1] Lipsius, *AR* 302 f.

[2] Plut. *Mor.* 834 a (the decree condemning Antiphon and Archeptolemos as traitors in 411 B.C.) *τούτοιν ἐτιμήθη τοῖς ἕνδεκα παραδοθῆναι καὶ τὰ χρήματα δημόσια εἶναι καὶ τῆς θεοῦ τὸ ἐπιδέκατον . . .· τὼ δὲ δημάρχω ἀποφῆναι τὴν οὐσίαν αὐτοῖν*, *An. Bekk.* (*Λέξ. Ῥητ.*) 199. 4 ff. *ἀπογράφειν· τοῦ μὴ βουλομένου ἐκτίνειν τὸ ὄφλημα ὃ ὀφείλει διπλοῦται τὸ ὄφλημα, καὶ ὁ δήμαρχος σὺν τοῖς βουλευταῖς τοῦτον εἰσπράττει, καὶ ἀπογράφεται αὐτοῦ τὴν οὐσίαν καὶ ἐνεχυριάζει. καὶ τοῦτο καλεῖται ἀπογράφειν*, 237. 8 ff. *δήμαρχος· . . . οὗτος δὲ καὶ ἀπεγράφετο τὰς οὐσίας ἑκάστου πρὸς τὰ δημόσια ὀφλήματα*, Harpokr. s.v. *δήμαρχος· . . . οὗτοι δὲ τὰς ἀπογραφὰς ἐποιοῦντο τῶν ἐν ἑκάστῳ δήμῳ χωρίων*.

the courts only intervened if a third party wished to establish the fact that he had a claim as owner or as hypothecator to the whole or a part of the property listed in the *ἀπογραφή*. This he did by the process known as *ἐνεπίσκηψις* (see pp. 215 f.). The resulting action was a *διαδικασία*, in which there might be several litigants, the state among them. Alternatively there might be cases where the *ἀπογραφή*, in the sense of a public announcement or denunciation, was the originating cause of the judgement imposing confiscation. This might occur in two different ways: a man might be denounced as holding property which did not belong to him, but to the state; or there might be grounds, not yet expressed in the form of a judgement against him, for a man's property to be wholly or partly confiscated. We know of a number of such grounds. The most important was owing money to the state (or to a public body such as a tribe, which for this purpose was treated as on a par with the state).[1] Another ground was embezzlement or other misappropriation of public goods.[2] In these cases the denunciations were read out at a *κυρία ἐκκλησία*.[3] This, so Lipsius suggests, was the last opportunity for anyone to contest in court the validity of the denunciation, whether it was the alleged offender whose goods were to be regarded as confiscated or a third party who laid some claim to those goods or any part of them. If no one came forward to assert such a claim (we have no idea within what time limits he had to move), the denunciation became equivalent to a judgement. It was the function of the Eleven either to introduce the case into a court or to pass on the property immediately to the poletai for public auction, as the case

[1] Lys. 9 *Soldier* 3, 21, Dem. 22 *Androt.* 54, 24 *Timokr.* 166, 40 *Boiot.* ii. 22, 53 *Nikostr.* hyp. and 1 ff., 59 *Neair.* 7, Hyper. 3 *Euxen.* 34; *An. Bekk.* (*Λέξ. Ῥητ.*) 198. 31 ff. (quoted on p. 211, n. 3). The following inscriptions are from the catalogues of the overseers of the docks: *IG* ii². 1631. 351–403 (the case of Sopolis, discussed in *IJ* ii. 146 ff.), 1631. 430–41 (the case of Stesileides), 1623. 218–23, 1628. 620–41, 1629. 1098–1132, 1631. 288–325 (all referring to the case of Demonikos, through the years 334/3 to 323/2 B.C.). Two poletai inscriptions are also important, particularly since they came to light after Lipsius wrote his account of *ἀπογραφή*: *Hesperia* 5 (1936) 393 ff., no. 10 (as emended in *Hesperia* 19 (1950) 244 ff., no. 16) and *SEG* xii. 100 (discussed by M. I. Finley, *Studi Arangio-Ruiz* (Naples, 1953) iii. 473 ff., with a note on the meaning of *ἀπογράφω* which he translates 'denounce', and by Kränzlein, *Eig. und Bes.* 125).

[2] Dem. 22 *Androt.* 61 *ἀπογράφειν ὅσ' ὑφείλετ' ἐξ ἀρχῆς*, Hyper. 3 *Euxen.* 34 *ὑπισχνουμένου τὴν Φιλίππου καὶ Ναυσικλέους* (sc. *οὐσίαν*) *ἀπογράψειν, καὶ λέγοντος ὡς ἐξ ἀναπογράφων μετάλλων πεπλουτήκασι.*

[3] Ar. *Ath. Pol.* 43. 4 *προγράφουσι δὲ καὶ τὰς ἐκκλησίας οὗτοι· μίαν μὲν κυρίαν, ἐν ᾗ δεῖ . . . τὰς ἀπογραφὰς τῶν δημευομένων ἀναγιγνώσκειν.*

might be; if the property was condemned in court, likewise they passed it on to the poletai.[1]

Gernet is probably right in suggesting that the distinction drawn by Lipsius, though a real one, had no juristic significance.[2] As we see in another connection (pp. 173 ff.), the moment a man was condemned to a fine payable to the state, he became a public debtor automatically. There needed to be no sentence of confiscation relating to the specific goods which were listed in the *ἀπογραφή* and were the object of the distraint.[3]

Neither Lipsius nor Gernet seems clear on the exact purpose of the *ἀπογραφή* and of the role played by *ἐνεπίσκηψις* in the whole procedure. Fundamentally *ἀπογραφή* served to mark out factually what objects belonging to an actual or potential defendant were liable to execution and therefore to sale by auction by the poletai. We know that such objects might be land or chattels; they might include claims, debts due to the defendant, or moneys deposited in a bank. When the list was published,[4] three things might happen:

1. If no one challenged the denunciation, the objects published were sold by auction by the poletai; the state collected one quarter of the sum realized, and the other three quarters went to the denouncer.[5] It is true that, if a denunciation followed this course, there might be distraint on goods with relation to which there had been no judgement; but juristically this was irrelevant. The official publication of the list, if it went unopposed, was equivalent to a sentence.

2. The person whose property was thus denounced might contest the validity of the denunciation. There must have been some

[1] Ar. *Ath. Pol.* 52. 1 *καθιστᾶσι δὲ καὶ τοὺς ἕνδεκα κλήρῳ τοὺς . . . τὰ ἀπογραφόμενα χωρία καὶ οἰκίας εἰσάξοντας εἰς τὸ δικαστήριον, καὶ τὰ δόξαντα δημόσια εἶναι παραδώσοντας τοῖς πωληταῖς.* [2] Gernet, *Dem.* iii. 82, n. 2.

[3] Thus in Dem. 53 *Nikostr.* Apollodoros denounces two slaves as being the property of Arethousios and liable to be distrained upon, since Arethousios is a public debtor.

[4] As stated in Ar. *Ath. Pol.* 43. 4 (quoted on p. 213, n. 3).

[5] Dem. 53 *Nikostr.* 2 *ἀπογράψας δὲ ἐὰν ἀποδείξω τὰ ἀνδράποδα Ἀρεθουσίου ὄντα, οὗπερ ἀπεγέγραπτο εἶναι, τὰ μὲν τρία μέρη, ἃ ἐκ τῶν νόμων τῷ ἰδιώτῃ τῷ ἀπογράψαντι γίγνεται, τῇ πόλει ἀφίημι, αὐτῷ δ' ἐμοὶ τετιμωρῆσθαι ἀρκεῖ μόνον*: Apollodoros states that, if successful, he will renounce the premium. So did Polyeuktos, *ὁ ἀπογράψας* in the Sopolis case, according to *IG* ii^2. 1631. 365 ff. The latter passage proves that the premium was not restricted to those who were prosecuting public debtors, as was suggested by Böckh, *Staatsh.* i. 467. Cf. Lipsius, *AR* 308, n. 27, D. M. Lewis, *Ancient Society and Institutions: Studies presented to Ehrenberg* (Oxford, 1966) 188.

limit of time within which such a defence had to be set up, but we do not know what it was. Lys. 19 *Prop. Arist.* was spoken for the defence in such a case. Aristophanes had been condemned to death and confiscation of property (this confiscation was not in issue here). The proceeds of the confiscation proved much less than expected, and his father-in-law was suspected of having diverted some of the property. The father-in-law's whole property therefore became the subject of ἀπογραφή. He made objection, but died before the trial came on; and the defence was taken over by his son, who was the brother-in-law of Aristophanes and for whom this speech was written. The speaker's arguments throughout are directed to proving that his father had been unjustly made the subject of an ἀπογραφή. At one stage he describes the proceedings as a γραφή, and he uses of his father the phrase ὥσπερ ἀδικοῦντος αἱ κατηγορίαι γεγένηνται.[1] Lys. 29 *Philokr.* was written for the prosecution in a similar case. Ergokles had been convicted in an εἰσαγγελία, probably for corruption, embezzlement of public money, and treason,[2] and condemned to death with confiscation of his property. Philokrates was suspected of having laid his hands on a great deal of this property, and *his* property was therefore subjected to an ἀπογραφή.[3] We can only guess at Philokrates' line of defence. According to the speaker, he had two only, to prove that someone else had Ergokles' property or to prove that Ergokles had been wrongly convicted.[4]

3. Some other person or group of persons might claim to have some right in the property stated in the ἀπογραφή to be public. The technical term for asserting such a claim was ἐνεπισκήψασθαι, and we may guess that action had to be taken in the same way and within the same time limit as action by the defendant against whom the ἀπογραφή was directed.[5]

It is probably a mistake however to assimilate (2) and (3) further and speak of both of them as ἐνεπίσκηψις, a term which,

[1] Lys. 19 *Prop. Arist.* 55 f.

[2] Lys. 28 *Ergokl.* 11.

[3] Both Aristophanes' father-in-law and Philokrates might have been attacked by way of εἰσαγγελία for malversation (κλοπὴ δημοσίων χρημάτων), for which the penalty might be death as well as confiscation of property. Procedure by way of ἀπογραφή was in that respect a milder alternative.

[4] Lys. 29 *Philokr.* 5.

[5] Dem. 49 *Timoth.* 45 ff., 53 *Nikostr.* 28, Lys. 19 *Prop. Arist.* 32, *SEG* xii. 100. 16 ff., Poll. 8. 61, *An. Bekk.* (Λέξ. Ῥητ.) 250. 14 ff.; vol. i, p. 54.

in contemporary documents at least, is restricted to the action of a third party. Certainly, even if the term ἐνεπίσκηψις was common to both, these two reactions against the ἀπογραφή were totally different in character. In (2) the objector was disputing the whole basis of the ἀπογραφή; in (3) he was asserting that he had some claim on a part of the property listed which rendered that part exempt from confiscation.

In the case of Apollodoros against Timotheos (the subject of Dem. 49 *Timoth.*) Apollodoros is claiming money allegedly lent to Timotheos by his father, the banker Pasion. Timotheos averred that some 1,300 drachmai of the alleged debt had been lent to Antimachos in his own right and not, as alleged by Apollodoros, to Antimachos as treasurer of Timotheos. Had this been so, Apollodoros argues, when Antimachos was condemned and his property confiscated, Pasion would have put in a claim by ἐνεπίσκηψις for repayment of the debt.[1] This shows incidentally that the state acknowledged the liability of a property which had been confiscated for debts resting on that property.[2] But the main point to be made here is that in this hypothetical case the issue whether Antimachos' property was rightly or wrongly subjected to ἀπογραφή was irrelevant; the only issue was whether such-and-such a part of the listed property was or was not rightly regarded as Antimachos' property.

The poletai records for 367/6 B.C. give a glimpse into an actual case.[3] A house was denounced by Theomnestos as belonging to Theosebes, who had been convicted in absence of sacrilege (ἱεροσυλία). Theomnestos seems to have recognized in the ἀπογραφή that 150 drachmai were owed to Smikythos on the house.[4] There were three other claims on the property, two deriving from πρᾶσις ἐπὶ λύσει and one from expenditure on funeral expenses for the previous owner of the house. All these three are recorded as having been recognized in the words ἔδοξεν ἐνοφείλεσθαι; presumably this meant that they had been the subject of a trial following upon ἐνεπισκήψεις, and that this trial took the form of a διαδικασία at which the various claimants stated their cases and ὁ ἀπογράψας could oppose the claims on behalf of the public

[1] Dem. 49 *Timoth.* 45 ff.

[2] Lys. 19 *Prop. Arist.* 32 shows that dowry money was exempt from confiscation. Pringsheim, *GLS* 164, n. 2, speaks of 'clear' debts without specifying what he means by the epithet.

[3] *SEG* xii. 100; vol. i, pp. 270 f.

[4] So Kränzlein, *Eig. und Bes.* 84 f.

treasury. Unfortunately we cannot tell from the inscription how and when these claims were going to be satisfied, nor whether, in reckoning the premium due to Theomnestos as *ὁ ἀπογράψας*, they were or were not deducted from the purchase price received from Lysanias, the purchaser.[1]

In Lys. 17 *δημ. ἀδ.* the speaker's grandfather had lent two talents to Eraton I. On the latter's death his three sons, Erasiphon, Eraton II, and Erasistratos, failed to keep up interest payments. The speaker's father obtained judgement against Erasistratos for the whole debt (he was the only one of the three brothers in Athens).[2] He did not succeed in getting execution of the judgement immediately, and in the meantime the property of Eraton was confiscated.[3] Several people entered *ἀπογραφαί* against it and, since the speaker's father had died in the meantime, he himself put in a claim (by *ἐνεπίσκηψις*, though the word does not occur here), modestly limiting it to one-third of the whole estate. He describes the ensuing case as a *διαδικασία* and the resultant decision as a *διαδίκασμα*.[4] It seems clear from this evidence that the term *διαδικασία* was certainly used where a third party asserted a claim; it is not so certain that it was used of cases like those dealt with in Lys. 19 *Prop. Arist.* and 29 *Philokr.*, which were straight contests between the treasury (represented by *ὁ ἀπογράψας*) and the putative public debtor.

There were sanctions against irresponsible appeal to the courts. The denouncer who failed to secure one-fifth of the votes was fined 1,000 drachmai.[5] On the other hand the objector who proceeded by way of *ἐνεπίσκηψις* had to deposit before the issue was tried one-fifth of the value of his claim, which became forfeit to the state if he lost (see p. 180).

[1] Perhaps the *ἐν-* in *ἐνεπίσκηψις* indicates that this procedure was basically different from that where the whole basis of the confiscation was challenged. Cf. the *ἐν-* in *ἐνοφείλεσθαι*.

[2] Strictly, under Athenian law, Erasistratos was only liable for one-third of his father's private debts. The speaker's language may be intentionally misleading when he says in paragraph 3 *λαχὼν ὁ πατὴρ παντὸς τοῦ συμβολαίου Ἐρασιστράτῳ*, but it is also possible that the estate of Eraton I had on his death remained undivided between his three sons. Gernet and Bizos, *Lys.* ii. 15 f.

[3] In all probability this was the estate of Eraton I; so Gernet and Bizos, *Lys.* ii. 18.

[4] Lys. 17 *δημ. ἀδ.* 1, 10. *ἀμφισβητεῖν* is used in Lys. 17 *δημ. ἀδ.* 9, Dem. 53 *Nikostr.* 28 (of a wife trying to recover her dowry out of property of her son being confiscated), *SEG* xii. 100. 26.

[5] Dem. 53 *Nikostr.* 1.

§ 4. *φάσις*

φάσις was a form of procedure[1] closely allied to *ἀπογραφή*. It may similarly be described as the denunciation of someone as having broken a law. As with *ἀπογραφή*, the word *φάσις* is used both of the document stating the charge[2] and of the resulting procedure.

Only certain breaches of the law laid a man open to *φάσις*. One of the principal breaches was of the law protecting orphans.[3] Others for which we have direct evidence were: misappropriating state property,[4] a special case of this being mining outside the area conceded by contract with the poletai;[5] other breaches of the mining law;[6] damage to public land or buildings;[7] digging

[1] Harpokr. (and Suda) s.v. *φάσις· λέγεται μὲν καὶ ἐπὶ δημοσίου ἐγκλήματος, ὅταν τις ἀποφαίνῃ τι τῶν δημοσίων ἔχοντά τινα μὴ πριάμενον, λέγεται δὲ καὶ ἐπὶ τῶν ὀρφανικῶν οἴκων. ὅτε γὰρ μὴ ἐκμισθώσαιεν οἱ ἐπίτροποι τὸν οἶκον τῶν ἐπιτροπευομένων, ἔφαινεν αὐτὸν ὁ βουλόμενος πρὸς τὸν ἄρχοντα, ἵνα μισθωθῇ· ἔφαινε δὲ καὶ εἰ ἐλάττονος ἢ κατὰ τὴν ἀξίαν μεμίσθωτο* (on the reading *ἀξίαν* see vol. i, p. 116, n. 4), Poll. 8. 47 *φάσις δὲ ἦν τὸ φαίνειν τοὺς περὶ τὰ μέταλλα ἀδικοῦντας, ἢ περὶ τὸ ἐμπόριον κακουργοῦντας ἢ περὶ τὰ τέλη, ἢ τῶν δημοσίων τι νενοσφισμένους, ἢ συκοφαντοῦντας, ἢ περὶ τοὺς ὀρφανοὺς ἐξαμαρτάνοντας*, *An. Bekk.* (*Λέξ. Ῥητ.*) 313. 20 ff. *φαίνειν· εἶδος ἐγκλήματος δημοσίου καὶ ἰδιωτικοῦ. ὅταν γάρ τις ἀποφήνῃ ἔχοντά τινα τῶν δημοσίων τι, μὴ πριάμενον, ἢ ἔμπορον ἀλλαχόθι ἐργαζόμενον, καὶ οὐχὶ εἰς τὸ Ἀθηναίων ἐμπόριον, δημόσιόν ἐστιν ἀδίκημα· ὅταν δὲ μὴ ἐκμισθώσωσι τὸν τῶν ὀρφανῶν οἶκον οἱ ἐπίτροποι, ἰδιωτικόν ἐστι τὸ ἀδίκημα*, 315. 16 ff. *φάσις· μήνυσις πρὸς τοὺς ἄρχοντας κατὰ τῶν ὑπορυττόντων τὸ μέταλλον, ἢ κατὰ τῶν ἀδικούντων χωρίον ἢ οἰκίαν ἤ τι τῶν δημοσίων, ἢ κατὰ τῶν ἐπιτρόπων τῶν μὴ μεμισθωκότων τὰς οἰκίας τῶν ὀρφανῶν*, *Lex. Cant.* s.v. *προβολή· . . . φάσις δὲ λανθάνοντος μήνυσις· Καικίλιος δὲ φάσιν φησὶν εἶναι ἣν κατὰ τῶν τὰ δημόσια μέταλλα ὑπορυττόντων ἀποφέρουσι καὶ καθόλου κατὰ τῶν τὰ κοινὰ κλεπτόντων· καλεῖσθαι δὲ οὕτω καὶ τὰς ἐμπορικὰς μηνύσεις*, Phot. (and Suda) s.v. *φάσις ἐστὶν ἣν ποιεῖταί τις πρὸς τὸν δοκοῦντα ὑπορύττειν δημόσιον μέταλλον ἢ χωρίον ἢ οἰκίαν ἢ ἄλλο τι τῶν δημοσίων· ἔτι δὲ καὶ οἱ τοὺς ἐπιτρόπους τῶν ὀρφανῶν αἰτιώμενοι παρὰ τοῖς ἄρχουσιν ὡς οὐ δεόντως μεμισθωκότας τὸν ὀρφανὸν οἶκον προφαίνειν λέγονται.* Lipsius, *AR* 309 ff., Paoli, *St. Dir.* 239, Bo. Sm. ii. 41, 71, Berneker, *RE* s.v. *φάσις*, Gernet, *Dem.* iv. 37 f.; Kahrstedt, *Klio* 32 (1939) 421, in a review of Bo. Sm., makes the odd assertion that *φάσις* was not a form of procedure at all, but merely the action of a prosecutor in stating the *τίμημα* of his charge.

[2] Dem. 58 *Theokr.* 7 f.

[3] See vol. i, pp. 115 ff.

[4] *IG* ii^2. 30*a*. 6 (386/5 B.C.), Isok. 18 *Kallim.* 6; Harpokr. s.v. *φάσις*, Poll. 8. 47, *An. Bekk.* (*Λέξ. Ῥητ.*) 313. 20 ff., *Lex. Cant.* s.v. *προβολή* (all four quoted in n. 1 above).

[5] Hyper. 3 *Euxen.* 35 *φήναντος γὰρ Λυσάνδρου τὸ Ἐπικράτους μέταλλον τοῦ Παλληνέως ⟨ὡς⟩ ἐντὸς* (*ἐκτὸς* Cobet) *τῶν μέτρων τετμημένον*, Dem. 37 *Pant.* 35 f.; Poll. 8. 47, *An. Bekk.* (*Λέξ. Ῥητ.*) 315. 16 ff., *Lex. Cant.* s.v. *προβολή*, Phot. s.v. *φάσις* (all four quoted in n. 1 above); vol. i, p. 203, n. 1, and works there cited.

[6] Poll. 8. 47 (quoted in n. 1 above).

[7] *An. Bekk.* (*Λέξ. Ῥητ.*) 315. 16 ff., Phot. s.v. *φάσις* (both quoted in n. 1 above).

up olive trees beyond the allowed number;[1] lending by an Athenian citizen or metic of money on a ship which was not destined to bring back corn to Athens,[2] or, being a resident in Athens, shipping corn to any destination other than Athens,[3] or more general breaches of import and export regulations;[4] evasion of a ten per cent customs duty;[5] certain, not further identifiable, acts of impiety.[6] Pollux states that *φάσις* was available against sycophants;[7] but Isokrates, in enumerating ways of proceeding against sycophants, makes no mention of *φάσις*, and it would have helped his argument to do so.[8] We may therefore disregard Pollux on this point.[9]

The denouncer had to lay a written denunciation with the appropriate magistrates. These were, in cases concerning public property, the syndikoi at the beginning of the fourth century (see pp. 34 f.), later the Eleven;[10] in cases concerning shipments of corn, the overseers of the market (see p. 27); in mining cases, commercial and tax cases (and, if these are to be included, cases

[1] Dem. 43 *Makart.* 71: not explicitly action by *φάσις*, but the successful prosecutor gets 100 drachmai for each tree, as against 100 payable to the public treasury.

[2] Dem. 35 *Lakrit.* 51 (quoted on p. 121, n. 2).

[3] Dem. 58 *Theokr.* 5 ff.; cf. Dem. 34 *Ag. Phorm.* 37, 35 *Lakrit.* 50, Lykourg. *Leokr.* 27 (all three quoted on p. 221, n. 3); *An. Bekk.* (*Λέξ. Ῥητ.*) 313. 20 ff. (quoted on p. 218, n. 1).

[4] *IG* i². 45 (Tod, *GHI* no. 44) 1 (referring possibly, though not certainly, to regulations on trade with the new colony at Brea, *c.* 445 B.C.), *IG* ii². 1128 (Tod, *GHI* no. 162) 18 (referring to the Athenian monopoly of ruddle from Keos, mid fourth century), Aristoph. *Ach.* 819 ff., 908 ff.

[5] Aristoph. *Knights* 300 ff. *καὶ φανῶ σε τοῖς πρυτάνεσιν ἀδεκατεύτους τῶν θεῶν ἱερὰς ἔχοντα κοιλίας*, Poll. 8. 47 (quoted on p. 218, n. 1). The immediate losers by such an evasion were those who had bought the right to collect the tax, but for this purpose their rights were treated as the state's rights.

[6] Dem. 22 *Androt.* 27 *τῆς ἀσεβείας κατὰ ταὔτ' ἔστ' ἀπάγειν, γράφεσθαι, δικάζεσθαι πρὸς Εὐμολπίδας, φαίνειν* (Weil: *φράζειν* codd.) *πρὸς τὸν βασιλέα*, schol. ad loc. *ἵνα ὁ βασιλεὺς τὴν φάσιν λαβὼν (φάσις δὲ κατηγορίας ὄνομα) τοῖς θεσμοθέταις φανερὰν καταστήσῃ καὶ παρὰ τῶν θεσμοθετῶν γνωρισθῇ τοῖς δικάζουσι τὰ ἐγκλήματα* (which confirms Weil's conjecture).

[7] Poll. 8. 47 (quoted on p. 218, n. 1).

[8] Isok. 15 *Antid.* 314.

[9] There is a compromise view, taken by Lofberg, *Sycophancy* 92, and Lipsius, *AR* 314, that *φάσις* was available not against sycophants generally, but only against those who made a business of attacking merchants and traders. It is true that merchants and traders were protected against sycophants, according to Dem. 58 *Theokr.* 11; but that passage mentions only *ἀπαγωγή* and *ἔνδειξις* as available for that purpose. Bo. Sm. ii. 71.

[10] There is no direct evidence for the Eleven's function here, but it is probable by analogy with *ἀπογραφή* (Ar. *Ath. Pol.* 52. 1, quoted on p. 214, n. 1).

against sycophants), the thesmothetai;[1] in cases of impiety, the basileus;[2] in cases concerning orphans, the archon.[3]

The man being denounced had to be summoned to be present when the denunciation was laid before the magistrate; the magistrate at that stage could be represented by a secretary.[4] The denunciation carried the names of the prosecutor and defendant and of the witnesses to the summons, and the prosecutor's assessment of the proper penalty.[5] As opposed to procedure by *ἀπαγωγή* or *ἔνδειξις*, the defendant was not compelled to find sureties or, failing that, go to prison. There is some doubt as to the payment of *πρυτανεῖα* in a *φάσις*. On the whole the better view is that they were paid by the denouncer (and probably also by the denounced) in every type of case (cf. p. 94). According to Pollux the court was 201 strong for cases involving 1,000 drachmai or less, 401 if the amount was larger;[6] the amount must have been that stated in the prosecutor's *τίμημα*.

If the denouncer won his case, he received a premium of one half of the sum accepted by the jury in its vote on the *τίμημα*.[7] The statement of Pollux that the penalty (he presumably means in its entirety) went to the wronged individual if another was prosecuting on his behalf may perhaps be a rule applying only to actions on behalf of orphans, which Pollux has wrongly generalized.[8] If the prosecutor failed to secure one-fifth of the votes, or failed to bring the case to court after he had filed his denunciation, he was liable to a fine of 1,000 drachmai (see

[1] See p. 16. Some of these cases are assigned conjecturally to the thesmothetai.

[2] See the passages quoted on p. 219, n. 6 above.

[3] Ar. *Ath. Pol.* 56. 6.

[4] Dem. 58 *Theokr.* 8 *ταύτην τὴν φάσιν, ὦ ἄνδρες δικασταί, ἔδωκεν μὲν οὑτοσὶ προσκαλεσάμενος τὸν Μίκωνα, ἔλαβεν δὲ ὁ γραμματεὺς ὁ τῶν τοῦ ἐμπορίου ἐπιμελητῶν, Εὐθύφημος.*

[5] Poll. 8. 47 *ἐδίδοσαν δὲ ἐν γραμματείῳ γράψαντες τὴν φάσιν, τά θ' ἑαυτῶν καὶ τὸ τοῦ κρινομένου ὄνομα προσγράψαντες καὶ τίμημα ἐπιγραψάμενοι,* 49 *ἔδει δὲ καὶ κλητῆρας προσεπιγράφεσθαι τὸν φαίνοντα, εἰ εἰσὶ μάρτυρες.* In face of this evidence Paoli, *St. Dir.* 239, should not in this respect differentiate *φάσις* from *γραφή*.

[6] Poll. 8. 48.

[7] *IG* ii². 412. 7 ff. *τῶν δὲ φανθέντ[ων τὸ μὲν ἥμυσυ ἔστω] το[ῦ φ]ήναντος, τὸ δὲ ἥμυσ[υ τοῦ δημοσίου],* Dem. 58 *Theokr.* 13 *τίς γὰρ ἄν, παρεὶς τὸ δίκαιως πράττοντα λαβεῖν τὸ μέρος τῶν χρημάτων κατὰ τὸν νόμον, διαλυσάμενος ἐβουλήθη μικρὰ κερδᾶναι . . ., ἐξόν, ὅπερ ἀρτίως εἶπον, τὰ ἡμίσεα τῶν φανθέντων λαβεῖν;*

[8] Poll. 8. 48 (quoted on p. 184, n. 1). Or perhaps he means that in such a case the half that normally went to the state went to the wronged individual; cf. the rule in Plato, *Laws* 928 c *γιγνέσθω δὲ τὸ μὲν ἥμισυ τοῦ παιδός, τὸ δ' ἥμισυ τοῦ καταδικασαμένου τὴν δίκην.*

p. 83). We may safely reject the statement of Pollux that in these circumstances the prosecutor incurred *ἐπωβελία*.[1]

It is implicit in the above rules that in most cases *φάσις* was an *ἀγὼν τιμητός*; perhaps in all cases, since in the supposed exception, the case where the limit of olive trees stubbed up had been exceeded, although the penalty per tree was fixed,[2] there might surely have been a difference of opinion between the parties on the number of trees which had been uprooted, which could only be settled by *τίμησις* and *ἀντιτίμησις*. In certain cases, where for example corn had been carried elsewhere than to Athens, a convicted defendant might suffer an extreme penalty,[3] possibly the death penalty with confiscation of property. Here we may guess that the prosecutor had to rely for his reward on collecting one half of the confiscated property.

§ 5. *ἀπαγωγή, ἔνδειξις, ἐφήγησις*

(i) *Introduction*

These three procedures[4] were closely related, and the two first are often found mentioned together.[5] It was common to them that there was no *πρόσκλησις* of the defendant; either he was haled before the magistrate or reported directly to him, or the magistrate was brought to confront the defendant. The defendant was incarcerated unless he could furnish three sureties from his own census class.[6] A necessary condition of the act or wrong for which the defendant was to be charged was that it was *in*

[1] Poll. 8. 48 (quoted on p. 184, n. 1).

[2] See p. 219, n. 1.

[3] Dem. 34 *Ag. Phorm.* 37 *τῶν δὲ νόμων τὰ ἔσχατα ἐπιτίμια προτεθηκότων, εἴ τις οἰκῶν Ἀθήνησιν ἄλλοσέ ποι σιτηγήσειεν ἢ εἰς τὸ Ἀττικὸν ἐμπόριον*, 35 *Lakrit.* 50 *ἴστε γάρ, ὦ ἄνδρες δικασταί, τὸν νόμον ὡς χαλεπός ἐστιν, ἐάν τις Ἀθηναίων ἄλλοσέ ποι σιτηγήσῃ ἢ Ἀθήναζε, ἢ χρήματα δανείσῃ εἰς ἄλλο τι ἐμπόριον ἢ τὸ Ἀθηναίων, οἷαι ζημίαι περὶ τούτων εἰσίν, ὡς μεγάλαι καὶ δειναί*, Lykourg. *Leokr.* 27 *οἱ ὑμέτεροι νόμοι τὰς ἐσχάτας τιμωρίας ὁρίζουσιν, ἐάν τις Ἀθηναίων ἄλλοσέ ποι σιτηγήσῃ ἢ ὡς ὑμᾶς.*

[4] H. Meuss, *De ἀπαγωγῆς actione apud Athenienses* (Breslau, 1884), Glotz, *Solidarité* 425 ff., Lipsius, *AR* 317 ff., Calhoun, *Criminal Law* 59 ff., Paoli, *St. Dir.* 237 f., Bo. Sm. ii. 212 ff., MacDowell, *Homicide* 130 ff. For the procedures in relation to the law of property see vol. i, pp. 206 f.

[5] Plato, *Apol.* 32 b, Andok. 1 *Myst.* 91, Dem. 20 *Lept.* 156, 24 *Timokr.* 146, 58 *Theokr.* 11, Hyper. 5 *Athenog.* 29, Ar. *Ath. Pol.* 29. 4.

[6] Dem. 24 *Timokr.* 146 *ἐν τοῖς νόμοις "τὸν δ' ἐνδειχθέντα ἢ ἀπαχθέντα δησάντων οἱ ἕνδεκα ἐν τῷ ξύλῳ"*, 144 *τοῦ νόμου . . .*, *ἐν ᾧ ἔνι "οὐδὲ δήσω Ἀθηναίων οὐδένα, ὃς ἂν ἐγγυητὰς τρεῖς καθιστῇ τὸ αὐτὸ τέλος τελοῦντας, πλὴν ἐάν τις ἐπὶ προδοσίᾳ τῆς πόλεως ἢ ἐπὶ καταλύσει τοῦ δήμου συνιὼν ἁλῷ, ἢ τέλος πριάμενος ἢ ἐγγυησάμενος ἢ ἐκλέγων μὴ καταβάλῃ"*.

flagrante delicto (ἐπ' αὐτοφώρῳ). How this condition was interpreted is discussed below.[1]

We have several speeches delivered in cases falling under one or other of these procedures, but their evidence on the details of the procedures is not as clear as we could wish, and the grammarians' articles do not help much in clearing up the points of difficulty. Ant. 5 *Her.* was delivered for the defence in a murder charge brought, wrongfully so the speaker urges, by way of ἀπαγωγή. Lys. 13 *Agorat.* was written for the prosecution in a similar case (it is wrongly described in the title as ἐνδείξεως). Andok. 1 *Myst.* is a speech for the defence in an ἔνδειξις. Lys. 6 *Andok.* (without doubt wrongly attributed to Lysias) is part of one of the speeches on the other side in the same case. Dem. 25 and 26 *Aristogeit.* i and ii purport to be speeches for the prosecution in an ἔνδειξις, but must be used with extreme caution, as they are not genuine.[2] Lys. 22 *Corn-dealers* is very likely a speech for the prosecution in an ἀπαγωγή.[3] Perhaps most important of all is Dem. 58 *Theokr.*, a speech in an ἔνδειξις against Theokrines.[4]

(ii) ἀπαγωγή

Taken strictly, ἀπαγωγή was the haling before the competent magistrate of one taken *in flagrante delicto* committing certain acts. The magistrate was usually one of the Eleven, but where a man exiled for murder or treason was apprehended in Attica it was the thesmothetai. If a man so caught confessed, the magistrate administered at once the appropriate penalty (see pp. 17 f.). If he

[1] Lipsius, *AR* 318, 812 (cf. also 320), defines the condition thus: either the defendant had to be caught in the act, or the action complained of had to be so notorious that the issue was not whether it had been perpetrated but whether it was punishable. That the procedure was not restricted to those literally caught in the act is shown for example by Andok. 1 *Myst.* 91 (part of the bouleutic oath) καὶ οὐ δέξομαι ἔνδειξιν οὐδὲ ἀπαγωγὴν ἕνεκα τῶν πρότερον γεγενημένων, πλὴν τῶν φυγόντων.

[2] Lipsius, *Leipziger Studien* 6 (1883) 317 ff.

[3] Gernet and Bizos, *Lys.* ii. 82 f.

[4] Of lost speeches, there was one by Antiphon for the defence in an ἔνδειξις laid by Kallias (Harpokr. s.v. διάθεσις). Speeches for the prosecution in ἐνδείξεις were Lys. *Against Kallias* (*An. Bekk.* (Ἀντιαττ.) 95. 25 f.) and *Against Aristagoras* (Harpokr. s.v. ἀμωσγέπως), Lykourg. *Against Aristogeiton* (Harpokr. s.vv. ἀγραφίου, ἡλικία, μητρῷον, ὄρυγμα, etc.), Dein. *Against Deinias* (Harpokr. s.v. παραφρυκτωρεῖν) and *Against Polyeuktos* (Harpokr. s.v. παλιναίρετος). Then there was a speech of Pytheas (Harpokr. s.v. ἀγραφίου) and one of Aristogeiton *Against Demosthenes and Lykourgos* (Phot. *Bibl.* 491 a 36; genuine according to Lipsius, *Leipziger Studien* 6 (1883) 331), which were for the defence in an ἔνδειξις. A speech for the prosecution in an ἀπαγωγή was falsely attributed to Deinarchos (D.H. *Dein.* 11).

did not, his accuser had to present to the magistrate a written indictment, also called *ἀπαγωγή*, on the basis of which the magistrate or magistrates introduced the issue for trial by a dikastery.[1] It is generally assumed that there was no stage in *ἀπαγωγή* corresponding to the *ἀνάκρισις* in other types of case, and this procedure is therefore thought to have been more summary and expeditious. But it must be noted that in the Agoratos case the Eleven compelled one of the prosecutors to add the words *ἐπ' αὐτοφώρῳ* to the written indictment; they acted in fact very like magistrates at the *ἀνάκρισις* in other types of case.[2]

The acts which rendered a man liable to *ἀπαγωγή* fall into three main categories.[3] First were acts done by those classed under the general head *κακοῦργοι*. These were listed as thieves (*κλέπται*), clothes-robbers (*λωποδύται*), kidnappers (*ἀνδραποδισταί*), burglars (*τοιχωρύχοι*), and cutpurses (*βαλλαντιοτόμοι*).[4] It is rather

[1] Lys. 13 *Agorat.* 85 "*ἐπ' αὐτοφώρῳ*" *τῇ ἀπαγωγῇ ἐπιγέγραπται*, *An. Bekk.* (*Συν. Λέξ. Χρησ.*) 414. 19 ff. (and Suda s.v. *ἀπαγωγή*) *ἀπαγωγή· μήνυσίς ἐστιν ἔγγραφος, διδομένη τῷ ἄρχοντι περὶ τοῦ δεῖν ἀπαχθῆναι τὸν δεῖνα. ἀπάγειν καὶ ἀπάγεσθαι τὸν κακοῦργον. ἀπήγοντο δὲ εἰς τὸ δεσμωτήριον πρὸς τοὺς ἕνδεκα.*

[2] Lys. 13 *Agorat.* 86 (quoted on p. 224, n. 2).

[3] Lipsius, *AR* 320 ff., speaks of two categories, but treats of our first two as subdivisions of a single category. His approach is confusing, particularly on the question of homicide.

[4] Ar. *Ath. Pol.* 52. 1 *καθιστᾶσι δὲ καὶ τοὺς ἕνδεκα κλήρῳ τοὺς ἐπιμελησομένους τῶν ἐν τῷ δεσμωτηρίῳ, καὶ τοὺς ἀπαγομένους ⟨κακούργους τούς τε⟩ κλέπτας καὶ τοὺς ἀνδραποδιστὰς καὶ τοὺς λωποδύτας, ἂν μὲν [ὁμολογῶ]σι, θανάτῳ ζημιώσοντας, ἂν δ' ἀμφισβητῶσιν, εἰσάξοντας εἰς τὸ δικαστήριον, κἂν μὲν ἀποφύγωσιν, ἀφήσοντας, εἰ δὲ μή, τότε θανατώσοντας*, Ant. 5 *Her.* 9 *καὶ ὡς μὲν οὐ κακοῦργός εἰμι οὐδ' ἔνοχος τῷ τῶν κακούργων νόμῳ, αὐτοὶ οὗτοι τούτου γε μάρτυρες γεγένηνται. περὶ γὰρ τῶν κλεπτῶν καὶ λωποδυτῶν ὁ νόμος κεῖται, ὧν οὐδὲν ἐμοὶ προσὸν ἀπέδειξαν. οὕτως εἴς γε ταύτην τὴν ἀπαγωγὴν νομιμωτάτην καὶ δικαιοτάτην πεποιήκασιν ὑμῖν τὴν ἀποψήφισίν μου*, Andok. 4 *Alk.* 18 *οὐδὲ τοὺς κακούργους ἀσφαλὲς εἰς τὸ δεσμωτήριον ὂν ἀπάγειν*, Lys. 10 *Theomn.* i. 10 *ἀλλ' οὐδ' ἂν τῶν ἕνδεκα γενόμενος ἀποδέξαιο, εἴ τις ἀπάγοι τινὰ φάσκων θοἰμάτιον ἀποδεδύσθαι ἢ τὸν χιτωνίσκον ἐκδεδύσθαι, ἀλλ' ἀφείης ἂν τὸν αὐτὸν τρόπον, ὅτι οὐ λωποδύτης ὀνομάζεται*, Dem. 35 *Lakrit.* 47 *παρὰ τοῖς ἕνδεκα; ἀλλὰ τοιχωρύχους καὶ κλέπτας καὶ τοὺς ἄλλους κακούργους τοὺς ἐπὶ θανάτῳ οὗτοι εἰσάγουσιν*, 54 *Kon.* 24 *τοὺς νόμους, τόν τε τῆς ὕβρεως καὶ τὸν περὶ τῶν λωποδυτῶν*, Isok. 15 *Antid.* 90 *τοῦτον ἀπαγαγὼν ἀνδραποδιστὴν καὶ κλέπτην καὶ λωποδύτην*, Xen. *Mem.* 1. 2. 62 *κατὰ γὰρ τοὺς νόμους, ἐάν τις φανερὸς γένηται κλέπτων ἢ λωποδυτῶν ἢ βαλλαντιοτομῶν ἢ τοιχωρυχῶν ἢ ἀνδραποδιζόμενος ἢ ἱεροσυλῶν, τούτοις θάνατός ἐστιν ἡ ζημία*, Plato, *Rep.* 552 d *κλέπται τε καὶ βαλλαντιοτόμοι καὶ ἱερόσυλοι καὶ πάντων τῶν τοιούτων κακῶν δημιουργοί*, 575 b *κακὰ δρῶσι σμικρὰ πολλά . . . οἷα κλέπτουσι, τοιχωρυχοῦσι, βαλλαντιοτομοῦσι, λωποδυτοῦσιν, ἱεροσυλοῦσιν, ἀνδραποδίζονται*, *An. Bekk.* (*Λέξ. Ῥητ.*) 200. 25 ff., (*Συν. Λέξ. Χρησ.*) 414. 19 ff., Hesych. s.v. *ἀπαγωγή*, Suda s.v. *ἀπαγωγή*. We cannot be certain that this list is exhaustive; for example, it has been suggested that a *μοιχός* could be regarded as a *κακοῦργος* for the purposes of this law (see vol. i, p. 35, n. 1).

strange to us that these acts are described not in terms of the wrong itself, but rather in terms of the wrongdoer, as though it was not so much the quality of the act which was relevant as the kind of man who did it. For this kind of man the generic term was *κακοῦργος*, which presumably had much the same connotation as the word 'felon' had till fairly recently in English law.

Two conditions were required to enable this procedure to be followed. First, a man had to be caught in the act (*ἐπ' αὐτοφώρῳ*).[1] Whatever the rules had been when this procedure was first instituted, by the fourth century 'being caught in the act' was very widely interpreted, and any act which was sufficiently notorious was in danger of being brought under it, though the act might date from the relatively distant past. A notable instance was the employment of *ἀπαγωγή* against Agoratos, dealt with in Lys. 13 *Agorat.* He denounced Dionysodoros under the Thirty, and Dionysodoros was executed. Some five years later Agoratos was haled before the Eleven by the relatives of Dionysodoros for his murder. The Eleven consented to the *ἀπαγωγή*'s being brought before a court on condition that the accusers added to the indictment the words *ἐπ' αὐτοφώρῳ*.[2] The circumstances of this case were peculiar, owing to the constitutional upheavals of the time and the ambiguities arising out of the amnesty. But it is significant that Agoratos, though he obviously questioned the propriety of the procedure as applied to his case, did not, as he presumably might have done, enter a *παραγραφή*. He thus conceded that the Eleven were not acting outrageously in accepting the indictment with the addition of the words *ἐπ' αὐτοφώρῳ*. In another case, Ariston claims that he might have proceeded against Konon by way of *ἀπαγωγή* for clothes-robbing some considerable time after the alleged incident.[3] It is to be noted that the defendant in Ant. 5 *Her.*, against whom procedure by *ἀπαγωγή* for murdering Herodes has been taken, though he takes exception to the use of the procedure, does not make the point

[1] Isai. 4 *Nikostr.* 28 *εἰς τὸ δεσμωτήριον ὡς κλέπτης ὢν ἐπ' αὐτοφώρῳ ἀπήχθη*, Dem. 45 *Steph.* i. 81 *εἰ κλέπτην σ' ἀπῆγον ὡς ἐπ' αὐτοφώρῳ εἰληφώς, τὴν οὐσίαν ἣν ἔχεις, εἴ πως οἷόν τ' ἦν, ἐπιθείς σοι*: the latter passage suggests that the stolen object was brought before the magistrate also.

[2] Lys. 13 *Agorat.* 86 *δοκοῦσι δ' ἔμοιγε οἱ ἕνδεκα οἱ παραδεξάμενοι τὴν ἀπαγωγὴν ταύτην . . . σφόδρα ὀρθῶς ποιῆσαι Διονύσιον τὴν ἀπαγωγὴν ἀπάγοντ' ἀναγκάζοντες προσγράψασθαι τό γε "ἐπ' αὐτοφώρῳ"*. MacDowell, *Homicide* 131 ff.

[3] Dem. 54 *Kon.* 1, 24.

that, whatever else was the case, he was certainly not caught in the act. This may be either because at that time (*c.* 415 B.C.) this would not have been a defence to the charge or, more probably, because the defendant was arguing that he was not a *κακοῦργος* and felt that he would weaken his case if he went on to argue that he had not been caught in the act either.[1]

The other necessary condition for an *ἀπαγωγή* of this sort was that it was committed by a *κακοῦργος*. The speaker in Ant. 5 *Her.* argues that, though he is not a *κακοῦργος*, as defined by the law, the procedure of *ἀπαγωγή* has been employed against him.[2] He admits that murder is a great *κακούργημα*, but holds that there is a special procedure to deal with it (the *δίκη φόνου*), and that his trial by *ἀπαγωγή* might mean that, though acquitted as a *κακοῦργος*, he could still be tried by a *δίκη φόνου*.[3] In this case too it is noteworthy that the defendant does not enter a *παραγραφή*.[4]

According to a law attributed to Solon, the use of *ἀπαγωγή* in cases of theft was restricted to the following: (1) any theft by night, (2) thefts in daylight (*a*) from a gymnasium whatever the sum, (*b*) of sums over ten drachmai in a harbour, (*c*) of sums over fifty drachmai wherever the theft was. The penalty on conviction was death.[5] It is unlikely that *ἀπαγωγή* could be used for other kinds of theft and the defendant punished less severely.[6] Aristotle

[1] K. J. Maidment, *Minor Attic Orators* i (Loeb, 1941) 155, suggests that the condition *ἐπ' αὐτοφώρῳ* applied only to alleged killers who were citizens; the defendant was a *ξένος*. See also MacDowell, *Homicide* 136 f., Wolff, *Paragraphe* 112 ff.

[2] Ant. 5 *Her.* 9 (quoted on p. 223, n. 4).

[3] Ant. 5 *Her.* 16 *ὥστε μηδέν μοι ἐνθάδε πλέον εἶναι μηδ' ἀποφυγόντι, ἀλλ' ἐξεῖναί σοι λέγειν ὅτι κακοῦργος ἀπέφυγον, ἀλλ' οὐ τοῦ φόνου τὴν δίκην*, 10, 85, 90, 94.

[4] Wolff, *Paragraphe* 112 ff., argues that it is a mistake to look upon the speaker's objections to the procedure as analogous to those appropriate to a *παραγραφή*, though this is how it struck even the writer of the Hypothesis. For Wolff *ἀπαγωγή* is not itself a kind of charge, but a more direct way than others of getting a case into court; once a case is there, the fact that it was initiated by *ἀπαγωγή* says nothing as to its content or procedural treatment (ibid. 116, n. 23a). This proves too much; surely, at the very least, the fact that Euxitheos had been subjected to *ἀπαγωγή* meant negatively that the case was not a *δίκη φόνου*.

[5] Dem. 24 *Timokr.* 113 f. *ὁ Σόλων . . . νόμον εἰσήνεγκεν, εἰ μέν τις μεθ' ἡμέραν ὑπὲρ πεντήκοντα δραχμὰς κλέπτοι, ἀπαγωγὴν πρὸς τοὺς ἕνδεκ' εἶναι, εἰ δέ τις νύκτωρ ὁτιοῦν κλέπτοι, τοῦτον ἐξεῖναι καὶ ἀποκτεῖναι καὶ τρῶσαι διώκοντα καὶ ἀπαγαγεῖν τοῖς ἕνδεκα, εἰ βούλοιτο. τῷ δ' ἁλόντι ὧν αἱ ἀπαγωγαί εἰσιν, οὐκ ἐγγυητὰς καταστήσαντι ἔκτισιν εἶναι τῶν κλεμμάτων, ἀλλὰ θάνατον τὴν ζημίαν. καὶ εἴ τίς γ' ἐκ Λυκείου ἢ ἐξ Ἀκαδημείας ἢ ἐκ Κυνοσάργους ἱμάτιον ἢ ληκύθιον ἢ ἄλλο τι φαυλότατον, ἢ εἰ τῶν σκευῶν τι τῶν ἐκ τῶν γυμνασίων ὑφέλοιτο ἢ ἐκ τῶν λιμένων ὑπὲρ δέκα δραχμάς, καὶ τούτοις θάνατον ἐνομοθέτησεν εἶναι τὴν ζημίαν.*

[6] So Lipsius, *AR* 321, n. 16, refuted by Kaser, *Z* 64 (1944) 144, n. 29.

says that those who were convicted under this procedure were condemned to death.[1] It was therefore an *ἀγὼν ἀτίμητος*. This causes some difficulty in connection with Ant. 5 *Her.*, where the speaker says that his opponents have entered a *τίμησις* (he does not say what it is), whereas the law prescribes that the killer should answer with his life.[2] The safest hypothesis here is that Aristotle states the law correctly, at least for his day, and that the procedure followed by the prosecution in the Herodes case is not known with sufficient exactitude for us to be sure whether the rule was the same when that speech was delivered.[3] One would imagine that, if the resulting *ἀγών* was of necessity *ἀτίμητος* with death as the penalty, the use of the procedure would have been restricted by the danger that a jury would acquit for small offences, just as it became difficult to procure convictions for sheep-stealing in England in the eighteenth century. But this is mere speculation.

Quite distinct from the *ἀπαγωγή* of felons was the use of the procedure against those guilty of homicide who, despite their blood guilt, were found in the holy places or the Agora. Any such person could be killed out of hand or haled off to prison, but no further action taken against him till he had been tried. If convicted, he was put to death. If the prosecutor failed to secure one-fifth of the votes, he was fined 1,000 drachmai.[4] It is not quite certain that we should say, with Lipsius,[5] that here the qualification *ἐπ' αὐτοφώρῳ* did not apply. The wrong done here was not the homicide in itself, but the defiance of the ban on entering the

[1] Ar. *Ath. Pol.* 52. 1 (quoted on p. 223, n. 4).

[2] Ant. 5 *Her.* 10 *τίμησίν μοι ἐποίησαν, ἀνταποθανεῖν τοῦ νόμου κειμένου τὸν ἀποκτείναντα.* *Pace* Maidment, *Minor Attic Orators* i. 156, it is not certain that this *τίμησις* was a monetary penalty. It may be that his opponents, by a technical error, included in their indictment a proposal that death should be imposed and this gave the speaker the technical opportunity to put in a counter-estimate of less than death. Cf. Gernet, *Ant.* 113, n. 1.

[3] According to MacDowell, *Homicide* 137, the Eleven had to accept the *ἀπαγωγή*, since the prosecutors alleged that the defendant was a *κακοῦργος*. It was for the jury to decide whether he was or not; but the fact, if it was a fact, that he had killed Herodes did not of itself make him one. However, the prosecutors may have based their indictment on *κλοπή* or *λωποδυσία* rather than homicide; Wolff, *Paragraphe* 115, n. 23, suggests that they did.

[4] Dem. 23 *Aristokr.* 80 *εἰ πάντα ταῦτά τις ἠγνόηκεν . . ., τὸν ἀνδροφόνον δ' ὁρᾷ περιιόντ' ἐν τοῖς ἱεροῖς καὶ κατὰ τὴν ἀγοράν, ἀπάγειν ἔξεστιν εἰς τὸ δεσμωτήριον . . . κἀνταῦθ' ἀπαχθεὶς οὐδ' ὁτιοῦν, πρὶν ἂν κριθῇ, πείσεται, ἀλλ' ἐὰν μὲν ἁλῷ, θανάτῳ ζημιωθήσεται, ἐὰν δὲ μὴ μεταλάβῃ τὸ πέμπτον μέρος τῶν ψήφων ὁ ἀπαγαγών, χιλίας προσοφλήσει.*

[5] Lipsius, *AR* 325.

Agora and the holy places, and it may be that, for the procedure to apply, the defendant had to be apprehended in one of the banned places. One would certainly suppose that it would not be an issue at the trial whether he had in fact been in one of the prohibited places. What might be in issue was whether he had in fact killed somebody. He might have already been warned by a proclamation of the basileus, as a result of action by the dead man's relatives, to keep away from *τὰ νόμιμα*, in which case the issue would be whether he was in fact the same person as the one named in the proclamation. But he might not have been so proclaimed, and in that case one issue would be whether he had killed the dead man.[1] A third possibility would be that he was a man who either had or should have gone into exile, as a result of a *δίκη φόνου*, and had not done so or had returned illicitly; here again the issue would be whether he was X or not. The law allowed such a man to be put to death by his finder without reference to the Eleven. However, the finder might then himself be charged with homicide; his defence would be that it was justifiable homicide, but he would none the less run some risk. In practice, therefore, we should imagine that the tendency would be to resort to *ἀπαγωγή*, in which the risk he ran was only a fine of 1,000 drachmai if he failed to secure one-fifth of the votes.[2] When Lipsius suggests that this use of the procedure covered the possibility that the relatives of a dead man might not act against his killer,[3] one must make the qualification that the procedure was only available against the killer if and when he

[1] Dem. 23 *Aristokr.* 80 (quoted on p. 226, n. 4) implies that it was open to the relatives of the dead man to proceed in this way rather than by a *δίκη φόνου*, though they risked the penalty of 1,000 drachmai if they did not secure one-fifth of the votes. It is not clear why MacDowell, *Homicide* 140, who suggests the three possibilities, uses in connection with this one the phrase 'if a man was "manifestly" a killer'. The passage from Demosthenes certainly does not suggest that for this use of the procedure the provision *ἐπ' αὐτοφώρῳ* would have to be attached to the *killing*; the wrong which justified the procedure (and in relation to which the *in flagrante delicto* provision therefore applied) was entering the prohibited place.

[2] Dem. 23 *Aristokr.* 28 *τοὺς δ' ἀνδροφόνους ἐξεῖναι ἀποκτείνειν ἐν τῇ ἡμεδαπῇ καὶ ἀπάγειν, ὡς ἐν τῷ ⟨α'⟩ ἄξονι ἀγορεύει, λυμαίνεσθαι δὲ μή, μηδὲ ἀποινᾶν, ἢ διπλοῦν ὀφείλειν ὅσον ἂν καταβλάψῃ. εἰσφέρειν δ' ἐς τοὺς ἄρχοντας, ὧν ἕκαστοι δικασταί εἰσι, τῷ βουλομένῳ. τὴν δ' ἡλιαίαν διαγιγνώσκειν*, Dein. 1 *Dem.* 44. Lipsius, *AR* 328 (cf. MacDowell, *Homicide* 140) should not say of this kind of *ἀπαγωγή* that it gave no opportunity for a trial: there is no need to suppose that the usual rule did not apply, execution in case of confession but a trial otherwise.

[3] Lipsius, *AR* 326.

visited one of the prohibited places. It seems relatively clear that an act of unjustifiable homicide was not, *as such*, sufficient ground for the use of ἀπαγωγή.

Analogous to these cases is the use of ἀπαγωγή provided for by a decree by which in the Peloponnesian war traitors who had deserted to the enemy camp at Dekeleia could be haled before the thesmothetai for execution.[1] They had, as it were, condemned themselves to permanent banishment. It is difficult to believe that in such a case the man could not assert his innocence before a court.

A third category of acts rendering a man liable to ἀπαγωγή was the use of rights from which he had been debarred by ἀτιμία. According to a law quoted in Dem. 24 *Timokr.* a man who had been convicted of maltreating his parents or of failing in his military duties or a man who had gone into the forbidden places was liable to be haled before the Eleven, who would imprison him and bring him before a dikastery, where he would be accused by ὁ βουλόμενος; if he was convicted, the penalty should be determined by the court and, if it was a fine, the defendant was to be detained in prison till he had paid.[2] In Dem. 58 *Theokr.* we are told that a prosecutor who dropped a prosecution by φάσις against a trader or shipmaster was liable to a fine of 1,000 drachmai and to ἀπαγωγή or ἔνδειξις.[3] Under this heading

[1] Lykourg. *Leokr.* 121 ἀκούετε, ὦ ἄνδρες, καὶ τούτου τοῦ ψηφίσματος, ὅτι τῶν ἐν τῷ πολέμῳ μεταστάντων εἰς Δεκέλειαν κατέγνωσαν, καὶ ἐψηφίσαντο, ἐάν τις αὐτῶν ἐπανιὼν ἁλίσκηται, ἀπαγαγεῖν Ἀθηναίων τὸν βουλόμενον πρὸς τοὺς θεσμοθέτας, παραλαβόντας δὲ παραδοῦναι τῷ ἐπὶ τοῦ ὀρύγματος.

[2] Dem. 24 *Timokr.* 105 ἐὰν δέ τις ἀπαχθῇ, τῶν γονέων κακώσεως ἑαλωκὼς ἢ ἀστρατείας ἢ προειρημένον αὐτῷ τῶν νόμων εἴργεσθαι, εἰσιὼν ὅποι μὴ χρή, δησάντων αὐτὸν οἱ ἕνδεκα καὶ εἰσαγόντων εἰς τὴν ἡλιαίαν, κατηγορείτω δὲ ὁ βουλόμενος οἷς ἔξεστιν. ἐὰν δ' ἁλῷ, τιμάτω ἡ ἡλιαία ὅ τι χρὴ παθεῖν αὐτὸν ἢ ἀποτεῖσαι. ἐὰν δ' ἀργυρίου τιμηθῇ, δεδέσθω τέως ἂν ἐκτείσῃ. Wayte ad loc. is very suspicious of this document. Some of the points which here concern us are confirmed in the text of the speech at paragraphs 60 and 103; but there is the difficulty that the document includes ἀπαγωγή of the homicide found in holy places among those in which the penalty was fixed by the court.

[3] Dem. 58 *Theokr.* 10 f. ὅτι δ' οὐ ταῖς χιλίαις μόνον ἔνοχός ἐστιν, ἀλλὰ καὶ ἀπαγωγῇ καὶ τοῖς ἄλλοις ὅσα κελεύει πάσχειν ὁ νόμος οὑτοσὶ τὸν συκοφαντοῦντα τοὺς ἐμπόρους καὶ τοὺς ναυκλήρους, ῥᾳδίως ἐξ αὐτοῦ τοῦ νόμου γνώσεσθε. βουλόμενος γὰρ ὁ τὸν νόμον τιθεὶς μήτε τοὺς ἀδικοῦντας τῶν ἐμπόρων ἀθῴους εἶναι, μήτε τοὺς ἄλλους πράγματ' ἔχειν, ἁπλῶς ἀπεῖπε τοῖς τοιούτοις τῶν ἀνθρώπων μὴ φαίνειν, εἰ μὴ πιστεύει τις αὐτῷ δείξειν ἐν ὑμῖν γεγενημένα περὶ ὧν ποιεῖται τὴν φάσιν· ἐὰν δέ τις παρὰ ταῦτα ποιῇ τῶν συκοφαντούντων, ἔνδειξιν αὐτῶν εἶναι καὶ ἀπαγωγήν. The rule is stated to be directed against sycophants; it may have been so by intent, but it is unlikely that it was so expressly. Bo. Sm. ii. 71.

the procedure could be used against slaves or metics who were exercising the rights of free men or of fully qualified citizens.[1]

We need not concern ourselves with certain exceptional cases which are recorded, where by a popular decree some particular act or acts were forbidden and those who committed them were to be liable to procedure by *ἀπαγωγή*.[2]

As we have seen, the consequences of conviction in a case arising out of *ἀπαγωγή* differed according to the type of case. In cases coming under our first two categories the penalty in the event of conviction was always death. In the third type of case the penalty was fixed by the court after *τίμησις* and *ἀντιτίμησις*.[3] The prosecutor in any of the categories was liable to a fine of 1,000 drachmai if he failed to secure one-fifth of the votes or withdrew from the case.

(iii) *ἔνδειξις*

ἔνδειξις was naming an offender and his offence in writing (the plaint itself was also called *ἔνδειξις*)[4] to a magistrate. It differed procedurally from *ἀπαγωγή* in that it was the magistrate's duty then to arrest the offender and imprison him or exact sureties from him.[5] In most cases the appropriate magistrates were the Eleven, but in certain cases it was either the basileus or the thesmothetai.[6]

The grammarians give the impression that *ἔνδειξις* was confined to cases covered by our second and third categories of cases rendering a man liable to *ἀπαγωγή* (pp. 226 ff.), those who visited places from which they were banned or who exercised rights of

[1] If *ἀπήγαγεν* has its technical meaning in Dem. 25 *Aristogeit.* i. 57, and if that speech can be used as evidence, *ἀπαγωγή* could be used against a metic who was evading payment of the *μετοίκιον*. Paoli, *St. Dir.* 237.

[2] For example Ar. *Ath. Pol.* 29. 4, Plato, *Apol.* 32 b, Dem. 20 *Lept.* 156.

[3] There may have been uncertainty even at the time as to whether *τίμησις* was or was not appropriate. A good deal must have depended on the framing of the written *ἀπαγωγή* in each case. Cf. p. 226, n. 2 and p. 228, n. 2.

[4] Dem. 58 *Theokr.* 1; cf. Poll. 8. 49.

[5] Dem. 53 *Nikostr.* 14 and passages cited on p. 221, n. 5.

[6] Ar. *Ath. Pol.* 52. 1 . . . *τὰς ἐνδείξεις εἰσάξοντας· καὶ γὰρ ταύτας εἰσάγουσιν οἱ ἕνδεκα. εἰσάγουσι δὲ τῶν ἐνδείξεών τινας καὶ οἱ θεσμοθέται*, Dem. 24 *Timokr.* 22 (if we may take this law as genuine) *καὶ ἔνδειξις αὐτῶν ἔστω πρὸς τοὺς θεσμοθέτας, καθάπερ ἐάν τις ἄρχῃ ὀφείλων τῷ δημοσίῳ· οἱ δὲ θεσμοθέται τοὺς ἐνδειχθέντας εἰσαγόντων εἰς τὸ δικαστήριον κατὰ τὸν νόμον*. The *ἔνδειξις* of Andokides for attending the Eleusinian Mysteries when he was *ἄτιμος* was laid with the basileus (Andok. 1 *Myst.* 111).

which they had been deprived by *ἀτιμία*.[1] The most frequent case may well have been that of the man who was technically *ὀφείλων τῷ δημοσίῳ* (on whom see pp. 172 ff.);[2] but some of the grammarians' definitions are too narrow,[3] and others possibly too wide.[4] Of the five surviving speeches concerned with *ἔνδειξις* three (Dem. 25 *Aristogeit.* i, 26 *Aristogeit.* ii, 58 *Theokr.*) were directed against men who had brought prosecutions in spite of being state debtors.[5] The other two (Andok. 1 *Myst.*, Lys. 6 *Andok.*) deal with the case of Andokides. He was charged with infringing the decree of Isotimides, which had bidden all who were guilty of impiety and had admitted it to keep away from the temples and the Agora at Athens.[6] Andokides had by his own admission attended the Eleusinian festival. We have also contemporary evidence for the use of *ἔνδειξις* against those who had gone into exile as a result of a *δίκη φόνου*, whether for homicide or for wounding with intent to kill (*τραῦμα ἐκ προνοίας*), and were found in any of the forbidden places.[7] We learn that anyone

[1] Harpokr. (and Suda) s.v. *ἔνδειξις· εἶδος δίκης δημοσίας, ὑφ' ἣν τοὺς ἐκ τῶν νόμων εἰργομένους τινῶν ἢ τόπων ἢ πράξεων, εἰ μὴ ἀπέχοιντο αὐτῶν, ὑπῆγον*, schol. Dem. 20 *Lept.* 156 (and Suda s.v. *ἔνδειξις*) *ἐάν τις ἄτιμος ὢν ἢ ὠφληκὼς τῷ δημοσίῳ καὶ μὴ ἐκτετικὼς ἄρχειν ἢ δικάζειν ἐπιχειροίη, τοῦτον ἐνδείκνυσιν ὁ βουλόμενος τῶν πολιτῶν· ὁμοίως καὶ τὸν ἀντιποιούμενον πράξεων ἢ τόπων ἀπηγορευμένων τοῖς νόμοις, οἷον τὸν ἡταιρηκότα τῆς ἀγορᾶς καὶ τοῦ λέγειν ἐν τῷ δήμῳ, ἔτι τὸν κακῶς λέγοντα τοὺς τετελευτηκότας ἀδίκως.*

[2] Dem. 20 *Lept.* 156 "*εἶναι δὲ καὶ ἐνδείξεις καὶ ἀπαγωγάς· ἐὰν δ' ἁλῷ, ἔνοχος ἔστω τῷ νόμῳ ὃς κεῖται, ἐάν τις ὀφείλων ἄρχῃ τῷ δημοσίῳ.*" *θάνατον λέγει· τοῦτο γάρ ἐστ' ἐπ' ἐκείνῳ τοὐπιτίμιον*, 24 *Timokr.* 22 (quoted on p. 229, n. 6): in both passages the debtor to the treasury is taken as a paradigm.

[3] Poll. 8. 50 *μάλιστα δὲ τοὺς ὀφείλοντας τῷ δημοσίῳ ἐνεδείκνυσαν, ἢ τοὺς κατιόντας ὅποι μὴ ἔξεστιν, ἢ τοὺς ἀνδροφόνους*, Suda s.v. *ἔνδειξις* (1)· *δίκη κατὰ τῶν ὀφειλόντων καὶ δημηγορούντων. οὐ γὰρ ἐξῆν λέγειν, οὐδ' ὅλως ἐπίτιμον εἶναι ὀφείλοντα. ὥστε εἰ καὶ ἦρχέ τις ὀφείλων, ἐνεδείκνυτο. ἤδη δὲ καὶ ἐπὶ τῶν φυγάδων ὅπου μὴ ἔξεστι κατιόντων, ἡ ἔνδειξις*, schol. Dem. 22 *Androt.* 33 and 24 *Timokr.* 146.

[4] Schol. Aristoph. *Knights* 278 (and Suda s.v. *ἐνδείκνυμι*) *ἐνδεικνύναι δὲ ἔλεγον τὸ καταγγέλλειν τινὰ κακουργοῦντα περὶ τὰ κοινά.*

[5] Dem. 58 *Theokr.* 14 tells us that the procedure was also available against debtors to sacred treasuries: *κελεύει* (sc. *νόμος*) *κατά τε τῶν ὀφειλόντων τῷ δημοσίῳ τὰς ἐνδείξεις τὸν βουλόμενον ποιεῖσθαι τῶν πολιτῶν, καὶ ἐάν τις ὀφείλῃ τῇ Ἀθηνᾷ ἢ τῶν ἄλλων θεῶν ἢ τῶν ἐπωνύμων τῳ.*

[6] Andok. 1 *Myst.* 71, Lys. 6 *Andok.* 9, 24.

[7] Dem. 23 *Aristokr.* 51 *ΝΟΜΟΣ. φόνου δὲ δίκας μὴ εἶναι μηδαμοῦ κατὰ τῶν τοὺς φεύγοντας ἐνδεικνύντων, ἐάν τις κατίῃ ὅποι μὴ ἔξεστιν.* Note that the orator when referring to the law substitutes the word *ἀνδροφόνους* for *φεύγοντας*: either word would cover unpremeditated as well as premeditated homicide (Lipsius *AR* 334, n. 62). Lys. 6 *Andok.* 15 *ἐὰν μέν τις ἀνδρὸς σῶμα τρώσῃ, κεφαλὴν ἢ πρόσωπον ἢ χεῖρας ἢ πόδας, οὗτος μὲν κατὰ τοὺς νόμους τοὺς ἐξ Ἀρείου πάγου φεύξεται τὴν τοῦ ἀδικηθέντος πόλιν, καὶ ἐὰν κατίῃ, ἐνδειχθεὶς θανάτῳ ζημιωθήσεται.*

who harboured a returned exile was subject to the same procedure as the exile and therefore, we must assume, to this kind of *ἔνδειξις*.[1] As we saw above (p. 228), *ἔνδειξις* was available against a man who dropped a prosecution by *φάσις* against a trader or shipmaster.

In all this evidence we find no direct connection between *ἔνδειξις* and *κακοῦργοι*, and this leads Lipsius to state categorically that it did not apply to those cases where *ἀπαγωγή* of the first category applied.[2] This may be a legitimate argument from silence; but Lipsius offers no rationale of the difference, and it is hard to see why the alternative procedure by *ἔνδειξις*, in which the magistrate was required to play a more active part than in *ἀπαγωγή*, was not just as much needed against the common criminal as elsewhere.

If *ἔνδειξις* was available against *κακοῦργοι*, we may assume that conviction meant the death penalty. Death was also the penalty when a public debtor or an *ἄτιμος* held a magistracy,[3] or when an exile returned illicitly,[4] or when an *ἄτιμος* entered a forbidden place.[5] But when an *ἄτιμος* sat as a dikast, the court decided the penalty after *τίμησις* and *ἀντιτίμησις*;[6] so too with the *ἄτιμος* who addressed the assembly or acted as prosecutor in the courts.[7]

(iv) *ἐφήγησις*

ἐφήγησις was the act of bringing a magistrate to the place where some wrong was being perpetrated and requiring him to

[1] Dem. 50 *Polykl.* 49 (quoted on p. 186, n. 3). [2] Lipsius, *AR* 331.

[3] Dem. 20 *Lept.* 156 (quoted on p. 230, n. 2).

[4] Lys. 6 *Andok.* 15 (quoted on p. 230, n. 7).

[5] Andok. 1 *Myst.* 33 *ἐὰν γὰρ μὴ μεταλάβῃ τὸ πέμπτον μέρος τῶν ψήφων καὶ ἀτιμωθῇ ὁ ἐνδείξας ἐμὲ Κηφίσιος οὑτοσί, οὐκ ἔξεστιν αὐτῷ εἰς τὸ ἱερὸν τοῖν θεοῖν εἰσιέναι, ἢ ἀποθανεῖται.*

[6] Ar. *Ath. Pol.* 63. 3 *ἐὰν δέ τις δικάζῃ οἷς μὴ ἔξεστιν, ἐνδείκνυται καὶ εἰς τὸ δικαστήριον εἰσάγεται· ἐὰν δ' ἁλῷ, προστιμῶσιν αὐτῷ οἱ δικασταὶ ὅ τι ἂν δοκῇ ἄξιος εἶναι παθεῖν ἢ ἀποτεῖσαι*, Dem. 21 *Meid.* 182 *ἀλλὰ Πύρρον, ὦ ἄνδρες Ἀθηναῖοι, τὸν Ἐτεοβουτάδην, ἐνδειχθέντα δικάζειν ὀφείλοντα τῷ δημοσίῳ, θανάτῳ ζημιῶσαί τινες ὑμῶν ᾤοντο χρῆναι, καὶ τέθνηκεν ἁλοὺς παρ' ὑμῖν.*

[7] There are two cases, both probable, neither certain. One is that of Aristogeiton in Dem. 25 *Aristogeit.* i. 92, which is subject to the doubts about this speech: *μάλιστα μὲν αὐτῷ θανάτου τιμῆσαι, εἰ δὲ μή, τοσοῦτον ἀναθεῖναι τίμημα χρημάτων ὅσον μὴ δυνήσεται φέρειν*. The other is that of Theokrines, of which Gernet, *Dem.* iv. 37, says cautiously that it appears to have been *τιμητός*; neither of the two passages advanced by Lipsius, *AR* 337, n. 74, to prove it (Dem. 58 *Theokr.* 47, 69) seems conclusive.

take the action which in ἀπαγωγή was taken by the private citizen himself. In one of the two places where the procedure is referred to in the orators Demosthenes is speaking of theft: if the victim of a theft can rely on his own strong right arm, he will arrest the thief by the procedure of ἀπαγωγή; if he is weaker, he will bring the magistrate to the thief and the magistrate will arrest him.[1] Although this was no doubt a survival of an archaic procedure, the fact that Demosthenes can cite it in the way he does indicates that it did still survive in his day. How literally we should interpret the procedure is another matter. Lipsius says that naturally the magistrate was accompanied to the scene by his servants;[2] we may agree, though there is no evidence. But we might also be tempted to guess that in the fifth and fourth centuries it would hardly have been possible for the magistrates personally to travel round Attica in such cases, and to suppose that they could delegate such a task to subordinates. We have unfortunately no idea how frequent such cases might be, and therefore how improbable it would be that magistrates could act thus.[3]

§ 6. *Procedures connected with liturgies*

(i) *Introduction*

There is no obviously proper place for the discussion of these procedures.[4] They deal with an alleged wrong, the imposition

[1] Dem. 22 *Androt.* 26 . . . οἷον τῆς κλοπῆς. ἔρρωσαι καὶ σαυτῷ πιστεύεις· ἄπαγε· ἐν χιλίαις δ' ὁ κίνδυνος. ἀσθενέστερος εἶ· τοῖς ἄρχουσιν ἐφηγοῦ· τοῦτο ποιήσουσιν ἐκεῖνοι. Cf. Dem. 26 *Aristogeit.* ii. 9 ἐφ' οἷς οἱ νόμοι κελεύουσι τὸ λοιπὸν μὴ γράφεσθαι μηδ' ἀπάγειν μηδ' ἐφηγεῖσθαι, schol. Patm. on Dem. 22 *Androt.* 26 ἐφηγεῖσθαι· τὸ ἐπάγειν ἄρχοντα ὅποι δεῖ ἐπὶ τὸ δεῖξαί τι παράνομον. εἰ γάρ τις ἔλεγεν εἶναί τι ἔν τινος οἰκίᾳ τῶν πολιτῶν, ἢ ἐὰν ὑποδεδεγμένον τινὰ φυγάδα ἐδείκνυεν, ὃν οὐ χρή, ἢ ἀνδροφόνον, ἔδει τὸν ἄρχοντα ἐπάγεσθαι καὶ ἐπιδεικνύειν, Poll. 8. 50 ἐφηγεῖσθαι δέ ἐστιν, ὅταν τις δι' ἀσθένειαν ἀπαγαγεῖν οὐ θαρρῶν ἐπάγῃ τὸν ἄρχοντα ἐπ' οἰκίαν οὗ τις τούτων ἀποκρύπτεται, *An. Bekk.* (Λέξ. Ῥητ.) 312. 31 ff. (under ὑφήγησις, but the ὑφ- is probably just a mis-spelling for ἐφ-; the same mis-spelling occurs in *Lex. Cant.* s.v. πρόστιμον) and Suda s.v. ἐφήγησις· δίκη ἐστὶν εἰσαγομένη κατὰ τῶν ὑποδεξαμένων τὸν εἰργόμενον ὑπὸ τῶν νόμων ἐπιβαίνειν τῆς χώρας, οἷον φυγάδα ἢ ἀνδροφόνον· ἢ ὅταν τῶν δημοσίων τι κατέχειν δοκῇ τις κρύφα.

[2] Lipsius, *AR* 337.

[3] In Lys. 7 *Sacr. Ol.* 22 there is a suggestion that a prospective prosecutor might have taken the nine archons to look at the allegedly uprooted olive stump; cf. Gernet and Bizos, *Lys.* i. 115, n. 2. It is not clear why Paoli, *St. Dir.* 238 wishes to regard ἐφήγησις not as a procedure in its own right, but simply as a preliminary stage in ἔνδειξις.

[4] Beauchet iii. 722 ff., W. A. Goligher, *Hermathena* 14 (1907) 481 ff., Lipsius, *AR* 588 ff., Gernet, *Dem.* ii. 71 ff.

upon a citizen of a liturgy which he claims should not have been imposed on him, or the exaction of more than should be exacted. The opposing party might be the state, or it might be another citizen alleged to be in a better financial position to bear the liturgy. Since, however, the whole subject-matter in dispute was concerned with a man's public duties, it is perhaps better to consider the procedures in the context of public wrongs.

A man who was trying to evade a liturgy might proceed on one of two grounds: either that he was not liable to the liturgy at all (*σκῆψις*), or that, although he might be in principle liable, another citizen, whom he specified, ought to undertake it in his stead (*ἀντίδοσις*). Whichever course he took might, though it did not necessarily, lead to a legal process. If it did, the presiding magistrate was in each case the magistrate in whose sphere the liturgy fell: the archon for choruses at the Great Dionysia and the Thargelia, and for choruses sent to Delos;[1] the basileus for choruses at the Lenaia and for the gymnasiarchy;[2] the strategoi (later the *στρατηγὸς ἐπὶ τὰς συμμορίας ᾑρημένος*) for the taking up of trierarchies and for the *προεισφορά*;[3] the overseers of the docks for trierarchs' responsibility for ships and ships' gear during their holding of the trierarchy and on handing over to their successors.[4]

Lack of detailed information compels us to treat together the procedures arising out of various liturgies. But we must try to keep in sight the fact that liturgies were of very different kinds. Procedurally the most significant difference was the degree to which a particular liturgy was nothing more than a money payment (the limiting case was here the *προεισφορά*) or also involved some personal service (as did the trierarchy, at least in its earliest form). Clearly a court had a much more difficult and delicate

[1] Ar. *Ath. Pol.* 56. 3 *ἔπειτα χορηγοὺς τραγῳδοῖς καθίστησι τρεῖς ἐξ ἁπάντων Ἀθηναίων τοὺς πλουσιωτάτους· πρότερον δὲ καὶ κωμῳδοῖς καθίστη πέντε, νῦν δὲ τούτοις αἱ φυλαὶ φέρουσιν. ἔπειτα παραλαβὼν τοὺς χορηγοὺς τοὺς ἐνηνεγμένους ὑπὸ τῶν φυλῶν εἰς Διονύσια ἀνδράσιν καὶ παισὶν καὶ κωμῳδοῖς, καὶ εἰς Θαργήλια ἀνδράσιν καὶ παισίν (εἰσὶ δ' οἱ μὲν εἰς Διονύσια κατὰ φυλάς, εἰς Θαργήλια ⟨δὲ⟩ δυοῖν φυλαῖν εἷς· παρέχει δ' ἐν μέρει ἑκατέρα τῶν φυλῶν) τούτοις τὰς ἀντιδόσεις ποιεῖ καὶ τὰς σκήψεις εἰσ[άγει, ἐά]ν τις ἢ λελῃτουργηκέναι φῇ πρότερον ταύτην τὴν λῃτουργίαν, ἢ ἀτελὴς εἶναι, λελῃτουργηκὼς ἑτέραν λῃτουργίαν καὶ τῶν χρόνων αὐτῷ τῆς ἀτελείας μὴ ἐξεληλυθότων, ἢ τὰ ἔτη μὴ γεγονέναι· δεῖ γὰρ τὸν τοῖς παισὶν χορηγοῦντα ὑπὲρ τετταράκοντα ἔτη γεγονέναι. καθίστησι δὲ καὶ εἰς Δῆλον χορηγοὺς καὶ ἀρχιθέω[ρον τ]ῷ τριακοντορίῳ τῷ τοὺς ᾐθέους ἄγοντι.*

[2] Ar. *Ath. Pol.* 57. 1, Dem. 35 *Lakrit.* 48, 39 *Boiot.* i. 9.

[3] See p. 32, n. 7.

[4] See p. 34, n. 2.

task to perform if its competence extended beyond the realms of simple finance.

(ii) σκῆψις

Bearing in mind this caution, we may look at what Aristotle says about those claims to exemption which came before the archon in connection with the χορηγίαι for which he was responsible.[1] His use of the definite article (τὰς σκήψεις) seems to imply that this kind of procedure would have been expected wherever a magistrate was in general control of the administration of a liturgy, though we cannot go further and assume that the particular grounds for σκῆψις which he goes on to mention were common to all. These grounds are:

1. That the man named had performed that particular liturgy before. It seems certain that men did perform the same liturgies more than once, but this may well have been because they did not choose to exercise their right of σκῆψις.[2]
2. That he was generally exempt (ἀτελής), because he had recently performed another liturgy and the period of exemption which that gave him had not elapsed.[3]
3. That he had not reached the age of forty. This rule applied only to χορηγίαι for choruses of boys. Here we have one certain case where the court would have before it considerations which were not financial.

We cannot say whether this list of grounds for σκῆψις is exhaustive even for the χορηγίαι, let alone other liturgies. It is strange that it does not refer to a possible objection by the man named that his property fell below some legally fixed minimum.

[1] Ar. *Ath. Pol.* 56. 3 (quoted on p. 233, n. 1).

[2] Lipsius, *AR* 589, n. 2, is not clear, though he rightly draws attention to the fact that Aristotle leaves some doubt whether the rule meant, by 'that liturgy', a χορηγία as distinct say from a trierarchy, or a particular χορηγία as distinct from another χορηγία.

[3] According to Dem. 20 *Lept.* 8 a law specifically prescribed that an interval of one year should intervene between the completion of one liturgy and the taking up of another: ἐνιαυτὸν διαλιπὼν ἕκαστος λῃτουργεῖ. *A fortiori* a man could not be required to perform two liturgies simultaneously: Dem. 50 *Polykl.* 9 οὐκ ἂν δυναίμην δύο λῃτουργίας λῃτουργεῖν οὐδὲ οἱ νόμοι ἐῶσιν. Isai. 7 *Apollod.* 38 implies that, when that speech was composed (about 354 B.C.), an interval of two years might be claimed between trierarchies; the rule for these may have differed from that for other liturgies.

It seems fairly certain that there were such minima, though we cannot say what they were.[1]

As regards the trierarchy, there seem to have been two kinds of *σκῆψις*, not always sufficiently distinguished by commentators. A man might try to evade the trierarchy altogether on grounds (1) or (2) above, or conceivably on some other grounds which we cannot specify. In such a case the strategoi, or one of them, had to bring his case before a dikastery, which decided the issue. This seems to have happened to certain men who wished to be excused from an expedition to the Adriatic in 325/4 B.C.[2] *σκῆψις* however was used in quite a different way in connection with the trierarch's obligation at the end of his term to hand over his ship and gear in a proper state of repair. This obligation bound him both towards the state and towards the trierarch who was going to take over from him, and it is not easy to disentangle exactly how these two obligations were legally enforceable. The state in this matter was represented by the overseers of the docks (see p. 34). A trierarch might claim that his ship and gear had been damaged or lost in a storm; a court decided by *διαδικασία* whether this was so.[3] Or he might claim loss by enemy action; on this the ekklesia decided.[4] If the trierarch won, he had to return to the state no more than the prow (*ἔμβολος*) of the vessel; if he lost, he had either to provide a new ship, retaining the old ship except for the prow, or to return the old ship and pay 5,000 drachmai towards the building of a new one.[5] The court might order a penalty less than the complete replacement of the ship;[6] we must suppose

[1] They are definitely implied in Dem. 20 *Lept.* 19.

[2] *IG* ii². 1629. 204 ff. (quoted on p. 32, n. 7).

[3] *IG* ii². 1613. 202 ff. *[αἱ δ]ὲ δύο τριήρει[ς αἷδ]ε ἐ[πὶ] Διοτίμου [δι]εδικάσθησαν κ[αὶ ἔδοξαν] κατὰ χειμῶνα δ[ιαφθαρῆναι]*, 1629. 746 ff. *αἷδε τῶν τριήρων καὶ τετρή(ρων) τῶν σκηφθεισῶν κατὰ χειμῶνα ἔδοξαν ἐν τῶι δικαστηρίωι κατὰ χειμῶνα διαφθαρῆναι*, 1631. 116 ff., 343 ff.

[4] *IG* ii². 1627. 241 ff. *τριήρεις τάσδε ἱππηγοὺς εἰς πλοῦν δοθείσας ἐκ τῶν νεωρίων ὁ δῆμος ἐψηφίσατο αὐτὰς καὶ τὰ σκεύη κατὰ πόλεμον ἀχρήστους γεγονέναι κατὰ ψηφίσματα, ἃ Δημάδης Δημέου Παιανι(εὺς) εἶπε*, 1628. 460 ff., 1629. 722 ff., 804 ff.: but these all refer to the same instance, which may have been an isolated one, and we ought not perhaps to base on it any general rule. Bu. Sw. 1130, n. 3.

[5] *IG* ii². 1623. 6 ff. *ταύτην ὡμολόγησεν ἐπὶ τοῦ δικαστηρίου καινὴν ἀποδώσειν τῆι πόλει Εὐξένιππος Ἐθελοκράτους Λαμπτρ(εύς), τὴν δὲ παλαιὰν διαλύσειν καὶ τὸν ἔμβολον ἀποδώσειν εἰς τὰ νεώρια* (and several more instances in the same inscription), 1629. 826 ff., 1631. 184 ff.

[6] *IG* ii². 1631. 442 ff. In *IG* ii². 1612. 91 ff. the trierarchs have to repair the ships. Böckh, *Urkunden über das Seewesen des attischen Staates* (Berlin, 1840) 199 f., U. Köhler, *Ath. Mitt.* 6 (1881) 33 ff.

that this was done by a process of τίμησις. The usual rule covering state debtors (on which see pp. 172 ff.) seems to have been waived in these cases, since we find in the records of the overseers of the docks undischarged obligations carried forward from year to year. A court might however impose a penalty of double the original penalty.[1]

(iii) ἀντίδοσις

The alternative course open to a man who wished to evade a liturgy was to challenge some other citizen, alleging that he was financially better able to discharge it. The challengee might accept the liturgy, in which case the matter was settled. More probably he would wish to resist the challenger. In this case what then transpired had the general title of 'exchange' (ἀντίδοσις). Unfortunately the precise meaning of this word (and of the corresponding verb, ἀντιδιδόναι), as used in this context in the fourth century, is not certain; but it is generally agreed that in origin it must have described a real exchange of some kind. There is however an unresolved controversy as to whether in the fourth century an actual exchange of property was an even remote possibility. On the most straightforward view of what is actually said about the procedure by the orators and grammarians, an actual exchange was always a possibility and provided the necessary sanction for the working of the system.[2]

On this view, the challengee, if not prepared to take over the liturgy, might accept the proffered exchange. If he did, the procedure described in Dem. 42 *Phain.* 5 ff. was set in motion.[3] The challenger could at once proceed on to the challengee's land and inspect it to find out its extent, what stocks or cattle there were and, negatively, to establish that it was not in any way encumbered with mortgages.[4] The challengee had the right to do the same on the challenger's estate. Each party then swore to furnish

[1] *IG* ii². 1623. 50 ff., 60 ff., 106 ff., 144 ff. In *IG* ii². 1628. 339 ff. the boule doubles certain obligations.

[2] This view was originally worked out in detail by Böckh, *Staatsh.* i. 673 ff., and is adopted, with minor variations, by Dareste, *Dem.* i. 181 f., Lipsius, *AR* 590 ff.

[3] Phainippos let his opponent think he was going to accept the exchange, but was really fooling him, and intended from the first to have the matter tried by διαδικασία. So Goligher; but it is hard to accept that, by acting as he did, he did his case 'no injury whatever' (Goligher, *Hermathena* 14 (1907) 509).

[4] See vol. i, pp. 268 f.

the other within three days with an inventory of all his property. The inventory itself was also given on oath. Mineral concessions were by law excluded.[1] If both parties declared themselves satisfied, the exchange of properties then took place, and the challenger performed the liturgy.[2] Or the challenger might withdraw the challenge and undertake the liturgy without exchange of property: this possibility is nowhere referred to in our sources, and it may not have been open to the challenger to withdraw in this way without the permission of the challengee; but if the challengee's permission was required, it is not likely that it would often have been withheld.[3]

The other possibility was that the challengee might decline the exchange. In this case the procedure of visitation and inventory had no place, and the challengee excluded the challenger from his estate.[4] The issue went before a dikastery as a *διαδικασία*.

[1] Dem. 42 *Phain.* 18 *τὸν νόμον, ὃς διαρρήδην οὕτω λέγει, "τοὺς δ' ἀντιδιδόντας ἀλλήλοις, ὅταν ὀμόσαντες ἀποφαίνωσι τὴν οὐσίαν, προσομνύειν τόνδε τὸν ὅρκον, 'ἀποφαίνω τὴν οὐσίαν τὴν ἐμαυτοῦ ὀρθῶς καὶ δικαίως, πλὴν τῶν ἐν τοῖς ἔργοις τοῖς ἀργυρείοις, ὅσα οἱ νόμοι ἀτελῆ πεποιήκασι'*", 23.

[2] The following passages are deemed, with varying degrees of cogency, to entail the possibility of an actual exchange of properties. Dem. 42 *Phain.* 27 *ἐῶ μετέχειν τῶν ἐμαυτοῦ τὴν μητέρα, ἄν τε τὴν Φαινίππου ἄν τε τὴν ἐμαυτοῦ ἔχω οὐσίαν*, 19 *ἐγὼ γὰρ καὶ πρότερον προὐκαλεσάμην Φαίνιππον, καὶ νῦν, ὦ ἄνδρες δικασταί, δίδωμι αὐτῷ δωρεὰν καὶ ἀφίσταμαι μετὰ τῆς ἄλλης οὐσίας καὶ τῶν ἐν τοῖς ἔργοις, ἐάν μοι τὴν ἐσχατιὰν μόνην ἐλευθέραν παραδῷ*: this, as Lipsius, *AR* 594, n. 16, rightly points out, is not the original summons of Phainippos (if it were, it would not be cited as it is in paragraph 23), but rather an offer by the speaker to throw his mining concession into his own property (which he was not bound to do) for the purposes of the exchange. Lys. 4 *Wound* 1 f. *θαυμαστόν γε, ὦ βουλή, τὸ διαμάχεσθαι περὶ τούτου, ὡς οὐκ ἐγένοντο ἡμῖν διαλλαγαί, καὶ τὸ μὲν ζεῦγος καὶ τὰ ἀνδράποδα, καὶ ὅσα ἐξ ἀγροῦ κατὰ τὴν ἀντίδοσιν ἔλαβε* (Scaliger: *ἔλαβον* codd.), *μὴ ἂν δύνασθαι ἀρνηθῆναι ὡς οὐκ ἀπέδωκε, φανερῶς δὲ περὶ πάντων διαλελυμένον ἀρνεῖσθαι τὰ περὶ τῆς ἀνθρώπου, μὴ κοινῇ ἡμᾶς χρῆσθαι συγχωρῆσαι. καὶ τὴν μὲν ἀντίδοσιν δι' ἐκείνην φανερός ἐστι ποιησάμενος, τὴν δ' αἰτίαν δι' ἣν ἀπέδωκεν ἃ* (Taylor: *ἣ* codd.) *ἔλαβεν, οὐκ ἂν ἄλλην ἔχοι εἰπεῖν (βουλόμενος τἀληθῆ λέγειν) ἢ ὅτι οἱ φίλοι περὶ πάντων ἡμᾶς τούτων συνήλλαξαν*: the emendations are highly probable, and it seems reasonably clear that an actual exchange of property was being contemplated and was averted by a reconciliation between the parties; but the passage is too doubtful to be conclusive. Dem. 20 *Lept.* 40 is even less conclusive: all that Demosthenes is saying there is that Leukon has property in Athens which would enable a citizen to bring the procedure of *ἀντίδοσις* against him; it is a *petitio principii* to argue that an actual exchange is implied, since on any view an identifiable estate or property was needed for the court to work upon. Equally inconclusive is Lys. 24 *Invalid* 9 (in any case a suspect speech).

[3] It would only have been tempting to withhold it if the challenger had grossly miscalculated and his property was very much greater than that of the challengee.

[4] Dem. 28 *Aphob.* ii. 17 *ἀπέκλεισα δ' ὡς διαδικασίας τευξόμενος*.

The court decided which litigant was possessed of the greater fortune. If they named the challenger, he had to discharge the liturgy and (we must presume) could not challenge a second man. If they named the challengee, he had to perform the liturgy.

Even when the διαδικασία was started, the challenger could withdraw the challenge, or the challengee could accept the liturgy. It has been much discussed whether the challengee could also stop the trial by accepting the exchange of property. One view is that he could not, because *ex hypothesi* he had, in demanding a διαδικασία, prevented the visitation of his property which would have tested the accuracy of his inventory.[1] On another view, though an exchange of properties might take place, it could only do so before the court actually pronounced judgement. That judgement was a direct mandate to the person named to perform the liturgy, and once it was pronounced he had to perform it.[2]

[1] Goligher, *Hermathena* 14 (1907) 511.

[2] Isok. 15 *Antid.* 5 ἔγνωσαν ἐμὴν εἶναι τὴν λειτουργίαν. Isokrates had been challenged to undertake a trierarchy. He demurred, and the issue went for trial. The sentence quoted describes the result of the trial; the subject of ἔγνωσαν is the Athenians in general, here personified in the dikasts. For Böckh, *Staatsh.* i. 675, the words state the effect of the decision, but do not rule out the possibility that Isokrates might have accepted the proffered exchange, in which case the challenger would have taken over his property and discharged the liturgy.

APPENDIX F

The manning of the courts at the end of the fifth and beginning of the fourth centuries

IN the mid fifth century dikasteries of varying size were drawn from among a body of men known as heliasts, so called because Solon had created a single popular court known as the heliaia. The antiquity of the court is proved by Lys. 10 *Theomn.* i. 15 f.: *καί μοι ἀνάγνωθι τούτους τοὺς νόμους τοὺς Σόλωνος τοὺς παλαιούς. ΝΟΜΟΣ. δεδέσθαι δ' ἐν τῇ ποδοκάκκῃ ἡμέρας πέντε τὸν πόδα, ἐὰν [μὴ] προστιμήσῃ ἡ ἡλιαία.* (The readings are confirmed by Dem. 24 *Timokr.* 105.) According to Ar. *Ath. Pol.* 24. 3 there were six thousand dikasts at the height of the Athenian empire, and Aristoph. *Wasps* 662 suggests that this was the number still in 422 B.C. Suda s.v. *πρυτανεία* also assumes six thousand as the regular number of dikasts at any one time. We have no information how these six thousand were selected out of the total number of qualified citizens, and the fact that the number is not mentioned in the very full account of the working of the courts in Ar. *Ath. Pol.* 63 ff. suggests that by Aristotle's day it had no significance (Hommel, *Heliaia* 36, n. 82). A. W. Gomme, in a review of Hommel in *CR* 44 (1930) 66, doubts whether the figure was ever anything but a rhetorical approximation.

The following two passages from Aristoph. *Wasps* make it clear that in 422 B.C. jurors were assigned by lot to particular courts under particular magistrates for the whole year.

303 ff. *ἄγε νυν, ὦ πάτερ, ἢν μὴ*
τὸ δικαστήριον ἄρχων
καθίσῃ νῦν, πόθεν ὠνη-
σόμεθ' ἄριστον;

1107 ff. *ξυλλεγέντες γὰρ καθ' ἑσμοὺς ὥσπερ εἰς τἀνθρήνια*
οἱ μὲν ἡμῶν οὗπερ ἄρχων, οἱ δὲ παρὰ τοὺς ἕνδεκα,
οἱ δ' ἐν ᾠδείῳ δικάζουσ'.

Whether *ἄρχων* in line 304 means the eponymous archon or the particular one of the nine archons to whose court this juror belongs, in either case the assumption is that each heliast knew in advance in whose court he would be sitting.

At that date there were probably ten sections of approximately (or exactly) six hundred jurors each. The sections were formed at the beginning of each year, and each was allocated to its own magistrate. A court of five hundred or multiples of that number could always be found by selecting the required number by lot. Ar. *Ath. Pol.* 27. 4 (κληρουμένων ἐπιμελῶς ἀεὶ μᾶλλον τῶν τυχόντων ἢ τῶν ἐπιεικῶν ἀνθρώπων) implies the use of the lot for the selecting of juries in Perikles' time. Under such a system it would have been comparatively easy to identify a very large proportion of the jurors who would sit on any given case, and this was a necessary precondition of bribery. We know that bribery was occurring. Anytos bribed his way out of condemnation for the loss of Pylos in 409 B.C.; Ar. *Ath. Pol.* 27. 5 states that he was the first to bribe a jury, but a roughly contemporary source (Ps.-Xen. *Ath. Pol.* 3. 7, reading συνδεκάσαι) argues that smaller juries would increase the danger of bribery, an unlikely argument if Anytos had been the pioneer of bribery. Jurors seem to know whom they will be trying in Aristoph. *Wasps* 157, 240, 288 f., for example. Ant. 6 *Chor.* 23 shows that the same dikasts sat in the same court on two successive days. Lipsius, *AR* 138, n. 14, is wrong in arguing that the identity of the jurors here mentioned underlines the number of persons able to witness to the events narrated; this identity was a limiting factor in that number. But he is right to insist that we should not deduce from this passage that a case could at that time run over two days; two different trials are being described (see p. 161, n. 4).

It is probable that certain modifications in the system were made during the archonship of Eukleides (403/2 B.C.) with the object of lessening the changes of corruption, and also of dealing with the possibility of a scarcity of jurors. Aristoph. *Ekkl.* 682 ff., *Pl.* 277, 1166 f. make it clear that when they were performed the assignment of jurors by lot to the various courts took place on each separate day when the courts were sitting. All qualified jurors were divided into ten sections known by the letters of the alphabet from *A* to *K*. The sections were sometimes called γράμματα (as in Aristoph. *Pl.* 1167). Membership of a section may at first have been for one year, but later it lasted for life. Each of the ten sections was of approximately the same size, and each contained an approximately equal proportion of each of the ten tribes. Each day jurors were assigned to courts by drawing from one urn a letter from *A* to *K* which designated one of the sections of jurors, and from another a letter from *Λ* onwards which designated the court to be manned. The assumption is that each of the ten sections contained something like six hundred names and that each of the ten courts needed a complement of five hundred. A further process of allotment must have been required to reduce the number of those who presented themselves if they were in excess of five hundred, as also if a particular court needed a complement of less than five hundred. If a court needed a complement of 1,000 or 1,500, for example, two or three letters could be drawn from the first urn against one from the second. There must also have been provision for a case where less than the needed complement in a particular section turned up; but perhaps this risk was obviated by a curious provision under which it seems that a man could be registered in more than one of the ten sections (Aristoph. *Pl.* 1167 σπεύδουσιν ἐν πολλοῖς γεγράφθαι γράμμασιν).

The system which obtained in Aristotle's time and which is briefly described above (pp. 45 f.) was again somewhat different. When it was introduced is a matter of conjecture. B. Keil, *Anonymus Argentinensis* (Strassburg, 1902) 266, connects it with the foundation of the second Athenian confederacy in 378/7 B.C.; cf. Hommel, *Heliaia* 120 ff., Bo. Sm. i. 373. It has been held, but with more firmness than the passage justifies, that Isok. 7 *Areop.* 54 (τίς οὐκ ἂν ἐπὶ τοῖς γιγνομένοις τῶν εὖ φρονούντων ἀλγήσειεν, ὅταν ἴδῃ πολλοὺς τῶν πολιτῶν αὐτοὺς μὲν περὶ τῶν ἀναγκαίων, εἴθ' ἕξουσιν εἴτε μή, πρὸ τῶν δικαστηρίων κληρουμένους) is only compatible with the system as described by Aristotle, and that therefore 355 or 354 B.C. is the *terminus ante quem* for the introduction of that system. The remark of Isokrates would surely apply to any system under which a substantial body of would-be jurors were sent away on a given day as a result of an allotment, and something of the kind must have happened under any of the systems described.

APPENDIX G

Kahrstedt on imprisonment

Kahrstedt, *Staatsg.* 141 ff., discusses remedies open to a man or woman (primarily citizens, though the rights of foreigners and metics are also touched on) who was wrongfully imprisoned. A man who caught another in adultery with his wife *in flagrante delicto* could either put him to death or hold him to ransom. If he did the latter, the supposed adulterer might bring an action against him for wrongful detention. Kahrstedt believes he did this by a δίκη εἱργμοῦ, vouched for only in *Lex. Cant.* s.v. εἱργμοῦ δίκη. The only direct evidence is in Dem. 59 *Neair.* 66, where the alleged adulterer's action is described in the words γράφεται πρὸς τοὺς θεσμοθέτας γραφὴν Στέφανον τουτονί, ἀδίκως εἱρχθῆναι ὑπ' αὐτοῦ, which rules out a δίκη (cf. vol. i, p. 33). It is to be noted that in that case the alleged adulterer was a foreigner, so that, in this context at least, a foreigner's liberty was protected equally with that of a citizen (unless we are to suppose that it was a γραφή *because* he was a foreigner, and that it would otherwise have been a δίκη).

In *IG* ii². 32. 9 ff. (385/4 B.C.) a man who is being granted the privileges of a *πρόξενος* is guaranteed against imprisonment as though he were an Athenian, which implies that a foreigner did not normally enjoy this guarantee.

Slavery (and by implication imprisonment) for private debt was abolished by Solon (see vol. i, p. 164), as was the selling into slavery of a child by its parents (Plut. *Solon* 23; Plut. *Mor.* 834 f says that Andokides was liable to trial for having as guardian sold a cousin to the king of Cyprus).

In relation to public debt, on the other hand, there is comparatively frequent reference to imprisonment, for example Dem. 22 *Androt.* 34 *ὡς οὖν οὐκ ὦφλ' ὁ πατήρ σου, τοῦτ' ἐπίδειξον, ἢ ὡς οὐκ ἀποδρὰς ἐξῆλθεν ἐκ τοῦ δεσμωτηρίου, ἀλλὰ τὰ χρήματ' ἐκτείσας,* 56 *τὸν μὲν ἑαυτοῦ πατέρα ᾤετο δεῖν, δημοσίᾳ δεθέντ' ἐπὶ χρήμασιν ἐν τῷ δεσμωτηρίῳ, μήτ' ἀποδόντα ταῦτα μήτε κριθέντ' ἀποδρᾶναι,* 53 *Nikostr.* 14 *παρεσκευάζοντο . . . ἐνδεικνύναι με ὡς ὀφείλοντα τῷ δημοσίῳ καὶ ἐμβάλλειν εἰς τὸ δεσμωτήριον.* The boule was empowered (but not bound) to imprison those reported to them by the apodektai as in arrear with certain payments, such as payments for rights to collect taxes, for mining rights, and for the purchase of confiscated goods: Andok. 1 *Myst.* 93 *ὁ γὰρ νόμος οὕτως εἶχε· κυρίαν εἶναι τὴν βουλήν, ὃς ἂν πριάμενος τέλος μὴ καταβάλῃ, δεῖν εἰς τὸ ξύλον,* Dem. 24 *Timokr.* 96 ff., Ar. *Ath. Pol.* 48. 1. Since the boule could not by *ψήφισμα* confiscate the goods of such defaulters, further action was needed to recover the state's dues. This further action must have been the bringing of a suit (as *εἰσάγουσα ἀρχή*—a remnant of the power of the boule as a magistracy to decide *αὐτοτελής*), and imprisonment, if imposed, will have been the equivalent of remand in custody. Similarly in *ἔνδειξις* against state debtors (on which see p. 230) imprisonment was remand in custody.

We have something different when in Ar. *Ath. Pol.* 63. 3 we find the rule that a public debtor who sat as a juror, and was informed against by *ἔνδειξις* and convicted and fined by a court, was imprisoned until he paid both the original debt and the fine. We have at least one example of a public debtor thus held (and held for a long time) in Andron, father of Androtion (Dem. 22 *Androt.* 34, 56, 68, 24 *Timokr.* 125, 168). In the same category come those cases where, for those who were convicted and fined for certain offences, imprisonment was prescribed until the fine was paid. Examples are *ὕβρις* (Dem. 21 *Meid.* 47), *κάκωσις γονέων*, and *ἀστρατεία* (Dem. 24 *Timokr.* 103), and defaulting tax-collectors (the last clause in Dem. 24 *Timokr.* 63, to be distinguished from the remand in custody mentioned in the first clause). These passages suggest that the debtor would be imprisoned immediately the verdict had been given. How does this square with the evidence about the ninth prytany (p. 173)? According to Plato,

Apol. 38 b, Sokrates (accused of ἀσέβεια) at one stage estimated his penalty at 3,000 drachmai and named sureties, Plato among them, for payment. The decree proposed by Timokrates (Dem. 24 *Timokr.* 39 f.) laid down that henceforward a man convicted of malversation could by providing sureties remain free until the ninth prytany, which implies that hitherto he was immediately incarcerated. It is clear that for Sokrates the same law stood as was contemplated for those convicted of malversation in Timokrates' decree: sureties secured freedom from imprisonment ἐπὶ χρήμασι (to use the phrase of Dem. 24 *Timokr.* 132) till the ninth prytany. We can also see from the possibility of imprisonment and sureties in Sokrates' case that ἀσέβεια must be added to the list of offences (ὕβρις, κάκωσις γονέων, ἀστρατεία) for which a money fine with imprisonment in case of default without sureties was imposed. Kahrstedt goes on to the *non sequitur* that this held in the period before Timokrates for all money penalties save those arising out of malversation, and he thinks this generalization is borne out by the probable fact that all those known to us as prisoners thus held were guilty of some form of malversation, namely Miltiades (Plut. *Kimon* 4, *Aristeides* 26, though Hdt. 6. 136 says nothing of this imprisonment, and Miltiades' offence may have been ἀπάτη τοῦ δήμου: see p. 54), Andron (see p. 242), Agyrrhios (Dem. 24 *Timokr.* 135), Aristogeiton (Dein. 2 *Aristogeit.* 2, 9), and Demosthenes himself (Plut. *Dem.* 26).

The decree of Timokrates (Dem. 24 *Timokr.* 39 f., the text of which is mostly confirmed by references later in the speech) laid down that public debtors threatened with detention by νόμος or ψήφισμα could name sureties in the ekklesia, or have them named by a third party. If the assembly accepted the sureties, the debtor remained free till the ninth prytany. If he had not paid by then, he was imprisoned and the property of the sureties was distrained upon. Expressly excepted from this privilege were tax-collectors, the eklogeis, the lessees of leasable revenues, and their sureties; for these the existing law was to persist. The only debts affected by this decree were money penalties and penalties for malversation. What was new was granting the extended time for payment to a new category of debtors who had not enjoyed this privilege before. But those liable to money penalties already enjoyed the privilege of the extended term (Andok. 1 *Myst.* 73, 78), and Sokrates the privilege of sureties.

The law regarding the imprisonment of state debtors was therefore as follows. There was no imprisonment ἐπὶ χρήμασι for payment of sums due to the state from purely financial debtors, lessees of taxes, mines, etc., but only against criminal debtors, those condemned to a money penalty. Whether the conviction was for default in payment of tax-purchase, desertion from the army, or impiety, was indifferent, as was whether the wrong was to the public chest or to some quite different interest. The only difference in categories was that, until the decree of Timokrates (353 B.C.), those condemned for malversation were always imprisoned, while any others could remain free until the ninth prytany on furnishing sureties. From 353 this milder rule was extended to all cases. It was in line with this principle that it was only the qualified ὀφείλων (the man who was convicted of sitting as a juror when he was not entitled to, as being a state debtor) who was imprisoned, not one who was, for example, simply in arrear with his rent payment.

APPENDIX H

ἐνεχυρασία

There is the same ambiguity in the use of ἐνέχυρον, ἐνεχυράζω, and ἐνεχυρασία as in the use of the German word 'Pfand'. The object mentioned may be either (*a*) one that has been given in pledge as security for a loan (see vol. i, p. 254), or one that is seized either (*b*) in satisfaction of a judgement or (*c*) by some administrative right on the part of him who distrains.

The words are certainly used of administrative execution (sense (*c*)) in two passages in Demosthenes. In 47 *Euerg.* 37 f. a trierarch distrained upon property of the trierarch whom he had succeeded, alleging that the latter had not delivered to him the equipment due: ἠξίουν πάλιν τὸν Θεόφημον ἢ αὐτὸν ἀκολουθεῖν πρὸς τοὺς ἀποστολέας καὶ τὴν βουλὴν . . . ἢ ἀποδιδόναι τὰ σκεύη· εἰ δὲ μή, ἐνέχυρα ἔφην λήψεσθαι κατά τε τοὺς νόμους καὶ τὰ ψηφίσματα. . . . εἰς δὲ τὴν οἰκίαν εἰσῄειν, ἵνα ἐνέχυρόν τι λάβοιμι τῶν σκευῶν. In 24 *Timokr.* 197 female slaves were allegedly seized against taxation debts to the state: θύρας ἀφαιρεῖν καὶ στρώμαθ' ὑποσπᾶν καὶ διάκονον, εἴ τις ἐχρῆτο, ταύτην ἐνεχυράζειν· ἃ σὺ πάντ' ἐποίεις ἐνιαυτὸν ὅλον μετ' Ἀνδροτίωνος.

The verb is used in two passages in Aristoph. *Clouds*, but the contexts do not make it certain in either case whether the kind of seizure at (*a*) above or at (*b*) is intended. One passage is 239 ff.:

> *Σω.* ἦλθες δὲ κατὰ τί;
> *Στ.* βουλόμενος μαθεῖν λέγειν·
> ὑπὸ γὰρ τόκων χρήστων τε δυσκολωτάτων
> ἄγομαι, φέρομαι, τὰ χρήματ' ἐνεχυράζομαι.

Here the seizures are currently going on, and Strepsiades is going to test their validity in court; hence his need for instruction. The other passage is 33 ff.:

Στ. ἀλλ' ὦ μέλ' ἐξήλικας ἐμέ γ' ἐκ τῶν ἐμῶν,
ὅτε καὶ δίκας ὤφληκα χἄτεροι τόκου
ἐνεχυράσεσθαί φασιν.

K. J. Dover ad loc. translates: 'I have lost lawsuits ⟨brought by some of my creditors⟩ and other ⟨creditors⟩ say that they will have securities taken for ⟨the⟩ interest ⟨which I owe⟩.' The point here is simply Strepsiades' parlous financial state. *Pace* Dover, it is not entirely clear that the reference here is to objects pledged in advance against non-payment of interest; it might be to eventual seizure after judgement. Fine, *Horoi* 170, points out that in the two scenes with creditors (*Clouds* 1214–1302) there is no hint of any pawning or hypothecating activity. Finley, *Land* 222, n. 6, however, should not support his view that ἐνεχυράζω always means execution and never refers to a security transaction by arguing that the scenes in the *Clouds* would lose all point if there was any hint of Strepsiades' having hypothecated or pawned property; conversion by a creditor of a pawn into his own property, e.g. by selling it (was the term for this ἐνεχυράζω?), was as much liable to lead to action in court as was seizure of a piece of property allegedly in execution of judgement.

Aischin. 3 *Ktes.* 21 uses the verb figuratively to describe the property of magistrates held, while they are still under εὔθυνα, to cover a possible judgement against them: ἑνὶ δὲ λόγῳ ἐνεχυράζει τὰς οὐσίας ὁ νομοθέτης τὰς τῶν ὑπευθύνων, ἕως ἂν λόγον ἀποδῶσι τῇ πόλει.

There is considerable controversy on the interpretation to be given to the words in three inscriptions:

IG ii². 2492 (lease from the deme Aixone, 346/5 B.C.) 7 ff. εἶναι ἐνεχυρασίαν Αἰξωνεῦσιν καὶ ἐκ τῶν ὡραίων τῶν ἐκ τοῦ χωρίου καὶ ἐκ τῶν ἄλλων ἁπάντων τοῦ μὴ ἀποδιδόντος (sc. τὴν μίσθωσιν).

IG ii². 1241 (lease from the phratry Dyaleis, 300/299 B.C.) 33 ff. ἐὰν δὲ μὴ ἀποδιδῶι τὴν μίσθωσιν ἐ[ν] τοῖς χρόνοις τοῖς γεγραμμένοις ἢ μὴ [ἐ]ργάζηται τὸ χωρίον κατὰ τὰ γεγραμμέ[ν]α, ἐξεῖναι τοῖς φρατριάρχοις καὶ Δυα[λεῦ]σιν ἐνεχυράζειν πρὸ δίκης καὶ μισθῶσαι ἑτέρωι τὸ χωρίον ὧι ἂν βούλωντα[ι], καὶ ὑπόδικος ἔστω Διόδωρος (the tenant) ἐάν τι π[ροσ]οφείλει τῆς μισθώσεως ἢ καθέλε[ι] τ[ι τ]ῆς οἰκίας ἢ κόψει τι τῶν ἐκ τοῦ χωρίου.

IG ii². 1168 (lease by a tribe) 10 ff. ἐὰν [δ]ὲ [μὴ ἀ]ποδιδῶσιν κατὰ τὰ[ς] γενομένα[ς συγγραφὰς ἐ]νεχυρασίαν εἶναι αὐ[τῶν καὶ] τῶ[ι ταμία]ι καὶ τοῖς ἐπιμεληταῖς· τὰς δὲ [ἐνεχυρ]ασίας ἐκ τῶν τοῦ μι[σ]θωσαμένου [εἶναι κα]ὶ τοῦ ἐγγυητοῦ αὐτοῦ τρό[π]ω[ι ὁπο]ί[ωι] ἂν βούλωνται. (For the restoration of the last few words see Wilhelm, *AP* 11 (1935) 205.)

In the event of certain defaults, these leases provide for ἐνεχυρασία to be carried out respectively by the demesmen (perhaps acting through their demarch), by the phratry members and phratriarch, and by the epimeletai and tamias. In the first and third cases the default is simply failure to pay the rent in due time; in the second, failure to maintain and cultivate the leased property is a further default which may lead to ἐνεχυρασία.

The first point of controversy is whether it is by chance or not that all these three instances refer to leases by public or semi-public bodies. In the opinion of some scholars, we should not conclude that a similar procedure would have been open to a purely private individual lessor; this is an administrative act by or on behalf of public bodies, which almost *ex hypothesi* could not be performed by a private citizen. Thus Partsch, *GB* 223, n. 1 (following Böckh, *Staatsh.* i. 597) believes that the demarch in making a seizure acted as a police officer (cf. p. 189, n. 2). If this was so, it is strange that in the Aixone inscription ἐνεχυρασία is to be undertaken by the demesmen and the demarch is not explicitly mentioned. It seems more likely that it is only chance that there has not survived a lease in which a private lessor is allowed to distrain for his rent.

Secondly, Mitteis, *RV* 406, takes πρὸ δίκης in the Dyaleis inscription to mean 'as though on the ground of a court judgement', and thus to be on all fours with clauses like that in the contract in Dem. 35 *Lakrit.* 12 (ἔστω ἡ πρᾶξις τοῖς δανείσασι . . . καθάπερ δίκην ὠφληκότων καὶ ὑπερημέρων ὄντων). Another view is that it means 'before judgement'; but this again can be taken in two ways. It can imply that a δίκη would be expected to supervene after the seizure (so *IJ* i. 333, n. 4, Beauchet iv. 441); but then we might expect the words to be πρὸ τῆς δίκης. The alternative is to take πρό as equivalent to ἄνευ: the seizure dispenses with the need for a civil action altogether (so Partsch, *GB* 221, n. 2). This view commits us to regarding this form of seizure as an administrative act not open to the private individual.

Lastly we have to ask upon what object or objects could distress be levied under these contracts. In the first inscription it is from the fruits (of the rented property presumably) and the rest of the property of the defaulting tenant. In the third it is from the property of the tenant and from that of his guarantor. The Dyaleis inscription is different in two ways. In the first place the condition precedent for the seizure is not merely failure to pay the rent, but also failure to work the land in the way the contract lays down. Secondly, seizure seems to be limited to the reoccupation of the rented land, with the view to letting it to another tenant. However, Partsch, *GB* 223 f., denies that the seizure mentioned as permissible πρὸ δίκης is restricted to the property rented. Other property must have been open to distress; otherwise what is the point of the phrase ἐάν τι προσοφείλει τῆς μισθώσεως? That phrase implies that the seizure may result in recovery of some of the rent in arrear. Partsch believes that the ordinary executive clause in a contract (such as the contract in Dem. 35 *Lakrit.*) was only appropriate for claims based on failure to pay specific sums or discharge specific duties. But it is difficult to see why failure to keep the property cultivated could not be so regarded. The contract seems to contemplate the possibility of a further legal proceeding (*ὑπόδικος ἔστω Διόδωρος*) to recover arrears of rent and damages for failure to maintain the house or for cutting timber. For all these reasons it is probably better to regard this Dyaleis inscription as *sui generis*.

The use of the word in the Brea decree (*IG* i². 45. 2) cannot be fully elucidated.

INDEX OF SOURCES

Where an entry refers to a note the page given is that on which the note begins.

INSCRIPTIONS

LEXICA

LITERARY TEXTS

PAPYRI

GENERAL INDEX

Where an entry refers to a note the page given is that on which the note begins.